Bob Paisley

Manager of the Millennium

Bob Paisley
Manager of the Millennium

John Keith

Foreword by Kenny Dalglish

ROBSON BOOKS

This edition first published in Great Britain in 2001 by Robson Books, The Chrysalis Building, Bramley Road, London W10 6SP

Fifth printing 2004

An imprint of **Chrysalis** Books Group plc

British Library Cataloguing in Publication Data
A catalogue record for this title is available from the British Library

ISBN 1 86105 436 X

Typeset by FSH Ltd., London
Printed in Great Britain by Creative Print & Design (Wales), Ebbw Vale

Contents

Foreword by Kenny Dalglish   1

Acknowledgements   5

1. The Building Bricks of Greatness   7
2. Anguish . . . Then a New Role   41
3. Decline, Fall and Revolution   56
4. Success and the Seven-year Itch   80
5. The Axe Finally Falls   97
6. Abdication and Succession   111
7. Double Up for Glory   129
8. Treble Chance   143
9. The Glory of Rome   185
10. The Capture of Dalglish   204
11. Genius in a Flat Cap   237
12. Title Deeds for a New Decade   257
13. Munich Magic, Paris Triumph   280
14. The Ruthless Quest   308
15. Sadness and Success   319
16. Farewell   330

The Statistics   349

FOREWORD
by Kenny Dalglish

If anyone in football owes Bob Paisley a greater debt than me, I would like to meet him. Bob brought me to Liverpool and then pointed me in the right direction as a manager.

His greatest asset, in my opinion, was his ability to make the right decisions. Bob used to describe himself as 'a modest Geordie'. Sure, he was totally unassuming. But underneath he had a huge bank of football knowledge and intelligence.

The number of his decisions that subsequently proved to be correct was unbelievable, ranging from team selection to injuries. He went right through the card in football – player, trainer, coach, physiotherapist, assistant manager to Bill Shankly, manager and director.

His great strength was that he knew something about everything. He could look at you and say: 'You did this wrong, you did that wrong.' He would look at an opposition team and spot individual flaws in it. He would inform us about their strengths and weaknesses and how we should try to counter them.

In the field of injuries alone, he was remarkable. Somebody could walk across a room in their best suit and he would spot a potential problem. He would watch a game, even on television, and forecast that a player was going to have an injury and invariably he would be right. If a player was hurt going into a tackle, Bob could tell almost immediately what type of injury he had.

He was a tremendous lieutenant to Shanks, who I am sure had a lot to thank him for. Then as manager he made decisions that affected the team and very, very seldom were they bad decisions. The massive success he had reflects that fact. Sometimes you would wonder why he did this or that – results provided the answer.

People said that Bob, with his Durham accent, was difficult to understand. As a Glaswegian, they said the same about me. Maybe that's why we could understand each other! The truth was, it wasn't difficult to understand Bob's words but rather what he was trying to say. But if you listened you could work it out. And most of the things he said about football were very intelligent. Every Friday morning we had a team meeting and there was always something in it you could pick up and learn from. He was brilliant.

There were not many people who had any dislike for Bob. That's not a bad thing to have going for you as a manager. Obviously he had to chop and change, leave people out and bring people in. But I don't think anyone ever lost respect for him. He had a tremendous ability at making substitutions. You saw him take a decision to bring someone on and at first you would think he had done it on a whim. In fact it had been a carefully considered decision, although he didn't have to explain it because the results proved him right most of the time.

Bob was like an uncle to many people. They looked at his face and thought he was a smashing fellow. Everyone liked him. The players also saw the other side of him, when he had to shout if somebody stepped out of line. But they liked him, too, and had total respect for him. He worked as a consultant to me for two years after I was appointed Liverpool manager in 1985. He brought all his knowledge and experience to bear, which was magnificent for me. The help he gave me was untold. He taught me some tricks of the trade but the greatest lesson I learned from him was in his overall thoroughness and preparation for matches. He treated me superbly and I would like to think I always try to treat people the way Bob treated me.

I first met Bob at around midnight on an August day in 1977 at Celtic Park. My mind was already made up to join Liverpool. He spoke to me and within two minutes I told him I would be signing. I was fortunate to get that opportunity and also that Bob sat with me for those two years after I became manager. That was no problem to Bob. He had enjoyed massive success but his ego was not massive. He wanted to come in and help, which he certainly did, along with Tom Saunders, Ronnie Moran and Roy Evans.

I can remember being in the office one summer's day just after becoming manager. Bob and I were sitting there. I said to him: 'What are we doing here, Bob? There's nothing happening and the phone's not ringing.'

He said: 'No, but you've got to be here in case something does happen.'

Overall, he was just a magnificent person, invaluable to Liverpool Football Club and a marvellous servant for them.

If you label someone as the greatest manager of all time, I suppose it is open to debate. What is not open to debate is that Bob Paisley was the country's most successful football manager of all time, and I was deeply privileged to have known him and played for him.

Acknowledgements

My thanks to all those, too numerous to mention, for their assistance, but in particular to Jessie Paisley and her family, BBC Radio Merseyside, Kenny Dalglish, John Watt, Albert Stubbins and Mal Scott-Taggart.

1

The Building Bricks
of Greatness

Bob Paisley, the man with the Midas touch, took football management into a new dimension of achievement with an incredible nineteen trophies in nine seasons commanding English football's most successful club. If, as they say, you judge a man by his friends, then football managers are judged ruthlessly on the prizes they win and the players they sign. Honours cascaded on Paisley and they were captured through the brilliance of the world-class performers he assembled in the Liverpool team.

The man who humbly served his time as an apprentice bricklayer in his native North East also built football teams of bewitching power, pace and precision. Yet he was very much a reluctant hero. Liverpool had to go down on bended knee to persuade this reticent anti-publicist to follow the outrageously extrovert Bill Shankly when the legendary Scot sensationally quit as manager in the summer of 1974. But for Shankly's still mysterious decision there would have been no outlet for the genius of Paisley, who would have been destined to remain in the shadows as a gifted assistant and physiotherapist until his own retirement, thus robbing our national game of a unique and glorious epoch.

But at the age of 55, when many men look to their pipe and slippers and contemplate the slow lane of life, he took on the massive task of leading Liverpool, proceeding to upstage every previous English club manager. Sir Matt Busby, a man Paisley admired immensely, Herbert Chapman, Bill Nicholson, Brian Clough and others had their outstanding haul of trophies outstripped by the stocky man in a flat cap, whose penchant for woollen cardigans gave him the appearance of your favourite uncle rather than the football maestro who conquered England and Europe.

Treble-winning Sir Alex Ferguson, whose subsequent deeds in charge of Manchester United have installed him as one of football's all-time great managers, admits to learning from Paisley when he was in charge of an Aberdeen side sent packing from the European Cup by Liverpool. It is a scandalous injustice that Paisley, a deeply patriotic man who loved his country and fought for it, never received the Royal tap on the shoulder. Knighthoods have been dispensed for contributions dwarfed by his flag-flying exploits with Liverpool.

Ferguson, himself, acknowledged that Paisley's achievements, too, deserved the accolade of a knighthood. 'He was a down-to-earth, uncomplicated man and it was wonderful to see somebody as modest as Bob have the success he had in football,' said Sir Alex.

If a single triumph among Paisley's glittering feats stood out for this unassuming son of Durham, it was the one that occurred on a magical night in May 1977. The Holiday Inn St Peter's Hotel in Rome reverberated to the sound of wild celebration. Champagne corks popped, bubbly was sprayed from balconies by ecstatic revellers and songs with a distinct Scouse flavour rent the balmy air of the Eternal City. Amidst this Roman carnival one man sat without a drink in his hand but with a broad, satisfied smile on his face and pride pumping through his veins. Bob Paisley had, just a few hours earlier, become the first English-born manager to win the coveted European Cup, thanks to Liverpool's epic 3–1 win over Borussia Moenchengladbach.

For Paisley and Liverpool it was the culmination of a dream. Bob recalled: 'There were so many things that pleased me. Rome was a place I'd been to after its liberation during the war and I had a soft spot for the city. The setting, the weather, the immaculate behaviour of the supporters and the performance we gave, which was praised throughout Europe, made it the greatest moment of my life.'

That triumph in the Olympic Stadium on 25 May 1977 was also the greatest night in the Anfield club's history. Players, their wives and friends, Liverpool officials, members of the media and those few supporters fortunate and intrepid enough to gatecrash the party, celebrated the majestic win until the wee small hours.

Their glee was evident by the riotous conga that snaked its way around the hotel swimming pool and gardens. One man at the heart of the festivities was comedian Jimmy Tarbuck, a life-long Liverpool fan: 'It was a night of wonderful enjoyment and fun,' he remembers. 'I celebrated with people I'd never seen before and never seen since. It was fantastic.'

Yet for Bob Paisley the glory that was Rome was something on which to quietly reflect. The most successful manager in the history of British football quipped in those distinctive County Durham tones: 'You won't find anyone sober in Rome tonight apart from me, the Pope and Horace Yates.' Horace was a teetotal sportswriter from the *Liverpool Daily Post* and Bob added: 'This is the second time I've beaten the Germans here...the first time was in 1944. I drove into Rome on a tank when the city was liberated. If anyone had told me I'd be back here to see us win the European Cup 33 years later I'd have told them they were mad! But I want to savour every minute of it...which is why I'm not having a drink tonight. I'm just drinking in the occasion.'

He later said: 'I just want to cherish the moment. I knew it was something special. I certainly wasn't begrudging anyone else celebrating. I just wanted all my faculties so I could reflect on what Liverpool had achieved that night. Inwardly I was drunk even though I hadn't taken a drink.'

Shankly, who had launched Liverpool's mission to win the European Cup back in 1964, was in the stadium to witness the fulfilment of that quest under Paisley and hailed his former club's triumph within seconds of the final whistle. 'This is the greatest night in Liverpool's history,' he declared. 'This is the result of planning, of simplicity, of how to play the game in a simple manner. I think the whole world now realises that it's the way to play. I would advise England to try to copy them now.'

Yet the brilliance of Paisley was embodied in his success not only in following Shankly – an act many believed was impossible in itself – but in leading Liverpool to even greater feats. Former Manchester United manager Ron Atkinson, whose rivalry with Paisley nurtured within him a glowing admiration and respect for the Liverpool boss, conveyed as well as anyone ever has done the scale of his fantastic achievements: 'If Bob Paisley had been on the Continent or in America, in whatever capacity or field he worked, and achieved what he achieved, I think he'd be rated higher than the President, the Lord Mayor, the King or the Queen or whatever. In a few years, when the inevitable quiz questions fly around about who was the greatest manager of all time, they will mention the achievements of men like Sir Matt, Stan Cullis, Bill Nicholson, Shanks, Don Revie – and then they will say: "Yes, but Bob did it all."'

And Graeme Souness, the superb midfielder signed and appointed captain by Paisley and who went on to manage Liverpool in a career embracing several countries, also places his former boss at the pinnacle, saying: 'People talk about other managers being great but there's only one, isn't there, if you look at the record? Bob achieved more than anyone else has or ever will do. Without a doubt in my opinion, Bob Paisley should have had a knighthood.'

Another Paisley signing, Alan Hansen, the imperious centre back who brought artistry and grace to the task of defending and now imparts his football knowledge and expertise to millions on television, says concisely: 'I go by records and what people have achieved. Bob's achieved more than anyone else so he's got to be number one.'

As the new millennium dawned, the *Rothmans Football Yearbook*, that respected and prestigious bible of football, named Paisley as the finest manager of the twentieth century in a poll of members of the Football Writers' Association. 'The manager was chosen for his overall achievements between 1900 and 2000,' said Rothmans' joint editor Jack Rollin. 'There were strong challenges from Sir Alex Ferguson and Bill Nicholson but in terms of success Bob Paisley is still out there on his own and he was voted Manager of the Century.'

Ferguson's feat in leading Manchester United to a hat trick of Premiership titles in 2001 brought him his seventh championship with the club and meant that he had won 14 major trophies at Old Trafford compared with Paisley's 13 at Anfield.

Yet the fact that Ferguson had been in charge since November 1986 and that Paisley's haul had been gathered in just nine seasons as Liverpool boss – and included three European Cup triumphs – surely leave him pre-eminent amongst managers in English football, although in overall British terms Ferguson is without peer through his feats at Aberdeen, where he lifted nine major trophies.

Paisley's European Cup successes came in an era when only national champions or the trophy winners could enter the competition which ran on a sudden death home and away basis rather than the somewhat cosy and protective group basis of the Champions League. There are more European games now but many lack a knife edge and fail to excite the public. And, domestically, Paisley's teams played 42 League games a season compared to 38 today.

Most of the Paisley years, too, preceded the fall of the Iron Curtain and the arrival of satellite television and a lack of information and intelligence on opponents made some European ties journeys into the unknown. Today the communications revolution has shrunk the world to a global village.

Ferguson's fellow Scot and one of his United managerial predecessors, Tommy Docherty, believes Paisley is at the top of English football's rostrum, saying: 'Alex is such a different character from Bob yet they have both achieved fanastic success. Bob was very quiet and modest but his players respected him. Alex is more boisterous and gets results in a different way.

'But if you ask me to say who was the greater, I would say Bob. I think Bob was the greatest manager ever if you take the length of time he was manager and the number of trophies he won. He was in charge of Liverpool for nine years and won 13 major trophies.

'Don't forget that he won the European Cup three times, as well as the UEFA Cup, which was a tough competition in those days. United's Champions League win in 1999 was a fantastic achievement but for me they shouldn't have been there because they did not win the league. In Bob's days only champions or the holders could play and if you lost you were out.

'Neither did Bob have the money that Alex has now, which has seen him spend £19 million on Ruud van Nistelrooy. Instead, Bob picked up real bargains like Hansen, Rush and Souness for peanuts. Both Alex and Bob are geniuses. But, for me, Bob stands alone.'

Docherty's powerful tribute to Paisley is echoed by Tommy Smith. 'Bob is simply the greatest manager this country has produced,' declared the former Liverpool captain. 'If Bill Shankly put the foundations in place then Bob Paisley built the empire. I don't think his achievements have been fully appreciated outside Liverpool but he remains untouchable.'

To have lost the great talent of Shankly only to find in Bob Paisley someone who would surpass his achievements makes you think that someone up there was smiling on Liverpool Football

Club. Peter Robinson, who arrived as club secretary in 1965 and later became chief executive and then vice-chairman, put into perspective Liverpool's first European Cup win, one that finally confirmed their status as one of the giants of world football.

'There were 27,000 of our fans at the game and I think about half of them turned up at our hotel banquet,' said Robinson. 'I remember going back to my room at about five o'clock in the morning and thinking that I didn't really want to go to bed. So I sat on the verandah looking out over Rome as the sun was coming up on a beautiful morning, feeling very proud both for the club and the city of Liverpool.

'I thought: "Here I am, a representative of Liverpool Football Club, from a city with problems, one that's in economic decline – yet here we are dominating European football."'

Robert Paisley was born in the County Durham mining village of Hetton-le-Hole, seven miles from Sunderland, on 23 January 1919, the second of four sons. And on the very day he entered the world, the harsh economic climate of the time was underlined on the doorstep of his family's small terraced house at 31 Downs Lane.

An estimated 150,000 of the country's miners, including many in Hetton, joined a nationwide strike for a shorter working week. Life in Hetton revolved around the pit. Bob was to recall that his father Samuel, a miner known to all as Sam, and his mother Emily managed to eke out the family budget so that they never went short of essentials, but had little or no money left at the end of the week.

Life for the Paisley family was far from luxurious, as Bob's widow Jessie describes: 'It was a little two-up, two-down colliery house with a small yard and toilet at the back. Every year they would redecorate the house and that was his mother's job. The women did everything up in that village. The men came home, had their meal and then went to the working men's club.

'Hanging on the wall at the back was a great big tin bath. At that time there were no pit baths so when Bob's dad came home from a shift at the pit he was very sooty. It meant that everyone had to clear out of the way as Bob's mum filled the big bath with hot water from a boiler and his dad had his bath in front of the fire.

'When I went to the house in Hetton on Sundays with Bob, who was then a player with Liverpool, all the uncles used to gather from round about and sit by the fire with their caps on and talk about football. In the same room, while this was going on, Bob's mum would be making Yorkshire puddings in a big old-fashioned oven in the wall.'

As a seven-year-old during the miners' strike of 1926, young Bob scrambled over pit heaps with his father to make crude fuel from coal dust and water to help keep the family warm. And along with all the other children of the village, during the strike he depended on school or soup kitchens for meals to supplement the family's sparse food resources. He would recount later, perhaps only partly in jest, that the basis of his speed and fitness on the football field was provided by his daily 100-yard dashes from the school to the soup kitchen across the road.

He also recalled that the dominant interests in the community were racing, pigeons and football, and Bob's flair and passion for soccer was evident when he was a mere toddler. He used to pester teachers to let him into school so he could play football with the older boys. And every Monday morning he would visit an uncle on a rather unusual mission. 'My uncle was a slaughterman for the Co-op and I used to get pigs' bladders off him to use as footballs in the street,' Paisley recounted. 'They did the job. They were quite good and if one went through a window I'd go to him and get another!' If no pig's bladder was forthcoming then rolled-up pieces of paper or cloth would do instead.

Little did I know then that not only would he swell tiny Hetton's remarkable total of top class players but he would be hailed as the greatest son of the village that was once the domain of a Norman knight.

Bob's father was reluctant for any of his four sons to follow him down the pit, even though there was little option. So keen was Samuel Paisley, who died in 1978 at the age of 83, that football should give Bob an escape route from a life down the mines that he bought him a pair of football boots when he was just four years old at a cost of 6 shillings, about half the family's weekly income. He also instilled in his son a burning desire for physical fitness. Years later Bob was to reveal proudly: 'It was because of my father that I lived the life of an athlete. He was an immensely strong man who worked at the Hetton Lyons colliery filling the coal tubs. There were no ponies or machinery to pull them out and nobody ever beat my father's record for the weight he shifted!'

Bob's upbringing fostered in him a keen sense of right and wrong, a fact illustrated by his fellow North Easterner, Albert

Stubbins, who recognised that quality when they were team-mates at Liverpool. He recalled: 'We were on a club tour of America and we were due to fly by charter plane from New York to St Louis. The pilot was impatient to take off when one of the players found he was 50 dollars short. He didn't know what had happened to the money.

'One of the lads suggested that we had a whip round amongst all the players to make up the missing amount. I remember myself, Billy Liddell, Willie Fagan, Cyril Sidlow, Ray Lambert, Laurie Hughes and the others digging into our pockets to throw a few dollars in. But when it came to Bob he just shook his head. He would not contribute that few dollars. He felt very strongly that if we paid the money, it inferred that one of the players had maybe taken the missing amount. Bob would not be swayed. He wouldn't deviate. It was a perfect illustration of his strength of character. You couldn't try any silly fiddles or mind games with Bob. He just wouldn't wear it. He had such very high principles.

'As it turned out, after the match in St Louis we returned to New York and the player concerned found the 50 dollars at the back of a drawer in his hotel room.'

There was plenty of scope in Hetton for young Bob's physical development. As a boy, one of his tasks was to help elder brother Bill, also known as Willie, push a barrow-load of coal two miles up the hill to his grandmother's house. They used to take turns, changing over at every telegraph post. Bob trained himself to push the barrow 80 yards while holding his breath, so boosting his lung power. Jessie Paisley remembered: 'Willie was the oldest so he got preferential treatment. When they got the coal up to the top, the grandmother always paid them. She was very particular. She paid Willie a penny and an apple and Bob a halfpenny and half an apple. When Willie left and started work it was Bob's turn, as the older one, to get the penny and apple while his other brother Hughie got half pay.'

Bill, four years older than Bob, worked at the local pit and Bob and the third son Hughie eventually followed him to the mine. Hughie spent his whole working life as a bricklayer down the pit. The youngest of the four lads, Alan, tragically died from diptheria and scarlet fever during World War Two at the age of 15 while Bob was on active service in Italy and unable to return home for the funeral. On hearing the news of his brother's death, Bob wandered down the road stunned, trying to come to terms with his loss. Seconds later, a shell dropped on the very spot where he had been standing. His life had been saved by the tragic message.

Although Bob was a more than useful cricketer as a fast bowler and proficient batsman, even attracting overtures from clubs, his overpowering sporting love was football. It filled his dreams and ambitions from an early age, a fact underlined when he recounted this particular childhood memory: 'In the North East at New Year's Eve they let the New Year in well and my first recollection of it as a boy was kicking a football around as the bells chimed midnight. The saying was that if you did something from the old year into the new one, you'd do it all your life.' This passion for football found a welcome outlet at Barrington School, where his skill and determination at left-half more than compensated for his small stature. And when he moved on to Eppleton Senior Mixed School, his football talent really blossomed. He was later to salute the school as years ahead of its time in coaching and encouraging the pupils to play the game. More importantly, it provided the young Paisley with an invaluably wide grounding in the sport. Mustard baths and massage were provided in the school's boiler house by the caretaker Bowler Burns, while the training and administration of the team were supervised by sportsmasters Barty Rowe, Jimmy Johnson and Alec Wright. So dedicated and efficient were the teachers that the school football team was the next best thing to a professional set-up.

'Barty Rowe was so keen that we lived and breathed the game through him,' Bob recalled. 'He passed on so much enthusiasm I'd have played for nothing. He was a legend in Hetton.' And with that sound common sense that was to characterise his playing and management career, he added: 'When I think of Barty, I think of what the game has lost – natural enthusiasm. Teachers today have got too many theories. It's all systems and formations. I'm sure they're talking above the kids' heads. Probably above the heads of professionals, too.'

Humility was something ingrained in Bob Paisley from an early age. It was a quality that endured throughout his life and one recognised immediately by his last signing as Liverpool manager, Republic of Ireland international Jim Beglin. 'He just struck me as a very ordinary man, an ordinary man with a football gift,' said Beglin. 'Despite all the success he'd had, he was also a very humble man.'

Even in an area and era when money was hard to come by, it was nothing extraordinary for a youngster to be called from the classroom at Eppleton when a big game was looming and be given a sherry and egg tonic prior to donning the school football jersey. The school certainly had the formula for landing trophies and Bob collected a host of medals during his spell in the Eppleton team, in which he started by facing boys three years his senior. He also digested a piece of advice that proved invaluable in his later days in management: 'My headmaster told me that if you want to tell anyone anything speak softly. You'll find that they'll try to listen to you to find out what you're saying. If you shout they probably won't be interested.' Each Eppleton pupil paid sixpence a season of their family's money for the upkeep of the team, while the local Co-op supplied boots and footballs.

Playing for Eppleton introduced Bob Paisley to the winning habit, something he recounted with affection: 'We won seventeen trophies in the schoolboy teams I played for from eleven to fourteen. When I went to play for two years with Hetton Juniors we won five trophies and when I joined Bishop Auckland we won a treble for the first time ever.'

At that time Bishop Auckland was a little further on in Paisley's football odyssey. But his progress to county recognition with Durham, and an England Schoolboy trial in 1933, had been noted in influential circles. Jack 'Ginger' Hill, a centre-half who played for Newcastle and England and captained his country during the 1920s, was one of Hetton's incredible production line of top-rank professionals, some fifty in all. So one can imagine the pride in Samuel Paisley when Hill told him that a big football future beckoned his son. Hill's opinion was echoed by Newcastle's Jack Kelly and Billy Graham. All three were heroes of Bob's, who was thrilled by their encouraging words.

Bob's friend Jackie Wilson taught him the 'Sammy Weaver Throw', which meant hurling the ball from the touchline to goalmouth in the style of the England and Newcastle left-half. By the age of eleven his football technique was impressive and his eagerness to learn from others was a talking point. He would always listen, a policy he adhered to throughout his life.

'I listen to everyone,' he said. 'My philosophy is that if there's any rubbish being talked you can discard it and never think of it again. It's best to let people say things and hear them out. I was always taught that the tongue is in a slippery place and it's liable to slip. I learn every day. I'll learn something today. I don't know what it's going to be, but I'll pick up something. And in life I do that. Someone, somewhere – and it doesn't have to be the most intelligent or knowledgeable person – will give you a lead into something, if you can listen.'

One particular Paisley display for Eppleton startled the football wiseacres of the day. It was a schoolboy final against Usworth, who included in their ranks an elegant player who had already appeared for England Boys. His name was Jimmy Hagan, later to find fame with Sheffield United, Derby and England as a player and who would go on to manage West Bromwich Albion, Benfica, Sporting Lisbon and Oporto. Ironically, Hagan would also spend sixteen months as an amateur with Liverpool, the club that was to become a home for Paisley. But that day in the North East, Eppleton's teachers gave Bob Paisley the task of marking Hagan and switched him from left-half to right-half with orders not to leave the young star's side. Watched by a capacity 4,000 crowd, Paisley stuck to his opponent like glue. So successful was he in his mission that Hagan hardly touched the ball and he sportingly led his smaller adversary off the field by the hand at the final whistle, more like a proud father than a football rival.

Bob followed in the footsteps of Ginger Hill and company by joining Hetton Juniors, later known as Eppleton Colliery Welfare. The club had a novel way of announcing the results of their away matches, sending them by a special form of air mail. And on one particular occasion, Paisley recalled, the excitement of the club officials got the better of them. 'In those days the teams sent their results to the local paper by homing pigeon and our president was given the job. We took the pigeon with us. After one game he was so excited he "launched" the bird, realising, too late, that he'd forgotten to put the ring on it containing the vital slip of paper with the score. As it flew off, he shouted: "Gan on, hinny, tell 'em we won 2–1!"'

One of his team-mates was Harry Potts, another native of Hetton, who would turn professional just eighteen months before Bob by joining Burnley in November 1937 and later play for Everton before returning to Turf Moor as manager. Another was Ned Blenkinsop, who revealed that even a trip to the fish and chip shop had a fitness connotation for the young Paisley. 'Whenever we made a trip to the fish and chip shop or the cinema, Bob would set off at a cracking pace,' he said. 'Often he'd put his watch on it to clock us. He was a real heel-and-toe man, just as keen to win the race for fish and chips as he was to win the European Cup.'

Bob's first football love was Sunderland and his first hero was their skilful, tricky winger Jimmy Connor. Later, the brilliant inside-forward skills of England star Raich Carter would also illuminate the Sunderland side and capture Paisley's admiration. One Wednesday afternoon in March 1933 he played truant from school to watch his idols take on Derby County in an FA Cup sixth-round replay. The biggest ever Roker Park crowd of 75,118 was recorded, although Bob was adamant that a further 20,000 attended unofficially. "They were hanging from the roof and the rafters,' he recalled. But it was not a happy day for Bob or Sunderland. They were beaten 1–0 and lost their England centre-forward Bobby Gurney, another idol of the young Paisley, with a broken collar-bone sustained in an early collision with Derby centre-half Jack Barker.

Bob's great dream of becoming a Sunderland player was crushed when they rejected him for being too small after a trial as a fifteen-year-old. He was turned down by Sunderland manager Johnny Cochrane and the club's chief scout Tommy Irwin. 'They said I was too small, yet what made me smile was that neither of them was more than 5ft 4in and that was allowing for Johnny's Trilby!' Bob recounted with a laugh. Tottenham also rejected him as too small while Wolves, then managed by the famous Major Franklin Charles Buckley, also dithered about signing him as a schoolboy and preferred to wait until he filled out physically. Buckley asked him to stay on at school for a while when he reached the leaving age, which at that time was 14. But after six months Wolves finally turned him down. It was a bitter disappointment to Bob, who had spent hours of extra training jumping at a swinging ball to improve his performance in the air. And it meant that Bob had to start earning his living elsewhere, and he took a surface job at the local pit.

Just three months later, his father was badly hurt in an underground accident and Bob had the heart-rending experience of seeing him brought up from below on a stretcher. Samuel Paisley had suffered arm injuries so horrific that his wife was asked to give permission for amputation. She refused, acutely aware of what her husband's decision would be. 'My mother didn't dare give her permission,' Bob recalled. Samuel's arm was eventually saved by a surgeon called Ritson who, ironically, was also a Sunderland director. But the injury prevented him working for five years and made him even more determined that Bob would not follow him down the mine. The accident also drew more attention to the dangerous state of some of the old shafts at the Hetton pit, as more modern mining methods were introduced.

Shortly afterwards the pit was closed but Bob quickly found another job by the rather bizarre route of handicap foot-racing, which was highly popular in the North East and drew some heavy betting.

One of his close friends was George 'Geordie' Oxley, later to become a Hartlepool footballer but at that time a well-known local runner, taking part in colliery fete and gala races. He would train in shoes with lead weights, with Bob acting as pacemaker. Oxley had won three major races and, in so doing, helped a group of local builders pick up some substantial winnings of their own. The outcome was that they offered jobs to Bob and his pal as apprentice bricklayers. Every day they had to cycle nine miles there and nine miles back – and Bob still played football!

His performances now attracted the attention of that renowned club of the amateur era, Bishop Auckland, who signed him prior to the start of the 1937–38 season for the princely sum per match of three shillings and sixpence – seventeen and a half pence today – which was all that was allowed under the amateur rules. A year later, one of the great talking points in Hetton was the style of young Paisley's Saturday morning departure. A Rolls-Royce would smooth its way into Downs Lane, stop at number 31 and whisk off Bob to play for Bishops later that day! Such was the stature of England's most famous amateur club that they arranged for private hire cars to collect their players from all over the county to take them to the ground where the Bishops were playing, home or away, either in the Northern League or cup competitions. But in Bob's first season at Bishops, the taxi service was unreliable so the next season they switched to a pick-up service in a Rolls-Royce.

The Rolls was driven by Dave Ward, who was reacquainted with Bob at the height of his success with Liverpool in 1980. Another reunion for Bob that year was with Bobby Wilson, who was the seven-year-old Bishops mascot in their treble-winning 1938–9 season. They became the first amateur club to win ten championships, a feat Liverpool were to match at professional level under Paisley's management in 1977, and scooped two cups.

Although football dominated Bob's life, he did go to the cinema with his pals at nearby Houghton-le-Spring on a Saturday night and on the way home used to call at the fish and chip shop in Hetton.

Fish and chips cost three halfpence and the young woman who befriended and served Bob and his friends was called Sarah Ann. She was to marry and have a son called Alan Kennedy, a player Bob would sign for Liverpool from Newcastle United for £330,000 more than forty years later. Sadly, she died shortly before her son's move to Anfield in August 1978. Kennedy, now a successful after-dinner speaker and soccer coaching school organizer, reflects on that long arm of fate stretching from Hetton to Anfield and spanning more than four decades: 'My mother, who was one of seven daughters, used to remind me that she lived in Hetton and worked in the local fish and chip shop during the 1930s and that one of the people who came in for his fish suppers was Bob Paisley. I'm not sure if he only wanted fish and chips – perhaps he had eyes for my mother or my auntie, as she was to become. My mother's family were very much into football. The game was an important part of the community. Bob was a player for the local team and my mother used to go along to watch him. It's amazing to think that Bob would sign me all those decades later, just after my mother had died. She'd have been very proud that I went to play for Bob at Liverpool. I always felt that Bob was like a father figure to me. My mother often said: "Wouldn't it be nice for you to go and play for Bob Paisley?"'

Paisley's successful career with Bishop Auckland reignited Sunderland's interest in him. But this time it was their turn to be disappointed because he had already promised Liverpool manager George Kay that he would join them at the end of Bishop's crowded season, which concluded with 13 games squeezed into the final fortnight as they won the Amateur Cup. After beating Wimbledon in the semi-final they lifted the trophy with a 3–0 win over Wellington after extra time at Roker Park to add to their Northern League championship. Inside-right Laurie Wensley scored a hat-trick and heard Bob had double cause for celebration as they stood at opposite ends of the Roker Park boardroom table signing as professionals – Wensley for Sunderland and Paisley for Liverpool.

'I imagine Bob got the same as me,' Laurie recalled. 'That was £25 to sign plus £8 a week in the season and £6 in the summer.

I also got 15 shillings from a director who had offered five bob a goal to the Amateur Cup Final scorers!' Both teams went to Sunderland's Grand Hotel for an after-match dinner then Bob and his colleagues headed back to Bishop Auckland with the cup. There was no open-top bus – the victors walked the streets parading the trophy.

The pair had signed professional forms with the arrangement that they would play their final game for the Bishops on Saturday 6 May against South Shields in the Durham Challenge Cup Final, also staged at Roker Park. They duly helped Bishops collect another pot to complete an unprecedented local treble. Some 48 hours later on 8 May 1939, a new chapter unfolded for twenty-year-old Paisley when he boarded a train for Liverpool to begin an amazing association with the Anfield club that was to span half a century. His first wages, though, were somewhat less than his former colleague Wensley was earning with Sunderland. Bob received a £10 signing-on fee and his weekly pay was £5. But on the very day that he was met at Liverpool's Exchange station by Andy McGuigan, a former Anfield forward who had joined the club's scouting staff, Pope Pius XII was making a public appeal to Germany, France, Britain, Italy and Poland to attend peace talks in the Vatican. The peace moves collapsed and before the year was out, World War Two was underway, delaying Paisley's League debut until 1946 and robbing him and his contemporaries of a huge slice of their chosen careers.

Bob began pre-season training at Liverpool in the July and had played just two reserve games for his new club when football and life as everyone knew it came to a halt when Britain and France declared war on Germany on 3 September. Yet that brief spell at Anfield prior to his army call-up made a deep impression on him, especially the presence of a cultured Scottish wing-half called Matt Busby, who was Liverpool's captain. 'Matt was skipper, and in the short period I was at Anfield before the war began he was always ready to give advice,' Paisley said. 'Even in those early days, lasting just two or three months, he gave me quite a few words of encouragement. He was a man you could look up to and respect. He'd played the game and people like him weren't solely tied down with tactics, which was a valuable lesson for me.'

Liverpool boss Kay, who had been recruited from Southampton in 1936 after appearing as West Ham captain against his former club Bolton in the famous White Horse FA Cup Final of

1923, wanted Busby to stay at Anfield and offered him a coaching job. But Busby, like Paisley a son of mining stock, politely declined Liverpool's overtures. When the war was over he became manager of Manchester United, proceeding to build at Old Trafford one of the great empires of world football. Said Paisley: 'It was unfortunate for us that Matt didn't carry on with Liverpool after the war, electing to go to Manchester United instead. He didn't do too badly there!'

Another player had joined Liverpool a year before Paisley and the pair were to become lifetime friends. This other aspiring youngster was one William Beveridge Liddell who had been recommended to Kay by Busby. The great Billy Liddell was one of the immortal legends of Liverpool history, a hero figure to later stars such as Tommy Smith and Ian Callaghan. He joined Liverpool as a sixteen-year-old amateur in 1938 from the exotically named Scottish junior club Lochgelly Violet, turning professional in April 1939 with Liverpool's agreement that he could continue his accountancy studies. He and Paisley struck up an instant rapport.

'I palled up with Billy, who was good-living, respectable and keen to get on in the football world,' said Paisley. 'The rest of the players were a good set, too. This was very lucky for me. I could have been pitched into a gang of fly-boys who couldn't care less about the game and you might have drifted. You're fortunate when you meet people like that.'

As King and country called for the fight against Hitler, Liddell entered the RAF as a navigator while 'Gunner' Paisley was called up in October 1939 and joined the 73rd Regiment of the Royal Artillery. He was initially stationed at several British camps including Rhyl in North Wales and Tarporley in Cheshire and through a welcome twist of fate, his football talent ensured that he failed to keep an unwanted date with Japanese 'hospitality'. His battery was sent to the Far East and although Bob was in line to go with them, he was transferred to another battery because he was the regimental soccer captain. It was a stroke of personal fortune. His unit was captured soon after it arrived and spent the rest of the war in a Japanese prison camp.

The lure of football was still irresistible to new recruit Paisley and it was while he was at Tarporley that he played in his first Mersey derby match at Goodison. To get there, he borrowed a bicycle and pedalled almost thirty miles to Merseyside. He left his bike at the Birkenhead side of the Mersey Tunnel, hitched a lift through to Liverpool then caught a tram to the ground, where the Lancashire Senior Cup Final drew a crowd of 30,000. An Everton team including Scottish pair Torry Gillick and Jimmy Caskie, who had helped bring the 1939 League championship to Goodison, won 4–2. Bob then had to make the return trip to Birkenhead and cycle all the way back to camp. 'I was as stiff as a board afterwards,' he admitted. He once broke camp rules by leaving without permission to play for Liverpool at Wrexham and scored in a 3–2 win, which was duly printed in the Sunday papers. When a sergeant questioned him, he swore he wasn't there and said the papers must have got his name wrong!

August Bank Holiday, 1941, saw Bob packing his bags. That was when he was posted to Egypt, which meant a ten-week voyage via South Africa because it was impossible to go through the Mediterranean. He was to be overseas for four years and two months. Although he had only ever had one driving lesson, when the order came for drivers to 'fall out', Bob fell out with them! And despite his inexperience and unfamiliarity with vehicles, he was given the job of driving a reconnaissance officer. One day the staff car broke down, as it did frequently. Bob had a simple solution – he would open the bonnet, tighten up everything he could find, then give it a kick! Amazingly, it usually worked, earning him the back-handed compliment from one of his superiors: "You're a bloody awful driver but a great mechanic!' He soon picked up the basics and become adept at driving a 15 cwt. truck.

Bob's regiment set up camp south of Cairo and it was November before he received any mail. Two sacks arrived for his unit and Bob carried the bulging mail bags a mile across the sands from the military post office to his barracks. But the only letter for Paisley R. was a postcard from George Kay telling him he had been picked to play for the reserves at Preston North End three months earlier! Even in Egypt, sport was a priority in his life. He once captained the regimental hockey team in a match and then played in cricket and football matches all on the same day. According to Bob, he had never played hockey in his life until then. But his commanding officer was a hockey fanatic and Bob ended up being made team captain.

Strangely, it was also in the desert that his interest in racehorses was first kindled. A jockey called Reg Stretton was in the same regiment. 'He didn't eat much and gave me his rations,' Bob revealed. When Reggie was switched to the Veterinary Corps in Cairo, Bob visited him and rode a few horses, a brief equine acquaintanceship that was to blossom in later life through friendships with those famous British racing figures Frank Carr and Frankie Durr. Frankie, a successful jockey and trainer, recalls one occasion when a Paisley visit caused a stir at his Newmarket yard.

'I would ring Bob and tell him where I was riding and he'd come to see me when he could. He always liked Haydock, York and Newmarket. One day when I was a trainer we'd just come back from Newmarket to my stables and Bob fancied a cup of tea. I had to go off to look at a horse and left Bob having his drink. My head man came in, saw Bob sitting in the corner and asked: "Who are you?" He came out, found me and said: "There's a funny chap in the office and when I asked him who he was, he didn't answer. Then I asked him what he did. He told me he looked after a small football team. When I asked which one he said Liverpool."'

In wartime Egypt, after a month's training on anti-tank guns, Bob was sent into the desert for nine months and was with Montgomery's Eighth Army, the Desert Rats, at the relief of Tobruk, which had been under siege from Rommel's Afrika Korps for eight months. British units involved in that action had spells of leave in Cairo and during these welcome breaks, Bob played for the Combined Services and regimental football teams as well as keeping his eye in at cricket and hockey.

The Eighth Army's watershed victory at El Aleamein took place in 1942, securing access to the trade routes and oil supplies of the Mediterranean, and Bob Paisley, footballer-cum-soldier, was there with them as the British fought their way through North Africa, Sicily and Italy. But during his time in the Western desert there was one particular alarming moment for Bob and his fellow Desert Rats, and it came straight out of a clear blue sky, as his former colleague Captain Norman Whitehouse related many years later when Bob was the subject of Thames TV's *This Is Your Life*: 'A plane came over and sprayed the dug-out with explosive bullets and when it was gone Bob had his hands over his eyes, shouting: "I can't see, I'm blind." We took him off to the medical officer as quick as we could. He came back twenty-four hours later wearing dark glasses but, thank goodness, he was alright.'

The war also gave Bob an insight into the Merseyside

personality and character, something in which he would be
immersed for the rest of his life. He explained: 'I love the city and
the people here. I've been with them for many years and I fought
alongside them. Ninety per cent of the regiment were from the
Merseyside area. So I got to know the Liverpool character. From a
psychological point of view, that was a big asset. I've had a fair time
to judge the Liverpool people and I think they're tremendous.'

In June 1944 the Allies liberated Rome and Bob travelled
through the Eternal City aboard a tank, to the delight of the joyful
civilians. Women threw flowers, men proffered wine to the
liberation forces and the cry went up: 'Ingles Viva, Americano
Viva!' Further up Italy, on the long route home for Gunner Bob
Paisley and his comrades, was the beautiful city of Florence,
where they set up camp at the local football stadium. It was there
in Florence that Bob saw boxing legends Joe Louis and Sugar Ray
Robinson in the ring, fighting exhibitions against the best the
American army could throw at them. Bob, for whom boxing was
yet another sporting interest, was a keen spectator at these bouts
and by a quirk of fate, he had something in common with the
great Joe Louis, because the 'Brown Bomber' had also signed
professional forms for Liverpool FC! It happened in July 1944
and proved an inspired publicity coup for George Kay. Louis
boxed a three-round exhibition bout at the old Liverpool Stadium
and Kay persuaded him to sign for the club. Louis went along
with the idea as a goodwill gesture. The registration forms,
however, were never submitted to the Football League.

A keen student of ring craft and the physical requirements of
boxers, Paisley put it to good use later in his career. He became a
master on the punch ball and all the other equipment in the
Liverpool gym and tutored the club's goalkeepers on how to
strengthen their hands. He said: 'I work it with the hips on the
punch ball. You weave over and hit. You're using the whole side
muscles and you use the elbows to get a continuity. You hit it,
follow through, hit it back and follow through again. It keeps the
hips going. That's one of the best exercises of the lot for
goalkeepers because it's essential their hands are no weak touches.
Some of the movement of a boxer can be useful for keepers, too,
because they often have to rely on instinctive work.' Bob's
technique with a punch ball made an impact with subsequent
generations of Liverpool players. Striker John Aldridge recalled:
'The first time I ever really spoke to Bob was in the Liverpool gym

when I was injured. He'd retired as manager but he saw me struggling with the punch ball. I was useless at it. Bob came over and said: "Out of the way, son. I'll show you how." He was magnificent at it, better than a boxer.'

On his return to Britain after more than four years abroad, Paisley was stationed at Woolwich Arsenal. VE Day, 8 May 1945, also happened to be the same date on which he had joined Liverpool six years earlier and at last, with hostilities over, he could again turn his thoughts to playing football. He had made thirty-three appearances and scored ten goals in wartime games prior to his departure overseas in 1941, and resumed in 1945–46 in the North and South Divisions set up by the Football League. He also made his FA Cup debut for Liverpool as the competition resumed on a two-leg home and away basis up to the semi-finals. Liverpool failed to progress that far, going out to Bolton Wanderers on a 5–2 aggregate after disposing of Chester on a 4–1 aggregate in round three.

He teamed up again with Billy Liddell and others like Laurie Hughes and Ray Lambert whose full Liverpool debuts had also been long delayed by the war. Lambert, originally a centre-half who switched to full-back and went on to represent Wales, was believed to be the youngest player ever to join a Football League club, putting pen to paper at the age of thirteen-and-a-half to sign for Liverpool as an amateur in January 1936 before signing professional forms in July 1939. He recalled: 'Bob and I shared digs and we grew up together at Liverpool. After one match, when we won 2–0 at Newcastle, Bob asked the manager, George Kay, if he and I could stay the weekend with Bob's family at Hetton, which wasn't far away. He gave permission as long as we were back at Anfield at ten o'clock on Tuesday morning. I met his parents, who were lovely people. On the Sunday morning, when we went for a walk, Bob took me to this dip in a field where there were a group of men playing cards. Gambling like that was illegal then, and there were look-outs posted in case a bobby was spotted!

'Bob was a good, strong, hearty player and a very good tackler. When we played Stoke he and I hatched a plan to stop Stanley Matthews. Bob said to me: "You take him on the outside and if he comes inside I'll catch him!" It was a double cover and you needed that with Stan because he was outstanding.'

Centre-half Laurie Hughes, who went on to win England recognition, added: 'Bob was a very underestimated player. He never looked classy but he was brilliant defensively and read the game so well. He would put in the initial effort to start moves for Bill Jones and I. Bob would get the important tackle in to make things easier for us. He was an unsung hero and a wonderful guy.'

Before he was demobbed, the army gave Paisley permission to travel on Fridays to report for weekend match duty with Liverpool. Sometimes, Bob would breach regulations by breaking his journey. He would get his pass made out to Durham, stop off to play for Liverpool and then head home to the North East before returning to barracks. It was on one weekend in 1945 that the paths of Bob and Jessie first crossed, fate taking a bizarre hand in engineering their meeting. Jessie recalled: 'I was teaching in Maghull, just outside Liverpool, at the time. It was the half-term holiday and I was going with a friend to her relatives in London. We went on the Saturday midnight train and this soldier came into the compartment, threw his greatcoat on my sandwiches and sat by me. I looked at him and I wasn't very pleased. He apologised, we got talking – and that was it!'

Bob's impish sense of humour swiftly bubbled to the surface when Jessie asked him about his wartime experiences. She remembered: 'Bob showed me a scar on his arm which he said had been caused by a bayonet during a desert battle. I found out later he was having me on. He'd cut it on a tin opener!' Jessie also has another enduring humorous memory of her father Arthur's reaction when she first told her family she had met Bob and asked if she could bring him home to meet them.

'My dad asked me what job Bob did. I told him he was a footballer.

'"But what does he do?" my Dad asked again.

'"He's a professional footballer," I replied. The atmosphere just went flat. Then I had the presence of mind to add: "Well, he did serve his time as a bricklayer.'

'My Dad's response was: "Oh, that's a proper job, that's alright then!"'

Arthur, a Mancunian by birth and an organ builder by trade, had a lifetime's pride in his work on the organs at Liverpool's Anglican Cathedral and St George's Hall, even though he could not play a note on them. Early in life he had a leaning towards Manchester City but when he moved to Merseyside he would cycle from his West Derby home to watch Liverpool play one week and Everton the next. 'Nobody had cars in those days and my dad and many others would park their bikes in the yards of one of the terraced houses near the grounds and the residents would charge them three pence,' said Jessie. 'When we moved across Liverpool to Springwood he used to go to nearby Holly Park and watch non-league club South Liverpool. I can still hear my dad and his pals saying: "Let's go and see the South." After I'd met Bob my dad liked to watch him play for Liverpool. He didn't go to Everton at all after that!'

The couple were married at All Souls Church, Springwood, Liverpool, on 17 July 1946, and in the ensuing years would celebrate the arrival of two sons, Robert and Graham, and a daughter, Christine. Bob's dislike of fuss persuaded him to keep quiet about his wedding, which took place on a Wednesday. Then he received an invitation from his pal and team-mate Billy Liddell to be a wedding guest three days later at the Scotland winger's own marriage to Phyllis in Garston.

'Very sorry, Bill,' Bob replied, 'but I'll be away on honeymoon!'

Jessie could understand Bob's pronounced Durham accent, but she observed a change when she returned with him to his native North East. 'His accent got stronger if you went up there, particularly if you were in his family's house,' she said. 'He used to just slip back into it. It was quite funny, really.'

Their wedding came after Bob's return from an American tour with Liverpool and just six weeks before football dusted itself off following its enforced wartime disruption. Up went the shutters on a new beginning, the long-awaited resumption of the Football League proper in season 1946–47. It meant that Paisley, Liddell, Hughes, Jones and the rest could finally make their League debuts in a squad of many new faces.

'Billy Liddell was blossoming as an international player and a great winger, after appearing for Scotland during the war,' said Paisley. 'We'd signed goalkeeper Cyril Sidlow and the full-backs included Ray Lambert, Jim Harley, Barney Ramsden and Eddie Spicer. In the half-back line we had players like versatile Bill Jones, Phil Taylor and Laurie Hughes. Laurie was a bit younger than the other lads and got a speck in the team during the war. He was coming good and he was a bit of a character, too. Up front we had a fine goalscorer in Jack Balmer.'

Bob sat out the opening two games of the new campaign, which opened on 31 August with Liverpool snatching a 1–0 win at Sheffield United thanks to a 90th-minute goal from Len Carney.

It was the only goal he scored in just six outings for the club, but just how valuable it was would be seen some ten months hence. For little did Liverpool know that it would be mid-June before they knew their First Division fate. Despite heavy rain around the country, massive crowds turned out to see the return of League football. It attracted a total of 950,000 spectators, with six clubs pulling in 50,000-plus crowds: Everton, who had reigned as champions because of the war, Chelsea, Sunderland, Tottenham, Aston Villa and Wolves.

Paisley also missed the home defeat by Middlesbrough the following Wednesday, but was called up to pull on a Liverpool jersey for the first time in League football against Chelsea at Anfield. Although Kay was manager, the directors picked the team, a system that would continue until Bill Shankly's arrival in 1959. Bob made his debut on Saturday 7 September 1946, and this was the Liverpool line-up: Charlie Ashcroft in goal, full-backs Jim Harley and Barney Ramsden, wing-halves Phil Taylor, Laurie Hughes and Bob Paisley, and a forward line comprising the South African Berry Nieuwenhuys, Jack Balmer, the highly versatile Bill Jones at centre-forward, Willie Fagan and Billy Liddell on the left wing. During the war, Nieuwenhuys had a distinguished campaign in the RAF and was awarded the Czech Medal of Merit, while Jones won the Military Medal for rescuing wounded comrades under fire.

The launch of Paisley's League career at Liverpool was dramatic. Watched by a crowd just five short of 50,000, he helped them to a whopping 7–4 win, Liddell, Fagan and Jones each scoring twice with Balmer notching the other. Paisley produced an assured debut, and Liddell was very impressed by his committed, uncompromising new team-mate.

'Bob was a hard-tackling player and one of the first fellows with the long throw-ins,' he said. 'He could throw the ball from the touchline to the near post, which was a valuable weapon in our armoury. He was an honest grafter and a great man to have on your side, tremendously strong and rugged. He never gave up. Despite his size he was a hard tackler and in those days the tackling was hard. We also used the shoulder charge, which you never see nowadays. When Laurie Hughes was playing centre-half, with Bob at left-half, Bob used to do all the tackling so that Laurie could step in on to the ball. I played in front of him for years at Liverpool and it was a great comfort to have him there, pushing the ball through for me. As players, we used to live opposite each other and the day my wife and I moved in, Bob was the first person across our doorstep to welcome us.'

Said Paisley: 'I was aggressive but I played the game because I loved and enjoyed it. I might have hurt people – and I got hurt myself a few times – but not with any malice. When I went on to the field I just wanted to play football. I didn't go out to kick anybody purposely. I just enjoyed playing and if that's aggression, then I'm guilty of that.'

By a strange quirk, while the first team were going goal-crazy and demolishing Chelsea 7–4, Liverpool reserves lost by an identical score at Preston! Yet Liverpool's strength in reserve was formidable. Wales international Cyril Sidlow, who had been absent after playing in the opening two games, established himself as Liverpool's first choice goalkeeper, Lambert became the regular right back and fellow defenders Eddie Spicer and Jim Harley, who had won Glasgow's Powderhall Sprint at 18 under the assumed name of A.B. Mitchell and was fined £10 for missing training, also appeared. Cyril Done and Bob Priday were also among the total of 26 players used by manager Kay during that comeback season for League football.

Paisley was building a sound football philosophy as he keenly observed how Liverpool played the game and how the club was run: 'I got to know the routine and I think the game's one of understanding, both from a player's and manager's point of view. The perfect man has never been born and players, like everyone else, have their weaknesses. It was on this theme, later, that I tried to select sides and pick players. I think foremost in my mind when I went on to the coaching side was to consider what I couldn't do as a player. I thought to myself, now where did I go wrong, where did I go adrift? I won the ball as much as anyone but I didn't always distribute it correctly. It was something I tried to instil into other people. With great respect to them, I think it is one of the failings of many great professionals who have had their day. Men like Raich Carter, Tommy Lawton and many more could never move away from their own skill bracket. This is where some of the great players have suffered.'

Four days after that thrilling win over Chelsea, Bob was in the side which lost 5–0 away to Manchester United, now managed by Matt Busby. That emphatic reverse prompted instant action by Liverpool, whose chairman, W. H. 'Billy' McConnell, dashed to the North East with manager Kay to sign Albert Stubbins, the red-haired 28-year-old Newcastle United centre-forward who was the leading marksman in English wartime football with 244 goals. Stubbins had joined Newcastle in April 1937 but, because his later career clashed with those of Tommy Lawton, Jackie Milburn and Nat Lofthouse, his England recognition was restricted to a victory international appearance against Wales at West Bromwich in October 1945, although he did represent the Football League, once scoring five against the Irish League at Blackpool. With Newcastle in the Second Division, he was keen for a move and was top of Liverpool's wanted list. But they were desperate to prevent news of their transfer mission leaking out and alerting Everton manager Theo Kelly. The operation was so cloak-and-dagger that McConnell and Kay attended a midweek reserve game at Everton before surreptitiously slipping out of Goodison at half-time and driving straight to Tyneside! They reached agreement with Newcastle overnight on a club record fee of £12,000 as Theo Kelly was still on the road to the North East, unaware that Liverpool were hours ahead of him.

A pleasant surprise awaited Stubbins when he popped into a Newcastle cinema. 'I was sitting in Newcastle News Theatre when a notice suddenly came up on the screen saying: "Would Albert Stubbins please report to St James's Park",' he recounted. When he got there he found both Merseyside parties waiting there with permission to speak to him. Kelly even topped Liverpool's bid by £500. So it was up to the player to decide whether his future lay with the red or blue half of Merseyside.

'When I got to the ground representatives of both Liverpool and Everton were there,' Stubbins said. 'Stan Seymour senior, in charge of Newcastle, said to me: "Who do you want to speak to first?" I knew they were both good clubs so I spun a coin and it came down heads to meet Liverpool first. I came to an agreement with them and when I met Theo Kelly of Everton I told him I'd made up my mind to go to Liverpool, and he was very courteous about it. It was a very happy time for me. Although Everton are a good club I'm glad the coin came down heads because I couldn't have had a better move.'

Stubbins was to prove an inspired acquisition, a player whose goals would help secure Bob Paisley his first silverware as a professional. 'The fact that I'd scored goals for Newcastle gave me the confidence to think I could do it for Liverpool,' said Stubbins.

'In contrast to some players who later moved for bigger fees, I never felt any sense of strain over the price Liverpool had paid. It was never a worry to me and, in fact, it was an incentive for me. I got off to a good start by scoring on my debut and the crowd were so good to me, as they were in all the years I was there.' That scoring debut by Stubbins in a 3–1 win at Bolton avenged Liverpool's FA Cup knock-out by the Lancashire club the previous season. Paisley was an injured spectator for the new signing's third Liverpool outing and saw the power of a Stubbins penalty-kick fracture the arm of Leeds United goalkeeper Johnny Hodgson as he pulled off a brave but painful save. Liverpool still went on to a 2–0 win.

The arrival of Stubbins not only sparked a twelve-match unbeaten run through to late November, which sent them to the top of the League, but also signalled the beginning of a life-long friendship between Wallsend-born Stubbins and Paisley, two sons of the North East who became key figures of Merseyside football. Stubbins went on to score 83 goals in 180 Liverpool appearances and during his Anfield career wrote a column for the *Liverpool Echo*. He took up journalism professionally in the North East after hanging up his boots.

Stubbins also had another claim to fame. His Anfield deeds thrilled a certain Liverpudlian called Paul McCartney and led to his being included on the montage cover picture of the celebrated Beatles album *Sergeant Pepper's Lonely Hearts Club Band* some two decades later. 'I got a telephone call one day from a young lady who said she was ringing on behalf of The Beatles' management,' he said. 'She asked if I would consent to my photograph being used on the cover of the *Sergeant Pepper* album. I said of course I would and told them to go ahead. I'd never met Paul at that time but it seemed obvious he was a Liverpool supporter.'

After joining Liverpool, Stubbins swiftly became aware of Paisley's qualities, on and off the field. 'Bob was not averse to having a discussion and to analyse a game in the after-match bath,' he said. 'Most of us were just glad to get the mud off us and relax in the warm water. But if we'd conceded a goal we shouldn't have done, for example, he'd want to go into detail and try to work out how the other team had found a gap in our defence. He wasn't trying to be clever or score points off anybody. He simply wanted to know so that maybe in the next game such a situation might be averted. I have to say that when he did analyse matches in the bath, he was pretty accurate too!

'As well as his high principles and his deep thinking, Bob also had great tenacity and total commitment. We lost to Everton at Goodison Park in a typical gruelling, hard-fought derby and at the end Bob had given so much he struggled to negotiate the steps back to the dressing room. He was just ahead of me and he could hardly walk. He was so exhausted he had to grab hold of the hand rail. I've never seen a man more drained.'

Liverpool's march was halted by a 3–2 defeat at Blackpool and a week later, on 7 December, they suffered the humiliation of a 5–1 home hiding by Wolves, watched by 52,512, Anfield's biggest crowd of the season. That put Wolves top, and apart from a weather-hit spell during a fierce winter when they were prevented from playing, they stayed in pole position until facing Liverpool in the return fixture at Molineux, their last game of the season.

As for Liverpool, the emphatic defeat by Wolves, in which Wallasey-born Everton reject Dennis Westcott scored four, was followed by successive 4–1 wins over Sunderland and Aston Villa which saw the prodigious Jack Balmer, attack partner to Stubbins, complete a run of scoring in seven consecutive League games, including three successive hat-tricks against Portsmouth at home, Derby County away – when he scored four – and Arsenal at home. He became the first player to achieve that feat in one season, Everton's Dixie Dean having scored consecutive hat-tricks at the end of season 1927–28 and a third treble in the opening game of the 1928–29 campaign.

George Kay's refusal to make his players tactical slaves had an impact on Paisley and influenced him in later years. 'This has always been the Liverpool way,' said Bob. 'The players have always been allowed to go out and express themselves. I don't mean individuals just going off willy-nilly without some organisation – they have to have some inkling of what's expected of them. Having said that, there's no way we'd tie down an individual at Anfield.'

Stubbins shared Paisley's views about life at Anfield in the immediate post-war era. 'The thing that struck me most about Liverpool was the common-sense attitude that persisted then and which continued, carrying the team and the club to so much success,' he said. 'There was such a sensible approach to things. The players got on so well and you weren't hauled over the coals for silly misdemeanours. They treated you like men and I think that policy was maintained over the years.'

The 1946–47 winter was a bleak one for a Britain still coming to terms with the massive drain of the war years, which meant continued rationing. The average weekly wage was £6 and most players earned little, if anything, more than that. Yet match attendances reached record levels. Ivan Sharpe, in the *Sunday Chronicle Football Annual*, observed: 'Reaction after years of war has sent Britain into a football boom. Attendances have reached new heights, with crowds flocking to games as never before and this is reflected in the balance sheets of the more successful clubs.' Consequently, in February 1947 the players threatened to strike in pursuit of what they passionately felt was a justified pay increase. The BBC reported: 'Members of the Professional Footballers' Association have been meeting in Manchester to discuss their request for a £12 season wage and a £10 summer wage. The Football League have already turned down their request and the players decided to submit their case to the Ministry of Labour. If the Football League opposes this decision, then the players say they will strike.'

The strike threat was averted and a new agreement hammered out which meant a new maximum wage for players of £12 during the season and £10 in the summer and a minimum level for a full-time player over 20 of £7 and £5 respectively. An increase in what was termed 'talent money' for players helping clubs to success on the field, was also agreed, meaning that players winning the championship could share a pay-out ranging between £275 and £550. Although Paisley and his team-mates never enjoyed the heady financial rewards that came the way of later generations of footballers, he felt that playing for Liverpool brought its own rewards. 'People have earned a lot more than me but nobody has enjoyed the game more than me,' he declared. 'By and large I like the approach and outlook of the ordinary Liverpudlian and I'm proud to have been able to help in providing them with a little bit of entertainment over the years.'

In 1947 a pint of beer cost seven pence in old money and a family saloon car cost around £400. But many commodities were either scarce or simply not available. Bananas, for instance, were an exotic luxury. The weather added its own icy gloom with blizzards and sub-zero temperatures playing havoc with life in general and football's fixture list in particular. England and Middlesbrough full-back George Hardwick vividly recalls that season and one particular FA Cup tie at Burnley: 'It was the most ridiculous situation I ever ran across in football. When we arrived at Turf Moor from Middlesbrough there were groups of men with crowbars and they were actually chipping out the ice from the lines and putting sawdust down. I didn't think for one moment the game would be played. But the referee thought otherwise and it went ahead.'

The backlog of fixtures caused by the severe winter was to conjure an incredible climax to the season for Paisley and Liverpool. But they had a dismal ten-match sequence between late November and the end of January in which they lost seven times and won on only three occasions. Their title ambitions, it seemed, had perished in the big freeze. In the FA Cup, however, they marched to the semi-final by toppling Walsall, Grimsby Town, Derby County and then Birmingham, who crashed 4–1 at Anfield thanks to a Stubbins hat-trick that included a still fondly remembered diving header from a free kick by Billy Liddell.

'In the second half, Billy was about to take a free kick and I took a position on the edge of the box,' said Stubbins. 'The Birmingham defence felt that as I'd gone back there, I wasn't going to cause any problem and left me more or less unmarked. It was one of Billy's low free kicks and when he struck it I started running at full speed. As the ball came flashing across I just dived at it and I was able to direct it to the keeper's left. Given the power of Billy's kick and the pace at which I met it, the velocity of the ball was terrific. It just flew in! It was an icy ground and both my knees were lacerated and bleeding. But it was certainly worth it!'

Liddell developed a productive understanding with Paisley on Liverpool's left flank and, as well as weighing in with his own quota of goals, provided much of the ammunition for Stubbins, Jack Balmer and Cyril Done, whose first Liverpool goal had come on the last Saturday of peace back in 1939. The fantastic versatility of Liddell was underlined by the fact that over the span of his Liverpool career he played in every department of the team apart from in goal – and he missed out on that only because he lost on the toss of a coin with Ronnie Moran after the recognised keeper had been injured during the match. Stubbins and Paisley drooled over Liddell's talents.

'We were playing Preston at Deepdale and got a free kick just outside the box,' Stubbins remembered. 'Billy was aiming to hit it with his right foot when the wind rolled the ball away. He just let it run and hit it with his left and it went in like a rocket. He was fast, courageous and very strong. When we got to Newcastle one day, I popped into their dressing room to say hello to my old team-mates. Newcastle had a very good full back in Bobby Cowell, who said to me: "Albert, how do I play against Billy Liddell?"

'I replied: "I'll say one thing: if Billy picks up the ball and you're not close to him when he does, you're dead!"'

According to Paisley, Liddell had qualities adored by the Kop. 'As well as being very skilful, Billy had a physical quality that was exciting,' he said. 'He would battle, challenge and show tenacity. The Liverpool crowd respond to that, and always have done.'

Liddell's majestic wing play was recognised at the end of the season by his selection for the Great Britain side that crushed the Rest of Europe 6–1 at Glasgow's Hampden Park. He wore the number 11 jersey to complete a mouth-watering forward line that also included the England trio of Stanley Matthews, Wilf Mannion and Tommy Lawton as well as inside-forward Billy Steel, who was selected after playing just nine games for Morton and one for Scotland. Steel was set to join Liddell, Paisley, Stubbins and company at Anfield, but after talking to Liverpool his proposed £15,000 British record-breaking transfer fell through and he joined Derby County instead. The Steel deal collapse had a direct impact on the lifestyle of Bob and Jessie Paisley. Liverpool had put Steel next in line for a club house if the transfer had gone through. When it fell through, the Paisleys took Steel's place on the Anfield housing list.

Liddell, meanwhile, went on to share with Matthews the distinction of being the only two players to represent Great Britain twice. They appeared again for the Combined British side against the Rest of Europe in Belfast in August 1955, to celebrate the Irish FA's 75th anniversary, a game which drew a 58,000 crowd who provided receipts of £13,000. But the celebrations belonged to the Continental visitors who won 4–1 against a team captained by Northern Ireland's Danny Blanchflower and which also included Wales giant John Charles.

Liverpool's FA Cup progress in 1947 was halted by Burnley, who beat them 1–0 through a Ray Harrison goal in a semi-final replay at Maine Road after a goalless extra-time deadlock at Ewood Park. But with their Wembley hopes ended, Liverpool dramatically revived their championship prospects. A sequence of five wins and two draws from seven games was interrupted by a 3–2 home defeat by Blackpool on 5 April. Five of their eight remaining matches were away from home and many pundits believed the championship was beyond them – it seemed their best chance was in snatching the runners-up spot in a four-club battle at the top that also involved Wolves, Manchester United and Stoke City. Liverpool's response was to reel off five straight wins which included a crucial 1–0 home defeat of Manchester United, thanks to an early Stubbins strike. Now they had four consecutive away games to finish their programme in what proved to be the longest season in football history. The Arctic winter had accounted for the postponement or abandonment of 146 League games and it meant that instead of Liverpool going to Wolves on 12 April, as scheduled on the fixture list, the game was not staged until 31 May.

Victories at Charlton and Arsenal and a draw at Brentford dramatically maintained Liverpool's title momentum to send them to Molineux with the championship up for grabs. Wolves had 56 points, the same total as Manchester United, who had completed their programme, while Liverpool and Stoke were on 55. But as they faced Wolves in their formidable Molineux fortress with the title at stake, there was a triple blow for Liverpool with Paisley, Phil Taylor and Willie Fagan ruled out with injuries. None the less, the spirit in the camp was undimmed, as Albert Stubbins recalled.

'We had been well behind and had a daunting and demanding run-in,' he said. 'It was really nerve-wracking. We got to the last game at Wolves, which was played on a very hot day. With Bob and Willie Fagan unfit we had to make a switch, with Billy Liddell playing in the unusual position for him of inside-left, even though he wore number seven and Billy Watkinson came in wearing the number ten jersey. Bob Priday, a young South African winger, came in at outside-left. I said to Bob Priday before the game: "If you lie deep and pick up the ball just hit a long pass, not to my feet but past me and past Stan Cullis. I'll see what I can do with it."'

The game was a farewell for Wolves captain Cullis, who was desperately hoping to end his quest for a championship medal before hanging up his boots. Alas, the Merseyside-born centre-half had his heartfelt ambition wrecked by the Liverpool strike force of Balmer and Stubbins. Skipper Balmer put Liverpool ahead after 21 minutes and with seven minutes of the first half remaining, Stubbins had the travelling Liverpool fans ecstatic by making it 2–0, as he described: 'Sure enough, Bob Priday was able to pick up the ball in his own half and, without wasting any time,

I was ready for it. Bob hit a long pass over the head of Stan Cullis, who went after it. So did Billy Wright, while the two full-backs tried to close the gap. I got the ball, accelerated, and took it past them. And as goalkeeper Bert Williams came out, I just rolled it past him into the net.'

Wolves pulled a goal back in the second half through Jimmy Dunn and mounted a series of furious attacks. But Liverpool, with former Wolves goalkeeper Cyril Sidlow in inspired form against his old club, and Liddell dropping back to bolster the defence, held out for victory. They had to wait a further fortnight before learning if they would be champions. If Stoke, who were two points behind but with a superior goal average, won their final game at Sheffield United in mid June then the title would go to the Potteries. What was certain was that Cullis's last hope of a championship medal as a player had gone, although he would go on to collect three as a manager as well as guide Wolves to two FA Cup triumphs. And he was quick to congratulate Stubbins, as the Liverpool centre-forward recalled: 'When Stan and I shook hands there were tears rolling down his face. We respected each other. We played hard but there was never any ill feeling. That goal I scored plagued him. Wherever he went people asked him about it and why he hadn't tugged my shirt. I think he deserves a lot of credit for the fact that he didn't, because he might have got away with it.'

The fortnight's wait must have seemed an eternity for Liverpool and Paisley. He had figured in 33 of Liverpool's 42 League fixtures which, in itself, was highly satisfactory from a personal standpoint. But how much more satisfying it would be if there was a championship medal to crown it. When, finally, Sheffield United met Stoke on Saturday 14 June, racegoers were preparing for the start of Royal Ascot three days later! And while the game was in progress at Sheffield, Liverpool faced Everton at Anfield in the delayed Liverpool Senior Cup Final, which drew a 40,000 crowd and kicked off fifteen minutes later than the title decider at Bramall Lane. A tannoy announcement that Sheffield United had won 2–1 sparked some amazing scenes on and off the field. Both teams stopped playing and the Everton players walked round the pitch offering congratulatory handshakes to their Liverpool opponents. Albert Stubbins will never forget that day.

'Midway through the second half we heard a hubbub amongst the crowd,' he remembered. 'We knew something was happening. Then we heard cheers and the news was brought to us in the centre of the pitch that we were champions. It was great for the city of Liverpool that we kept the title on Merseyside. Everton had held it right through the war after being champions in 1939 and we had become the first post-war champions. The Everton players immediately shook our hands to congratulate us on the pitch.'

Sheffield's amazing win over a Stoke side that had been unbeaten in the previous 11 games was achieved thanks to a winner by 40-year-old Jack Pickering who, to pile drama on to drama, was making his only League appearance of the season! Liverpool's win over Everton to lift the Liverpool Senior Cup completed a foursome, the Lancashire Cup and the Lancashire Combination championship having already been secured. For Paisley, the League triumph brought him the first of an incredible ten championship medals in his various roles over the span of his amazing Liverpool career.

'I'd won a lot of cups and medals up in the North East and then I found myself winning a championship in my first season of League football with Liverpool,' Paisley recalled. 'I don't know about my ability but I must have been a lucky mascot!'

Almost 30 years later another dramatic, heart-pounding Liverpool victory at Wolves would also provide a momentous milestone in Bob's remarkable football odyssey.

The final First Division placings that summer of 1947, as gloriously sun-kissed as the winter had been harsh, were: Liverpool, champions with 57 points from 42 games, runners-up Manchester United on 56, just pipping Wolves on goal average, with Stoke City fourth on 55 points.

Liverpool's thrilling title win was reflected in the club's balance sheet, which showed a profit of £17,208, the third highest in England just behind Burnley but way short of Stoke's whopping £32,207. The championship was the crowning glory for a squad that had a family atmosphere, recalled by Jessie Paisley: 'We lived at the beginning in club houses at Bowring Park, for which we paid 25 shillings a week rent. Billy Liddell was opposite and Albert Stubbins, Willie Fagan, Cyril Done, Phil Taylor and others were also neighbours. It really was fun and enjoyable in those days. The wives went to the games together and Phyllis Liddell and I used to sit on the wall outside the Anfield ground waiting for Bob and Billy to come out. There was no ladies' lounge or anything like that! Then we'd go to the sweet shop before we got the tram home.'

And, providing a wonderful illustration of what luxuries were like in that early peace-time era, Jessie added: 'Billy and Phyllis Liddell were the first ones to get a washing machine, so we all went to see it! Then Albert Stubbins got a new bedroom suite that wouldn't go up the stairs. So the window had to be taken out upstairs and we all spent a morning watching them get the suite into the house. We'd hardly got two halfpennies to rub together but we had great fun.'

Fun was the name of the game for that Liverpool team. Paisley was often in the mood to play practical jokes and Billy Liddell revealed what happened on one occasion: 'Just after the war we had a commissionaire at Anfield called Paddy Walsh and he used to clean the manager's car. One particular day Paddy was doing his usual immaculate job and went to get a new bucket of water. While he was gone Bob nipped in, opened the car doors and wound down the windows. Unsuspecting Paddy came back and when he threw the water it went through the windows and saturated the whole of the inside of the car.'

2

Anguish... Then a New Role

After the heady success of 1947, the next two seasons were ones of anti-climax for Liverpool. The 1947–48 campaign got underway a week after India's independence from Britain as a separate state from Pakistan. Liverpool were soon in a state themselves – one of deep depression. After winning two of their first three games, they scraped just two victories from their next 12 outings. And by October, when American test pilot Chuck Yeager became the first man to break the sound barrier, Liverpool had been brought completely down to earth as they languished in the bottom half of the First Division.

October was also the month when the Football Association first addressed the issue of television and football. The game's ruling body agreed that League games could be televised and that the individual clubs, as promoters, could make the final decision. But, quaintly, the FA added that given the limited number of households that owned a TV set, television was unlikely to affect attendances. There was no stampede by clubs to have their games screened on the box. Although Arsenal had been the first club televised, when a specially arranged 1937 friendly between the Highbury first and reserve teams was shown, and screening of FA Cup Finals had started pre-war, League football stayed shy of the TV cameras.

It was not until September 1960 that a League game was televised live, a dull Friday night Lancashire derby between Blackpool and Bolton, who won 1–0. The plan to make it a regular feature was instantly scrapped.

Although the BBC launched *Match of the Day* in August 1964, featuring recorded highlights of Liverpool's 3–2 home win over Arsenal, live League football remained off the nation's TV screens until 1983, another significant year in the life of Bob Paisley.

But the picture for him and his Liverpool colleagues in the first week of March 1948 was decidedly murky. By that stage they had collected just eight League wins and the fear of relegation was real.

Compounding their woes was an early exit from the FA Cup. They emphatically overcame Nottingham Forest in round three with a 4–1 home win, Stubbins scoring twice and Liddell and Priday also on the mark, but in the fourth round there was a painful reunion with Matt Busby when his Manchester United team toppled Liverpool 3–0. The match was played at Everton's Goodison Park due to Old Trafford being closed through wartime bomb damage.

It was Mersey derby action against Everton that was to give Liverpool their only crumbs of comfort from a bitterly disappointing season. One of their victories had come at Goodison in September, a 3–0 success achieved through goals by Balmer, Stubbins and Fagan, and on 6 March they beat Huddersfield at home to set off on a run of five straight wins that helped dispel worries about dropping into Division Two. Indeed, they lost only one of their last 11 games to finish in mid table. They happily completed the double over Everton with a 4–0 Anfield win in April, and their final fixture was especially memorable for Paisley, who scored his first Liverpool goal in a 2–1 home win over Wolves, ending a season in which he made 39 senior appearances.

A measure of Liverpool's continued box office attraction was provided when they played Newcastle, on their way to promotion from Division Two, in a Valentine's Day friendly and almost 45,000 turned up! The year also saw transfer and attendance records set. Tommy Lawton's move from Chelsea to Notts County in November 1947 set a new English record fee of £20,000, only to be surpassed by just £50 three months later when Sunderland signed Len Shackleton from Newcastle.

And the First Division clash between Manchester United and Arsenal at Maine Road in January 1948, a contest between the eventual runners-up and champions respectively, drew a crowd of 83,260, the biggest ever for a League game in England.

The following season, 1948–49, was frustratingly similar to the previous one for Bob Paisley and Liverpool.

Without Stubbins for many of the games, Liverpool finished 12th and bowed out of the FA Cup at Wolves in the fifth round. They would have made their exit at the initial hurdle had it not been for Paisley's first FA Cup goal, scored in the 90th minute at Nottingham Forest in round three to make it 2–2. That sent the game into extra time and then a replay, which Liverpool won.

It was the days of leather footballs, which were like a lump of rock when wet, and reinforced boots. And as Albert Stubbins recalled, Paisley was to witness a revolution in the weight and design of both: 'With the lighter boots and shin guards, the injuries the players received in later years were of a different nature. Bob was very much aware of this when he moved into the physiotherapy side of the game later in his career. When he and I played the ball was heavy and the boots were very strong, with hard toe-ends. If you got a kick from one and your shin wasn't protected it could break your leg. When the boots and shin guards became lighter, so the types and risk of injury changed with them.'

Paisley had a painful experience when he returned to the North East with Liverpool in October 1948 to play promoted Newcastle. Shortly after kick-off he was knocked out by a full-blooded shot from Norman Dodgin. After treatment he moved to the wing, swapping positions with Liddell, but he was still dazed and ten minutes before the interval he was carried off by trainer Albert Shelley and 12th man Cyril Done.

Nine minutes into the second half he was back in action at outside-left, resuming briefly in his left-half role before returning to the wing. But late in the game he rose to head a powerful Liddell cross, collapsed to the turf and was carried off a second time. He spent the weekend in hospital suffering from concussion and said he could remember only the opening ten minutes of the match. But he missed only one game and was back in action a fortnight later. He also collected another League goal that season, scoring in the 3–2 April defeat at champions-elect Portsmouth, in a campaign that saw him pass a century of Liverpool appearances. The fixture with Pompey at Anfield the previous November was memorable for Billy Liddell's 20-yard headed goal in Liverpool's 3–1 win.

The events of the following season, 1949–50, proved unforgettable for Bob, for both the right and wrong reasons, and almost forced him to leave the club. Yet ironically, the season could hardly have started better. He scored Liverpool's first goal in their 4–2 opening-day win over Sunderland, and the club made their best start to a season since their inaugural League campaign in the Second Division more than half a century earlier in 1893–94, when they were unbeaten in all 28 games then won a Test match for promotion. In 1949 they went on to clock up 19 League games unbeaten before suffering their first defeat at Huddersfield on 10 December. It was then the longest unbeaten run from the start of a season by any side since the First Division was enlarged to comprise 22 clubs.

That record endured until Leeds United strung together 29 matches undefeated in 1973–74, later equalled by Liverpool in 1987–88 when the top flight contained 21 teams. But Liverpool's record was the more impressive, including 22 wins to 19 by Leeds.

Bob Paisley appeared in the first 11 games of the season before losing his place through injury. And when a player was hurt in those days there was little in the way of recovery aids provided today by sophisticated machines.

Albert Stubbins recalled: 'Newcastle United were the only club I've ever known to pass the whisky around in the dressing room before we went out on the pitch! The captain took the bottle off the trainer, had a sip, said "Good luck, boys", passed it on to the next man and eventually to me, and I was only about 18.

'When it reached the end of the line it was passed back up to the captain, who had another sip, said "Good luck, boys", and the bottle was passed along all over again.

'On the pitch one day, our great Scottish wing-half Jimmy Gordon got a nasty kick on the shin and I just couldn't believe what happened. The trainer came on, loosened Jimmy's sock and poured whisky inside the pad on to the shin. The trainer who did it, Andy McCombie, was a former Scottish international himself and he really believed that if you poured whisky on to the shin it worked wonders. If you said something like that to people in the professional game today, with all the sophisticated equipment and methods, they'd be horrified.'

Paisley returned during the Christmas programme in the 2–2 home draw with Chelsea but missed out on the club's final game of the decade. That was against Arsenal on 31 December when two Liddell goals gave Liverpool a 2–0 home win — the second of them direct from a corner — to put them top of the League.

Bob was back in action early in the New Year and soon showing the form that won a glowing salute from no less a figure than Danny Blanchflower, who would later captain and manage Northern Ireland. The future Tottenham skipper recalled: 'My first match at Anfield was at right-back for Aston Villa. The roar from the Kop was awesome as Billy Liddell waltzed down the wing making us look like idiots. Then I began to recognize the source of Liddell's magic. He was Liverpool's inconspicuous craftsman at left-half, Bob Paisley.'

Injury forced Paisley to miss the opening of Liverpool's 1950 FA Cup campaign, a goalless draw at Blackburn, but he was back in the team for the replay, taking over from another casualty Bill Jones, and helped the team achieve a 2–1 win. Indeed, he stayed in the side through every round right up to the gates of Wembley – only to then see them slammed shut in his face.

Exeter fell 3–1 in round four and Stockport were then beaten 2–1 at Edgeley Park before Blackpool, without Stanley Matthews, were knocked out 2–1 at Anfield. That brought a semi-final collision with Everton at Maine Road. Merseyside was agog at the prospect of the first such semi-final meeting between Everton and Liverpool since 1906 and their first at any stage of the FA Cup since 1932.

'I remember my dad and I sharing a place in a day-long queue at the station just to get his train ticket to go to Manchester for the game,' Jessie Paisley recalled. 'You didn't think anything of it. There were no privileges then. Nobody in the queue knew who I was and I remember one chap behind me saying to another: "I'm just a bit worried about that Paisley fellow in case he handles the ball again." I assume that in a game not long before that Bob must have handled it for some reason! It was quite funny to hear him say that.'

That same supporter would probably have been raising a glass to Paisley after his telling contribution to the semi-final. This is how the teams lined up on Grand National day, Saturday 25 March: Everton had George Burnett in goal, full-backs Eric Moore and Jack Hedley, a half-back line of Jackie Grant, Dave Falder and Peter Farrell, and an attack comprising Ted Buckle, Eddie Wainwright, Harry Catterick, Wally Fielding and Tommy Eglington; Liverpool had Cyril Sidlow in goal, Ray Lambert and Eddie Spicer the full-backs, Phil Taylor, Bill Jones and Bob Paisley as the half-back trio, with a forward line of Jimmy Payne, Kevin

Baron, Albert Stubbins, Willie Fagan and Billy Liddell.

A 73,000 crowd descended on Manchester, generating gate receipts of £13,497, and the red section were jubilant in the 29th minute when Liverpool went ahead, with Paisley the unlikely marksman. As 10–1 shot Freebooter was romping to victory at Aintree, forty miles away Bob unleashed a 'freebooter' of his own. Jimmy Payne delivered a high cross which Everton keeper Burnett could only punch straight out, and it fell fortuitously to the feet of Paisley, who lobbed it back into the goalmouth, and with Burnett distracted by a double challenge from Stubbins and Liddell, the ball sailed into the Everton net. A mistake by Peter Farrell then presented Liddell with a chance to clinch victory for Liverpool after 62 minutes with a shot from an acute angle, and it was a night of jubilant celebration for Paisley and Liverpool as the club savoured the prospect of their first ever game at Wembley and their first appearance in an FA Cup Final since losing 1–0 to Burnley at Crystal Palace in 1914, when King George V became the first reigning monarch to attend the event.

The club standing between Liverpool and their first FA Cup success was Arsenal. But Liverpool had beaten the Gunners in both League games that season, and although title hopes had collapsed with a dismal run of just three wins and eleven goals scored in their last thirteen First Division fixtures, to finish eighth, optimism was high that they could triumph at Wembley at the end of April.

The joyful build-up to the final turned to anguish for Paisley, however, when he found himself omitted from the Wembley team, a decision made not by manager George Kay but by the nine directors who picked the side. A knee injury had prevented Paisley from playing in the four League games leading up to the final, but he was fit and available for Wembley – and left out. There was not even a place on the bench, because no substitutes were then allowed. In the only change in personnel from the semi-final team, Laurie Hughes, an England centre-half, returned to the side in a half-back line that also included two other England men: Bill Jones, who took over Paisley's left-half role, and skipper Phil Taylor, who had succeeded Jack Balmer as captain that season. The directors voted by a 5–4 majority to play Jones rather than Paisley, who was devastated by his omission.

Said Paisley: 'I knew that George Kay didn't pick the team but I was so disappointed I could hardly look at him when he got on the team bus. I was with the lads at the time so I didn't say anything. I didn't want to upset them because I wanted them to win the Cup. I had a good heart-to-heart chat with Albert Stubbins, who was a good friend, and I told him I was thinking of leaving Liverpool. I also had an offer from a Sunday paper offering quite a bit of money to have a go in print about being left out and saying publicly how I felt. I was tempted but I turned them down. I didn't want the big headlines.'

Stubbins confirmed: 'He really was very despondent over being left out, especially after scoring one of the semi-final goals that got us to Wembley. Mentally, he was a very strong man, but he was really shattered when he got the news. He and I were chatting and I said: "Don't leave Liverpool. I know it's an awful disappointment to be missing such a big game. But you're settled on Merseyside and if you leave it's going to affect your whole life."

'He was at the lowest point in his career. But I told him to think very hard about it. "Don't make a hasty decision, don't leave the club on a sudden whim, however disappointed you feel," I told him. Fortunately for Liverpool, he stayed. Just imagine how different football history would have been if he had left! Ironically, his bitter experience helped to equip him even more for the decisions he had to take later as a manager.'

The impact of Bob's absence from the Wembley team was felt deeply by his family, as Jessie Paisley recalled: 'I remember going to the match and I can't say that I particularly wanted to go after what had happened to Bob. It was like an ante-natal clinic on the train, because there were about six of the wives all expecting. Football-wise it was a very disappointing time. Bob didn't kick up any fuss officially about being left out. But he was awfully upset and his father was furious. Up in Hetton they would have nothing to do with the final. The whole town was up in arms over Bob being dropped.'

Ultimately, it was a gloomy day all round for Liverpool. The Arsenal side was superbly marshalled by left-half Joe Mercer, the Hoylake-based former Everton star who trained at Anfield following his move to Highbury six years earlier. He continued to train there during the build-up to Wembley but to avoid having a 'spy' in the camp, Liverpool told Joe he had to go through his paces on his own in the afternoons after the club sessions had finished.

In those days when there was a Cup Final colour clash, both

clubs had to change. So Liverpool wore white shirts with red collars and cuffs and black shorts that afternoon, while Arsenal played in old-gold shirts and white shorts. This was how the teams lined up:

Arsenal: George Swindin; Laurie Scott, Walley Barnes; Alex Forbes, Leslie Compton, Joe Mercer (captain); Freddie Cox, Jimmy Logie, Peter Goring, Reg Lewis, Denis Compton.

Liverpool: Cyril Sidlow; Ray Lambert, Eddie Spicer; Phil Taylor (captain), Laurie Hughes, Bill Jones; Jimmy Payne, Kevin Baron, Albert Stubbins, Willie Fagan, Billy Liddell.

Liverpool retained Baron at inside-right even though Jack Balmer had recovered from a long battle against injury. Manager Kay was taken ill on the journey south but attended the game, clearly unwell and suffering from stress. That was certainly not relieved by Liddell's early clattering from his fellow Scotland international Forbes, a physical attention that the great winger attracted throughout the match. Arsenal went ahead through a 17th-minute goal after Leslie Compton and Barnes combined to find Logie, as Goring set off on a decoy run that took Hughes with him. Logie simply played the ball through the subsequent gap and Lewis slipped it past Sidlow.

Liverpool had their chances to draw level, notably when Arsenal goalkeeper Swindin palmed an effort from Payne on to the bar. He also had to make a last-ditch save after missing a Liddell centre. But in the 63rd minute Arsenal – and Lewis – scored a second goal. Goring, the young centre-forward in his first season in top-class football, linked with Denis Compton and Cox to release Lewis, who hit a first-time shot into the left-hand corner of Sidlow's net. Increasingly desperate, Liverpool frantically strove to get back in the game but when Taylor's header hit the bar and Fagan missed another chance, it was clear that the cup was destined for North London. Tom Whittaker's Arsenal, average age 31, became the oldest team to win the trophy, and when Footballer of the Year Mercer received the cup from King George VI, he became, at 35, the oldest winning captain. Two years later, when he was 37 years 268 days old, he tasted the other side of the Final's emotional scenario when he skippered injury-hit Arsenal in their 1–0 defeat by Newcastle.

Recriminations and inquests following Liverpool's Wembley defeat focused on the absence of Paisley. Many pundits felt that on a pitch made greasy by a pre-match downpour and subsequent

April showers, Paisley's combative talents and incisive tackling would have helped to quell the threat of Logie. As it was, Liverpool's renowned half-backs never did themselves justice and as the *Sunday Times* reported, the Anfield side 'were gallant losers but were outmatched by a better all-round team'.

Liverpool's Wembley captain, and later manager, Phil Taylor, was one who believed that if Paisley had played against Arsenal the cup would have gone to Merseyside rather than North London. 'Bob must have been the unluckiest player ever not to be in the team and if he had been I'm sure we'd have won,' said Taylor. 'That is no reflection whatsoever on any of those who did play, but Bob's qualities would have been invaluable at Wembley. He would never shirk or pull out of a tackle. If he thought it was his ball, it was his ball.'

Winger Jimmy Payne echoed Taylor's sentiments: 'We might have won the Cup if Bob had played because he was such a hard worker. I played at inside-forward as well as on the wing and Bob played like two men. He was always feeding you the ball. Without that supply you can't play and Bob was a great supplier. I think the game today needs his type very much.'

Paisley, to his credit, came to terms with his Wembley anguish and reflected on it philosophically. 'Probably missing a European Cup Final is the only thing that matches being left out of the FA Cup Final,' he said. 'It hit me so hard in 1950 that if a club had come in for me and Liverpool had wanted me to go then I would have left. But during the summer I thought about it and came to the conclusion that even if I had left, the same thing could happen somewhere else. So I stayed put and the odd thing was that the following season I not only captained the side but I played in 41 of the 42 League games.

'And the experience did serve its purpose. As a manager I had to tell players they were left out and at least when I say I understand how they feel, I really do understand and I'm more patient if they fly off the handle, which I was tempted to do in 1950.'

It was typical of Merseyside supporters that they turned out in their thousands to welcome home the defeated Wembley team. Crowds lined the streets and turned up en masse at Anfield to see the losers parade around the pitch before attending a civic reception at the town hall. But it was to prove a watershed weekend in Liverpool fortunes, signalling the start of the club's wilderness years. Liverpool, stripped of Laurie Hughes for a lengthy spell after he sustained knee damage appearing in the Charity Shield for an England XI, finished ninth in the First Division in 1950–51, a position made to look more respectable by neighbours Everton's relegation after finishing bottom. But the warnings of decline at Anfield were clear. In the FA Cup they suffered an embarrassing third-round exit at Third Division Norwich, 3–1, and in the League they were kept afloat by 15 goals from Liddell and ten from Balmer but conceded four on three occasions at Anfield, to Huddersfield, Newcastle and Wolves.

Two of those games marked the end of the careers of two Liverpool players. The 4–2 defeat by Newcastle in November saw the curtain fall for goalkeeper Cyril Sidlow. He was beaten four times in a ten-minute period spanning the half-time interval and the Wales international never appeared again after 165 senior appearances. Sidlow's own protégé, Rusell Crossley, replaced him and went on to dispute the goalkeeping berth with Charlie Ashcroft. When Wolves won 4–1 in front of the Kop a month later it spelled the end of a much briefer First Division career for a Scottish centre-half called Joe Cadden. His arrival at Anfield had been the result of Liverpool's strong American links which were forged through a series of club tours of the United States, Bob Paisley being the only man to travel on every one.

Paisley's first American trip with the club was in 1946 when he helped Liverpool win all ten tour games as the first English team to travel Stateside since the end of the war. Bob was a member of the playing squad that returned two years later and won all 11 games and also had their interest alerted in Glasgow-born Cadden, a defender then playing for Brooklyn Wanderers, who returned to Britain to sign for Liverpool. He made his debut in the autumn of 1950 but the demands of top-flight English football were too great on him and his fourth First Division outing was also his last. He made just one FA Cup appearance the following season before being transferred to Grimsby.

In February 1951, George Kay retired on medical advice. The toll that the pressures of top-class football had taken on him, so evident at the previous year's Cup Final, made it impossible for him to continue in charge. A little over three years later he was dead at the age of 62. Liverpool turned to another Mancunian, Don Welsh, to succeed Kay. A former England international, he had guested as a player for Liverpool, among other clubs, during the war before hanging up his boots to enter management as boss of Brighton and Hove Albion. He took over at Liverpool in March at the age of 40.

In his first full season in charge, Welsh recruited 18-year-old right-winger Brian Jackson from Leyton Orient, for a then substantial fee for a teenager of £6,500. But the new manager lost a batch of senior Anfield professionals to injury. Stubbins who had scored five goals for the Football League in a 6–3 win over the Irish League the previous season, had to undergo thigh surgery and made only 13 League appearances in 1951–52, full-back Spicer missed the whole campaign after breaking a leg on the club's summer tour to Sweden, while Taylor and Hughes missed large chunks of the programme through knee damage.

But the durable, consistent Paisley missed only five League games and weighed in with two goals. One of them helped gain a point in a 3–3 draw at West Brom and the other set his side en route to a 2–1 home win over Stoke. He also earned deserved representative recognition when he was named in the England B party that beat Holland 1–0 in Amsterdam. Although he was not included in the team, his place on the trip showed that his unspectacular but solid contribution to the Liverpool cause had not gone unrecognised.

It was the season when the white football, introduced by the great Arsenal manager Herbert Chapman in the 1930s, received official Football League approval. But the dominant colour of the campaign was red, with a distinct Old Trafford hue. Matt Busby's Manchester United marched to their first post-war championship as Liverpool finished a nondescript 11th. Paisley's most memorable contribution came in the FA Cup when a club record 61,905 crowd crammed into Anfield and saw him score the first goal in Liverpool's 2–1 fourth-round knock-out of Wolves, who were completely hoodwinked by a tactical numbers game. Stan Cullis, now managing the club, gave his celebrated captain and England star Billy Wright the task of marking Billy Liddell. But Liddell, despite wearing number eleven, played at centre-forward, with number nine Cyril Done on the wing. Wolves never came to terms with it and were on their way out after Paisley had struck after five minutes, with Done scoring a second just four minutes later. But Liverpool dreams of Wembley were ended at the next hurdle when they lost 2–0 at Burnley.

The club's fortunes were even gloomier the following year of 1952–53, after the team flattered to deceive with a run of five straight League wins in a seven-match unbeaten run from the start of the season. Birkenhead-born centre-forward Jack Smith, drafted into the side the previous season, started the campaign as Liverpool's number nine and scored four times in the opening six games, but added only another four goals over the rest of the season from a total of 27 League appearances. Stubbins, at the end of his Anfield career before returning home to the North East, failed to score in five outings. His last appearance, in a 3–1 defeat at Stoke City on 3 January, coincided with the debut of Northern Ireland international Sammy Smyth, a forward for whom Welsh had paid Stoke £12,000. The new signing responded with seven goals in 19 games but once again the ever-reliable Liddell was Liverpool's top scorer, for the fourth consecutive season. In the previous campaign his 19-goal total in 40 outings included his first hat-trick, struck against Tottenham at White Hart Lane, when his direct opponent was a certain full back called Alf Ramsey, later knighted for managing England's 1966 World Cup winners.

This time Liddell weighed in with 13 goals in 39 games. But even the great Scot's massive talent, which earned the club the nickname 'Liddellpool', could not halt the almost inexorable Anfield decline.

New faces including Alan A'Court, Louis Bimpson and Ronnie Moran emerged but the overall strength of the squad was woefully weak. The Kop's most painful experience in the League that season came on 15 November when they saw their side crash 5–1 at home to Arsenal, four of the London club's goals coming in the second half. The Gunners went on to complete a double by ramming another nap hand of goals past Liverpool in a 5–3 Highbury win in April. Paisley played in 26 of Liverpool's 42 League games, scoring twice, but because of injury he was spared the ignominy of being in the team that was bundled out of the FA Cup by lowly Gateshead of the Third Division North. Roy Saunders came in for his debut in Paisley's left-half berth for the third-round tie, which was played on a gluepot pitch in swirling fog at Redheugh Park. Many felt the game should not have started – across the Tyne at St James's Park, Newcastle's tie with Swansea was abandoned after only eight minutes – but referee F.B. Coultas of Hull allowed the match to start and finish, although the 15,000 spectators saw only fleeting glimpses of the action. Gateshead had what they felt was a perfectly good goal disallowed in the 73rd minute, but the reprieve for Liverpool was short lived. Six minutes from the end, Ian Winters connected with one of a series of Gateshead corners to head past Russell Crossley and signal an undignified end to Liverpool's Cup hopes. Their exit occurred on the same day as Isthmian League side Walthamstow Avenue beat Stockport to become the first amateur club to reach the fourth round since Corinthians in 1929. Gateshead, meanwhile, went on to reach the quarter-final for the only time in their history, where they lost to Bolton. The Cup run was their last taste of glory. Seven years later their 40-year Football League status was ended when they were surprisingly voted out in favour of Peterborough.

Liverpool's own grip on their First Division tenure was becoming increasingly weak. They made a desperate escape from relegation in the final game of the 1952–53 season, when a vociferous 47,000-plus crowd roared them to a 2–0 home win over Chelsea, in which Paisley filled his usual left-half role. It lifted them to 17th place and safety. But it was merely a stay of execution. The following season, despite Welsh and the directors making transfer market sorties to sign Charlton pair John Evans and Frank Lock, Geoff Twentyman from Carlisle and goalkeeper Dave Underwood from Watford for a total of £37,000, Liverpool crashed through the trap door into Division Two. Remarkably, they did manage to score 68 goals, 17 more than tenth-placed Cardiff. Sammy Smyth, whose career had peaked prior to his arrival at Anfield, finished as joint top scorer on 13 goals with Louis Bimpson, before the Belfast-born player returned to his native Northern Ireland to join Bangor for £2,000 the following January. But Liverpool's respectable scoring output was wrecked by an appalling defensive record. They conceded 97 goals, more than any club in all four divisions that year. And their search for success away from home reached embarrassing proportions. They had finished the previous season without a win on opposition soil since February and that dismal sequence stretched to 24 games and 14 months until they prised a 2–0 win at Manchester City on 7 April 1954, to set an unwanted all-time club record. During that gloomy run they lost their opening 13 away League games in 1953–54 as well as slipping out of the FA Cup in the third round at Bolton. They were deservedly relegated after finishing bottom with 28 points from their 42 games, ending the club's half-century of unbroken First Division membership. To complete their black season, in which a huge total of 31 players were used, they suffered the loss of Spicer, whose second broken leg of his career, sustained in a 5–1 defeat at Manchester United in December, ended his playing days. Spicer, decorated for wartime bravery in the Royal Marines, was originally a left half, winning England Schoolboy recognition, but switched to left back to accommodate Paisley at number six. The Old Trafford match marked the debut of new signing Underwood, and Spicer's fate made it an even sadder occasion for the former Watford goalkeeper.

His collision with team-mate Spicer in a three-man pile-up with United's Tommy Taylor caused the break that forced the Liverpool defender to hang up his boots at the age of 31.

For Liverpool and their fans, the bitter pill of relegation was even harder to swallow because, as they went down, Everton returned to the top flight as Second Division runners-up to Leicester. But if it was a defining moment for the Anfield club, it was also a massive landmark in the career of Bob Paisley. After his final season as a player, in which he had 20 outings and scored twice for a grand total of 278 Liverpool appearances bringing him 13 goals, he was ready to depart Anfield and football. Once again, he might have been lost to the club and the game.

Bob was considering returning to his native North East and a job in bricklaying, in which he had served an apprenticeship. And Albert Stubbins remembers Bob telling him of another route fate might have taken him: 'Immediately after retiring as a player, Bob talked about going into the fruit and veg business and he also considered taking a newsagents. It was a massive wrench in life to finish playing. It could be frightening for a married man with a family suddenly finding himself without a job in his thirties.'

But Paisley's interests in muscles and bones rather than oranges and lemons or trowels and mortar pointed him in another direction. He recalled: 'Four of us finished playing; Phil Taylor, Bill Jones, Eddie Spicer and myself. Eddie was forced to retire and the other three of us were granted free transfers. We were due our accrued share of benefit money, which was £750 for five years. I saw Will Harrop, who was then chairman, who said that if I wanted to move perhaps to a lower division club the money would still be there for me. But I wasn't interested in playing anywhere else and I was ready to go back to bricklaying, which was my trade.

'But I'd studied physiotherapy through a correspondence course and I'd always fancied getting a trainer's job if that was possible. Fortunately, Liverpool asked me to join the coaching staff and I took over the reserves. I was delighted to be able to stay in football doing something I wanted to do.'

The backroom job offer to Bob came from director T.V. Williams (the initials stood for Thomas Valentine) and was to prove inspired. Williams, a cotton broker who remembered the Liverpool fans singing at Anfield for the first time as they celebrated promotion in 1905, had been a shareholder since 1918 but business commitments prevented him joining the board until 1948. He later became chairman for eight years and, eventually, was made the club's first life president. Three years before recruiting Bob to the training staff, Williams had been responsible for another major decision – to buy land in the West Derby district of Liverpool to use as the club's own Melwood training ground. Prior to that the players had trained at various sites including Prescot Cables, Penny Lane and Longmoor Lane, as well as at Anfield itself.

Williams also proved instrumental in fuelling Paisley's interest in injuries and their treatment. One of the Liverpool director's close friends was the Everton benefactor and Littlewoods founder John Moores, later to be Sir John, whose name opened most doors on Merseyside and way beyond. Williams obtained a letter, signed by Moores, requesting that Paisley be granted access to hospitals in the area where he could study medical methods and operations.

'I'd always had an interest in physiotherapy and psychology. The physio side probably stemmed from the knocks I got as a player. I found that valuable later on,' said Paisley. 'It stood me in good stead. If anyone pinned me down I'd say that was my greatest asset. I could speak to players and give them examples of injuries and how they heal.'

Jessie Paisley remembers how welcome Bob's backroom job was at the time: 'When Bob was offered the post of second-team trainer by T.V. Williams, we had two kiddies. The money was less than he'd been getting as a player, which wasn't much anyway, but it was a job and he was so thankful still to be in football.'

3

Decline, Fall
and Revolution

As Paisley began the new chapter of his career as physiotherapist and reserve-team coach, the Liverpool first team found Second Division life harsh. They finished 1954–55 in 11th place, the lowest position in the club's entire League history. During the season, John Evans scored all five goals in a 5–3 home win over Bristol Rovers but Liverpool also sank to their record defeat, a 9–1 drubbing at Birmingham on 11 December.

But the following month they had reason for special celebration, with a shock fourth round FA Cup win over the old enemy across Stanley Park. Without an away win all season after 12 attempts, they went to newly promoted Everton, lying sixth in the First Division, and caused probably the biggest sensation in the long history of Mersey derbies by winning 4–0. Liddell opened the scoring, A'Court made it two before half-time, and a couple of second-half goals from John Evans completed the shock scoreline. But Liverpool went out to Huddersfield 2–0 at home in the next round, a disappointment that would be echoed at Anfield for the remainder of the 1950s.

A return to the top flight remained agonisingly elusive and after a near-miss third place in 1955–56, Don Welsh became the first Liverpool manager to be sacked. That season had also included an embarrassing, desperately-gained 3–3 home FA Cup draw with Third Division Scunthorpe, Billy Liddell sparing even greater blushes with a 90th-minute equaliser. Liverpool needed extra time to win the replay before being knocked out by the eventual winners Manchester City. That midweek replay against City, on a snow-covered pitch following a goalless duel at Maine Road, will remain in Anfield folklore forever because of Liddell's famous late 'goal'. He raced in and drove a fierce shot past City's German goalkeeper Bert Trautmann, which the Kop celebrated as the equaliser to make it 2–2 and signal extra time, only to see it disallowed by referee Mervyn Griffiths because he had blown for full-time seconds earlier.

Against this backdrop, Bob Paisley was filling a valuable and successful role in charge of the reserves. He remembered: 'I had three years with the Central League side and in the second year we finished runners-up to the brilliant youngsters of Manchester United, most of them tragically to be killed in the Munich air disaster. The next year we won it, for the first time in Liverpool's history.'

A man destined much later to find himself in the opposite camp to Bob in two Wembley finals came under the Paisley influence. Keith Burkinshaw spent four years at Anfield and, because of his Wales-based National Service in the army and intense competition for wing-half places, he spent most of it in the reserves, making just a single first-team appearance. But playing under Paisley helped shape his career, which continued with Workington and Scunthorpe before becoming first-team coach at Newcastle (sitting on the opposite bench to Paisley in the 1974 FA Cup Final) and blossoming as manager at Tottenham, with whom he lost to his mentor in the 1982 League Cup Final but guided them to two FA Cup triumphs and a UEFA Cup success.

'I think Bob just got wiser and wiser and wiser,' said Burkinshaw. 'There was absolutely nothing fancy about Bob. He just got right to the meat of the problem immediately. There were no fancy words with him and he stripped everything to the bone. The players knew this and they responded and reacted to the honesty that shone through and the plain way he said things. Liverpool had tremendously good habits. I think that Bob Paisley was responsible for that as much if not more than anybody else at Anfield. Those good habits paid them handsomely over the years.'

The departure of Welsh led to the promotion of Paisley's friend and ex-team-mate Phil Taylor as his managerial successor. Taylor had also joined the backroom staff, becoming first-team coach, and stepped up to the manager's chair in May 1956. He soon began recruiting new talent in the club's quest to climb out of

Division Two. Scottish international goalkeeper Tommy Younger was bought from Hibs for £9,000, and wing-half or inside-forward Johnny Wheeler cost a similar amount from Bolton, with whom he had won an England cap. They linked up with defenders Dick White and John Molyneux, who had been signed the previous year from Scunthorpe and Chester respectively for a total of around £10,000.

But it was to be a case of so near yet so far for Taylor. In his first season as boss Liverpool went out of the FA Cup to Third Division Southend but staged a grandstand finish to their League programme, winning nine and drawing two of their final 12 games. Yet they finished third again, just a point behind second-placed club Nottingham Forest. Anfield great Liddell made his 400th League appearance in December of that season and celebrated with a goal from the penalty spot in a 2–0 win over Bury, one of his twenty-one in the campaign as the club's top scorer. Liddell topped the Liverpool scoring charts again the following season, for the eighth time in nine years, with twenty-two goals. He also surpassed Elisha Scott's club record of 429 League appearances when he played and scored in a 4–0 Anfield win in November 1957 over a Notts County side managed by former Everton and England centre-forward Tommy Lawton.

Liddell's feats thrilled Liverpool fans, who idolised the quietly spoken, self-effacing player who modestly let his talents do his talking. Among Liddell's legion of admirers was a certain youngster called Jimmy Tarbuck, whose pal Bobby Campbell progressed to the first team from Paisley's reserves. 'I was very lucky in that I started supporting Liverpool as a kid and the great Billy Liddell was a hero of mine,' Tarbuck said. 'What a player, what power! With my pal Bobby playing for the club I used to bunk in pretending to be a player myself. The ground was nothing like the great stadium is today. It was a bit decrepit and the dressing rooms were not like you'd expect them to be.'

The year of 1957 was also a milestone year for two other young Liverpudlians who would take the entertainment world by storm. That July the paths of Paul McCartney and John Lennon first crossed at a fete at St Peter's Church Hall in Liverpool's Woolton district. As well as providing the moment that signalled the coming of The Beatles, that church would figure large in the lives of Bob and Jessie Paisley.

The long and winding road of Bob Paisley's Liverpool career

would soon take another highly significant turn. During 1957–58, Taylor's playing staff was supplemented by three more signings. Winger Tony McNamara crossed Stanley Park from Everton for £4,000, inside-forward Jimmy Harrower arrived from Hibs for £11,000 and another forward, Fred Morris, cost £7,000 from Mansfield. But McNamara's stay, after being signed in December 1957, was short. He left for Crewe the following July and then switched to Bury in the September, completing within a year a remarkable tour of duty embracing the four divisions of the League, the Fourth having just been introduced after the ending of the Third North and Third South.

Meanwhile, another of Bob Paisley's reserve-team charges, locally born left-back Gerry Byrne, who would go on to become one of the heroic figures in Liverpool history and play for England, graduated to the first team. He made his debut at Charlton Athletic in September 1957 but it was a day to forget. A depleted, flu-hit team, in which Laurie Hughes replaced Dick White to make the last of his 326 appearances, lost 5–1 and Byrne put through his own goal. It proved to be his only appearance of the season and he was eventually transfer listed until his career was rescued by the momentous event in Anfield fortunes that would occur before the decade was out.

That season was another case of 'so near yet so far' as far as Liverpool's aim of returning to the First Division was concerned. They finished fourth and reached the FA Cup sixth round, losing 2–1 to promoted Second Division rivals Blackburn at Ewood Park. But the event of 1958 that overshadowed not only the national game but also Britain's national life happened on Thursday 6 February. That was the black day when the aircraft carrying the young Manchester United side after their European Cup game at Red Star Belgrade crashed on the runway at Munich. Twenty-three people perished, including eight of the team built by Matt Busby. The United manager himself was left critically ill and fighting for his life.

The Munich disaster left the nation in deep shock and a minute's silence was observed at football matches throughout the country 48 hours later, when Liverpool had a home fixture against Charlton. Busby's eventual triumph in leading United to Europe's greatest prize in 1968 pointed the way for Paisley, and Bob's qualities of leadership brought a memorable tribute from Sir Matt. Saluting Paisley on TV's *This Is Your Life* after Liverpool's first

European Cup triumph, he said: 'Bob, I knew you first as a very dedicated player, one who always put club before himself. It didn't surprise me at all when you took over the helm at Liverpool and led this great club to the greatest prize in football.

'One might get the wrong impression about Bob. Yes, he is a very quiet person, I would agree with that. But he has this inner steel to motivate his players to great heights and this is a wonderful thing in his favour. He is prepared to give everyone else the limelight rather than himself. This is a very rare thing these days.'

European football was not even a pipedream for Liverpool and their fans in 1958, although if their latest promotion near-miss was a less than illuminating experience for the Kop, they did at least have something brighter to cheer. Two seasons earlier the first League game played under floodlights in England has been staged at Fratton Park when Newcastle beat Portsmouth 2–0. And on 30 October 1957, floodlit football came to Anfield when the big switch-on took place for a game against Everton, the second of two games to celebrate the Liverpool County FA's silver jubilee. Liverpool had provided the Goodison Park opposition at the opening of Everton's floodlights, a match the visitors lost 2–0. They won the Anfield return 3–2 but Everton lifted the commemorative trophy as aggregate winners.

The following campaign, 1958–59, was to be Taylor's last full season in charge at Liverpool. A disappointing start, which saw them win only four and lose five of their opening 11 games, was climaxed by a 5–0 hiding at Huddersfield, whose manager was a certain Bill Shankly. Liverpool's 13th game proved unlucky for Liddell, who was dropped for the first time in his long and illustrious Anfield career having scored nine times in as many appearances that season. The fact that Fulham were the opposition was especially ironic as Liddell had scored more goals against the London club than any other. As it transpired, his replacement, Louis Bimpson, stepped up from Paisley's reserve team to score the only goal at Craven Cottage and inflict Fulham's first defeat of the season.

That victory fuelled a surging Liverpool run which brought 14 wins from 16 League games up to early February and revived their promotion hopes. But in the FA Cup their fortunes reached a new low when they suffered the humiliation of third-round elimination by a team of Southern League part-timers. Their tie at Worcester City, postponed from the previous Saturday because of a frozen pitch at St George's Lane, was played on 15 January 1959. Liddell was still out of favour and his role on that fateful Thursday afternoon was as 12th man, helping trainer Albert Shelley stud the boots. It was his first Cup absence after an unbroken post-war run of forty appearances. Liverpool went behind after only nine minutes on the icy surface, after defensive mistakes by John Molyneux and Dick White allowed winger Tommy Skuse to score. Worse was to follow. White, attempting to clear a square pass, sliced the ball over goalkeeper Tommy Younger into his own net to make it 2–0 to the home side in the 81st minute. Geoff Twentyman, later to become Liverpool chief scout, pulled a goal back from the penalty spot but Worcester completed the greatest victory in their history.

The impact of that defeat stunned Liverpool. Taylor and the directors tried to come to terms with it in the fortnight they had to wait before resuming League action. The team responded with a 3–2 win at Charlton and scored a similar victory next time out, at home to Bristol City. But a run of only one win from the next five games dented their promotion hopes and Liddell, who had made just a single appearance since October, was recalled at the age of 37 in place of injured A'Court for the Good Friday home duel with Barnsley on 27 March. It was his 466th League appearance, setting what was then a new record for Merseyside's two senior clubs, and he celebrated with two goals in the last 11 minutes to give Liverpool a 3–2 victory, following an early strike from Jimmy Melia.

Liddell played in all but one of Liverpool's remaining games and finished with the impressive return of 14 goals from 19 appearances. But for the club it was the same old story of promotion being close but not close enough. They finished fourth for the second consecutive season, following two third-place spots, and the patience of the fans was now frayed.

Before the 1959–60 season dawned, there was a significant change on the backroom staff. Already arrived was Reuben Bennett, a craggy Scot who was a physical education expert and devotee. A former goalkeeper who had played for Hull City, Queen of the South and Dundee, he briefly managed Ayr United as well as coaching Dundee, Third Lanark and Motherwell. He was a man of iron who would say to players who were injured and needed treatment: 'Just rub it down with a kipper!' Or if one of them had a cut, his tongue-in-cheek response would be: 'It's only a pin-prick – clean it up with a wire brush!' In August 1959, eight months after Bennett's addition to the coaching staff, the directors elevated Bob Paisley to work alongside manager Phil Taylor a first-team trainer in succession to Albert Shelley.

That same summer saw the departure of goalkeeper Tommy Younger, who had given Liverpool valuable service in 120 games over a three-year span. Younger, at 15 stone a formidable figure between the posts, had been last line of defence for Hibs in the inaugural European Cup campaign of 1955–56 and helped the Scottish club reach the semi-final where they lost to French club Rheims, who, in turn, were beaten 4–3 in the final by Real Madrid. He returned to Scotland, as player-manager of Falkirk, with fellow keeper Bert Slater moving in the opposite direction in an exchange deal. Slater, small for a keeper at 5ft 8¹/₂in, was chosen for the Reds against the Whites in Liverpool's pre-season public trial game at Anfield and was beaten twice in a 2–2 draw. The Whites, recognised as the reserves, had in their ranks two players who would fill massive roles in the looming rebirth of Liverpool, Gerry Byrne and Roger Hunt, as well as Liddell and a player who would find fame across Stanley Park with Everton, Johnny Morrissey.

None of that quartet was selected for the opening League game in which Liverpool crashed to a 3–2 defeat at Cardiff City, where even both their goals were own goals by Scottish centre-half Danny Malloy! Liddell, nearing the end of his playing days, was recalled and scored in a 4–2 home win over Bristol City in the next game and went on to make 17 appearances over the season, scoring five goals. But new arrival Slater was dropped after three games and Doug Rudham recalled to a side which was now captained by Ronnie Moran, after Johnny Wheeler relinquished the job following a season as skipper.

Hunt made his debut against Scunthorpe in September and scored in a 2–0 win, the launch of a glittering career. But just three wins from their next 11 games left Liverpool languishing in mid-table mediocrity. Sections of the Anfield crowd gave vent to their frustration with a bout of slow handclapping when the final whistle sounded on a 1–1 home draw with Portsmouth, an action condemned by the *Liverpool Daily Post*.

'Nobody can pretend that the squandering of yet another home point was not disappointing, but this was no possible justification for the slow handclap to which the players left the field at the end,' the newspaper chided, adding: 'The last thing that could be said against them was that they had failed for want of effort.'

Ironically, amidst the growing crisis of League form, Liverpool went to Goodison Park and beat their First Division neighbours Everton 3–0 – Hunt scoring two of the goals – in the first leg of the Merseyside Floodlight Challenge Cup, a competition devised to give the two clubs the opportunity to cross swords. Although Everton won the Anfield return 2–0, the aggregate victory went to Liverpool. But their failure to make an impact in the Second Division promotion race prompted them to make a dramatic plunge into the transfer market which had Merseyside agog. They signed centre-forward Dave Hickson from Everton, a player who had become synonymous with Goodison Park fortunes during two spells at the club and was a key figure in their return to the First Division four years earlier. Salford-born Hickson had signed professional for Everton in May 1948 after arriving as a 15-year-old and also played for Aston Villa and Huddersfield. Hickson, a notable header of the ball who once played in an army cadets team coached by the legendary Everton centre-forward Bill 'Dixie' Dean, was a totally committed player. Sometimes he overstepped the mark, as his three dismissals indicate, but he never gave less than 100 per cent. That season, though, he had been dropped three times, prompting him to ask to leave Goodison.

Leslie Edwards reported in the *Liverpool Echo* of Friday 6 November, 1959: 'Liverpool FC today signed Dave Hickson for a fee of about £12,000. Thus the impasse of a week between the senior clubs of this city has been broken by compromise. Liverpool stepped up their original offer and Everton toned down the £15,000 fee they set on Hickson's worth when agreeing to his transfer request.'

Hickson made a superb debut the following day, scoring both Liverpool goals in a 2–1 home win over Villa, one of his former clubs. He scored again in his second outing, but Liverpool fell to a 4–2 defeat at Lincoln City – a landmark result. Two days after Liverpool's demise at Sincil Bank, manager Phil Taylor resigned, citing the strain of the unfulfilled promotion quest. He handed in a letter to chairman Tom Williams at noon on Monday 16 November and it was amicably accepted at a board meeting the following night.

'I made promotion my goal,' said Taylor. 'I set my heart on it and strove for it with all the energy I could muster. If the strain of the constant battle for promotion has told a tale on the players, it has told also on me. Great though my devotion to Liverpool has been and is, I don't think any alternative was left for me.'

Years later, Taylor reflected on his departure from the club and told me: 'Resigning as manager was a very moving experience. I had been at Liverpool since I was 17 and had so many good years at Anfield. But that's life, that's how things go, and it was very pleasing to see my old club enjoy so much success later.'

Taylor's departure left his assistant Bob Paisley, chief coach Reuben Bennett and the rest of the backroom staff wondering what their futures were. Paisley needed to find out. 'When Phil finished I put a letter into the board asking to clarify my position,' he said. 'They said I would be staying at the club. Then Shanks came.'

In those three words, Paisley was heralding a revolution – the arrival of Bill Shankly as the new Liverpool manager. Life at Anfield would never be the same again, on or off the field, although Jessie Paisley recalls Bob's initial fears over his Anfield future: 'Bob and everyone else didn't know what was going to happen after Phil Taylor had left. They thought they might be finished by the club because so many managers wanted to bring their own staff with them.' But any fears that Shankly would bring in his own coaches and dispense with the services of any current backroom members were instantly dispelled.

'My first priority was to try to make the directors think along the same lines as me about the potential there was for Liverpool because, candidly, it was a shambles of a place when I came,' Shankly declared. 'The team wasn't a very good team, the ground was rundown and it wasn't good enough for the people here. I knew the people here because I'd played here and the crowd were fantastic.

'I had to assess the players, seeing who could play and who couldn't, and the directors. But above all, I had to get the training staff together. Normally, a new manager takes his own men with him to safeguard himself. I could have done that. We'd just beaten Liverpool at Huddersfield. But I didn't do that. I already knew Bob Paisley, Joe Fagan and Reuben Bennett – in fact, I'd once tried to sign Joe Fagan. The first thing I did was to have a meeting with them. I told them that I'd lay down the plans, then they'll pick them up and we'll all work in harmony. Then, one day, we might get the players we need and that will be it.'

For Paisley, the arrival of Shankly was the start of a gloriously fruitful and successful association that would take Liverpool from

Second Division mediocrity to the pinnacle of achievement in England and Europe. With Paisley initially first-team trainer and later assistant to the manager, it was the perfect partnership – Shanks the often outrageous front man with a wisecrack for every occasion, and Paisley the coach and physiotherapist with a wealth of injury knowledge, happy to stay in the background. And both of course, rich in football wisdom.

'Shanks was very fortunate when he went to Liverpool in that Bob was there with his wealth of injury knowledge,' Albert Stubbins believes. 'I'd say that Bob was ahead of quite a few in the field of physiotherapy and study of injuries even then. I could have visualised Bob staying as a physio for the rest of his career. I never gave a thought to him becoming manager.

'There's the famous story of Shankly going into the dressing room and saying: 'Nobody's injured!' It says a lot for Bob that he had such a strong character and strong opinions that if he told Shanks someone wasn't fit, Bill reluctantly accepted it. He had so much respect for Bob. It was a wonderful combination, yet one that was so unlikely.'

Paisley made a swift analysis of some of Shankly's personality traits which contrasted sharply with his own yet dovetailed so perfectly into a mighty partnership. 'Bill never gave advice, he gave an order,' he observed. The alliance between Shankly and Paisley became a football phenomenon and Bill's widow Nessie recognised the qualities in their working relationship: 'If you asked Bob a question, he wouldn't come out with the answer right away. He waited. He always thought before he spoke and Bill depended a lot on Bob. They were like the terrible twins when they got going. I think Bill needed Bob. I think he calmed him down a bit.'

Of the 784 matches in which Shankly was in charge with Paisley at his side during the ensuing fourteen and a half years, they each missed only one game, a record of consistency that matched the quality for which the Liverpool teams became famous. Bob's single absence was through illness while Bill's happened when he went to spy on European opponents Cologne on the day in 1965 when Stockport, then rock bottom of the old Fourth Division, held out for an incredible 1–1 FA Cup draw at Anfield.

Liverpool's first game with Shankly as manager was against Cardiff City at Anfield on 19 December 1959, but as Paisley underlined, it was not an auspicious start to the new era: 'In Bill's first game we got beaten 4–0 at home by Cardiff. We knew we needed players and he wanted to assess the ones we had. He always said he wanted strength through the middle, a strong 'spine'. It took him a year or so to sort things out and then we were on the beat. From then on it was pretty good going.

'I was first-team coach until 1971 when I was given the title of assistant to Bill, until 1974. You just couldn't visualise the success that would be achieved. I don't know how you explain that. One thing I did know though, right away, was that Bill and the supporters were made of the same stuff.'

The end of Shankly's first half-season at the helm saw Liverpool finish third in the Second Division and bow out of the FA Cup to Manchester United with a 3–1 fourth-round home defeat. The conclusion of that 1959–60 campaign marked the retirement of the player Shankly idolised and held up as an example to aspiring youngsters everywhere. England's Tom Finney, a younger team-mate of Shankly's at Preston, hung up his boots. Players and officials joined hands in the centre circle at Preston's game against Luton to say farewell to the Lancashire genius as a brass band played 'Auld Lang Syne', although Finney did make a special reappearance for Northern Ireland club Distillery in a European Cup duel with Benfica in 1963.

The air of change and transformation at Anfield also embraced the retirement of another post-war great, the magnificent Billy Liddell. He made the last of his 12 outings under Shankly in a 1–0 home defeat by Southampton on 31 August 1960, taking his total of Liverpool League and Cup appearances to 536 with a remarkable goals total of 229. The following month his majestic contribution to Liverpool was recognised at a testimonial match between Liverpool and an All Stars team at Anfield, when a crowd of 38,789 paid £6,340 to salute him. Liddell's decision to end his illustrious career coincided with a Shankly clearout of the playing staff. It was in stark contrast to his vote of confidence in the backroom staff, which already included Joe Fagan, recruited on a recommendation from his Rochdale manager Harry Catterick the previous year. Some 24 players left Anfield in the early stages of the Shankly regime while one, put up for sale before his arrival, was swiftly removed from the transfer list by the new manager and went on to become one of Liverpool's all-time heroes. His name was Gerry Byrne.

Tommy Lawrence, the goalkeeper who graduated through the ranks of Anfield to displace Jim Furnell as Shankly's first choice in October 1962 and went on to make 390 senior appearances and also play for Scotland, recalled that Byrne was already installed at Anfield when he arrived. And Lawrence remembers that they both went through a special ritual with the revered Liddell: 'I signed in 1956 as an amateur but Gerry was here in 1953. We saw a lot together. When I signed, you had your picture taken with Billy Liddell. Everyone who joined the club did that. It was the great moment of shaking hands with Billy and having your picture taken with him. I've still got the photograph.'

Shortly after Liddell's departure, Liverpool's Scottish contingent – an integral ingredient at the club since the first team they ever fielded contained nine Scots and two Englishmen – was extended by two more prospective stars as Shankly recruited Ian St John for a then club record £37,500 and Ron Yeats for £30,000. Yeats and St John arrived in the summer of 1961 from Dundee United and Motherwell respectively and were joined a year later by Willie Stevenson, snapped up from Glasgow Rangers reserves for a bargain £7,000.

'St John's debut was in the Liverpool Senior Cup Final at Everton,' Shankly recalled. 'We lost 4–3 but he scored three goals and set the place on fire. That was in the May. In July we were after Yeats. We went up to Dundee United but we got no joy. Next day the phone rang and they said: "You can have him for £30,000." I said: "Right, we'll meet you in Edinburgh tomorrow." We met them and we got Yeats. Those two were the greatest signings. They were the beginning of Liverpool.'

Shankly's first full season in charge, 1960–61, had seen the abolition of the maximum wage for players, with Fulham's Johnny Haynes becoming the first £100-a-week British footballer. But there was only more frustration for Liverpool, who again finished third in the Second Division. However, the acquisition of St John and Yeats, who was installed as the new club captain, brought instant results. Ten wins and a draw from their opening 11 games of 1961–62 launched Liverpool towards promotion, while the team behind the team, Shankly, Paisley and company, were also winning friends and admirers.

Jessie Paisley recalls just what an effective partnership Bill and Bob forged: 'They never quarrelled. They argued and discussed things. But they never fell out.' And this is what Shankly said on

Bob's *This Is Your Life*: 'Bob and I never had any rows. We didn't have time for that. We had to plan where we were going to keep all the cups we won. Bob was a dedicated, loyal man, efficient as well. And like me, he wanted to win things.'

Paisley's genius for diagnosing and treating injuries became famous and his healing hands and knowledge attracted people of both sexes from far beyond the confines of Anfield. Former world light-heavyweight boxing champion John Conteh was among a host of sportsmen who sought a treatment room consultation. Stars from showbusiness and entertainment also knocked at Paisley's door. Help was happily given until one day, remembered by Jessie, even the unflappable Paisley was stumped!

'Bill got the idea that anyone could come and be treated by Bob,' she explained. 'And he did. He treated all kinds of sportsmen, showbusiness people and even ballet dancers. But he did object one day when a man turned up at Anfield with his greyhound for Bob to treat. Bob explained that he wasn't a vet!'

By now the Paisleys were the proud parents of a daughter, Christine, as well as sons Robert and Graham, and Jessie's return to teaching some years earlier was preceded by another illustration of Bob's wry sense of realism. She recalled: 'In the days when things had seemed a bit dicey at the club, it wasn't too common for the wife to go back to work. And if he'd gone from the club, we couldn't have the house. So I said to Bob: "I think I ought to go back to teaching."

'He said: "I think so, too." No messing, no trying to dissuade me. He agreed and that was it!'

The 1961–62 season saw Shankly's new side finally secure promotion back to the top flight after eight seasons in the Second Division. Jim Furnell, an £18,000 buy from Burnley, took over in goal from Bert Slater for the final 13 games, with the Scot leaving Anfield that summer to join Dundee.

Liverpool won the Second Division title in style with 62 points from 42 games, eight ahead of second-placed Leyton Orient, and they were unbeaten at Anfield for the first time since 1905. More than half of their 99-goal tally was provided by their new attack of Roger Hunt and Ian St John, a bludgeon and rapier combination that would become one of the great spearheads in Anfield history. Hunt hit a club record 41 goals in 41 League appearances, while St John weighed in with 18 and local product Jimmy Melia scored 12.

The team included another Scot, Tommy Leishman, a £9,000

recruit from St Mirren just before Shankly's arrival, and two more of his signings: Gordon Milne, who cost £16,000 from Preston, and Kevin Lewis, a £13,000 buy from Sheffield United, both of whom had arrived in the summer of 1960.

This was the line-up that began that 1961-62 campaign so powerfully: Bert Slater; Dick White, Gerry Byrne; Gordon Milne, Ron Yeats (captain), Tommy Leishman; Kevin Lewis, Roger Hunt, Ian St John, Jimmy Melia, Alan A'Court.

During the campaign, Ronnie Moran was recalled at left-back as White's Anfield career ended, and a young man became a first-team regular after making his senior debut as an 18-year-old in place of his boyhood idol Billy Liddell just four months after Shankly's arrival. His name was Ian Callaghan, a former Anfield groundstaff boy destined to become Liverpool's marathon man by making a club record 856 appearances over an 18-year span.

Years later, following Shankly's retirement as manager, he saluted Callaghan on his chat show on Merseyside's independent radio station, Radio City:

Shankly: 'The record books show, Ian, that you made your first team debut for Liverpool at Anfield against Bristol Rovers in 1960 replacing your big idol Billy Liddell.'
Callaghan: 'Yes, boss, Billy was my hero when I weas at school and I was always a Liverpool supporter. I played in the A and B teams and then you came along, I signed professional and packed my job in.'
Shankly: 'I'm glad you didn't pack football in!'

The Second Division title was clinched on an overcast, rainy April day with a 2–0 home win over Southampton, Lewis scoring both goals in the absence of the suspended St John. The Scot had been sent off in the home League duel with Liverpool's FA Cup conquerors Preston, who triumphed 1–0 at Old Trafford in a fifth-round second replay, their goal being scored by a brilliant winger called Peter Thompson. Thompson's talents were too great for Liverpool to ignore and the following year Shankly moved in to take him to Anfield for £37,000. Thompson's success at Liverpool, with Everton legend Dixie Dean hailing him and Callaghan as the best pair of club wingers in the business, prompted an intriguing exchange between Shankly and a group of fans during a *Daily Express* sports forum at Liverpool Supporters Club.

Shankly: Did Peter Thompson entertain you?
Audience: Yes!
Shankly: I developed him and made him a better player. But do you know who makes players?
Audience: Bill Shankly!
Shankly: The mothers and fathers make players. Not coaches. It's the mothers and fathers. But maybe I made him a better player because he came into a good team.

The angst-ridden eight-year quest for promotion was the subject of fascinating comment by journalist Ivan Sharpe in the match programme when Liverpool visited Wolves in their first campaign back in the top flight. Sharpe wrote: 'When Liverpool were relegated in 1954, their late secretary said to me: "It does you good if you get back the following year." Well, they didn't. It took them eight solid seasons to regain the right to meet such as the Wolves again. That is 336 matches or 504 hours of sometimes excruciating effort – exactly 21 days, each of 24 hours, of intensive endeavour. Someone at Anfield should write a new book with the old title *Three Weeks*. No love scenes. No heart-throbs. All heart-breaking hard labour.'

Despite two goals from Jimmy Melia, Liverpool lost 3–2 on that visit to Molineux on 29 September 1962. But their first season back in the First Division was essentially one of bedding in. They finished a creditable eighth behind title-winning neighbours Everton, who had appointed Harry Catterick manager in April 1961 after Johnny Carey's famous sacking by John Moores in a London taxi when they were in the capital attending a Football League meeting. Liverpool also unluckily lost 1–0 to Leicester at Hillsborough in the 1963 FA Cup semi-final. But the biggest winner of the season was the weather, which played even greater havoc with fixtures than the fierce winter of 1946–47. All previous records for disruption were shattered, with more than 400 League and Cup games in England, Wales and Scotland postponed or abandoned. And the single worst day was 9 February 1963, with 57 games called off through snow or ice and only seven matches completed.

But the icy blast was instrumental in Bob Paisley forging a new and warm friendship. To maintain fitness and give the players match action during the big freeze, Liverpool travelled to Ireland for a friendly game. And it was while Bob was sitting with Shankly and other members of the Liverpool contingent in Dublin's Gresham Hotel that he first met the renowned racing trainer, the late Frank Carr. Frank, based at Malton in Yorkshire, had returned to his homeland to buy a horse called Gay Navaree and he and Bob, a keen racing fan, were soon deep in conversation.

'I liked Frank instantly and we talked into the early hours about footballers and racehorses,' said Bob, who discovered that the pair of them shared humble childhood backgrounds. 'Frank had bags of real Irish patter and I admired his personal honesty and attitudes. He made no bones about his early poverty, which I knew all about from my own experience. In fact, Frank made such an impression on me that I thought if I was starting all over again, I'd like to train horses, too!'

The friendship was deep and enduring, and whenever possible, especially in football's close season, Bob would visit Frank's stables and relax among the equine community. 'Where I come from in the North East, you are interested in horses, football and pigeons,' said Paisley. 'My father Sam was a racing man who studied form and I suppose that's where my interest first started. He liked to look for value in the ante-post market and so do I.

'The first Grand National I saw was in 1948. Shortly after, we played Blackpool and I was given the job of marking Stanley Matthews. To know that I had backed the 50–1 Aintree winner, Sheila's Cottage, helped me get through a difficult match! I am intrigued by the racing game and I love visiting the stables, going out on the gallops and messing about the yard. I take it all in. It's so absorbing. You might get an older horse, like the occasional old professional footballer, looking as if he is saying, "Oh, blimey, training again!" and just plodding around. But on big race day he'll be there showing himself off in front of the crowd and fairly flying in the race. We all know footballers like that, don't we! If you're edgy, the players will be edgy; if you're tense, they'll be tense. Players sense these things and I'm sure horses do, too. You can do too much with some horses in training and they've got nothing left for the race. Others love training and can't get too much. So it is with footballers. Some need the loud voice, some the soft. Some horses are good in any going the same as some players, whereas some are just not suited to heavy ground. Yes, players and horses share a lot of characteristics. I know, as a man keen on racing, that a real thoroughbred will often want a donkey or a goat to travel with it in its box. In the same way, the great players need lesser lights to support and bolster them.'

One of Bob's many visits to the Malton stables provided Frank Carr with what was literally a burning memory: 'Bob and I went out to cut some long grass on the gallops. It was a real hard slog. So I said to Bob: "I'll show you a countryman's trick." Bob stood back while I poured petrol over the long grass and dropped the match in it. "This cuts out all the hard work, Bob." I said. But I'd poured the petrol in a circle and I'd forgotten I was in the middle of it when I set it alight. I had to run for my life! Mind you, Bob didn't have the last laugh. I got him riding a racehorse one time and I have to say that as a jockey he made a great football manager!'

Paisley arranged for reciprocal visits by Frank as his guest at Liverpool matches, and his first appearance in the team's dressing room sparked laughter among the players, as Ian Callaghan explained: 'Frank was chatting to Bob, who introduced him to all the lads. After we'd been out to see the pitch, we came back in and all the lads were in bulk, laughing. They were tickled by the fact that Frank was sitting on the bench and his legs were dangling, not even touching the floor.'

Callaghan also recalled that Paisley's love of racing and a flutter at the bookies had other spin-offs: 'Ever since I knew Bob, he always had a hip pocket with a wad of money. I've never seen a wad like it. There were just notes wrapped around each other. If you were a bit short of cash or lost at cards, or what have you, we'd ask Bob for a loan and the wad would come out.'

Paisley's circle of racing pals also included Liverpool-born Frankie Durr, who as a jockey won the St Leger on 7–1 shot Sodium in 1966. And when Frankie steered Roland Gardens to victory in the 2000 Guineas in 1978, it was a profitable success for Paisley. He'd backed it at 66–1.

Durr, raised in the Everton Brow area of Liverpool, quit the saddle to become a Newmarket-based trainer in 1979 and several times had Bob Paisley as his guest at the stables before his retirement from racing in 1992. 'I first met Bob when Liverpool played at Ipswich, when Bill Shankly was manager,' he said. 'Bob knew who I was and invited me on to the team bus before it left. From then on we became very friendly. He'd always let me have a couple of match tickets. He was very generous but you couldn't say anything against Liverpool where Bob was concerned. All the jockeys were desperate to meet Bob when he came to the races.

He was terrific with everybody and so clever when it came to football. I'm glad he didn't ride horses – he'd have been champion jockey and I'd have been out of a job.'

With Peter Thompson recruited from Preston during the summer of 1963, Liverpool swept to the First Division championship in their second campaign back in the top flight. It was a time when the world reverberated to the Mersey Sound, with the birth of Beatlemania. The Fab Four stopped the traffic when they appeared at the London Palladium amid scenes of teenage hysteria, and had a similar impact in America after flying into Kennedy Airport to an amazing reception in February 1964, the same month that a certain Cassius Clay became world heavyweight boxing champion by knocking out Sonny Liston in Miami. But at Anfield, the Kopites proved quite a knock-out act themselves. They provided their own Mersey Sound with some raucous renditions of The Beatles' smash hit 'She Loves You' as the football machine assembled by Shankly and oiled and fuelled by Paisley powered the club's first League title since 1947.

Liverpool even overcame a decidedly false start, losing their first three home games to Nottingham Forest, Blackpool and West Ham, all by 2–1. That prompted the memorable pledge by Shankly to the board: 'I assure you, gentlemen, that we WILL win a home game this season!' Sure enough, a 2–1 home derby win over reigning champions Everton at the end of September set Liverpool on their way to seizing their title, and a run of seven straight victories spanning March and April, including an Easter double over Tottenham, helped them cross the finishing line with 57 points, four ahead of Manchester United, with Everton a further point adrift in third place.

The championship was clinched on a sun-kissed May afternoon with a 5–0 home demolition of Arsenal. And of the 17 players that figured in League combat for Liverpool that season, the usual team lined up like this: Tommy Lawrence; Gerry Byrne, Ronnie Moran; Gordon Milne, Ron Yeats, Willie Stevenson; Ian Callaghan, Roger Hunt, Ian St John, Jimmy Melia or Alf Arrowsmith, Peter Thompson.

The partnership of Hunt and St John proved devastating, with 31 and 21 goals respectively, and the new Liverpool were hot box-office attractions, drawing an average Anfield attendance of just under 50,000, with the club reporting a new record profit of £72,283. Their League success made their FA Cup fate that season even more astonishing. They lost 2–1 at home to Second Division strugglers Swansea Town, despite dominating the quarter-final contest. 'We should have scored 15!' roared a disbelieving Shankly.

The summer of 1964 saw Bob Paisley embark on his fourth trip to America with Liverpool. On his visits in 1946, 1948 and 1953 as a player, they had not only been unbeaten but won every match except one, a draw with Swiss side Young Boys of Berne.

The '64 trip was almost as successful although Liverpool's undefeated record on United States soil was finally broken when they lost to German side Hamburg, led by the great Uwe Seeler. But the Anfield club took their four-tour record to a scorching 42 wins from 44 games.

The trip provided some classic Shankly stories which Paisley, filling the role of Boswell to Bill's Dr Johnson, loved to recount at dinners or in relaxed moments amongst friends and colleagues. Like Shankly refusing to change his watch, insisting defiantly: 'No bloody Yank's going to tell me the time!' And, because of that, pinning up the team sheet at three o'clock in the morning! Boxing devotee Shankly also ordered the team to play a five-a-side on the very spot where Jack Dempsey fought Gene Tunney at Soldier's Field, Chicago. But the story with which Bob brought the house down at an Anfield dinner in his honour in November 1983 concerned the time he was called on to help chairman T.V. Williams solve a pressing problem. Colin Wood, who reported the tour for the *Daily Mail*, recalls it vividly.

'We'd been in New York a couple of days and T.V. Williams went to Bob and complained of being constipated. Bob told him not to worry and suggested he had a fruit salad every morning. Another couple of days went by and T.V. went to Bob again, complaining: "I still can't go, Bob. I'm in pain."

'So Bob said: "OK, I'll give you a tablet."

'We then moved on to Boston and T.V. came to Bob again, saying he couldn't go, so Bob gave him another tablet. This went on through Detroit and then St Louis. On the afternoon of the match, a group of us went out for a walk and when we got back Bob was standing there in the hotel lounge with a little smile on his face. We said: "What's happened, Bob?"

'He said: "I got back in after a stroll and was given an urgent message to go to see T.V. in his room. When I got there I've seen nothing like it! It was wall to wall. It was everywhere."

'The trouble is that T.V. brought only one pair of trousers with him. T.V. was a tall man and the only fellow in the party with trousers to fit him was Ron Yeats. So at the after-match banquet, in a temperature of more than 80 degrees, T.V. had to wear a pair of Ronnie's trousers tucked around him with a raincoat over them so nobody would see them! But that wasn't all. During the afternoon, when Ron Yeats told Ian St John that he had to loan T.V. a pair of trousers, the Saint fell off his chair laughing, hit his head and was ruled out of the match.'

In the curtain raiser to the 1964–65 season, Liverpool as champions contested the Charity Shield for the first time since 1922. They drew 2–2 at home to FA Cup winners West Ham, a game in which Alf Arrowsmith was injured challenging Bobby Moore and was destined never again to strike the scoring form that had marked him out as a menacing attacker.

The new campaign took Liverpool over the threshold into a world in which they would revel – Europe. It was the start of an odyssey that would last unbroken until the horror of the Heysel disaster some 21 years later, and it was the most prestigious of all Continental competitions, the Champions' Cup, that provided Liverpool with their European baptism. Gordon Wallace, a player whose talents were sadly sabotaged by brittle bones, had the distinction of scoring the first European goal in Liverpool's history when he netted after only three minutes against Reykjavik in Iceland. Their part-time opponents were beaten 5–0 on that August afternoon in 1964 and a 6–1 win in the return gave Liverpool an 11–1 aggregate triumph.

Next up were crack Belgian club Anderlecht, but Liverpool, donning the all-red strip for the first time and with Tommy Smith wearing number ten as a sweeper, overpowered them 3–0 and completed the job with a 1–0 win in the Brussels return to book a quarter-final place later in the season. The switch to all-red, or all-scarlet as Shankly called it, had a tremendous impact. And Ron Yeats had a special role to play in its unveiling.

'I can remember the day that Shanks came to me after training and said he wanted me to try on a shirt,' said Yeats. Then he said: "Put the whole scarlet strip on, and your boots, and come out on to the pitch." and I ran out there and Shanks, Bob, Joe and Reuben were all there. Shanks said: "Yes, yes. That's what we'll play in from now on. It'll make the whole team look huge." '

The night the new strip was worn for the first time prompted some typical and unforgettable Shankly hyperbole. He said: 'The introduction of the all-scarlet strip had a psychological effect. I went home that night and said to Nessie: "Do you know something? Tonight, when I went out on to Anfield, there was a glow like a fire was burning."' Proving that nothing is ever discarded in football fashion, as in fashion generally, more than three decades later in 1998 Liverpool returned to a round-collar style strip, the Reebok kit being inspired by that 1960s design which became world famous.

Smith's first-team graduation came just after that of fellow local boy Chris Lawler, a defender who settled at right-back but was also an assured performer at centre-half when the need arose. Both went onto play for England. They were joined in the November of that year by a player who cost £40,000 from Arsenal. Geoff Strong had to retire ill to bed after his first encounter with Liverpool's training methods, but became one of the greatest utility players ever to appear for the club.

Shankly's notorious dislike, perhaps even inner fear, of injuries, which he took to the extent of not talking to unfit players, placed a massive responsibility on Paisley's shoulders to ensure that he diagnosed fitness problems as early as possible and swiftly put remedies and recuperative treatments into operation for the players concerned. His thoroughness was a byword in the game and he did it all literally by the book – by keeping a daily log. He kept it updated right through to his last day in management and it might have been titled 'How to win trophies and dominate soccer'.

The fact that it rained on a March day in 1970 or that a certain player had two days off with a sore throat the following November might seem trivial. But nothing was trivial to Paisley. 'I observe training, watch movement, jot down any injuries, anything at all that may be relevant,' he explained. 'Everything that could possibly affect a player's performance is entered in the book, no matter how unimportant it may seem. If a player has a birth or death in the family it goes in the book. So do all the details of weights, injuries, performances and weather conditions, both in training sessions and in matches. If you want to know what the weather was like this time last year, it's down in black and white. We've even got details of players' appointments with people like solicitors and accountants.

'In fact, any observations made by the training staff and myself are recorded because it's amazing how helpful this information can be. You can see patterns emerge. In some cases you can see from the book that a player has good and bad spells of form at the same stage of each season. Details like this concerning experienced players can help in the development of the younger ones. Sometimes it enables you to nip problems in the bud.

'There's so much talk in the game about tactics and teamwork, but amidst all this it's so easy to overlook the simple things. The psychological and mental factors are equally as important to players as the physical side. If a player isn't tuned in mentally, he won't perform as he should, even if he is physically right. And vice versa. There has to be a balance and that's why this book is so invaluable to me. The slightest scrap of information is worth entering in the log. You never know when it might throw some light on something.'

Scottish wing-half Willie Stevenson was well aware of Paisley's massive contribution: 'They say behind every good man there's a good wife. In Bill Shankly's case, he not only had a good wife in Nessie but a good friend and colleague in Bob Paisley. Bob was very, very knowledgeable. He might not have been the most articulate of men but he got through to you what he meant. Sometimes with Shanks he'd bamboozle you and you'd have to listen so close to what he was saying. Bob would say: "Just watch that number six." He might not know their name but you'd be aware. That was the secret with Bob. He'd just say one or two words. And he'd be right. He would pick out if a guy was good at going inside and coming outside or outside coming in. He would forewarn you.'

Stevenson's words are echoed with a smile by his former team-mate Peter Thompson: 'Obviously Bill Shankly was the driving force and great motivator, but Bob Paisley had a fabulous tactical football brain. That's why his sides went on to win more than ours did. He learned a lot about motivation from Shankly and he had the football brain as well. Shankly once stayed away for a couple of days to devise a secret plan against Everton. When he came back he unveiled this plan but he had 13 men on the board. Bob had to diplomatically help him out. He was a lovely, lovely guy as well.'

In 1965 Liverpool at last lifted the trophy previous generations of supporters had lived and died without seeing them land – the FA Cup, the piece of silverware that had eluded the club throughout its 73-year history. And the year dawned with Liverpool in the midst of a sparkling sequence and on course for a possible successful defence of the championship. From November to February they went on a 14-game unbeaten League run and although their form subsequently dipped to see them finish seventh, there was drama and excitement in the two big cup competitions in which they were engaged. In the FA Cup they toppled West Brom and then Stockport but only after a replay following a shock 1–1 Anfield draw with the Fourth Division's bottom club while Shankly was away on his spying trip in Cologne. Bolton, Leicester (again after a replay) and Chelsea in the semi-final were also beaten to take Liverpool to Wembley for the first time since their defeat by Arsenal 15 years earlier.

The threat from Cologne to Liverpool's European hopes promised to be a massive one. And so it proved in a saga that stretched to a five-week marathon watched by a total attendance of 133,000. The first leg in Germany was goalless. Then when the teams ran out for the second leg at a blizzard-hit Anfield, the referee sent them back to the dressing room and called off the game, declaring play impossible on a pitch covered with more than two inches of snow. When the Germans returned for the rescheduled match, both defences were again impregnable and without a goal being scored over the two legs, the time went into a play-off at neutral Rotterdam. At last there were goals, with strikes from St John and Hunt giving Liverpool a 2–1 interval lead. But Cologne equalised in the second half and at the end of extra time the tie was still deadlocked. With no penalty shoot-outs then, the spin of a disc would decide who went through to the semi-final. One side of the disc was coloured red for Liverpool, the other white for Cologne. When it was first spun, however, it came down on its edge and stuck in the mud. The disc had to be tossed again. This time, fate smiled on Liverpool as it came down red to end the marathon collision, which had begun on 10 February and had now reached its climax on 24 March, in their favour. The leap of joy from skipper Ron Yeats told the story.

The team flew home to take on Chelsea in the FA Cup semi-final at Villa Park three days later and booked a Wembley date with Leeds United after a 2–0 victory, thanks to a goal from Peter Thompson and a penalty by Willie Stevenson. That game was unforgettable for comedian Jimmy Tarbuck.

'I got on very well with Shanks and I was already friendly with Ian St John,' he recalled. 'On the day we beat Chelsea at Villa Park, Shanks invited me into the dressing room which, of course, was a great thrill for me. Shanks made me feel very welcome. He did it again quite often after that and I remember taking Frankie Vaughan into the dressing room with me once. Liverpool's rise coincided with The Beatles and people like Cilla Black, Gerry and the Pacemakers and myself stepping on to this wonderful bandwagon.'

Liverpool were 90 minutes away from achieving the club's cherished dream and taking the FA Cup back to Anfield. And three days after Wembley, they would have to face Inter Milan in the first leg of the European Cup semi-final.

4

Success and the Seven-year Itch

The alliance of Shankly and Paisley had carried Liverpool to horizons that would have seemed fantasy at the start of the decade when the club languished in the Second Division entertaining the likes of Scunthorpe and Plymouth. And while there was a stark contrast in the personas of the two men, their views on the game and how it should be played and coached overlapped into a powerful, shared philosophy, as Bob outlined: 'Neither Shanks nor myself had ever been on a manager's course. I'm not saying there's anything wrong with them. But we'd gained our knowledge as we'd gone along.

'We did go on a coaching course. We went to Lilleshall to learn, but Shanks and the rest of the Liverpool staff who went ended up taking the classes ourselves. People say that Liverpool only play the simple way. Well, what's the simple way? It's giving the ball to the best advantage for a colleague. Then, it doesn't become simple because the man who's giving that ball has to sort out the best way for his team-mate to receive it. That's a thought process. Yes, we try to keep it as simple as we can and keep out the complications. There are certainly too many complications today. But at the same time you mustn't over-simplify it.'

Saturday 1 May 1965 is a glorious date in Liverpool history, the day they won the FA Cup and saluted an individually heroic performance that helped achieve it. They had to overcome a talented Leeds United side that included the formidable half-back line of Billy Bremner, Jack Charlton and Norman Hunter and the passing skills of Johnny Giles.

This is how Liverpool lined up: Tommy Lawrence; Chris Lawler, Gerry Byrne; Geoff Strong, Ron Yeats, Willie Stevenson; Ian Callaghan, Roger Hunt, Ian St John, Tommy Smith, Peter Thompson.

Hunt felt sure it was going to be Liverpool's afternoon: 'Going down the tunnel, obviously you're a bag of nerves – all the players were very nervous – but I was also very confident. What helped was the fact that when we went out to have a look at the Wembley turf beforehand, our supporters made such a terrific noise. The stadium seemed full of Liverpool supporters. You couldn't hear the Leeds fans. So I just couldn't see us losing.'

But to take the cup back to Anfield for the first time required a performance of raw courage from Hunt's team-mate Gerry Byrne, who had been on the transfer list and surplus to requirements when Shankly arrived as manager in December 1959. He promptly announced that Byrne was not for sale and if ever a single occasion proved the wisdom of that decision, it was Wembley 1965. Byrne produced one of the bravest displays the stadium has ever witnessed following a fierce sixth-minute challenge by Bobby Collins, for which the little Scot was penalised by referee Bill Clements. Paisley dashed on to the field to be told by Byrne that some skin had been taken off his shin. The left-back's real problem was not revealed until several minutes later, when the ever-alert Paisley seized the opportunity to have another look at him during a stoppage for treatment to a Leeds player. His instant – and correct – diagnosis was a broken collar-bone, and Bob had to think and act quickly in a crisis amidst the tense atmosphere of a Wembley Cup Final. He recalled: 'I felt Gerry's collar-bone and knew right away it was broken. There were no substitutes in those days and I told him that if I was in his place I'd have to have a wooden leg before I went off!'

Byrne recalled his dramatic injury: 'When Bob came on I told him about my leg and he gave me treatment for that. Then when I got on my feet I could feel my shoulder bone. But even though I was in pain, I was determined to play on.'

Not only did he complete the 90 minutes but also the entire half-hour's extra time.

Byrne and Paisley agreed that the extent of the damage must be kept secret from Leeds. But Paisley then had to break the news to Shankly, who was waiting anxiously on the sidelines. Bob recalled:

'I went back to our bench and I had to tell Bill about Gerry's injury very, very quietly, to avoid the Leeds manager Don Revie overhearing. He was sitting very close to us. Thank goodness Don didn't hear. In fact, nobody from Leeds had any idea of the massive handicap Gerry was playing under, or the agony he was suffering. Nobody in the 100,000 crowd knew, either. At half-time I put a figure-of-eight bandage on Gerry and he went out again and did tremendously well. He even went through and laid on the cross for Roger Hunt to score our first goal early in extra time.'

Liverpool's lead was cancelled out by a Leeds equaliser from Bremner. But they were not to be denied their destiny. In the 111th minute of the contest, Ian St John rose to meet a Callaghan cross and clinch the Cup for the Kop. 'I saw that Cally was going to cross it and I presumed it would be short,' said St John. 'So when I went short, the ball came and that was that.'

It was a goal acclaimed by St John's strike partner Roger Hunt. 'Ian's winner was a great goal,' he said. 'It looked at first as if Ian Callaghan was going to run the ball out of play. But Ian was very fast and he got to it down the right. When he crossed it, there was Ian St John to slot it home. That was Ian. He was great in the air. Once he'd headed that one in, I don't think Leeds were capable of coming back. There was more chance of us scoring another.'

The trophy was presented to Ron Yeats by the Queen, whose own colour choice was not lost on the exuberant Liverpool followers, who chanted: 'Ee Aye Addio, the Queen's Wearing Red!' Shankly even took off his famous raincoat in celebration. But behind the scenes the final twist of an incredible afternoon was taking place, involving Paisley and the heroic Byrne. Bob revealed: 'After the game I sent for the Wembley doctor to examine Gerry's collar-bone. He said there was no way it was broken. But I insisted that Gerry had X-rays. And, sure enough, it was broken.' It would not be the last time that Paisley's gift for diagnosis would put other medical assessments to shame. He was even affectionately dubbed 'The Witch Doctor'.

Shankly was hugely appreciative of Bob's range of injury knowledge and drooled over Byrne's defiant Wembley display and how the whole affair had been handled by him and Paisley: 'Who could have played at Wembley Stadium for two hours with a broken collar-bone? The bones were gritting together. It was unbelievable The greatest thing of all is that Bob and I never disclosed it. Apart from us, the Liverpool doctor and our players, nobody knew until after the game.'

The welter of inquiries about Gerry Byrne as the Liverpool party travelled back to Merseyside by train on the Sunday, to prepare for Tuesday's confrontation with Inter Milan, led to the club taking an unusual step, recalled by Ian Callaghan: 'On the train back we were putting bulletins out about Gerry Byrne. They were all asking how he was. We got that fed up we put a bulletin on the door saying, "Gerry's fine and feeling OK – but he won't be fit for Tuesday night"!'

Around half a million people turned out in a fantastic welcome home to Liverpool's FA Cup winners, who then retreated for a short break in Blackpool before facing the mighty Italians. When the team arrived at Anfield by coach on the Tuesday evening, Ron Yeats observed on how quiet the approaches to the stadium were. It was only when they disembarked that a steward told the players the gates had been locked on a capacity 54,000-plus crowd an hour and a half earlier. Those privileged to be present that night savour its memory as the greatest occasion Anfield has ever experienced. The emotion-charged atmosphere had a raw energy of its own, and the old stands reverberated from the roar that greeted injured duo Gerry Byrne and Gordon Milne parading the FA Cup around the running track before kick-off.

And when the action began, a vintage performance from Liverpool saw them put the reigning world and European champions to the sword with a 3–1 victory. Hunt's goal from a third-minute Callaghan cross put them ahead, only for Inter to equalise after ten minutes when a slip by Yeats let in Peiro for Mazzola to score. Liverpool regained the lead when Callaghan dummied a 34th-minute free kick. The winger jumped over the ball and kept on running as Stevenson found Hunt, whose sidefoot pass allowed Callaghan to make it 2–1. 'That's the most treasured goal of my career,' said Callaghan. 'What made it even more rewarding was that we'd practised the free-kick plan for some time. It was great to make it pay off like that.'

St John made it 3–1 after Hunt's shot had rebounded off goalkeeper Sarti 15 minutes from the end, and Liverpool felt they should have had a fourth goal. But Austrian referee Karl Kainer disallowed Chris Lawler's strike for offside, thus robbing the attacking full-back of a double celebration following his wedding the previous day. Said Lawler: 'It was one of the best "goals" I've ever scored, and it was with my left foot as well! It was disallowed for offside. But it would have stood today.'

England winger Peter Thompson recalled how that famous victory over the Italians could have been even more emphatic: 'It was the biggest night I ever knew at Anfield. There was a fantastic atmosphere. Shanks and Bob devised the tactics and we could have hit Inter for six. Chris Lawler scored a fabulous goal but the referee gave Geoff Strong offside. We also hit the post and the bar. It was an incredible performance against what was the best club team in the world.'

Armed with a 3–1 lead, Liverpool were optimistic of eliminating Inter in the second leg. But they walked into a nightmare in Italy. A hate campaign had been whipped up against them, with claims that the players were on drugs. There was a vicious atmosphere inside the San Siro Stadium and the performance of the Spanish referee Ortiz de Mendibil prompted Shankly and Paisley to strongly suspect corruption. Subsequent investigations, notably spearheaded by the *Sunday Times*, proved it beyond any reasonable doubt.

Inter won the return 3–0 and their first goal came from a swerving shot from Corso direct from a free kick. But to a man, the Liverpool camp insisted that the referee had signalled an indirect free kick. And despite the tendency of European referees to favour goalkeepers, the Spanish official then allowed Peiro to kick the ball away as Tommy Lawrence was bouncing it and steer it into the net for Inter's second goal. A brilliant piece of football involving Corso and Suarez saw Facchetti hit Inter's third goal to give them a 4–3 aggregate triumph and help maintain what was then a Latin monopoly of European football's greatest prize. Inter went on to beat Benfica 1–0 in the final at their own San Siro home, a previously appointed venue.

Shankly summed up the desperate disappointment of Liverpool as he reflected on the manner of their European dismissal: 'The second leg was a war. I've never seen such hostility, with purple smoke bombs being let off. Oh, it was an awful feeling. And the decisions on the pitch were queer. I don't think the Inter Milan players were cheats or anything like that. It was the decisions. Even if the decisions had gone in our favour there's a possibility Inter Milan might have beaten us. But of all the people I've seen and met in my life, the referee that night is the one man who haunts me.'

Peter Thompson believes that Liverpool's European

experiences in 1965 had positive repercussions for the club in general and Bob Paisley in particular, although, he frankly admits, not especially for his own Anfield career: 'I was in Yugoslavia with England and fell ill about four days before the second leg against Inter. They flew me from Yugoslavia to Milan and I was still suffering from the stomach bug. I wasn't fit but they talked me into playing, as only Shankly and Paisley could! "You're fit – you'll forget about your upset stomach when you get out there in front of all those people!" said Shanks. But I wasn't right and I didn't really perform.

'We went off the field very depressed that night. We thought we were going to win the European Cup. It would have been a wonderful thing for us. We thought Shanks would give us a good going over but he just stood there and said: "Don't worry, boys, they were drugged to the eyeballs! Nobody could beat us 3–0 without drugs!"

'That was Shanks. Bob was a character in his own right, too, I was an individualist as a player and, looking back, I was a bit too greedy on the field. I just played my own game. Bob talked to me about it, although I could never really understand him so I didn't take any notice. Bob got through to the rest of them, though, and he went on to fabulous success.'

Thompson, missing only two of 42 League games and weighing in with five goals, was an integral part of the team that completed a trophy hat-trick in 1965–66 by regaining the championship, which gave Liverpool a three-season return of title, FA Cup and title again. They hit the top of the table for the first time that season with a 5–2 home win over Blackburn on 17 November, briefly lost pole position after a goalless draw at Stoke but went back to the summit with a 2–1 home win over Burnley on 27 November and led the field for the rest of the season. They hit five goals on four occasions, including a sweet nap hand without reply against Everton at Anfield. They also played in front of the country's biggest League attendance of the season when they drew 0–0 at Goodison in the derby return in March, watched by 62,537.

Liverpool finished as champions with 61 points, six ahead of Leeds and Burnley, who were locked on the same total of 55. Hunt hit 30 League goals, with his partner St John bagging ten, and Liverpool set a new all-time League record of using only 14 players in their triumphant title campaign. Of those, Alf

Arrowsmith made only five appearances, two as substitute, and Bobby Graham had just a single outing. Five players, Lawrence, Byrne, Smith, Yeats and Callaghan, were ever-presents. Indeed, Callaghan had played in all 84 games of the two title campaigns of 1964 and 1966, an illustration of his amazing fitness and consistency.

The 14-player record, equalled by Aston Villa in 1980–81, was a tribute to the physical condition of the players, the training programme laid down by Shankly, and Paisley's uncanny diagnosis and treatment of injuries. Three players from that 1960s team, Hunt, Lawrence and Callaghan, revealed to me some vivid memories of Paisley and Shankly and their attitude to injuries. They also presented their own thoughts on Bob's knowledge of physiotherapy.

Hunt: Bob, when he finished playing, studied it and went into it. He did a good job really. He was far more knowledgeable than we gave him credit for at the time.
Lawrence: We just got pulled in when he got new machines.
Hunt: The new machines came from Germany.
Lawrence: And he got the books out, and started reading them.
Hunt: You made sure you weren't a guinea pig.
Callaghan: We were just talking about that before – when Jimmy Melia was the guinea pig.
Keith: Was it Jimmy Melia or Peter Thompson?
Lawrence: It was Jimmy Melia.
Hunt: Yeah, this new machine came and it was one where you had the pads on your legs. You had to actually do it yourself. So when you got a certain level of pain – that's it – OK. So Bob did the three or four dials. They were experimenting with Jimmy Melia and he said, 'Turn it up a bit. Do you feel anything?' Jimmy said, 'No, it's OK. Turn it up a bit more.' So Bob turned it up. Jimmy said, 'Can't feel anything, it's fine. A bit more, Bob'. So he turned it up right to the top and looked around at the plug. 'The ruddy thing's not switched on!' said Shanks giving the mains plug a firm kick. *'Boof!'* Up went Melia . . . (*Five minutes laughter*)
Keith: He always said he was good in the air!
Lawrence: But that's what happened when they got these new machines – they got books with them. Bob and Joe Fagan would be sitting reading these books, and if you were in there with these new machines you didn't want to go on the table!

Hunt: It's funny because Albert Shelley at that time was the first-team trainer and he was just helping out with the kit, the towels, baths and all that, and sometimes he'd give you a bit of a rub-down, Albert. And he wouldn't go near these machines, Albert. 'No, we'll 'ave the old lamp in,' he'd say. (*Laughter*) He was very suspicious of the machines, wasn't he?

Callaghan: We used to have an old box in the dressing room, where you put your knee in and they put Vaseline all over it, covered it with a towel, put the lid down and just left you there. You had two switches to go hotter and you just used to do it yourself. Just left there for an hour!

Keith: Who supervised that, was it Bob or Albert?

Callaghan: It was both, Bob and Albert.

Lawrence: Even that wax bath was terrible.

Hunt: Oh, the was bath was terrible, but the thing was Shanks hated you if you were injured. He got all these machines and if any of the lads were in the treatment room he wouldn't come in. He used to open the door very slightly and peep in and say, 'That bastard Callaghan's on the table!' But you'd get no sympathy if you were injured.

Lawrence: Never spoke to you. Wouldn't even speak to you.

Keith: He used to use Ian as the yardstick and used to say, 'There's nobody like Ian Callaghan, he's like a rubber ball. When he gets injured he just bounces back again.' And that was the yardstick – everybody should be like that and never get injured...

Hunt: Shouldn't get injured, yeah. Actually, it was good when you think of it. It was good thinking because you really felt guilty if you were injured, didn't you? Tommy, tell him about you.

Lawrence: I got injured at Wolverhampton on the Monday night and my leg was bad. Really was bad – the muscle had gone in it. Didn't speak to you, but on Tuesday morning he said, 'How is it?' But you didn't like saying there was anything wrong with you.

Hunt: But didn't Bob say to you, he knew you were unfit, but he said, 'Tell him you're fit'?

Lawrence: And Shanks left it till Friday – and he got me out. And he said, 'Right. Come on, run round the pitch!' I could hardly walk – never mind run! (*Laughter*) So Bob had said to me before I went out 'Tell him you're fit'. So, as soon as I'd run round the pitch he said, 'OK, son, how is it?' I said, 'I'm fit'. Shanks said, 'Fxxxxx fit!!!!! You're a cripple! A bleedin' cripple! Get out o' ma sight!!!!' (*Roars of laughter*) ... Before I'd started around the pitch I could've raced a dozen greyhounds with my kecks down, but as soon as I said I was fit... that was me finished!

Hunt: But Bob knew if someone got injured on the field, he knew if it was a bad one. He was pretty good on that.

Keith: Because Shanks didn't want to know that part of it, did he?

Hunt: Not at all, no.

Lawrence: He sent Alfie Arrowsmith to Coventry for about three months when Alfie had that bad leg, didn't he? Every time Alfie came out ... oh dear me ...

Hunt: I once overheard him talking to Tony Book outside the dressing room, when he used stand in the corridor on match days. Tony Book had come with City, but he wasn't playing and he had an Achilles tendon injury. I heard Shanks saying to him, 'Don't rush that, son. Don't rush it at all.' Now if it had been one of us with an injury he would've said we were malingering, wouldn't he?

Lawrence: He used to leave you all week, till maybe Thursday, Friday, and then if you said 'No' then that was it. You were out, you were away, you were nobody then. That were it.

Keith: But he used to ask Bob.

Hunt: He asked Bob. He didn't ask you, he asked Bob.

Keith: ... because he respected Bob's opinion. So, really, it was a very good thing that someone like Bob was about for Shankly. I suppose when Bob became a manager his knowledge of injuries ...

Hunt: Well, he was a lot better than Shanks on that side of it, on the injuries side.

Callaghan: One guy you haven't mentioned in all this is Reuben Bennett.

Hunt: Yeah, 'cause he was always in the dressing room.

Lawrence: He's the one who always spoke to us. The injured players could always go to Reuben Bennett when Shanks wouldn't speak to you.

Callaghan: Yeah, if you were injured and sent to the end of the training ground to do your own thing, it was always Reuben who came down and said, 'Keep going, keep going ...'

Keith: He gave you great encouragement?

Callaghan: Oh yeah. He was great, a lovely man.

The Liverpool dressing room of the 1960s was memorable not

only for the Scottish tones of Shankly and Bennett but also for Paisley's distinctive Durham accent and colloquialisms. One of them was Bob's use of the word 'doings', which could have a host of different meanings depending on the situation. Two other stars of that era, Ian St John and Ron Yeats, gave me some hilarious examples:

St John: You know they used to pull that gag at every game with Bob. They'd shout across to Bob, 'Pass us the doings, Bob!' and he'd throw over whatever they needed. And I used to say 'He's gonna ruddy well catch on to us one of these days, I'm telling you!' One day one of the lads, I think it was Smithy, needed a bandage and he yelled, 'Hey, Bob, throw us a doings,' and this bandage came flying over Bob's left shoulder. (*Laughter*) And then Hughes started doing it, a bit obvious, and he used to yell to Bob (*St John in soprano voice*), 'Pass us the doings, Bob!'

Yeats: He did it in a pre-season game at Doncaster, I'm no' joking. Somebody was on the table and Bob had his back to us. Emlyn sat down next to me and nudged me. (*St John laughing at the thought*) 'Listen to this,' he said. 'He doesn't know what I want, I'm gonna ask for a pair o' shinguards, but I'm gonna say doings.' I said, 'Bloody hell! For Christ's sake, Emlyn!' Then he said, 'Hey, Bob, throw us over that doings, will you?' and a bleeding pair of shinguards came flying through the air straight away! Bob never even turned round! (*Hysterical laughter*) I couldn't ruddy well believe it. I was laughing ma head off and Bob looked over as if to say, 'What the hell are you lot laughing at?'

Keith: That's incredible.

St John: He had a sixth sense.

But in the art of psyching out Shankly, nobody did it better than Bob Paisley when it came to players' injuries, as St John and Yeats illustrated:

St John: I remember that. Bob had Shanks sussed on that. Bob realized it. If you were unfit, Bob pronounced you as unfit but you had to say you were fit. And then let him talk you out of it. He did it with me one time. 'I think I'll be OK, boss.' When Shanks saw you it was, 'Christ, son! You can't play!'

Yeats: Or he'd say, 'How do you know you'll be OK?'

St John: (*Laughing*) Or you'd say, 'I think I'll get through the game.' And he'd say, 'Christ, son, no . . .' and then you'd go away.

While the 1965–66 season brought Liverpool championship
success, there was disappointment for them in the FA Cup and
sheer agony in the Cup-Winners' Cup, in which they went close
to lifting the club's first European trophy. Paisley's first absence
from duty since Shankly's arrival, due to an attack of tonsilitis,
coincided with Chelsea avenging their semi-final defeat of a
season earlier by knocking out the FA Cup holders 2–1 in the
third round in front of the Kop. But Liverpool extracted their own
revenge in Europe. Having lost to Inter Milan in the European
Cup the previous May, they went back to Italy and pegged
Juventus to a 1–0 win at Turin's Stadio Communale in their first
engagement in the Cup-Winners' Cup, and completed the job by
toppling the Italians 2–0 in the Anfield return, thanks to goals
from Chris Lawler and Geoff Strong.

Strong would prove a major figure in that season's European
campaign. A native of Northumberland and given his professional
chance by Arsenal, he rated his move to Liverpool as one of the
best decisions of his life. And he recalled how they were a team on
and off the field: 'There's nowhere in the world like Liverpool and
the boys of the sixties were very, very close. Wherever we went we
were together; we even went on holiday together. It was a gang of
guys with a fantastic camaraderie. It was tremendous.' It was that
still-prevailing spirit which, some three decades later, led to the
founding of the Liverpool FC Former Players Association, open
to all who have donned the Anfield jersey.

Belgium's Standard Liege, on a 5–2 aggregate, and Hungarian
side Honved, beaten 2–0 on aggregate, were next to fall in the
Cup-Winners' Cup to secure Liverpool a mighty semi-final
confrontation with Celtic. In the first leg, played on a windy night
at Parkhead, Liverpool were without the injured Roger Hunt,
which provided one of only eight first team outings for Phil
Chisnall, a £25,000 signing from Manchester United in April
1964. Liverpool were far from their best and lost 1–0 in front of
80,000 spectators to set up a tense, atmospheric second leg. It was
one of Anfield's unforgettable nights when a fire alert was
triggered by what seemed to be smoke rising from the stadium. It
turned out to be steam generated by a packed crowd of 54,208,
the club's biggest of the season for a game billed as 'The Battle of
Britain'. This time Strong replaced the still-injured Hunt but was

himself hobbling from the 20th minute with a ripped cartilage. Paisley bound up his knee with a bandage and Strong bravely stayed in the thick of the action.

The game was still goalless at the interval but a 61st-minute free kick swept in by Tommy Smith put the teams level on aggregate. And Strong, who dubbed himself 'Limpalong Leslie', swooped for victory six minutes later by rising on his one good leg to meet Callaghan's cross and head past keeper Ronnie Simpson. The hero's mantle was bestowed on Strong, whose versatility was remarkable. In his six-year Anfield career he wore every shirt except numbers one and seven.

The vast amount of empty bottles left behind by the hordes of Celtic fans who had travelled south for the game made an amazing sight in the cold light of the following morning. The collection prompted Celtic boss Jock Stein to quip to Shankly: 'Are you going to give us a cut of the takings or should we just take the empties back?'

Victory over Celtic booked Liverpool a return visit to Glasgow to face West German side Borussia Dortmund in the Cup-Winners' Cup Final at Hampden Park. But before that there was the little matter of the loose ends of the championship to tie up. Liverpool faced Chelsea in their last home game of the season, needing a point to secure the title for the second time in three seasons. They ran out of the tunnel on a sun-splashed Saturday afternoon to a guard of honour formed by the Chelsea players. Two Roger Hunt goals clinched a 2–1 win and landed the seventh championship in Liverpool's history. The Kop were ecstatic, turning their joy in the direction of the fifth-placed visitors with renditions of 'London Bridge Is Falling Down' and 'Show Them The Way To Go Home'.

A crowd of 53,754 witnessed that game, underlining that there really was a 'Boom at the Kop', as St John's book, published that year, was so colourfully titled, inspired by the famous British movie *Room at the Top*. There certainly wasn't much room at Anfield, which was packed for most games after the rebuilding of the Kemlyn Road Stand and the Anfield Road End during the previous three years cut the stadium capacity to less than 54,000. The number of 50,000-plus attendances climbed into double figures that season with an average of more than 48,000. It was reflected in the club's balance sheet, which showed a profit of £148,408 with some players in the £5,000-a-year wage bracket, a star salary by any standards in Britain in the mid 1960s.

Yet England winger Peter Thompson emphasised that it was the sheer enjoyment and personal achievement of playing for Liverpool that meant most: 'I was supposed to be a wonder boy at 17 and a has-been at 19. When I came to Liverpool within 12 months we were champions and I scored twice in our 5–0 win over Arsenal that clinched it. I'll never forget that game because I didn't score many goals. To run round Anfield in front of almost 50,000 people after winning the title is an incredible feeling. You can't really describe it unless you've actually been through it. I got picked for England, too, then we won the FA Cup for the first time in history and the League again. It was a fabulous time. They were super days. We played as a team and had a passion to win. There was a blend of Scots, local lads, and others like Gordon Milne and myself. Money never, ever came into it. It was just the thrill of going out there and playing.'

Shankly's insistence on being free to pick the team on his arrival in 1959 had been vindicated a thousandfold, a point on which Paisley reflected: 'People like me benefited from the fact that Bill was the first to have his say as a manager. Nobody ever queries my selections. Now some people make the manager bigger than the players. I don't go along with that. I don't look at it in that light.'

Liverpool's success became intertwined with the city's exploding pop and comedy culture and spawned the wonderfully enduring story of the evangelical sandwich-board man outside Anfield, with a poster posing the question: 'What would you do if the Lord came?'

One wag, clearly a fervent Kopite, scrawled underneath: 'Move St John to inside-right!'

The landing of the championship brought Bob Paisley his third title medal, following his initital triumph as a player in 1947. He also figured in a remarkable but bizarre salute to the team and backroom staff from one jubilant Liverpool fan, who named his newly born daughter: Paula St John Lawrence Lawler Byrne Strong Yeat's Stevenson Callaghan Hunt Milne Smith Thompson Shankley Bennett Paisley O'Sullivan...complete with those misspellings of Yeats with an apostrophe and, ironically, Shankly with an 'ey'!

After clinching the title, Liverpool headed to Scotland the following midweek for the Cup-Winners' Cup Final against Dortmund, who had knocked out trophy holders West Ham in the semi-final. Torrential rain restricted the crowd to 41,000, less than half Hampden's 100,000 capacity, and Liverpool's line-up was: Lawrence, Lawler, Byrne, Milne, Yeats, Stevenson, Callaghan, Hunt, St John, Smith, Thompson.

Liverpool were in the driving seat for most of the game without ever hitting peak form. When they did threaten they were denied by the defiant goalkeeping of Hans Tilkowski. And Dortmund were cheered on by Celtic fans still angry over an offside verdict that had ruled out a late Bobby Lennox strike in the semi-final at Anfield. The Hampden contest was goalless at half-time but Sigi Held put the Germans ahead after being put through by a superb pass from Lothar Emmerich, whose four goals over two legs had destroyed West Ham in the semi-final. Hunt prodded an equaliser for a jaded-looking Liverpool, but a cruel extra-time goal condemned them to defeat. Reinhardt Libuda, out near the touchline, floated the ball towards the net. It was too high even for Ron Yeats to clear and the ball went in off him, much to the Liverpool skipper's chagrin: 'He'd chipped Tommy Lawrence and I'd got back on the line. But instead of the ball hitting the bar and going over, it hit the bar, came down and went in off my chest.'

Roger Hunt would, at least, have the satisfaction later that summer of being on the winning England side against three members of that Dortmund team in the World Cup Final. Tilkowski, Held and Emmerich were in the West German line-up that lost 4–2 after extra time at Wembley. Two of Hunt's Anfield colleagues, Gerry Byrne and Ian Callaghan, were also in Alf Ramsey's 22-man squad and all three drew a £1,000 bonus in addition to appearance fees for helping England achieve their triumph. A fortnight later the trio were in the Liverpool team that beat FA Cup winners Everton 1–0, thanks to a Hunt goal, in the Charity Shield at Goodison. Paisley was, as usual, at Shankly's side for an occasion made unique by rival captains Yeats and Brian Labone parading around the ground with English football's two major domestic trophies while Hunt and Everton's England left-back Ray Wilson proudly displayed the newly won World Cup. But that grip on the championship was to be Liverpool's last on any major trophy for seven years, a gap on the honours board often overlooked by fans and pundits alike.

Not that Liverpool could be called unsuccessful during that period, in which their lowest finishing position in the League was fifth and they managed a runners-up spot, in 1969, and two third places. They were beaten finalists in the 1971 FA Cup, falling 2–1 in extra time to Double-winning Arsenal at Wembley after Steve Heighway had put them in front, ironically the first game they lost that season after taking the lead. During those seven years without a trophy, Liverpool also qualified for Europe every season. But they suffered the chastening experience of being beaten 7–3 on aggregate by emerging Dutch masters Ajax and their burgeoning star Johan Cruyff in the second round of the 1966–67 European Cup.

Liverpool had needed a play-off in Brussels to overcome Petrolul Ploesti, the team from the Romanian oil fields, to get through to meet Ajax, and in the first leg they were blitzed 5–1 in an Amsterdam fog. It was a night when the incorrigible Shankly ran on to the pitch without the referee's knowledge and also one that defined both the football rivalry and native wit of Merseyside, as an Everton fan telephoned the *Daily Express* sports desk in Manchester and proclaimed: 'Now we know – Ajax DOES kill 99 per cent of all known germs!'

Despite Shankly's bravado about the second leg, Liverpool could only draw 2–2 an Anfield, where Cruyff crowned a bewitching performance by scoring both the Dutch side's goals. It was a harsh lesson for Liverpool but Paisley was a keen student. The club adjusted to the demands of Europe, especially in their travel plans, which Paisley rated such a crucial factor.

'Travel, and its effects, is the most underrated part of the game,' he said. 'When English clubs first competed in Europe they went on their holidays. They were excited about going to exotic places and used to spend almost all week away. We cut it down to spending as little time as possible in the country – as late as we could get in and as soon as we could get out. That was our philosophy. We'd train until the last possible moment at home before starting our journey, because what training we did abroad was only going to be a light session. We'd take our own water, too. That's not to say the water was tampered with abroad. But it is different and you never know how people react. Different water can cause stomach upsets, for instance.'

After Ajax there were four consecutive seasons for Liverpool in the European Fairs Cup, later to be known as the UEFA Cup, and some new faces. Gordon Milne, one of the stars of Shankly's first great side, left to join Blackpool for £30,000 in May 1967, just three months after a raw 19-year-old called Emlyn Hughes made the trip in the opposite direction. Even for a club record £65,000, he proved a 'steal'. The infectiously enthusiastic young recruit went on to captain both Liverpool and England, and earn the nickname 'Crazy Horse' bestowed on him by Everton fans! A few months after Hughes arrived, another key player and future England star was recruited from Scunthorpe United. Ray Clemence cost just £18,000 in June 1967, although he had to wait two and a half seasons before ousting Tommy Lawrence as the club's first-choice goalkeeper and going on to prove himself arguably the best Liverpool have ever had.

Centre-forward Tony Hateley was another new arrival, his £96,000 signing from Chelsea in June 1967 taking Shankly's transfer outlay towards the £500,000 mark since his swoops for St John and Yeats six years earlier. Hateley figures in one of Ray Clemence's abiding memories of Paisley's unique medical methods: 'One of my favourite memories of Bob was late in the 1967–77 season at West Ham. Tony Hateley, who was great in the air but not always on the ground, was having one of his indifferent days. It was in the days when you brought substitutes on only for injured players. Tony threw himself into a challenge for the ball but ended up sliding off the pitch into the advertising hoardings, which were very close to the touchline. Bob was on like a flash to attend to Tony. He started tying his legs together.

'"No, no, Bob," said Tony. "It's not my legs, it's my back."

'Bob said: "I know it is son. But I'm tying your legs together so we can get you off and get the sub on."'

While Willie Stevenson ended his impressive five-year Anfield career by joining Stoke City for £48,000 in December 1967, the spending continued. In September 1968, as Hateley was sold on to Coventry for £80,000 after scoring 28 goals in 56 appearances during his 15 months at Anfield, another striker, Alun Evans, became the country's first £100,000 teenager when he joined Liverpool from Wolves. Centre-back Larry Lloyd was signed for £50,000 from Bristol Rovers in April 1969 and eventually took over at number five from Yeats, Shankly's first captain, who ended more than a decade of Liverpool service by crossing the Mersey to join Tranmere as player/assistant manager in December 1971. Another new capture was Alec Lindsay, who cost £67,000 from Bury in March 1969 and was brilliantly converted by Shankly and Paisley from a wing-half or inside-forward to a left-back who would go on to play for England.

Liverpool's first three campaigns in the Fairs Cup brought them little joy with the Hungarians of Ferencvaros knocking them out in the third round in 1967–68, Athletic Bilbao winning a first-round engagement on the toss of a disc the following season and then Portuguese side Vitoria Setubal eliminating Liverpool on the away-goals rule in round two in 1969–70. But all the time the club were storing up European know-how and becoming Continentally street-wise – none more so than Paisley, who was acutely aware of the pitfalls and potential dirty tricks to which opposing clubs could resort: 'There was a story that Ajax were 'gassed' in one of the Iron Curtain countries. There was a whiff of something pumped into their dressing room! So many of the foreign teams who come here, especially from Eastern Europe, are suspicious about things. It makes you wonder why they are. It throws it back on them. Are they suspicious of you because they get up to tricks themselves?'

Paisley was keenly aware that diet was a crucial factor: 'It's so important that we started taking our own food tasters with us to oversee and help to organise what the hotel kitchens were serving up. We also take our own supplies of various things. We tell our players to drink and eat only what's served or recommended. It's so easy for stuff to be tampered with.'

The approach of the 1970s heralded a time of change. Man set foot on the moon on 21 July 1969 and the age of supersonic air travel also beckoned with the prototype of the Anglo-French Concorde taking to the sky for the first time a year earlier. In 1968, Manchester United became the first English club to lift the European Cup, their 4–1 Wembley win over Benfica following Celtic's triumph the previous season, achieved with a 2–1 victory over Inter Milan in Lisbon. Nine years would elapse before another British club would claim Europe's most prestigious trophy. That club would be Liverpool – with Bob Paisley the manager.

5

The Axe Finally Falls

In common with global events, the start of the new decade was also a time for change at Anfield. Indeed, in Paisley's view, Shankly's loyalty to the players who had become legends in the sixties stretched too far, as Jessie Paisley revealed. 'Bob made his decisions and stuck to them,' she said. 'He believed that Bill kept some players in the team for too long, that he was too loyal to them. If Bob thought it was time for a player to move on then he would act on that. He didn't feel it was right for the player or club to keep them past their best.'

Judging the right time to part company with players was, in Paisley's eyes, 'one of the most important things in football. It's a huge mistake to keep someone when you know he isn't going to be suitable. It's not fair on him or on you. You do it in the right way, of course, and you try not to fall out about it. But it has to be done.'

Roger Hunt, dubbed 'Sir Roger' by the Kop left for Bolton in December 1969, after scoring a record 245 League goals for Liverpool in an overall total of 285. He was one of the greatest forwards ever to play for the club, and the same applied to his attack partner Ian St John. The Scot's 118 goals from more than 400 appearances put him in the list of Liverpool's all-time top scorers and his impact and influence on the team assure him of a place in the roll-call of Anfield's greatest players. His name inspired the fans to seize on the jazz classic 'When The Saints Go Marching In' and convert it into a Kop standard, before their adoption of 'You'll Never Walk Alone' as the Anfield anthem.

Indeed, songs became a trademark of the Kop and Shankly

himself was caught up in the musical fervour, as Paisley revealed: 'It was right up Bill's street. He'd often say to me after coming off the pitch and the Kop had been singing: "Bob, I wish they'd given us another verse!"'

So when the time came for long-serving players to leave Liverpool and the remarkable Anfield atmosphere, the break could be emotionally painful. St John recalled the day in October 1969 when he realized his great Liverpool career was nearing its close and the advice he received from Bob Paisley: 'I found out my name wasn't on the team sheet and I went looking for the boss. I was really wound up about it but, thankfully, Bob and Reuben saw me and told me to cool it. They calmed me down.'

Paisley believed it was in the best interests of team harmony if he could deal with players' problems before they even reached Shankly. 'Those few yards between the dressing room and the manager's office are vital,' he stressed. 'Once a player gets in there it's an argument. When Bill was manager, I rated a big part of my job as cutting things off before they reached the office. If I could sort out his beef, all well and good. If I couldn't, at least I could offer him some advice, even if it was just to delay things and take the heat out of the situation.'

The watershed for Liverpool and a batch of their 1960s stars came on 21 February 1970. The occasion was an FA Cup sixth-round tie at Vicarage Road against a Watford side labouring in the Second Division and who were to finish that season fourth from bottom. Liverpool, stripped of Tommy Smith and Peter Thompson through injury, lined up like this: Tommy Lawrence, Chris Lawler, Peter Wall; Geoff Strong, Ron Yeats, Emlyn Hughes; Ian Callaghan, Ian Ross, Alun Evans, Ian St John, Bobby Graham. They had won 2–1 at Watford earlier that season in the League Cup – a competition rooted firmly at the foot of Liverpool priorities in those years – but the FA Cup result left the club reeling. A single goal from the head of Watford's Barry Endean decided the game and Shankly was in no doubt that the time for change was overdue. He admitted that an era had come to an end.

'We were without Peter Thompson and Tommy Smith and if they'd played we might have won,' he said. 'But in a way it was a godsend they didn't, because after we'd lost I decided that was it. I'd bargained for the players going on longer than they did. Some of them waned a little bit. I realized I had to break up the team and start again.'

Shankly's delay in regenerating Liverpool's ranks until it was virtually forced upon him was a fate that would not befall Paisley, who observed candidly: 'It's essential to keep a turnover of players, by bringing in new blood. There's no pleasure in telling a player it's time for him to go. But if and when they go into management, they have to do the same themselves. Bill was living on what the team had done. I think it's got to be turned over year by year – an addition here, an addition there, sometimes several new faces at a time.'

And so finally the axe fell on a batch of Liverpool's 1960s greats. Out went Tommy Lawrence, the goalkeeper who had signed for Liverpool as a professional back in 1957 and made almost 400 senior appearances for them. Lawrence had earned two nicknames during his Anfield career. One of them, 'The Flying Pig', was accorded him affectionately by fans and team-mates because of his superb agility for a man of such a big frame weighing more than fourteen stone. He was also dubbed the 'sweeper keeper' by no less a football authority than Joe Mercer, who gave him that label after his marvellously effective display almost as an extra defender in the 1966 Charity Shield win over Everton at Goodison. Lawrence had set a First Division record of conceding only 24 goals when Liverpool finished runners-up to Leeds United in 1968–69, but after the Watford defeat he made only one more senior appearance before joining Tranmere Rovers in September 1971. He left Anfield with rich memories and an abiding dressing-room recollection of Shankly as kick-off time approached on match days: 'He would continually sip a cup of water and comb his hair all the time. Well, actually, he'd hold the comb still and move his head on to it!' The man who followed Lawrence, Ray Clemence, would go on, amazingly, to lower his predecessor's all-time goals-against record still further.

Also victims of Shankly's post-Watford axe were St John, Yeats and Ian Ross, a utility player whose value was in his versatility and his man-marking ability on the rare occasions Liverpool rated an opponent worthy of such close attention. He excelled in that role against Bayern Munich's Franz Beckenbauer in the 1971 Fairs Cup, crowning his display with a goal, and also shackled Everton's Alan Ball in a 3–0 Goodison derby win the previous season. But Ross could never hold down a regular place and was sold to Aston Villa for £60,000 in February 1972. A similar fate befell midfielder Doug Livermore, who would return to Liverpool as a coach more than two decades later. He was called up for his first senior start against Derby a week after the Watford debacle, but just nine months later moved to Norwich for £22,000 after 17 appearances. The great hopes Liverpool held out for Alun Evans after their record investment in his teenage talents also foundered. He never scaled the heights expected of him and after a return of 33 goals in 110 outings, a cartilage operation and a nightclub incident which left him facially scarred, he followed Ross to Villa for £70,000 in June 1972.

The attractions and temptations of nightclubs to players, and the inherent danger to their football careers, have echoed down the years. It was something of which Shankly, Paisley and colleagues were constantly vigilant, as Bob revealed: 'We know what goes on. We were players ourselves once. It's been like that over the generations. If there are any hangovers we can work them off on the training ground. We try to treat the players like men and we hope they'll act with responsibility. By and large, what few incidents there have been over the years we've managed to cover up and we've been fortunate to keep them out of the papers.'

The Watford watershed led to Shankly making a key signing later that year. In November 1970 he paid £110,000 for Cardiff City's towering centre-forward John Toshack, who had set a record for the Ninian Park club by becoming their youngest ever player in a senior game, making his debut as a 16-year-old against Leyton Orient in the Second Division in November 1965. Six months later another player arrived for the more modest fee of £35,000 from Fourth Division Scunthorpe. Anfield, then in the throes of renovation, resembled a building site on the May morning in 1971 when twenty-year-old Kevin Keegan arrived for transfer talks. He even sat on a dustbin outside the stadium offices, waiting to meet Shankly and sign the transfer forms.

Andy Beattie, a former Huddersfield Town manager who had worked with Shankly at the Yorkshire club and was then scouting, had been persuasively instrumental in securing Keegan for Liverpool and beating off competition for his signature. But even in Keegan's first meeting with Shankly, there was clear evidence that here was a youngster with a positive attitude and self-belief, qualities that would be major factors in Liverpool achieving new glories under both Shankly and Paisley. The youngster told Shankly he wanted a fiver increase on Liverpool's wage offer and made an instant impact on the Anfield manager. 'I've never seen such enthusiasm as Keegan showed when he joined us,' Shankly said. 'You could tell from the start he was out to prove a point because of his humble background and hard upbringing. His father was a miner. It was the kind of background I had. I was brought up in a mining village. Right from the start Keegan didn't want to lose. He was a winner.'

Paisley played a major role in the Keegan signing, as he revealed: 'Shanks had seen Kevin many times and he asked Joe Fagan and I to go and see him to make a final decision. Joe and I were satisfied with what we saw after just 20 minutes and highly recommended him. People thought Kevin would take Ian Callaghan's position (in midfield) because Cally had been injured and had taken some stick from the crowd.' As it turned out, the evergreen Callaghan stayed in the side to taste more success, much of it inspired by the cocky young player snapped up from football's bargain basement.

Keegan's arrival was overshadowed by Liverpool's Wembley preparations for the FA Cup Final against champions Arsenal, which he watched starry-eyed as Liverpool threatened to lift the trophy with a goal two minutes into extra time. It came from Warwick University graduate Steve Heighway, a BA who had broken into the Liverpool side early in the season after playing as an amateur for Skelmersdale United. His fast, high-stepping raids down the flank marked him out as an exciting forward of real menace. The Dublin-born raider's elevation into the Anfield side was achieved alongside that of fellow graduate Brian Hall, a BSc, whose industrious midfield play was also a feature of the new Liverpool. Heighway collected his first Republic of Ireland cap even before he had made his League debut for Liverpool and lined up in this Wembley team: Ray Clemence, Chris Lawler, Alec Lindsay, Tommy Smith (captain), Larry Lloyd, Emlyn Hughes, Ian Callaghan, Alun Evans (substitute Peter Thompson), Heighway, John Toshack and Hall.

But Heighway's shot that beat Arsenal goalkeeper Bob Wilson at his near post did not prove to be the winner. Eddie Kelly, sent on to replace Peter Storey in Arsenal's ranks, became the first substitute to score in an FA Cup Final with a scrambled 101st-minute equalizer which was originally credited incorrectly to George Graham. And Liverpool's torture in the sun at sweltering Wembley was complete when Charlie George beat Clemence with a spectacular winner to ensure that the North London club became only the fourth in the history of English football and only the second in the 20th century to land the coveted League and Cup double, the title having been secured five days earlier thanks to a headed winner at Tottenham from a certain Ray Kennedy.

Liverpool had finished fifth in the First Division that 1970–71 season and in Europe reached the Fairs Cup semi-final, losing to their great domestic rivals Leeds by the only goal of the two meetings, scored at Anfield by Billy Bremner.

The following year, despite making early exits from three knock-out competitions – to Leeds after a replay in the fourth round of the FA Cup, West Ham in the fourth round of the League Cup and Bayern Munich at the second hurdle in the European Cup-Winners' Cup – they finished third in the League, level on points with runners-up Leeds and only a point behind champions Derby County, who had a total of 58.

The club had embarked on that 1971–72 season with Kevin Keegan plunged straight into first-team action in the opening game against Nottingham Forest at Anfield. But instead of playing him in midfield, Shankly paired the stocky Keegan up front with lanky John Toshack to launch a partnership that would become a worthy successor to the glorious Hunt and St John combination of the sixties. The decision to pitch Keegan in at the deep end in an attacking role had been taken by Shankly after the new boy's superb display in a pre-season practice game, backed by his effervescent confidence in his own ability, and Keegan responded by scoring 12 minutes into his debut to help Liverpool to a 3–1 win.

As Paisley reflected, Shankly's bold move had paid off handsomely: 'Everything just clicked into place – Kevin was playing up front and Cally in the centre of midfield. Sometimes you're looking for something like that to guide your hand. It's not all genius, although saying that is probably taking some credit away from Bill. But Bill, like me, was the first to admit that you need a bit of luck. It's what makes football the game it is.'

Keegan went on to score 11 goals that season with Toshack netting 13. And if a Toshack strike from a Keegan pass a few minutes from the end of Liverpool's final League game at Arsenal had not been ruled out for offside – a decision which BBC television film showed to be a wrong one – the title would have gone to Anfield instead of Derby. The Derby players had completed their programme and were crowned champions while relaxing in Majorca after Liverpool's game at Highbury ended goalless and Leeds lost 2–1 at Wolves, just 48 hours after they had won the FA Cup by beating Arsenal 1–0.

The following season, however, did end Liverpool's seven-year itch for a trophy, with a unique double in the shape of the League title and the UEFA Cup, the club's first silverware in Europe. All those years in which Liverpool had achieved remarkable consistency in English football, even if there was no trophy to show for it, had been a period when the team behind the team, the backroom training and coaching staff, had elevated the Boot Room to fabled status. That stuffy, cramped, smelly, window-less room off the main dressing room corridor at Anfield became world renowned for the collective wisdom of its inhabitants. It was a place where men steeped in the game would chew the football fat over a bottle of beer or a tot of whisky. Bob Paisley, Joe Fagan, Reuben Bennett, Ronnie Moran, youth development officer Tom Saunders, youth coach John Bennison and chief scout Geoff Twentyman formed a rich mountain of knowledge, eventually supplemented by a young coach called Roy Evans. The melting pot of theories, ideas, opinions and reflections on the game in general and Liverpool matches in particular presented by this football brains trust was akin to a master class, and its value to the club's success incalculable.

The Boot Room grew out of a 'thank you' gift from Paul Orr, later to become Lord Mayor of Liverpool and formerly manager of local Merseyside amateur club Guinness Export. During his time in charge, the Guinness players were made welcome at Anfield for treatment to injuries and were even given team strips for some of their more important games. So as a token of his gratitude, Orr gave Paisley and Fagan a few crates of the renowned dark brew whose name his team carried. The first Boot Room fuel had arrived.

The Boot Room became Anfield's combat bunker where strategies and tactics were debated and devised even though Shankly, perhaps illustrating his own wisdom in letting his staff freely express their views without the pressure of his presence, dropped in only occasionally. But visiting managers and coaches were invited in for a drink after matches, win, lose or draw. Peter Robinson, then Liverpool secretary and later chief executive and vice chairman, recalls the birth of the Boot Room and one consequence of its hospitality. 'The Boot Room was started by Bob and Joe Fagan as a place to have a chat in the afternoon.

Shanks would only flit in and out. A brewery supplied Joe with some of its products and it just grew from that. Visitors had to be invited in and the manager of one club rather over-indulged on the hospitality and was fired on the team's journey home. Apparently he'd consumed a lot and told his chairman what he thought of him!'

On Elton John's first Anfield visit as Watford chairman, he accepted an invitation to cross the Boot Room threshold and emerged to relate a story that captured the spirit of the place perfectly: 'I've just played a live concert to thousands in America but I was much more nervous stepping into this world-famous holy of holies,' Elton admitted. 'When I was asked what I'd like to drink I said a pink gin. Joe Fagan said to me, "Sorry, lad. You can have a Guinness, a brown ale or a Scotch – and that's yer lot." I had a beer. It was great just being in there!'

Paisley had his own recollections of how the Boot Room legend began and the crucial role it fulfilled: 'It started initially with Joe and I as somewhere we could talk and air our views and, on match days, as a place to have a drink with visiting managers and backroom staff. We tried to win every game but, no matter how hard the match was, we liked to relax afterwards and have a drink with the opposition. Just talking about the game is a most interesting aspect of football. On Sunday mornings we'd go in and talk about the Saturday game. There were differing opinions and disagreements and everyone put their oar in. But it was all done in the right manner. We liked everyone to air their views and you probably got a more wide-ranging discussion in the Boot Room than you would in the boardroom. But nothing spilled out of there. What went on was within those four walls. There was a certain mystique about the place, which I also believe there should be about the dressing room. What's said in there should, by and large, be private, too.'

The original Boot Room disappeared into history amidst Anfield renovations in January 1993 during Graeme Souness's period as manager. It was demolished as part of the site of a new press room. But the essential flavour of the bolthole that achieved cult status was captured by Tony Adamson when he went inside the old Boot Room to record this memorable BBC radio interview with Paisley, Moran and Evans.

Moran: We have a Guinness or a lager. The opposition are invited in and we have a chat. Not necessarily about the match but how things are going generally in the game.

Adamson: You've got a 1955 team picture up there. It's falling to bits. Why did you put that up?

Paisley: I don't know what that was put up for...

Evans (jokingly): It's the year I was born.

Adamson: There's a fellow in a white coat on the picture – is that you, Bob?

Paisley: Yes, the trainers wore white coats then. We got them banished. We've improved everywhere!

Moran: I'm the one who put the picture up. I'm on the back row and someone's painted horns on me.

Adamson: What about these pictures here?

Moran: These are various ones taken after games and on visits by certain people to the club.

Adamson: We have boots hanging on the wall. But dare I ask you what's in these cupboards here?

Moran: It's the bar – and the tactics. Here's the bar and there's the tactics.

Adamson: A mass of noughts and crosses.

Moran: These cupboards here are our own private ones – Joe Fagan's, Roy's and my own. It's where we keep all our books and what-nots.

Adamson: You keep a daily book?

Moran: I keep a record of what we've done in training each day and on match days I write in who's scored, who's come off, and what type of injury. I keep this for first team and reserves.

Evans: I just copy Ronnie's book because I was like that at school!

Adamson: It's like visiting a shrine, isn't it?

Moran: People do come here and they want the Boot Room pointed out to them. It started a good thing in the game because when we go to other clubs, they invite us into their so-called boot room.

Evans: We keep ours a bit tidier than anyone else, don't we!

Adamson: There can't be many with a carpet in the Boot Room.

Moran: I think this carpet's been here as long as the boss.

Paisley: No, no, I had my own. This is one I think Joe brought in.

Adamson: With respect, Bob, it could do with a clean, couldn't it?

Paisley: Yes, well, we're just thinking about that. If we can win something this year we'll get it cleaned.

Tommy Docherty's memorable aside that all a visiting manager has to look forward to at Anfield is a cup of tea at half-time and a drink in the Boot Room at the end was borne out in cold figures. Although Liverpool's last major trophy was the 1966 championship, their own stadium had become a fortress and during the 1970s they became virtually invincible in front of the Kop. From January 1970 to December 1979, Liverpool played 210 League games at Anfield and, incredibly, lost only nine. They won 156 matches and drew 45. During the same period, for example, Manchester United suffered 41 League defeats at Old Trafford and also spent one season in the old Second Division after the ignominy of relegation. When Liverpool opened the 1972–73 campaign they had lost just three home First Division games since the turn of the decade, an amazing level of consistency – and even that would be surpassed during Bob Paisley's period of command.

If confidence was high that summer of 1972, the team was also boosted by the arrival of Scottish international Peter Cormack, who cost £110,000 from Nottingham Forest after a recommendation from Shankly's brother Bob. As well as talent, Cormack also possessed the spirit and attitude which, as Bob Paisley stressed, became a hallmark of Liverpool players: 'I can never remember anyone coming here and trying to rule the roost, or acting selfishly. We preach that it's a team game and ever since I've been at Liverpool the club has always been bigger than the individual.'

Cormack, a classy, skilful attacking midfielder, would, in years gone by, have been categorised as an inside-forward. The former Hibernian player was the last piece of the jigsaw to provide Liverpool with a double-winning team that captured the UEFA Cup and the championship, in which they staged a thrilling closing run that saw them plunder 29 points and suffer just one defeat in their final 17 games. Cormack made 30 League appearances and weighed in with a valuable eight goals, including a home derby match decider against Everton and the only goal in the win over Crystal Palace as Liverpool took over the title with 60 points, three ahead of runners-up Arsenal, with Leeds a further four points behind. Attack partners Keegan and Toshack scored 13 League goals apiece while at the other end Ray Clemence emerged as a goalkeeper of rich quality. He made his full international debut against Wales in Cardiff in November 1972 and during the ensuing years fought a battle royal with Peter

Shilton for the honour of filling the country's number one jersey. Bob Paisley, ever alert and vigilant, had his own observations on the rising goalkeeping star: 'Players are very different before games. Ray would sit in the corner dead quiet. But afterwards, if we've won, he went mad. It's the release of tension. In Ray's case he went haywire.'

Liverpool used only 16 players to land the League title, and of that squad, Trevor Storton made only four appearances while Clemence's goalkeeping deputy Frankie Lane had just a single outing. His one and only League game for the club was an unhappy experience, ending in a 2–1 defeat at Derby in September 1972 when he carried a seemingly innocuous left-wing cross from Alan Hinton over his line.

The usual Liverpool line-up in that 1972–73 campaign was: Clemence, Lawler, Lindsay, Smith (captain), Lloyd, Hughes, Keegan, Cormack (or Hall), Heighway, Toshack (or Boersma), Callaghan.

And after a single substitute outing the previous season, it was also the year when a gangling teenager made his big breakthrough with 12 starts and two substitute stints. Phil Thompson would go on to accumulate almost 500 Liverpool appearances, initially as a midfielder but making his reputation as a centre-back of true class. So slender was Merseyside-born Thompson that Bill Shankly delivered the famous aside about his physique: 'He tossed up for his legs with a sparrow – and lost!'

Thompson, strangely wearing the number nine jersey, was in the Liverpool line-up that clinched the championship against Leicester City – and Shilton – in the final League game of that 1972–73 season. They did it with this record: Played 42, won 25, drew 10, lost 7, goals scored 72, goals against 42, points 60. The match, watched by a 56,000-plus crowd, was a poor second to the occasion which brought Bob Paisley his fourth championship medal as coach and player. At the final whistle, as Shankly took the salute of the Kop, one man stood on the pitch in tears. Leicester forward Frank Worthington's emotion was understandable as he pondered what might have been. But for a medical verdict that caused the collapse of his proposed transfer to Anfield, he could have been a member of the jubilant Liverpool team.

The championship success was also a triumph for the complementary qualities of Shankly and Paisley, a view illustrated by Ian Callaghan: 'They were the perfect double act,' he said.

'Shanks was a motivator supreme. There was nobody beter. Bob's tactical knowledge, and of the game generally, was incredible. He could watch a match and recognise the qualities of every single player, spotting their strengths and weaknesses.'

After a few days basking in their title glory, Liverpool had to get down to more serious stuff, preparing for their two-leg UEFA Cup Final against West German side Borussia Moenchengladbach. A first European trophy beckoned after a campaign which had begun with a 2–0 first-round aggregate victory over another West German club, Eintracht Frankfurt, Keegan and Hughes scoring the goals in the Anfield leg. That was followed by a 6–1 aggregate trouncing of Greek side AEK Athens, then it was a trip behind the Iron Curtain to meet the East Germans of Dynamo Berlin, where Liverpool prised a goalless draw before winning the return 3–1. Their reward was a quarter-final duel with more East German opposition, this time the more formidable Dynamo Dresden. Goals from Brian Hall and Phil Boersma gave Liverpool a 2–0 first-leg win at Anfield, and then a Keegan goal in the return crowned one of Liverpool's finest away performances in Europe to clinch a 3–0 aggregate victory.

For Bob Paisley, the trip to Dresden also brought an enduring friendship, as Jessie Paisley recalled: 'Bob met an English teacher in Dresden called Wolfgang and he kept in regular touch by letter. But when the Berlin Wall came down he was able to visit England and had a great time.'

Liverpool's passage into the semi-final pitted them against Tottenham, with the chance to avenge their knock-out by the North London club in the League Cup quarter-finals earlier that season. They did so, but only by the skin of their teeth. Steve Heighway's strike in a 2–1 defeat at White Hart Lane took them through on the away-goals rule after Alec Lindsay had scored the only goal of the Anfield first leg. So Liverpool were through to their first European final since 1966.

The first leg against Moenchengladbach kicked off in a Merseyside downpour and after 27 minutes Austrian referee Erich Linemayr decided the Anfield pitch was unplayable and abandoned the game, to be restaged the following evening. One of the stadium maintenance staff revealed to me that a blockage was later found in one of the drain releases, which contributed to the massive build-up of surface water. On that twist of fate Liverpool's fortunes turned. Shankly, who had opted to play

Brian Hall first time round with John Toshack on the bench, reversed their roles the next evening after suspecting the Germans would be vulnerable to the big Welshman's aerial threat. Toshack, unhappy to be left out originally, was not shy of letting Shankly know his feelings, as Bob Paisley revealed: 'Tosh went in and laid the law down with Shanks about being left out. But after the game had been abandoned, Jock Stein, who was at Anfield, said to Bill that he should get a big man down the middle against the Germans when the game was restarted next night. He took Jock's advice and Tosh was back in the team!'

Toshack's belated appearance terrified Moenchengladbach and after two goals from his partner Keegan and another from Larry Lloyd, plus a superb Ray Clemence penalty save from the great Jupp Heynekes, Liverpool went to Germany for the second leg armed with a 3–0 lead. But how they needed that first-leg cushion! Thunder and lightning heralded the return game as Borussia, inspired by the midfield craft of their skipper Gunter Netzer, put Liverpool on the rack and by half-time had slashed the deficit to a single goal. But the visitors, roared on by their travelling fans and members of the German-based British Forces, held firm. Borussia ran out of steam and Liverpool at last lifted a European trophy. It was a proud moment for captain Tommy Smith, the players, Shankly, Paisley and the entire backroom staff – and Merseyside gave them a rapturous welcome when they toured the city on their return. It was the first time an English club had achieved the double of League championship and UEFA Cup.

The following season, 1973–74, Liverpool were given a harsh lesson in Europe with a rare home defeat and exit to Red Star Belgrade. They also relinquished their League title to old rivals Leeds United, to whom they finished runners-up, but brought home another piece of silverware in the shape of the FA Cup after an emphatic 3–0 Wembley conquest of Newcastle. The Tyneside club's England centre-forward Malcolm Macdonald, who talked a good game in the build-up to the final, was hardly given a kick by a dominant Liverpool side who won with a brilliant team display crowned by two goals from Kevin Keegan and one from Steve Heighway. They also had another apparently legitimate strike from Alec Lindsay disallowed for offside by referee Gordon Kew. Phil Thompson, who by now had established himself as a first-team regular, helped shackle Macdonald and joyously declared on the pitch within seconds of the final whistle: 'What about Supermac now? I'm going to take him home and put him on the mantelpiece for our kid to play with!'

Amidst the celebrations, Paisley lit up a cigar and said to Shankly: 'I'm smoking this to celebrate beating Doncaster in the third round!' His words were only partly in jest. The Yorkshire club, who finished that season third from bottom of the Fourth Division, had given them a mighty scare by drawing 2–2 at Anfield after leading 2–1 at half-time. But Liverpool won the replay, took two games to beat Second Division Carlisle, disposed of Ipswich and Bristol City then beat Leicester City 3–1 in a semi-final replay at Villa Park after a goalless draw at Old Trafford, to book their Wembley date.

The team that took the FA Cup to Anfield for the second time in the club's history lined up like this: Clemence, Smith, Lindsay, Thompson, Cormack, Hughes, Keegan, Hall, Heighway, Toshack, Callaghan. Substitute: Lawler.

But those players, in common with the entire football world, were stunned two months later at an announcement that still has an aura of incredulity despite the passing of time.

6

Abdication and Succession

A week after Shankly's great rival Don Revie of Leeds became England manager in succession to Sir Alf Ramsey, and five days after West Germany beat Holland 2–1 in the World Cup Final, media representatives were called to a noon press conference at Anfield on Friday, 12 July 1974.

I was present in the club's trophy room and can still hear the gasps of astonishment when the Liverpool chairman, John Smith, announced that Bill Shankly had resigned. At first, people simply refused to believe that Shankly had gone, at the apex of his career with the FA Cup newly won, having been decorated with the OBE for his services to the game and at a seemingly fit and healthy 60 years of age. But Shankly told the assembled journalists that he was feeling tired, and spoke of the intense pressures he faced. He said also that his massive commitment to football had been unfair on his wife Nessie.

I am convinced that Shankly regretted his decision within weeks of his departure, with which he went ahead despite desperate attempts by Smith, Paisley and club secretary Peter Robinson to persuade him to stay. I think even Bill under-estimated the hold the game had on him. It was a drug he could not kick, even though in an interview with me he stressed that his dramatic decision was not one he had reached quickly.

'I get guided by my conscience. My conscience is honest. So if I do something, I'm doing the right thing. People might think that when I do something it's quick and erratic. No, no – I'm being guided by my own conscience,' Shankly said. 'If you can't make decisions in life, you're a bloody menace. You'd be better becoming an MP! I left Liverpool because I was satisfied. I had proved a point. All the arguments were won. Nobody pushed me. It was my decision and it took a long time in the making, like waiting for the gallows, really. I'd like to think I've put more into the game than I've taken out and that I haven't cheated anybody.'

The momentous impact of Shankly's resignation was not lost on Paisley, the man who had been at his side for almost 15 years, overseeing Liverpool's rise from the Second Division to the summit of English football. Yet Paisley revealed that the topic of retirement – a word, incidentally, that Shankly loathed – was one he had regularly raised with Bob.

'Shanks often said he was going to leave,' he said. 'Every year, virtually, he'd say he was going to pack in. You didn't take him seriously. When he finally did it I was lost for words, shocked. It was the day I got back from holiday and it was like a bomb being dropped.

'I don't know why he left. But I enjoyed every moment of the time we worked together. We had our opinions and views, but there's no way you could have anything but great respect for a man like Bill. I had nothing but admiration for him.'

Jessie Paisley, then a schoolteacher, remembers the moment she heard the news of Shankly's retirement: 'I was teaching at school when I heard on the radio that Bill had resigned. Bob had no inkling of it and he certainly didn't feel they'd ask him to take over. He thought the club would go for someone like Ian St John, never thinking of himself.

'When he found out, he tried to persuade Bill not to retire but to have a break, go on a cruise and then come back. But Bill was adamant about his decision. It's still a mystery why Bill left. Nobody really knows.'

Paisley was the man Liverpool wanted to succeed Shankly, but there was just one problem: Bob was reluctant to take the job. Peter Robinson admitted that the situation was one of the most serious Anfield had ever faced: 'It was definitely crisis time when Bill left. It was a bombshell and Bob was very reluctant to take the position as manager. When we approached him he said no and that he wanted to talk to Bill. In the end the chairman, directors and I had to gang up on him.'

Paisley eventually decided to consider taking the job. 'If I took it, I thought I would just be a buffer until someone else came in,' he said. 'I wasn't afraid of the job but I'd been quite happy as I was. I hadn't wanted Bill to leave. There was no backbiting from me. In the end I had to be prepared to take it and I did so for the lads on the backroom staff. I told the chairman I'd talk to them. I thought that if I took the job it would prevent the whole backroom set-up being disturbed.'

John Smith, later knighted for his services to football, stressed that Paisley was the only man they wanted as their new manager: 'When Bill resigned, the only person we wanted to succeed him was Bob. We had no hesitation about that. We didn't advertise the job. We just wanted Bob because we believed in a policy of promotion from within.'

Jessie Paisley recalled how the family rallied round to help Bob reach his decision. 'He was very reluctant about taking it but the whole family got behind him and gave him plenty of encouragement,' she remembered. 'We said to him, "Go on, you can do it." That was the message he got from all the people up in Hetton, too!'

Paisley admitted that Shankly's abdication left him mystified and that he was keenly aware of the challenge posed in succeeding him. Said Paisley: 'Did he want to become a director and was he refused? Was the job becoming too demanding? Was it because he wanted to go out at the top? We had just won the FA Cup a year after becoming the first English club to win a European trophy and the championship in the same season. Or was he worried about having another team to build? Tommy Smith had been relieved of the captaincy in that season, Ian Callaghan was getting no younger and Chris Lawler was no longer a regular. As it turned out, Tommy and Cally had starring roles still to play but at that time it looked as if there could have been a problem replacing them. I tried to talk Bill into staying, have a holiday and then work something out together when he got back. But he said he'd had enough and that was that.

'I knew, taking over from him, there would be difficulties to combat because of the type of extrovert personality Bill was and the fantastic record he had. I knew comparisons would be made. I also knew some team rebuilding would have to be done. But when I took the job I knew one thing: I had to do it my way. You can't imitate anybody. You've got to be yourself. I couldn't go and do some of the things that Bill did. I'd do things less obviously than Bill, in a more cunning sort of way. We were very different people. I'm delighted if nobody recognises me, whereas Bill wore steel caps on his shoes so people could hear him coming!'

By the time Liverpool flew out of West Germany in early August for a pre-season warm-up game against Kaiserslautern, Paisley had been officially appointed. He was to take up his duties officially after the Charity Shield against Leeds on 10 August and the Billy McNeill testimonial game against Celtic in Glasgow two days later. But it was agreed that 55-year-old Paisley would pick the team for all three matches. His appointment was announced to shareholders by John Smith at the club's annual meeting in a Liverpool hotel on the evening of Friday 26 July, a fortnight to the day since Shankly's retirement.

'This is a very proud moment for me,' the new manager told the meeting. 'I hope I can justify the faith you have placed in me. I've enjoyed every minute spent with Bill and the stories about him are legendary. There was another one only today. A fan rang him to ask if he would accept a Golden Boot and Bill said: "Yes. Tell him I take size twelve and a half!"'

The decision to appoint Paisley was applauded by Shankly, who declared: 'In my place you have a man who, like me, is basically honest. Without having basic honesty you are nothing. I hope that Liverpool will be successful for a long time to come and that Bob Paisley and his staff will do a great job. He's been a very loyal man to me. When I decided to go I said to the chairman he should be very careful about bringing somebody in from outside the club, because there is a very capable staff inside who, over a 14-year period, have laid down a system and pattern of playing which some Fancy Dan might come along and break up with fancy phrases. Bob Paisley, of course, is the number one man – so I recommended him.'

The Liverpool dressing room took a while to come to terms with Shankly's departure. And Paisley's era, as Kevin Keegan revealed, had a bizarre launch: 'When Bob succeeded Shanks we thought he would be the fall guy and that someone else would be brought in later. We didn't like that. When he told everyone at Melwood that he'd just been appointed he added: "I didn't want the job anyway."'

'I don't think anyone from outside would have had the courage to follow Bill Shankly, and we all said to ourselves: "Let's help the guy become a great manager." It wasn't long before we realized he didn't need help. For someone who didn't want it, he did a terrific job!'

The shock and upheaval of the events at Anfield eclipsed the arrival of a player who would become a key figure during Paisley's reign. On the very day that Shankly quit, Liverpool signed Ray Kennedy for a club record £180,000 from Arsenal, where he had figured in a menacing attacking partnership with John Radford. A short time into his new reign in charge, Paisley was to find a brand new role for Kennedy, who like himself was a native of the North East, hailing from Seaton Delaval in Northumberland. The deal was set up and completed by John Smith, who had conducted negotiations with his Highbury counterpart Dennis Hill-Wood. But Kennedy's arrival earned only single-column reports in the national press and passing references on radio and television, the media consumed with the story of the legendary manager who had walked away from Anfield.

But even after he quit, Shankly would still turn up at the club's training ground and the players, quite understandably, continued to call him boss. That made the handover even more fraught. Ian Callaghan recalled those early days. 'We all knew Bob so well – and some of us for a long time – that it was difficult to suddenly adjust to calling him boss. We still called Shanks that! But we were delighted that Bob had been appointed rather than somebody from outside. The lads had always had a few giggles about the figures of speech Bob used, like "doins", but we had nothing less than total respect for the man and his vast knowledge.'

True to Liverpool tradition, there was no place for new acquisition Kennedy when the players who had lifted the FA Cup, minus the injured John Toshack who was replaced by Phil Boersma, went back to Wembley to raise the curtain on the 1974-1975 season. Led out by the departing Shankly, they faced champions Leeds in the Charity Shield. But the repercussions of the managerial handover were still rumbling, and the events at Wembley did no favours for Paisley. He reflected ruefully, some time later: 'My first steps in management were like walking blindfold through a minefield.'

Captain Emlyn Hughes revealed that Paisley told the players he did not expect his reign to be a long one: 'It's amazing, considering what he went on to achieve, that Bob actually said to us: "I'm in this job under sufferance and I won't be here very long." '

Indeed, so turbulent were the first few weeks that Paisley

admitted to me that he even considered relinquishing the reins he had just picked up from Shankly. He also believed that the shockwaves from the Charity Shield, the first to be staged at Wembley, went close to forcing Kevin Keegan to quit football prematurely. Goals from Boersma and Trevor Cherry tied up the game at 1–1 and Liverpool won 6–5 on penalties, with Ian Callaghan of all people putting the deciding spot-kick past David Harvey with only the second penalty of his long career. But the result went almost unnoticed.

During the week leading up to the Charity Shield, Keegan had been sent off in the friendly match at Kaiserslautern after reacting angrily to a fierce challenge by one of the German players on Ray Kennedy. Fortunately for Liverpool and Keegan, referee Gunter Quindeau could not attend the FA hearing in London and the matter was dropped. But it was the escape before the storm. The intense rivalry between Liverpool and Leeds pumped up the Charity Shield atmosphere at Wembley and a contest marred by fouls and niggling incidents exploded in the second half. Johnny Giles had already been booked for fouling Keegan before the Liverpool striker swapped punches with Billy Bremner, whose celebrated skill and tenacity were accompanied by a firebrand temperament, and referee Bob Matthewson sent off both players. It was Keegan's second dismissal in five days and as he and Bremner trooped back to the dressing room as the first British players to be sent off at Wembley, they hurled their shirts to the turf on the touchline in sheer frustration. The FA responded by charging both players with bringing the game into disrepute.

Keegan went straight back to his parents' home in Doncaster after the match but linked up with the Liverpool squad in Glasgow 48 hours later for the testimonial game at Celtic, where Shankly received an amazing farewell salute from the Scottish supporters. Next morning, Bob Paisley became Liverpool manager officially, unaware of the massive handicap the football authorities were about to inflict on him, Keegan and the club.

The following Saturday Liverpool won their first League game of the Paisley era, a 2–1 victory at Luton. The goals came from Tommy Smith and Steve Heighway, who took their places in this 4–3–3 line-up: Ray Clemence; Tommy Smith, Phil Thompson, Emlyn Hughes, Alec Lindsay; Brian Hall, Ian Callaghan, Peter Cormack; Phil Boersma, Kevin Keegan, Steve Heighway.

Smith, the Anfield Iron himself, recounted some of Paisley's qualities: 'In the team talks he'd tell you about the strengths and weaknesses of the opposition, a classic line of his being: "He's not fast but a bit nippy!" He often left us doubled up laughing. But only because of his delivery. He always got his message over and you didn't cross him. He demanded that everyone played to their maximum and gave their best. He was uncompromising in that aspect.'

After the Luton match, Keegan had to drop out to begin an automatic three-match ban for his Wembley dismissal, with Toshack passed fit to return in his place for the goalless midweek draw at Wolves. The day after that Molineux game, Paisley had to accompany Keegan to the FA disciplinary commission hearing of the disrepute charges against him and Bremner. The three-man commission was chaired by Vernon Stokes, sitting with former Aston Villa chairman Norman Smith and Paisley's lifetime friend and former Liverpool colleague Sir Matt Busby. They handed down a swingeing punishment in the form of a ban on the two players until the end of September, plus a £500 fine. It meant Keegan would miss eleven games, three for being sent off and a further eight for the shirt-throwing.

'I'm seething and Kevin is bitterly upset, angry and disillusioned,' was how Paisley responded to the FA sentence. 'What has rubbed salt in the wounds is that we've been told there's no appeal against it and learned that the Home Office have brought direct pressure to bear on the case.' A supporter had been stabbed to death the previous Saturday at Bloomfield Road at Blackpool's game against Bolton and Paisley was fuming to discover that there had been Government interference in the Keegan–Bremner affair.

'The two players and the clubs have been victims of the hysteria and the calls for examples to be made of them.' Paisley stormed. 'It's a savage, six-fold sentence.' He outlined those as 1) Keegan's three-match ban, 2) A club fine which Liverpool had been advised to impose by the FA, 3) The FA fine, 4) The further eight-match ban, 5) Keegan's name blackened throughout the country, and 6) His talents denied to the fans for 11 games.

It completed a miserable summer for Keegan. On an England trip to Yugoslavia in June, during Joe Mercer's brief but exhilarating stint in charge, he had been beaten up by police in Belgrade after an airport incident in which he was not involved. The player now vented his spleen on the FA commission when he insisted: 'The punishment is out of all proportion to the crime. I don't know how they had the nerve to impose it. I am bitter about it and I can't forget it.' Yet he was able, later, to reflect on that traumatic period of his career philosophically: 'It was a really bad time for me but things worked out for Liverpool because Phil Boersma came in and had a great scoring run. Then, when I came back, at least I was refreshed after a break from football! In fact, I was surprised that I came straight back in after my suspension.'

Paisley advised Keegan not even to turn up at the training ground during his long ban, as that would only deepen his frustration and increase the pressure on him after such a savage suspension. So Keegan spent his enforced absence from football looking up old friends, playing golf – and getting married! He tied the knot with girlfriend Jean and bought her a sheepdog as a wedding present.

But while the bells were ringing in celebration for the Keegans, the alarm bells had sounded for Paisley and Liverpool as they deliberated on how to deal with the blow of losing him for so long. The team that had drawn at Wolves, a game that marked Ian Callaghan's 500th League appearance for the club, beat Leicester 2–1 at home four days later thanks to a couple of Alec Lindsay penalties.

Anfield that Saturday afternoon also saw Shankly's emotional pre-match farewell to the Kop. A crowd of almost 50,000 watched him walk out on to the pitch, take the salute and walk off down the tunnel swathed in red and white scarves draped around him by fans. 'I remember when I first walked into Anfield how dilapidated it was,' Shankly recalled, sipping a cup of tea in the boardroom afterwards. 'It does me good to see how it looks today.'

The handover from Shankly to Paisley also turned out to be a landmark in the career of Bootle-born Roy Evans. He had been a player at Liverpool since joining as a schoolboy nine years earlier and had made his debut at left-back in a 3–0 home win over Sheffield Wednesday in March 1970. But competition for places was so intense that by the time Shankly quit, Evans had made only 11 senior appearances and the departing manager suggested that even at the tender age of 25, Evans should consider switching to a coaching role. Evans was receptive to the idea, which Paisley and John Smith took on board, and he became the youngest backroom man in the entire Football League as reserve-team coach. Evans, given valuable advice by fellow coach and close friend Ronnie

Moran, proceeded to win the Central League in each of his first three years in charge and a total of seven times in nine seasons, filling a key role in the development of the club's youngsters. Chairman Smith proved amazingly prophetic. 'This appointment,' he declared, 'is not for the present but for the future. One day Roy Evans will be our manager.'

Evans recalled Paisley's words at the time. 'He told me that although my play was steady I was never going to have a regular first-team place, and suggested I should look to the future and concentrate on coaching. I hesitated because it seemed very early to hang up my boots. But after a fortnight thinking it over, I agreed.'

Two decades later, a subsequent Liverpool chairman, David Moores, would hail Evans as 'the last of the Shankly boys' when he appointed him manager in succession to Graeme Souness.

Three days after the win over Leicester, another bumper crowd, more than 42,000, saw Paisley's unchanged side beat Wolves 2–0, with Heighway and Toshack on target. But Toshack's lingering battle against thigh problems caused by muscle calcification meant that Paisley had to change his winning line-up for the trip to Chelsea. There, Kennedy scored the opening goal in a 3–0 win, while Boersma, who had walked out of Wembley and threatened to quit the club the previous May after being omitted from the Cup Final squad, struck twice. So despite the absence of Keegan and Toshack, Liverpool had extended their unbeaten start to the season, and to Paisley's management career, to five games, comprising four wins and a draw, to go top of the First Division. And England goalkeeper Ray Clemence offered some intriguing observations about Paisley the manager: 'I think when he first succeeded Shanks he was a bit overawed. I'll never forget him standing in the dressing room in the summer of 1974 on the first day of pre-season training and telling us: "Shanks has gone and they're giving me the job even though I didn't really want it. But we must try to carry on what he's started."

'He saw it as his duty to take the job. Yet he set an incredible record that will never be beaten. Things just snowballed for him after the first season. For me, he was a better coach than motivator of men, but a shrewd judge of a player and very strong tactically.

'He could also pull a player apart. He was a decent man but he had a ruthless streak in him. 90 per cent of his signings were good ones and he could assess all positions, even my speciality of goalkeeping. He knew a fair amount about that and he would play in goal in five-a-sides.

'Although he was totally different from Shanks he could be very funny, with that dry type of North East humour. He told us the story of Jimmy Adamson saying after beating Liverpool that his Burnley team were in a different league. "At the end of the season they were . . . they were relegated," quipped Bob.'

A few days later after the win at Chelsea the new manager was feeling in something less than top form when he was the subject of enforced role reversal as a patient in the Anfield treatment room. He suffered stiffness in his neck and shoulders after the car he was driving collided with a petrol tanker. The Liverpool backroom staff, many of them tutored by Paisley himself, gave him physiotherapy to speed his recovery before the team on the field provided him with another timely tonic against Tottenham the following Saturday. Boersma, who almost two decades later would return to Anfield as a coach during Graeme Souness's period in charge, went one better than his brace of goals at Stamford Bridge a week earlier by scoring a hat-trick in a 5–2 win. Ray Kennedy weighed in with a goal on his home debut, with Hughes scoring the other.

Boersma's scintillating form not only softened the blow of Keegan's absence, it also went close to making one of Paisley's whimsical asides come true. Following his hat-trick against Spurs, Bob nicknamed him 'Johan' after the Dutch master Cruyff, and spies from the Netherlands descended on Liverpool games to consider the international claims of the Kirkby-born player who was eligible for Holland through his Dutch father.

Boersma was on the mark again in the 2–1 League Cup win over Brentford before Paisley suffered his first defeat as a manager, a 2–0 reverse at Manchester City on 14 September. It ended an unbeaten Liverpool run stretching back to the previous April under Shankly, when they had gone down 1–0 at home to Arsenal, when the goalscorer for the Gunners was none other than Ray Kennedy. Liverpool's response to their Maine Road reverse was a record-breaking 11–0 drubbing of Norwegian side Stromsgodset Drammen in the European Cup-Winners' Cup first-round first leg three days later. Apart from being the biggest win in the club's history, the game was also notable for the fact that Brian Hall was the only outfield player not to score. Boersma and Phil Thompson hit two goals apiece and the others came from Steve Heighway, Peter Cormack, Emlyn Hughes, Tommy Smith, Ian Callaghan, Ray Kennedy and Alec Lindsay.

The massive win smashed the club record which had stood since February 1896 when Liverpool beat Rotherham 10-1 in a Second Division match. A 1-0 win in the second leg in Norway a fortnight later, which saw Keegan's comeback from his marathon ban, ensured a 12-0 aggregate victory. It had been a smooth return to Europe for Liverpool after their jolting exit to Red Star Belgrade in the previous season's European Cup. When the Yugoslav champions beat Liverpool 2-1 in the second round first leg in Belgrade, there were high hopes at Anfield that Chris Lawler's away goal would prove a key factor in progressing to the quarter-finals. But Red Star, managed by the respected Miljan Miljanic, who guided Yugoslavia to the 1974 World Cup Finals and later moved to Real Madrid, stunned the Kop by fulfilling their pledge not to come to Anfield just to defend. Their second-half goals from Lazarevic and Jankovic crowned a menacing counter-attacking display. Lawler struck again, his 11th and last European goal, in what proved to be Shankly's final European game as manager. But the full-back's late effort, which took his goal haul in all competitions to a remarkable final total of 61 without the aid of penalties, could not prevent Liverpool's elimination on a 4-2 aggregate.

Their exit prompted a top-level Anfield inquest into playing tactics and style. Shankly, Paisley and their coaching colleagues in the Boot Room agreed that the era of the traditional British 'stopper' centre-half was being overtaken by players who could be creative as well as destructive, and that a more patient Continental playing pattern was on the way. Fate, as it happened, intervened. Larry Lloyd, one of those typical British centre-halves, who had been signed by Shankly as successor to Ron Yeats, ruptured a hamstring. Phil Thompson, originally a midfielder, took over from him at the heart of defence alongside Emlyn Hughes to form a more skilful centre-back partnership, with Tommy Smith taking over from Lawler at right-back and Alec Lindsay on the left.

Lloyd's injury was instrumental in his departure from Anfield. It had been five years since his £50,000 arrival from Bristol Rovers but he was still only 25.

He missed the 1974 FA Cup Final and although Paisley assured him there was still a future for him at Anfield, he insisted on leaving. So just three weeks into Paisley's reign, England international Lloyd was sold to Coventry for £240,000, the start of an unhappy two years for the big defender until Brian Clough gloriously revived his career at Nottingham Forest. Lloyd later reflected and admitted: 'I acted like a spoiled kid when I hit that first real problem with Liverpool. After Phil Thompson had taken my place when I was injured, I couldn't stand the idea of having to fight to get it back. I thought the club would collapse without me. It didn't. Bob Paisley urged me to stay but that wasn't good enough for old big-head. I thought I knew it all. I told him I wouldn't play in the reserve side again. And before I could catch my breath, I found myself at Coventry.' Lloyd was to prove a rarity, a player leaving Liverpool and going on to achieve great things elsewhere. Having sold him, Paisley's first act as a buyer in the transfer market was to dip into English football's lower reaches and scoop up Phil Neal from Fourth Division Northampton for £60,000 in October 1974.

In his opening fortnight as boss, Paisley had dispelled any notion that he would be an easy touch for people inside or outside the club. Chairman John Smith's comments to a local newspaper about possible future signings and opinions on players brought a stinging rebuke from the man he had just appointed manager. Paisley told him in plain terms that such matters were within his province and warned that if there were any further such public outbursts he would quit. His point was accepted without reservation, Smith apologised and cordial relations were swiftly resumed. But what was a matter of principle in Paisley's eyes had been established. Parameters had been set between himself and the board.

At dressing-room level, if some of the players he had inherited from Shankly wondered how Bob would made the adjustment from assistant boss to manager, there were also intriguing opinions on his credentials from men who had starred in past Liverpool teams. That fine Scottish wing-half, Willie Stevenson, for instance, said: 'I think a lot of us didn't feel Bob could make that step up to manager as he did. But he did things in such a subtle way perhaps we weren't aware of how he did it. I don't think we'll ever see his like again and I don't think anyone will be at a club the length of time Bob was.' Centre forward Tony Hateley, too, has glowing memories of Paisley: 'He was the man you went to because you couldn't approach Shanks. Bob was the cushion, the buffer. I was at Liverpool a season and a half, I got a couple of injuries and Shanks wouldn't speak to me. Bob knew about injuries. He'd tell Shanks you were injured... but Shanks still wouldn't speak to you. Bob and Bill were a partnership but I always felt that Bob could go on to become a great manager. With all due respect, he was a big part of the brains behind Shanks and the partnership anyway.'

Paisley was justifiably proud of his first signing as Neal proved one of the bargain buys of all time. Paisley described the qualities he and Liverpool were looking for. 'Some players can talk better than others but we look for character in players. Scouts talk and tend to stick together in their opinions. If one of them condemns a player they all tend to. If one says he's great they'll all follow suit. Geoff Twentyman had spotted Neal and I told him to keep tabs on him because we wanted cover with Chris Lawler nearing the end. We wanted a stand-in and general factotum. The last time we saw Phil play before signing him he ended up playing in goal!

'Apparently, Phil had been set to join Aldershot. He might have got into habits he couldn't break and finished his career in the lower divisions, instead of coming here and playing 50 times for England. I saw him as a natural player who understood the game.'

But shortly before Neal's arrival at Anfield, Phil Thompson sustained long-term knee damage. He was carried off against Stoke in Liverpool's next outing after the goal glut against Stromsgodset, and had to undergo cartilage surgery which ruled him out for eight weeks before he made his return at Coventry - ironically minus the injured Larry Lloyd - in the last game of November, during a spell that proved the most dismal and tortured in Paisley's entire managerial career. A run of eight games without a win and an outrageously inaccurate Sunday newspaper article compounded the inherent pressures on him in succeeding Shankly.

In five weeks, Liverpool dropped from pole position in the League to fourth, with Everton leapfrogging them into second place behind new pacesetters, Stoke City. November dawned in the wake of Muhammad Ali's feat in knocking out George Foreman in Zaire to recapture the world heavyweight boxing crown at the age of 32. Liverpool opened the month with a 1–0 defeat at title rivals Ipswich, a jolting setback for Paisley and his team which also spawned an appalling misquote from a sportswriter covering the game, which twisted the knife in Anfield wounds.

Paisley recalled: 'A Sunday paper report the day after the Ipswich game quoted me as saying that even in Bill's days I used to run the show. It was totally untrue. I never said any such thing. And anyone who knows me and my feelings about Shanks knows I'd never say anything like that. But Bill read it and took offence. I apologised, even though I was in no way to blame. He was still free to come to our training ground, where the players still called him boss. But he took the decision not to come to Melwood anymore. In the fullness of time we both agreed that his decision had been the right one even if it had been for the wrong reason. There is no way I'd have driven Bill away.'

Yet the build-up of problems in those early weeks of Paisley's management brought him to the brink of walking out. 'Just a few months after we persuaded him to take on the job Bob knocked on my office door one morning and said he felt he couldn't continue any longer,' revealed Peter Robinson, then club secretary and later chief executive and vice chairman.

'He said he found things too difficult to handle and that he had problems with a couple of critical journalists as well as the administration aspect of the job. Eventually, after some gentle persusasion, Bob agreed to stay as manager on condition that I spoke to the two pressmen he'd mentioned and that Tom Saunders, who had been our youth development officer, was drafted in to help with administration matters.

'It meant that we had an "inner cabinet" at the club, consisting of the chairman John Smith, Bob, Tom and myself, which made all the decisions on the buying and selling of players. And when you look at those we signed I don't think there were too many mistakes. But when Bob came to see me that particular morning he wanted to go. Just imagine the man who went on to become English football's most successful manager leaving so suddenly.'

An extra factor in a potentially fraught situation was the public clamour during Paisley's first season in charge for Shankly to be made a director or president of Liverpool, demands which the Anfield board, mindful of the overpowering legacy for his successors left by Sir Matt Busby's achievements at Manchester United, resisted. Paisley believed that, too, was the right decision.

'After working with him for 15 years I knew Bill well and I was very aware that it would be difficult for him to do anything but the top job at any club,' Paisley said. 'There were times when I had problems I'd have liked to have talked over with him. But I didn't, partly because it wouldn't have been fair on him, because he'd retired to get away from problems, and also because Bill was the type that if he offered advice, you'd have to take it! Bill was a boss man. If he'd been elected to the Liverpool board he'd have wanted to be in charge. And that's not a criticism. Being in charge was his strength and that's why Liverpool were so successful when Bill was manager. After he left, other clubs and managers thought they could get free advice from him and because he'd talk football to anybody, they exploited him. If I was guilty of anything it was of not doing more to discourage people who were using Bill. But at the same time I was in no doubt that I'd have to stand on my own two feet as Liverpool manager. I was following a legend and even if we had any success in those early days, I knew I would not get the credit for it.' But although Bill and I were very different people, he and I were the worst losers in the world. In that respect there wasn't a hap'orth of difference between us.'

After the Ipswich defeat, Liverpool's gloom deepened when they went to Hungary the following midweek and played a goalless draw with Ferenevaros to bow out of the Cup-Winners' Cup on the away-goals rule, after the Budapest club's 1–1 first-leg result at Anfield. That exit was followed by a 3–1 home crash to Arsenal on the Saturday, after which Paisley introduced a self-imposed ban on talking to the media as the Mersey derby at Everton loomed a week later. 'It wasn't that I'd fallen out with the press people,' Paisley explained later. 'It was just that the going was getting rough and it wasn't the right time to be shouting the odds. I had enough on my plate putting things right with the team.'

During the build-up to Paisley's derby as manager, his second new player arrived in the shape of Terry McDermott, the Kirkby-born midfielder who had impressed despite being in the Newcastle United side beaten by Liverpool in the FA Cup Final six months earlier. McDermott, hard-running with a fierce shot and a powerful athletic engine, made his debut at Goodison Park a few days later. But while the £170,000 acquisition was an expected debutant, another player's Liverpool baptism came as a total shock. Phil Neal woke up that Saturday morning and began preparing to play in the reserves when there was a knock at the door of his digs. It was Liverpool's youth development officer Tom Saunders with the message that Paisley wanted him to report, instead, to Goodison. Thinking he was just being called into the squad, Neal walked nonchalantly across Stanley Park, which separates Goodison from Anfield, carrying his boots in a plastic bag. When Neal arrived, Paisley asked him if he would like to walk out on to the pitch to sample the derby atmosphere. Even then, Neal assumed he was just being given a taster of things to come if he continued to impress in the reserves following his leap up the football ladder from Northampton. But on his return to the dressing room, Paisley told him: 'Get changed. You're playing.' For Neal it was the start of a majestic Liverpool career, comprising four European Cup medals, seven League championships, a UEFA Cup winner's medal and four in the Football League Cup. He also collected a half-century of England caps and remains forever grateful to Paisley's stewardship.

'I was Bob's first signing,' said Neal. 'He changed my life, as he did so many others. He gave us great memories and you can't put a price on that. He made me an adopted Scouser. He put together a team with so many leaders in it that I once said it could run itself. That's a tribute to Bob and his staff for signing them and assembling them.

'Bob taught us that nothing should come in the way of Liverpool having success. One of the things that springs to mind is that the players' Christmas party one year had already been booked at Tommy Smith's nightclub. We went ahead and had this party in secret on the Monday night, fancy dress and all, after drawing 1–1 with Fulham in a cup tie. We had another game on the Wednesday and drew again. Bob brought us in on Thursday morning and he was furious. We were sitting round a table with heads bowed when Bob came in, slammed the door and said: "Alright, who organised the bloody Christmas party then?" There was silence. Nobody was willing to respond to Bob's question. Then Steve Heighway, who was the PFA representative at the time, tried to explain that we'd booked it ages before. Bob's face dropped, then he said: "If you want a bloody Christmas party, have it in the summer." Then he slammed the door and was gone.'

In the first of Neal's 650 Liverpool appearances, which brought him 60 goals, he took over at left-back from the injured Lindsay and found himself facing his neighbour, Everton's Scottish winger John Connolly, who lived in digs 200 yards from his own. Neal, at home in any defensive role, would go on to make his reputation at right-back and his solid, composed display in the goalless draw at Everton convinced Paisley that he was first-team material.

Neal sat out the next three games before Paisley drafted him in for the home match with Luton in mid December. From then on he was a regular choice. Liverpool won that game 2–0, their first victory in nine games following black November which, as well as their European exit, had also seen them crash out of the League Cup through a 1–0 home defeat by Middlesbrough. John Toshack scored against Luton on his return from a lengthy injury absence, during which he had gone close to leaving the club. But fate worked in reverse for Phil Boersma. After his early-season scoring exploits during Keegan's suspension, he lost his place and a year later was sold to Middlesbrough for £72,000.

Liverpool went into the New Year of 1975 in third place with 29 points from 23 games, level with Everton and one point behind leaders Ipswich and Middlesbrough. January was marred by another 1–0 reverse at Ipswich, in the FA Cup fourth round, a result partly avenged by a 5–2 League win over the Suffolk club the following month. And for a while it seemed the title would be Merseyside-bound. Both Everton, managed by Billy Bingham, and Liverpool had spells at the top of the table. As late as 5 April, Paisley's side led the way on goal average from Everton, Stoke and Derby, with all four clubs locked on 47 points. But a 1–0 defeat at Jack Charlton's Middlesbrough was to cost Paisley the championship in his first season as manager. Derby, guided by Dave Mackay following the departure of Brian Clough, stole through to take the title for the second time in four seasons. Their 53-point haul was two more than Liverpool's total of 51, the same as Ipswich who finished third on goal average with Everton fourth, a further point behind. In a race where the lead changed a record 21 times, Liverpool had, in Paisley's horseracing parlance, been beaten by a neck.

'I felt disappointed at finishing second because I felt our squad was as good as anything else knocking around,' Paisley admitted. 'I considered it failure and I knew people would be judging me against Bill, a great manager. But we'd once gone seven years without winning a trophy and that tended to be forgotten. I felt in that first year as if I was an apprentice on a Derby horse who rode wide at the bends.' But that initial season in command, when his team did at least lift the Fair Play Trophy, was to prove a bedding-in period for Paisley, who swiftly broke his self-imposed ban on talking to the media to forge a relationship with a small corps of national newspaper football writers – including myself – that would grow and endure throughout and beyond Bob's days as manager. He revealed that the first year at the helm had been a voyage of discovery in many aspects. 'It's taught me that I've got to make decisions that may not be popular with everybody,' he admitted. 'But I've learned to be more relaxed and I've realised that some jobs can be done in an hour instead of sweating on them for days.'

Jessie Paisley recalled Bob's determination to succeed: 'Once he'd taken the job on, he wouldn't give up,' she said. 'After a poor result he would say: "That's my lot." But it wouldn't be at all. It would make him more determined.'

Paisley also finally bowed to the persuasive tongue of chairman John Smith and his fellow directors and agreed to accept a contract. Amazingly, he had insisted on working without one during the 21 years since he made the switch from player to backroom man in 1954. 'I've always believed in an honest day's work for an honest day's pay,' said Paisley characteristically. 'I've never felt the need to have the confirmation of a contract that I could do a good job. Now, I realise there are many people dependent on me and, in turn, I am dependent on many people. So I felt that perhaps I should have a contract for the first time.'

For Liverpool, the move could not have been better timed. For Paisley's management skills blossomed richly in the 1975–76 campaign to launch the club on the most successful period any British side has ever experienced.

7

Double Up for Glory

Paisley added a new defender to his squad for the launch of the 1975–76 season.

Left-back Joey Jones was recruited from Wrexham for £110,000, a deal that not only gave the club a player of unquenchable spirit but also one of the great characters of Kop folklore. And one example of his new manager's North East humour made a lasting impression on Jones, as he recalled years later: 'The boss – I still refer to him as that – was honest, genuine, humble, not flamboyant and often humorous. One day at the Melwood training ground I kicked a ball through a window and the boss asked to see me. I thought I was going to get my knuckles rapped. But he said to me: "You're leaning back too much – you should get your body over the ball!"

'I asked Phil Neal and Ray Clemence if they got telegrams from the boss when they were away on international duty. Phil said they did, with the message "Good luck". I told them that the boss sent them to me when I was away with Wales. The message he put on mine was: "Keep out of trouble."

'I owe him so much because he gave me the chance to play for the team of my dreams, the one I stood on the Kop cheering. What a great manager he was, and a fine example to some of them now. Some modern managers are more high-profile than the players. But Bob Paisley is up there with Busby, Shankly and Stein as the greatest ever. I don't think anyone will achieve what he did.

'He was also brilliant at knowing about injuries. Before he signed me he watched me play for Wrexham at Tranmere and I went off injured. The medical people said I had a Potts fracture but he said: "No, it's not. I'll wager it's ankle ligaments." Needless to say, he was right.'

The new recruit, who first donned a Liverpool jersey during the club's pre-season tour of Holland and Germany, made his senior debut in this line-up that opened the campaign at Queens Park Rangers on 16 August: Ray Clemence in goal, a back four of Phil Neal, Phil Thompson, Emlyn Hughes and Joey Jones; a midfield trio of Terry McDermott, Ian Callaghan and Peter Cormack; and a front three of Steve Heighway, John Toshack and Kevin Keegan, with Tommy Smith on the bench.

Liverpool did not begin well at Loftus Road, going down 2–0. However, it was a defeat by Dave Sexton's side that Liverpool would avenge doubly over the course of a memorable Anfield season. They responded by building a six-game unbeaten run which ended in a 2–0 reverse at Ipswich in mid-September, a third consecutive defeat at Portman Road which prompted Paisley to hold a no-holds-barred meeting with his players.

'I had a heart-to-heart talk to them,' said Bob. 'I told them we'd been setting out to please everyone but found we just couldn't do it. It's impossible. People talk about entertainment, but some-where along the line you've got to conserve energy if you want consistency. So we changed things a bit, tactically.'

The team suffered only one defeat in the next 23 League games as Paisley made influential changes over the course of the winter in defence and midfield. Phil Neal switched flanks to left-back, allowing Tommy Smith to reclaim a place at right-back, while a masterstroke by Paisley transformed Ray Kennedy's career. The player who had arrived as a Double-winning centre-forward from Arsenal on the day Shankly quit had failed to make a sustained impact at Anfield. But Paisley believed Kennedy had untapped talents. After tracking down and talking to one of his schoolteachers in the player's native North East he moved Kennedy from attack to midfield, beginning with a trial run in the reserves. The outcome was sensational. Kennedy, recalled to the first team against Middlesbrough in November, revelled in his new role. His brilliant response to the switch coincided with Peter Cormack's absence through cartilage damage and Kennedy became a fixture on the left flank wearing the number five jersey. Within four months he was called up by Don Revie to play for England, confirmation if any were needed of Paisley's innate football wisdom.

'Moving Ray was the best switch I ever made,' said Paisley. 'He had really lost his appetite for playing up front but he was surprised I'd found out that he'd played midfield as a schoolboy. He got his weight down from 14 stone to 12 stone 10 and went on to play for England, although his talent was never fully recognised in this country. He had a keen football brain and when he got in the box he was as dangerous as anybody.' What neither of them knew was that this powerful player sadly had already fallen victim to Parkinson's Disease, a fact made even more tragic and remarkable given Kennedy's subsequent deeds with Liverpool.

Kennedy celebrated his England debut with a crashing left-foot goal in the 2–1 win over Wales at Wrexham in March 1976. That game also heralded the international debuts of Phil Neal and Phil Thompson in a team captained for the first time by Kevin Keegan and with a fifth Liverpool player, Ray Clemence, in goal. But for Emlyn Hughes, appointed captain of his country by Joe Mercer during his caretaker spell in charge of England, there was only anguish over Revie's decision to discard him. It was the following season before he reclaimed his place.

Terry McDermott, too, later became an England player and evergreen Ian Callaghan, Footballer of the Year in 1974, was recalled by Revie's successor Ron Greenwood more than eleven years after his previous international outing as a raiding winger against France during the 1966 World Cup Finals. But there was never to be an England call for a new Anfield discovery, Jimmy Case. The former amateur had burst on the scene to claim Liverpool's right midfield berth while his close friend 'Razor' Kennedy patrolled the left with an aplomb that frightened every European coach Liverpool faced. An early season 3–2 victory over Tottenham saw Case, a 21-year-old former electrician, fire the first of his 46 Liverpool goals in 265 senior appearances. A local product of Northern Premier League club South Liverpool, he had been signed during the Shankly era in May 1973.

Case's first-team debut, delayed by a groin injury, had come in the final game of Paisley's first season in charge, when he made an eye-catching contribution to a 3–1 home win over Queens Park Rangers. His graduation to the Liverpool team had echoes of Paisley's own early experience because Case, too, was considered too small and rejected by both Liverpool Schoolboys and then Burnley, after a trial at Turf Moor. But as Paisley declared in typical pithy tones: 'If a player's good enough, he's big enough. Jimmy's got skill and he's filled out and got stronger since he was a boy. He'll do for me.'

A punctured lung sustained against Birmingham further

impeded Case's progress at Anfield, but he roared back with a hat-trick at home to Slask Wroclaw in the second round second leg of the UEFA Cup in December 1975, to seal a 5–1 aggregate victory following a 2–1 win in Poland when the temperature dipped to ten degrees below zero. He followed in the tradition established by players like Callaghan, Smith and Lawler of local boys who really had made good at Liverpool. Case reflected on his development at Anfield and saluted Paisley at a Variety Club tribute dinner staged in honour of the great Liverpool manager.

'When Bob became manager I was trying to catch his eye to get a first-team chance,' he said. 'I think I succeeded when I started fighting with Alec Lindsay in a game between the first team and reserves! I was going past Alec a few times and he had that scything left foot that kept coming out. It happened once or twice. Then I started kicking back and then it was the fists. I eventually got into the first team and my room-mate at Liverpool was Ray Kennedy. It was a known fact that we used to get into a few scrapes here and there. So for the rest of the time I was trying to avoid Bob Paisley! But he was always one step ahead of us and he made my career by picking me for the team.'

Liverpool had made early progress in Europe by dispatching Hibernian on a 3–2 aggregate, thanks to John Toshack's hat-trick of headers in the home leg, before a 9–1 aggregate demolition of Real Sociedad from Spain's Basque country, an October trip notable for a false alarm over the death of General Franco. During Liverpool's stay in San Sebastian the Spanish dictator, reviled by the Basques, was reported to have died. Suddenly the whole town was decked in bunting and street parties were about to celebrate his passing when it was revealed that he was, in fact, still alive. Franco lingered for another month before his death in Madrid a fortnight before his 83rd birthday and after 40 years of absolute rule, thus paving the way for the restoration of the Spanish monarchy. By then Sociedad had been humbled 6–0 at Anfield following their 3–1 defeat in their own Atocha Stadium with Toshack, who would later manage the Spanish club, among the Anfield scorers.

The game also heralded the first home appearance of a red-headed 18-year-old, David Fairclough. A local product like Jimmy Case, he had been given his debut by Paisley in the League game at Middlesbrough three days earlier in the absence of Steve Heighway, whose number nine jersey he filled at Ayresome Park in a 1–0 win. In the Anfield duel with Real Sociedad, the youngster was sent on as a half-time substitute for Callaghan and celebrated by scoring one of the six goals. The era of the 'super sub' had dawned. Of Fairclough's total of 153 Liverpool appearances, 61 were from the bench and, in all, he scored 55 goals, his two greatest both scored as a substitute.

The first of those immortal strikes came against Everton at Anfield in his first season and crowned a crucial spell of four goals in three consecutive League games. He scored the only goal of the game when he started at Norwich in place of unfit John Toshack, then went on as an early substitute for the injured Steve Heighway and hit both goals, one in each half, in the 2–0 home win over Burnley. Next up was the derby clash with Everton on 3 April, which kicked off at 11am to avoid a clash with that afternoon's Grand National. Fairclough was again on the bench but after 63 minutes, with the game goalless, Paisley sent him on as substitute for Toshack, who had been concussed colliding with Everton's derby debutant David Jones. With less than two minutes remaining, Fairclough took possession on the halfway line on the right wing and set off on a mesmerising run. Evading tackles and sweeping past a series of increasingly desperate Everton challenges, he cut in and unleashed a shot that rocketed past visiting goalkeeper Dai Davies.

A few hours later local hero Red Rum finished second at Aintree. But Fairclough's spectacular red run took his side past the winning post with a spectacular strike timed officially at 88 minutes, 38 seconds.

A year later the lean, lanky forward struck an equally unforgettable goal against St Etienne. But it is the derby winner that has pride of place in Fairclough's mental scrapbook. 'That goal against Everton is my all-time favourite and gave me most pleasure,' he said. 'I robbed Martin Dobson and just kept going. To beat five men and then finish with a low shot into the next was just fantastic for me. I think I surprised myself. Sometimes you look back and wonder how you did things! I showed the video of that goal to my son Tom and his reaction was: "Wow!"'

Liverpool's win over Everton was not enough to take them to the top of the League. Queens Park Rangers occupied pole position – putting Liverpool's opening day defeat at Loftus Road into a more respectable context – and were the bookmakers' favourites to land the championship for the first time in their history. QPR, who had lost 2–0 at Anfield earlier that season, had 53 points from 38 games with Liverpool on 51, having played a game fewer, and Manchester United and Derby both on 50 points.

Paisley and Liverpool had gone out of the FA Cup in the fourth round at Derby when home substitute Roger Davies scored the game's only goal, his fourth in six duels with Liverpool. They also made an early exit in the League Cup, losing 1–0 at Burnley in a third-round replay. But they still had a championship and UEFA Cup double in their sights. In Europe, their conquest of Slask Wroclaw booked them a quarter-final clash with Dynamo Dresden, the East German club they had beaten home and away en route to UEFA Cup triumph under Shankly three seasons earlier. This time they prised a goalless draw away from home, thanks to a magnificent penalty save by Ray Clemence from Peter Kotte, the England goalkeeper's second of that season's competition following his spot-kick stop in the first round at Hibernian. Clemence revealed that he had dived to his right thanks to information received on Kotte's penalty kicks from Liverpool's youth development officer Tom Saunders, who doubled as the club's European assessor and had seen the East German take a spot-kick on a spying mission behind the Iron Curtain. Goals from Case and Keegan steered Liverpool to a 2–1 win over Dresden in the Anfield return to secure them a glamour semi-final against Barcelona.

For Paisley, his staff and some of the players, the meeting with Barcelona meant a reunion with old adversaries. Hennes Weisweiler, who was manager of Moenchengladbach against Liverpool in the 1973 UEFA Cup Final, was now in charge at Barcelona and the Spanish club included in their ranks the great Johan Cruyff, who had tormented Liverpool in 1966 when he was a rising star in the Ajax side that dumped them out of the European Cup on a 7–3 aggregate. This time, however, Cruyff and his Dutch colleague Johan Neeskens, also in the Barcelona side, were overshadowed by the menacing combination of Toshack and Keegan. The first leg was at the magnificent Nou Camp stadium and the game was only 13 minutes old when Clemence's long clearance fell to Keegan. He flicked it on to his attack partner Toshack and the big Welsh international gave goalkeeper Mora no chance to score the game's only goal.

Not surprisingly, it inspired one of Toshack's many poems, which he called 'A Goalden Night', part of a collection which was published in book form under the title *Gosh It's Tosh*. One verse read:

A goalden night and what a thrill
It's Liverpool one Barcelona nil
One away goal will suit us fine
And I'm so pleased that it was mine.

Hardly Poet Laureate material! Nevertheless, Toshack's rhyming accounts of his experiences with Liverpool and Wales had wonderful novelty value and his goal at the Nou Camp ensured that Liverpool became the first English club to beat Barcelona on their own ground in Europe. At the time of writing, they remained the only one to do so. The Spanish club's 3–3 draw with Manchester United in the Champions' League in November 1998 was their 18th home game against English opposition, of which they had won 15 and drawn two, with their solitary defeat inflicted by Paisley's Liverpool. The margin of victory could have been greater, so commanding was Liverpool's performance. Their crisp, accurate passing, their teamwork and rapid switches from defensive containment to probing attack left Barcelona ragged and dispirited long before the end. It was a backhanded compliment and a tribute to Liverpool's grip on the game that many home fans in the 75,000 crowd hurled cushions at their own team, prompting a misunderstanding by the exuberant Joey Jones. The Welsh defender, sitting on the Liverpool bench, began to throw them back until Paisley stepped in to prevent a comical situation getting out of hand. As Jones remembered: 'I was on the substitutes bench and we kept getting hit during the game by hard-boiled sweets and it was annoying me. At the end, all these cushions came flying out of the stand. I started throwing them back like frisbees and they were bouncing off the Spanish fans' heads. Bob got hold of me and threw me down the tunnel, saying: "You'll start World War Three."

'I said: "Boss, they're throwing cushions at us."

'He said: "They're not throwing them at you. They're throwing them at them because they got beat!"

As if stung by the fierce criticism of their home display, Barcelona showed much more fire in the second leg in front of a 55,000-plus crowd, Anfield's biggest of the season. It was goalless at half-time. Then a rare goal from Phil Thompson, who turned in a Toshack shot after 50 minutes, gave Liverpool a 2–0 aggregate lead. But Paisley's side were pegged back after a move involving Cruyff, who sped down the left flank before delivering a measured cross, which Rexach drove past Clemence. It left Paisley and his players anxiously aware that another Barcelona goal would take the Spaniards through on away goals. They held out, though, for a 2–1 aggregate win to clinch a place in the two-leg final against Bruges of Belgium. But the pattern throughout that season of Liverpool being away first in Europe was broken. The first meeting with Bruges was to be at Anfield.

Prior to that, though, there was the little matter of the League championship to attend to. Liverpool had three First Division matches left – a home clash with Stoke and visits to Manchester City and Wolves. They beat Stoke 5–3 in a thrilling duel at Anfield – Fairclough enjoying another scoring substitute stint by hitting the clinching fifth goal – and two days later on Easter Monday, 19 April, the team went to Maine Road and demolished Manchester City 3–0, although the contest was goalless until 17 minutes from time. Then Steve Heighway struck and a brace of goals in the last two minutes from Fairclough, this time starting the game in the absence of Case, took the teenager's output to seven in seven League outings. It was a significant victory for Paisley's side, the value of it underlined 48 hours later when Manchester United's title hopes dissolved with a 1–0 home defeat by Stoke.

The tag of 'super sub' sat uneasily on Fairclough's shoulders. But he reflected on it philosophically in later years: 'Bob used to keep everything simple and when he wanted an opposition system to be broken up he would send me on and ask me to try and get a piece of it. He rarely sent me into situations from which there was little chance of recovery. He would also tell me to run up and down the line and say: "You're not going on but it might scare a few of them to see you."

'I was named as a substitute more times than I would have liked but, at the same time, I did enjoy a great deal of success. He did it for the benefit of Liverpool Football Club and he's certainly as great as any legend they've ever had.'

After their Maine Road win, Liverpool were without a game the following Saturday, the scheduled final day of the League season when they were due to meet Wolves. Call-ups for John Toshack and Joey Jones by Wales for the European Championship match in Yugoslavia the same day prompted the club to request a rearrangement of their trip to Molineux. Liverpool and Wolves failed to agree a new date so the League Management Committee stepped in to fix Tuesday 4 May as the night when the destiny of three clubs would be decided in a cliff-hanging climax to the season. QPR finished their programme with a 2–0 home win over Leeds to give them 59 points, one more than Liverpool, who therefore needed either a win or a low score draw up to 2–2 at Molineux to become champions, while Wolves had to win to have a chance of escaping relegation.

It was a remarkable coincidence for Paisley, whose first championship medal had come after Liverpool won their final game of the 1946–47 season at Wolves. Now he hoped that history would repeat itself.

The date switch meant that after the win at Manchester City, Liverpool had more than a fortnight to wait before the game at Molineux. But there was no opportunity to dwell on it. The UEFA Cup Final first leg against Bruges loomed on Wednesday 28 April. And this is how Paisley's side lined up: Clemence; Smith, Thompson, Hughes, Neal; Fairclough, Callaghan, Kennedy; Keegan, Toshack, Heighway. Substitute: Case.

Two Bruges goals early in the contest, by Lambert and Cools, stunned the Kop and Liverpool were still trailing 2–0 at half-time when Paisley withdrew Toshack and sent on Case. It proved an inspired decision. Case scored in a sensational comeback, with Ray Kennedy and a Kevin Keegan penalty providing the other goals in a 3–2 win. It meant that Liverpool had two games left in which they could win two trophies or see them slip away.

The match at Molineux the following Tuesday proved one of the most atmospheric in Liverpool history. An official crowd of 48,900 was recorded, but many more supporters clambered on to the roof of the stands, perched on floodlight pylons and even swarmed through the dressing room corridor at a ground that had witnessed many great nights during Wolves' halcyon days of the 1950s. That was the era of their trail-blazing exhibition matches against the likes of Honved and Moscow Spartak, which pointed the way for English clubs to enter European football competitively.

Just like the Bruges game at Anfield, it was the opposition who drew first blood against a Liverpool side in which Paisley made just one change, Case earning a starting place with Fairclough dropping to substitute. An early goal by Steve Kindon had Liverpool nerves jangling and with 14 minutes left Wolves still clung to the lead despite a furious second-half onslaught by the visitors. But then the tide turned. Keegan, with a goal almost inevitably set up by Toshack, equalised. And with a flourish befitting champions, Toshack added a second with Kennedy pouncing for another to clinch a 3–1 win and the championship. Wolves were relegated – and could not have saved themselves anyway as Birmingham took a point at Sheffield United – while QPR, less than a quarter of an hour from the title, were left to ponder on what might have been. But their manager Dave Sexton was gracious in his deep disappointment after his side's finishing flourish of 15 wins from their final 17 games had been denied the ultimate prize by Paisley's team. 'Cream,' said Sexton, 'always rises to the top, and that's what Liverpool have done.'

Paisley's first trophy as manager was hugely significant for Liverpool. It was the club's ninth League title, installing them as champions by putting them ahead of Arsenal who, at that stage, had won the title on eight occasions. And Bob himself was delighted to have joined the select band of men to have played in and later managed championship-winning teams.

'I'm proud to be a Liverpudlian tonight,' said a beaming Paisley, underlining his view that he was now an 'adopted' Scouser. The scenes in the dressing room were riotous and, amazingly, a group of gatecrashing Liverpool fans broke in and did a celebration conga past Paisley and his players before obeying instructions to leave!

Paisley's captain, Emlyn Hughes, saluted the manager's leadership qualities: 'Bob's greatest attribute as a manager was dealing with strengths and weaknesses, the opposition's and your own! He didn't talk any tactical rubbish, nothing about Christmas-tree formations and such like. He just spoke in plain and simple language.'

Jessie Paisley has her own memories of the mass exodus of fans from Merseyside to witness that glory night at Molineux: 'It was a remarkable night. Just getting there was a job because the whole of the city of Liverpool seemed to be travelling to Molineux. My son Robert drove me and we had to come off the motorway, which was clogged with traffic. But Bob was so pleased at winning his first championship.'

Sadly, amidst the celebrations that went on until dawn, Reuben Bennett, the hard-as-nails Scottish coach everyone said was made from girders, fell ill and had to be taken to a Liverpool hospital. Next morning Bob visited Ben, as he was affectionately known, and was told he was not in danger and on the mend. It was the cue for a little example of Paisley humour. Referring to the fact that Reuben was partial to a drop or two of Scotch, he quipped: 'When the hospital took a blood sample from him they thought he was Bell's Manager of the Year!'

The following week Paisley would be named as winner of that prestigious whisky-sponsored award, for his feat in leading Liverpool to the title and the UEFA Cup Final. It followed two divisional awards, in December 1975 and April 1976, and he would go on to lift a grand total of 23 Bell's awards. Amongst a shoal of congratulatory telegrams was one from Sunderland, Bob's first football love, and another from Bill Shankly which read: 'Well done, Bob. I'm very pleased for you. Liverpool have proved once and for all that we are the real champions of England.'

After the heady title clincher at Wolves, Liverpool had more than a fortnight to wait until their return UEFA Cup Final meeting with Bruges in Belgium on 19 May, holding what many believed was a fragile 3–2 first leg lead. Bruges coach Ernst Happel, a former Austrian international centre-half of great repute, was confident his team could win 1–0 and lift the trophy on the away-goals rule, thanks to the two they had scored at Anfield. Six years earlier Happel had led Feyenoord of Holland to the European Cup and World Club championship, overcoming Celtic and Estudiantes respectively. He looked on course for more success when, just 11 minutes into the return, East German referee Rudi Gloeckner awarded Bruges a penalty for a handling offence against Hughes, whose protests were in vain. Raoul Lambert, one of the Anfield scorers for the Belgian side, fired the spot-kick past Ray Clemence and things look bleak for Liverpool, who were unchanged from the team that had secured the title.

But within four minutes of that potentially crushing setback of having their first-leg lead so swiftly wiped out, Liverpool were back in front on aggregate. Bruges defender Eduard Krieger conceded a free kick just outside the penalty area and Hughes rolled the ball square for Kevin Keegan to blast a right-foot shot past goalkeeper Bert Jensen. And that was how the score remained to the end, with Liverpool victorious on a 4–3 aggregate, a reward for their composed defending under intense Bruges pressure. Ray Clemence displayed his familiar prowess in goal and shrugged off his nightmare slip that had allowed a certain Kenny Dalglish of Celtic to score for Scotland in their 2–1 win over England four days earlier.

Emphasizing Liverpool's strength, five of Paisley's team jetted straight out from Belgium to link up with the England squad for their games in the USA Bicentennial Tournament against Brazil,

Italy and Team America. Emlyn Hughes had again not been selected by England boss Don Revie to travel to Los Angeles with Clemence, Keegan, Neal, Thompson and Ray Kennedy. 'Revie can pick who he wants – but I think I deserve to be in the England squad,' insisted Hughes.

The addition of the UEFA Cup to the championship repeated Anfield's double of 1973 under Shankly. He was a spectator in Bruges as a guest of Liverpool, who had staged an emotional Anfield testimonial for their former manager a year earlier. But the League title, UEFA Cup and Manager of the Year award were only part of a cascade of honours that rained on Paisley's Liverpool. The club also lifted the European Team of the Year Award, the Central League title, Lancashire League Division 2 championship and, three months later, the Charity Shield when John Toshack's only goal at Wembley toppled Southampton, shock FA Cup Final conquerors of Manchester United.

Another massive honour also went to Anfield with Kevin Keegan being voted Footballer of the Year by the Football Writers' Association. Keegan was a darting bundle of inspirational skill and energy and contributed 16 goals in a partnership with Toshack that yielded a season's total of 39. With the help of Paisley's wise counsel, Keegan had put two career crises behind him – his lengthy ban for the shirt-throwing incident in the 1974 Charity Shield and an England walk-out after being dropped by Don Revie in May 1975 – to become the superstar of English football. Jessie Paisley recalled Bob's heart-to-heart talk with Keegan: 'When Kevin walked out of the England camp, Bob chatted to him all morning, not just about football but about their lives and background. It ended with Bob persuading Kevin to ring Don Revie and the situation was resolved. But their talk never became public knowledge. As far as Bob was concerned it was a private matter.'

Keegan's talents were also attracting foreign admirers, with Real Madrid and Barcelona among a batch of clubs linked with him. And he, in turn, made no secret of the fact that he would relish a lucrative new challenge abroad. The outcome was a typically British compromise. After talks with Paisley, chairman John Smith and secretary Peter Robinson, Keegan and Liverpool agreed that if he stayed at Anfield for another season, the club would not stand in his way if he wished to accept a foreign offer. Paisley had a characteristic response, saying: 'It's not all honey and cake abroad and I don't want to lose Kevin. But freedom of contract is looming and there could come a point when if he wanted to go, he'd just go. He says if he went abroad he could be a millionaire in five years. You couldn't deprive a player of his age that sort of opportunity. If you did, he wouldn't be happy. But we'll cross that bridge when we come to it.'

The public announcement of Keegan's intended departure sparked a year of intense speculation that only heightened pressure on him and Liverpool. And Keegan later admitted it was an error to reveal his plans that summer. 'My mistake was in announcing what I was going to do so far in advance,' he said. 'I should have just left when the time came. But I felt the fans should be told and that's something I tried to do later at Newcastle. I wanted to give supporters as much information as possible.'

The summer of 1976 also marked the end of Brian Hall's Liverpool career, after more than 200 appearances and twenty-one goals. Hall, having lost his place to Jimmy Case, joined Plymouth for £45,000 but was destined in later life to return to Anfield as the club's public relations executive. As Hall departed the Kop, a new face arrived. Centre-forward David Johnson cost Paisley a club record £200,000 from Ipswich and was already well known to Merseyside fans, having been born in Liverpool and begun his career at Everton before moving to Portman Road in October 1972. Shankly had tried and failed to sign him from Everton when Harry Catterick was manager, and since then Johnson, fast, mobile and menacing in the air, had become an England striker. Paisley viewed his acquisition as an important bolstering of his Liverpool squad. There was also a family link. Bob's wife Jessie, former deputy headmistress of St Mary's Church School in Liverpool's Grassendale district, had once taught Johnson's wife Carol.

Johnson arrived with a bizarre distinction – he was the last player to score for Everton against Liverpool, way back in November 1971! Signed less than 48 hours before the Charity Shield, he missed Liverpool's Wembley win over Southampton but made his debut in this team paraded by Paisley to open the League season at home to Norwich: Ray Clemence in goal, a back four of Phil Neal, Phil Thompson, Emlyn Hughes and Joey Jones; in midfield, Ian Callaghan and Ray Kennedy, with Kevin Keegan striking from deep to support a raiding party of Johnson, John Toshack and Steve Heighway. Jimmy Case was squeezed out on to the bench.

The only goal of the game, from Heighway, got Liverpool off to a winning start in a season which saw the Football League's introduction of goal difference to replace goal average and one in which Paisley's team intended to become the first side since Wolves 18 years earlier to retain the championship. As well as that opening day line-up, Paisley also called on battle-honed Tommy Smith, David Fairclough and Terry McDermott to underline the strength of his squad despite the departure of Peter Cormack, who ended his four-year Anfield career by joining Bristol City for £50,000.

'I've got to choose 11 from 16 but I hope they'll all be patient because, if the season goes as we hope it will, we're going to need all of them,' Paisley reflected in an unerring prophecy.

As Liverpool embarked on this quest for new glory, Jessie Paisley revealed how Bob would unwind at home: 'On Sunday afternoons at home, Bob would sometimes tinkle on the electric organ, although that was the day he also had the press to deal with. They would ring him and sometimes, especially if it was the southern press on the phone, it was best if you got the grandchildren out of the way until he had cooled down again! But he liked messing about on the organ and could actually play the tune of 'Amazing Grace', which was Bill Shankly's favourite hymn and which Bob chose when he was on *Songs of Praise*. As well as his great love of horseracing, Bob liked listening to Harry Secombe singing and he liked looking at the garden. I used to get him to mow the lawn but it would have been rather disastrous if his gardening went further than that. If I asked him to weed the path, everything would go – plants as well!'

There was little chance for Paisley to relax in the amazing campaign about to unfold.

8

Treble Chance

In the month that saw the death of Chinese leader Mao Tse-Tung and the landing of the unmanned spacecraft Viking 2 on Mars, to transmit the first close-up pictures of the planet, Liverpool showed their own power by landing on top of the First Division. They shrugged off a 2–1 defeat at Birmingham, and a swift exit from the League Cup in a second-round replay at West Brom, to win 3–2 at Derby on 11 September through goals from Kennedy, Toshack and Keegan, a game when Smith came in for knee casualty Thompson.

Four days later they opened their European Cup campaign with a 2–0 home win over Northern Irish side Crusaders, needing a Phil Neal penalty to set them on the way to a victory secured by a second-half John Toshack strike. The part-timers defended so doggedly that it prompted an acerbic, though humorous jibe from Paisley when one of the Irish side's players revealed he had lost a contact lens during the game. 'He'll find it in one penalty area or the other,' mused Paisley, whose team ran out 5–0 winners in the Belfast return, four of the goals coming in the final nine minutes after a first-half strike from Keegan.

A week after the win at Derby, the value of Ray Clemence was demonstrated again when he saved a Keith Osgood penalty to help his side win 2–0 against Tottenham. And although Liverpool lost at Newcastle next time out, by the game's only goal, they then embarked on an unbeaten domestic run stretching into December, which included a 3–1 Anfield win over Everton, for whom Martin Dobson ended their six-year derby goal drought. That game saw Joey Jones become the first Liverpool player to receive a yellow card in League football, after England aligned with Europe by introducing yellow and red cards to replace the referee's notebook and pointed finger.

In the European Cup, Paisley and his players faced the club's longest journey yet, a 5,000 mile round trip to play Trabzonspor in the remote Turkish town of Trabzon on the Black Sea. 'I think we'll need camels for this one,' quipped Paisley, who promptly dispatched European 'spy' Tom Saunders to vet the unknown opposition. Saunders' description of what he found – 'a different world' – was far from an overstatement. Hotel facilities were appalling (rats and cockroaches infested the two used by the Liverpool party) and stomach upsets were the norm. One member of the press corps was unable to shake off a bug he contracted until the second leg at Anfield a fortnight later, when the travelling Trabzon doctor gave him some tablets that worked like magic. Whoever doubted the value of local knowledge!

A clearly angry Paisley rapped: 'They've put us in a doss house. I've had better rations in my "bivvy" in the Western Desert!'

A few players had the foresight and wisdom to take their own provisions. Ray Clemence, for example, took a bundle of Cadbury's chocolate bars which he found far more appetising and energising than anything on the hotel menu! But food and accommodation were not the only problems. Those members of the party who could get to sleep were awakened in the early hours by chanting at a nearby mosque and a tannoy calling the faithful to pray. So it was a Liverpool squad far from its physical peak that had to go into action against a club that was only ten years old and which was fiercely proud of having upstaged its big-city rivals in Istanbul and Ankara to lift the Turkish championship.

The dilapidated stadium had only a 13,000 capacity, but its situation, and the pulling power of Liverpool, gave the match a setting reminiscent of the famous Battle of Rorke's Drift, the role of the Zulus being played by thousands of non-paying spectators massed on hills overlooking the ground. Liverpool's dressing room had moss growing on the walls and Paisley described the match ball as 'worse than a pig's bladder at a Durham miners' gala'. In the circumstances, Liverpool's 1-0 defeat, through a hotly disputed 63rd-minute penalty conceded by Emlyn Hughes, was highly creditable in a game that marked a new English record 79th European appearance by Ian Callaghan.

Paisley and the players were not the only ones to feel less than Turkish delight. I shared a full match Radio City commentary with

Elton Welsby only to discover afterwards, to our abject frustration, that the transmission had gone as far as Ankara and hit a dead end. Not a word reached Merseyside from that passionate football outpost in Anatolia, close to the old Soviet border with Georgia.

Given that arduous trip, as well as Paisley's conviction that the physiological demands of travel took an unappreciated toll on the mental and physical condition of players, Liverpool did well to take a point from their League game at Leeds three days later, thanks to a second-half Ray Kennedy goal. The manager was ever alert to the requirements and responses of his players and also, as Ian Callaghan reflected, very fair to them. 'Bob was firm when he had to be but he also had a softer side to his nature. As a player I felt that even if you didn't play well, if you gave 100 per cent, Bob would recognise that,' Callaghan said.

Liverpool ended the month of October 1976 with wins at Leicester, when Toshack scored the game's only goal against the club he had come close to joining two years earlier, and at home to Aston Villa when they hit three without reply, with Terry McDermott, Ian Callaghan and Kevin Keegan on target. All the goals came in the last 16 minutes, emphasising Liverpool's persistence and determination. The win over Villa meant that after 12 games Liverpool led the First Division, three points clear of a five-club pack locked on 15 points: Manchester City, Ipswich, Newcastle, Leicester and Middlesbrough.

McDermott's goal proved to be his only one in the League that season. But the Kirkby-born player, who was establishing himself at Anfield as a midfielder of pace and power, and would win his first England cap within a year in Ron Greenwood's first match as national manager, was overjoyed at his strike and sent a warning to Liverpool's rivals. 'When that chance came there was no way I was going to miss it. I was chuffed to score in front of the Kop. We showed that we will fight to the end. We did that today and got our reward. Once Villa got over-confident, there was nothing down for them.'

The Wednesday following the Villa game saw the return with Trabzonspor. Phil Neal, who missed the first leg through injury as Tommy Smith impressively deputised, returned to the team in time to help unlock the door to the European Cup quarter-final. Some 3,000 banner-waving Trabzonspor fans travelled to Anfield – the biggest influx of foreign supporters since Ajax a decade earlier – but their hopes of seeing their side progress swiftly evaporated.

Only eight minutes had gone when Steve Heighway seized on a Keegan flick from McDermott's cross to level the aggregate score. Two minutes later David Johnson, drafted into the attack in place of the injured Toshack, collected a slipshod back-pass from visiting captain Cemil for Liverpool's second. And with still only 18 minutes on the clock, Keegan put the contest beyond the Turks with a glorious header from a Callaghan centre.

'Our early goals killed them off,' observed Paisley. 'They did get a bit wild late on but whatever the deficiencies of the Turkish team, courage isn't one of them. They kept going and were much fitter than many foreign teams who've been here.'

Liverpool, having clinched their place in the last eight of Europe's greatest club competition, could now put their Continental campaign on ice until March and concentrate on those two big domestic targets, the League championship and FA Cup. They marched on with a 1-0 win at Sunderland, a 5-1 home hammering of Leicester and a 1-1 draw at Arsenal, the point at Highbury gained by a goal three minutes from time scored against his former club by Ray Kennedy. Paisley was angry, though, over referee Alan Turvey's booking of Ray Clemence, for his protests after being penalised for breaching the much-abused four-step rule for goalkeepers. 'Every keeper in the country's doing it and getting away with it, but Ray's been singled out,' he complained angrily.

The team completed an unbeaten sweep through November with a 2-1 home win over Bristol City, after which Keegan, despite scoring one of the goals, revealed that he felt exhausted and wanted to be substituted. He did in fact complete the match but his comments indicated that he was feeling added pressure caused by his summer disclosure that this was to be his last season at Liverpool. Speculation over his future was intense and incessant, but he played through it and missed only four of the 42 League games in his farewell campaign.

A severe winter was taking its toll on fixtures and as Liverpool embarked on their first outing of December, the Pools Panel had to adjudicate for the first time in three years on fixtures elsewhere. Liverpool, too, caught a cold with a 1-0 defeat by title rivals Ipswich, Paul Mariner heading the 75th-minute winner at Portman Road. It put Bobby Robson's second-placed East Anglian challengers to within a point of Paisley's team, who had taken 25 points from 17 matches. And when Ipswich won their game in hand the following midweek, with a 4–2 victory at Birmingham, they leapfrogged Liverpool to go top by a point. Liverpool went back to the top four days later with a 3–1 home defeat of QPR, on a day when Ipswich's game at Newcastle was weather-beaten and abandoned at half-time.

But what happened next was astonishing as Liverpool, who had conceded only 13 goals in their previous 18 League games, sank to a stunning 5–1 midweek defeat at Aston Villa, all the goals coming in the first half. They were 4–0 down in half an hour. Andy Gray, later to join Everton, scored two of Villa's goals and although Ray Kennedy scored a consolation for Liverpool, there was no way back for them. It was the club's heaviest League defeat since their 7–2 hiding at Tottenham on Easter Monday 1963, and the biggest in any competition since they slumped 5–1 to Ajax on a foggy night in Amsterdam in 1966.

'I can't remember many games like this one,' admitted Callaghan. 'Everything Villa did went in. But at least it will wake us up a bit.'

Clemence was smarting from having five goals put past him for the first time since a 7–1 hiding by Grimsby in his Scunthorpe days a decade earlier. 'Unlike that night at Grimsby, I don't think I could have done anything to prevent the Villa goals,' he said. 'We let Villa dictate the pace of the game instead of doing our usual away job by setting the pace ourselves.'

Paisley made no excuses, admitting: 'We got what we deserved. If they were suffering from any complacency, it should have been knocked out of them now. Looking at our team, you'd have thought they'd never played together before and that we had no experience. It was just too bad to be true. We've talked about it and some good can come out of it if they realise they get nothing for last season. It's not in my mind to make a string of changes, but they've got to show what they can do – or some of them are going to be in for a shock.'

The return of John Toshack, who had missed the Villa Park debacle through concussion sustained in the win over QPR, was the only team change for the game at West Ham three days later. He replaced David Johnson but it didn't change Liverpool's fortunes, as they went down to a 2–0 defeat which cost them the League leadership. But still Paisley refused to panic. He called his squad together for a heart-to-heart talk and named an unchanged side for the Christmas game against Stoke. After all, it was Bob's belief that a manager and his men had to stick together. 'The game is one of understanding between players and managers,' he said. 'You have to march in the same direction to achieve success, and you certainly have to do that to overcome problems.'

The team in whom Paisley kept faith gave their answer in the shape of a 4–0 conquest of Stoke, which they followed with a 1–1 draw at Manchester City, a point gleaned without Kevin Keegan, who had injured a shoulder. December also heralded another personal milestone for Paisley and secretary Peter Robinson, who had been at Liverpool since 1965. At a wide-ranging Anfield press conference, chairman John Smith announced that both men were to be given seven-year contracts to run until 1983, with Robinson having the new title of general secretary.

As the press conference was unfolding, Bob's wife Jessie was receiving Christmas wishes from her children in Class six on the last day of term at St Mary's School in the Grassendale district of Liverpool. Bob's own graduation with honours was saluted by Smith, when he said: 'These new contracts for Bob and Peter are a mark of the great esteem in which both are held not only at Liverpool but throughout the football world.' For Paisley it was a fitting accolade for his distinction of being the longest-serving one-club man in the English game, and he accepted it with his usual realism and humility.

'In football it's very flattering to be given a contract for seven days, let alone seven years,' he reflected. 'To be offered something like this makes you look for the definition of the word faith – and this seems to me a better definition than anything that appears in the dictionary. This club has been my life. I'd go out and sweep the streets and be proud to do it for Liverpool FC if they asked me to. A lot of good men in this game lose their jobs too early, and too many are forced to live in fear. Liverpool's attitude is very different. But there's no way it will make me complacent. I'm far too conscious of my duty to the supporters for that to happen.'

Paisley's new contract was worth a total of £105,000 over its seven-year span, less than some players now earn in a month, a dramatic illustration of the wildly spiralling finances of modern football. But at the same press conference in December 1976, Liverpool heralded the dawn of football's commercial age when Smith announced that they had launched an export drive to sell the club overseas and to market club goods throughout the world. He also revealed that Anfield was to have a new executive lounge for shareholders and that Liverpool's first ever sponsored match would take place later that season, when Bell's would back the clash with Manchester United.

Smith admitted: 'Clubs cannot manage on their takings through the turnstiles. Every other means of expanding revenue has to be used for clubs to exist. Sponsorship is one of the biggest.' And with an observation that now seems quaintly from another age, he added: 'We are the only club in the UK and, I believe, the only one in Europe not to have perimeter advertising around the ground. So we can offer what no other club can offer – exclusivity.'

Paisley's thoughts swiftly returned to the title battle and the FA Cup. The emphatic win over Stoke meant that Liverpool went into 1977 back at the First Division summit. However, because of the weather-ravaged programme, Ipswich now had three games in hand and were only two points behind. Liverpool's New Year's Day clash was with Sunderland, the club Paisley idolised as a boy. With Keegan still absent, the team won 2-0 to underline their recovery from the jolting reverses at Villa and West Ham. They were back on course, and only the weather was bothering Paisley. 'No other country in the world has such varying conditions for football as we have,' he said. 'Within six days we've played in rain against Stoke, on ice against Manchester City and in mud against Sunderland. So we've done well to take five points out of six. These kind of things can make or break championships.'

Keegan, minus his flu-hit partner John Toshack, resumed action in the FA Cup third round when Third Division Crystal Palace held out for a surprise goalless draw at Anfield, a game which saw Terry McDermott sustain a first-half ankle injury in a challenge by Phil Holder that would rule him out until March. But a brace of second-half goals from Steve Heighway, following a 19th-minute Keegan strike, gave Liverpool a 3-2 win in the Selhurst Park replay. The previous day, 10 January, Paisley's concerns about the perilous nature of football management had been underlined when Everton sacked Billy Bingham, who had been in charge at Goodison since the summer of 1973.

Steve Burtenshaw took caretaker charge until Gordon Lee's appointment at the end of the month. The cruel irony of Bingham's dismissal was that it followed a 2-0 home third-round FA Cup win over Stoke which helped set up a mighty all-Merseyside semi-final collision in the spring.

Liverpool's League fortunes dipped before their next FA Cup outing, a 1-1 home draw against West Brom being followed by a 2-1 defeat at Norwich. So although Ipswich lost at Tottenham, they were only a point behind with three games in hand, while Manchester City were only a further two points behind, having played the same number of games as the Portman Road club. But in the Cup, Liverpool cruised through against Carlisle, winning 3-0 at Anfield to earn yet another home outing, this time when they were pitted against Oldham, who fell 3-1 in front of the Kop. Fate was again kind to Paisley and his side when they were handed a home tie against Middlesbrough in round six. Second-half goals from Fairclough and Keegan secured a 2-0 win and that semi-final date with Everton at Maine Road, Manchester.

Prior to that, however, Paisley's team had to concentrate on their other two pursuits, the championship and European Cup. They toppled both Birmingham and Derby in the League at Anfield, the latter game notable for both teams lining up before kick-off to applaud Ian Callaghan on to the field to salute his 800th senior appearance in a Liverpool jersey. And as the fixtures and the pressure mounted, Callaghan revealed Liverpool's attitude and cited the Mersey derby win several months earlier as the game that ignited Liverpool's season.

'Sometimes just one result in a season can be like a spark, and that win over Everton certainly got us going. But as we always do at Liverpool, we're taking one game at a time,' he said.

Callaghan took his familiar place in the Liverpool team in his usual number 11 jersey for the next hurdle of the club's European Cup mission, a testing quarter-final first-leg trip to face crack French club St Etienne, who had lost 1-0 to Bayern Munich in the previous year's final in Glasgow. With players like the two talented Dominiques, Rochetau and Bathenay, and Argentine defender Osvaldo Piazza, it was clear they posed a massive threat to Liverpool's ambitions, which were not helped by Keegan being ruled out for the game in France after aggravating a thigh injury in the FA Cup win over Oldham. This absence meant a recall for Terry McDermott, for his first appearance since his January ankle injury.

Liverpool proceeded to give a magnificent performance against the French champions in the Geoffrey Guichard Stadium. Phil Thompson went close to scoring with a header and Steve Heighway, enjoying a superbly effective season, went even closer when his shot from a Jimmy Case pass hit a post. But Liverpool hopes of at least keeping a clean sheet, so valuable in European away games, dissolved ten minutes from time. St Etienne skipper Jean-Michel Larque floated a corner to the far post where full-back Gerard Janvion mishit the ball, only for it to bounce to Bathenay, who prodded it past Clemence.

As the squad flew home to prepare for their next challenge – a home League game against Newcastle – in what was now a succession of crucial games in their drive for honours on three fronts, Paisley revealed his recipe for overcoming St Etienne in the Anfield return. 'This French team have a very good defensive record and our task at Anfield could be a frustrating one, so we need all the vocal encouragement we can get from the supporters,' he said. 'But as well as being positive in the second leg, we've got to be guarded and very patient.'

Mention of the 'T' word – the Treble – was virtually banned within Anfield's portals, and certainly Paisley tended to become tetchy when media men mentioned the possibility. But he did observe: 'Our involvement in three competitions might not be a bad thing, because at least it means you just can't afford to become obsessed with one of them. I want 11 hungry players out there on the pitch against Newcastle. They gave everything they had against St Etienne. It was a hard stint and it catches in your throat to ask them to do it again. But that is what we have to do in every game.

'I admit it was hard for me to get up on Thursday morning after the match in France and start thinking about Newcastle. But every game we play demands that level of concentration and single-mindedness. It's a cliché, but we must take each game as it comes. This month of March is the decisive period – if we do well now, we're almost at the Lord Mayor's Show.'

A single goal from Steve Heighway was sufficient to topple Newcastle and keep Liverpool in pole position in the championship. But Phil Thompson's tussle with Alan Gowling ten minutes from the end proved costly for the player and the club, although it would set up an amazing twist in a dramatic climax to the season. Thompson suffered damage to his left knee which meant he had to undergo cartilage surgery for the second time in two years and would miss the remainder of the campaign. But his enforced absence meant a recall alongside skipper Emlyn Hughes at the centre of defence for veteran Tommy Smith, the man dubbed the 'Anfield Iron'. Former captain Smith, approaching his

32nd birthday, had already announced that he would retire after his testimonial at the end of the season. But he answered Paisley's call in typical committed, upbeat style.

'This is not a comeback – I've been around too long for that,' he growled. 'I didn't want to be a reserve, which is why I decided to retire. But that is all out of my thoughts right now. We're involved in three competitions and I'm concentrating on them.'

Paisley expressed the utmost faith in the old campaigner, saying: 'It's a blow to lose Phil, because with the demands on the squad we need as many players as possible fit and available. But Tommy knows his way round alright! He's got the nous to sort out situations less experienced players may lack. He can read things and react to them. The first few yards are in your head.'

Smith's return coincided with a 1–0 midweek defeat at Tottenham, a goal from Ralph Coates derailing Liverpool while title rivals Ipswich and Manchester City respectively drew and won. Paisley, looking to accentuate the positive, responded: 'The consolation for us was that Kevin Keegan came through alright after his return from injury. We've got to be thankful for that.' While the pace was getting hotter, the manager remained true to his principles and his personality by aiming to keep things low key: 'Keeping a low profile is an important part of football. I've always said that if you open your mouth too wide, somebody will want to close it for you. Some people in the game put petrol on the fire whereas we'd throw a bucket of water on it.'

Keegan's attack partner Toshack missed the next game at Middlesbrough through injury, which gave David Fairclough another outing on the Ayresome Park stage where he had made his senior debut the previous season. A Hughes goal – his only one of the season, struck ferociously from 30 yards – won the match for Liverpool, to leave them on top with 42 points from 31 games, with Ipswich ominously only a point adrift with two games in hand. Manchester City were lying third on 39 points from 30 games. But the championship struggle went on ice for Liverpool as they clicked back into European mode to resume combat with St Etienne on what was to be one of Anfield's most magical occasions, a night of sheer adrenalin-pumping theatre which still inspires tingling excitement whenever it is recalled.

Paisley named an unchanged side, which lined up in this 4-3-3 formation: Ray Clemence; Phil Neal, Tommy Smith, Emlyn Hughes, Joey Jones, Jimmy Case, Ian Callaghan, Ray Kennedy;

Kevin Keegan, John Toshack, Steve Heighway. On the bench were substitute goalkeeper Peter McDonnell, Brian Kettle, David Johnson, Terry McDermott and David Fairclough. St Etienne drafted in Alain Merchadier to replace the banned Osvaldo Piazza, the centre-back's first-leg foul on Callaghan having earned him his second yellow card of the campaign and an automatic suspension.

There was an intensity and electricity in the atmosphere that Anfield had not experienced since the Inter Milan first leg in the European Cup semi-final a dozen years earlier. A mass of St Etienne supporters in the 55,000-plus crowd, wrapped in their club's green and white, injected their own Gallic passion and flavour, saluting their team with the chant of 'Allez Les Verts'. But they suffered an early shock. A mere one minute and forty-two seconds had elapsed before Liverpool wiped out the French side's 1–0 first-leg advantage – with a goal Keegan admitted he did not even intend! The England star despatched the ball from the left, meaning it to be a cross. But it curled over visiting goalkeeper Ivan Curkovic and into the net to level the aggregate at 1–1.

That was merely the cue, however, for St Etienne to display their class and their character by launching a series of raids that sternly tested Liverpool's defence and drew breathtaking saves by Ray Clemence from Larque and Rocheteau. But even the England goalkeeper was powerless to stop Bathenay's brilliant, wickedly swerving long-range shot six minutes into the second half, which put St Etienne back in front on aggregate and meant Liverpool had to score at least twice more.

Now it was their turn, decisively as it proved, to display their own powers of recovery. Ian Callaghan's 58th-minute cross from the right found Toshack and when he breasted the ball down to Ray Kennedy, the former Arsenal striker steered a low shot past Curkovic to make the aggregate score 2–2. But if St Etienne held out without conceding another, they would go through on the away-goals rule. The tension mounted as time ticked away. There were only 18 minutes left when fate and an inspired decision by Paisley combined to turn the course of the contest.

John Toshack, who had returned to face St Etienne after missing the previous Saturday's game, collided with Merchadier. Paisley had already planned to throw Fairclough into the fray and as soon as Toshack needed treatment, it was the signal for the red-headed raider to replace him.

Fairclough will never forget that night. He recalled: 'I remember going on the team bus to the ground from the Adelphi Hotel and when we got to Anfield Road there were so many people and there was such an atmosphere I got this feeling that something special was going to happen. There was something different about it and when we got to the stadium and went out on to the pitch before the game that feeling was reinforced. I was feeling particularly nervous that night wondering how the game might go. We got off to a good start with Keegan scoring very early doors. But then as the game unfolded it got more and more edgy and I clearly remember feeling this might be a game to avoid having a run in as a substitute! I joked with Brian Kettle in the dug-out: "I don't fancy going on here. It might go to penalties." But once Bathenay scored St Etienne's goal I, like many, thought that perhaps the French had a little bit too much for us, because they were a special side. Bathenay's goal was extraordinary, and when goals like that go in, you think to yourself that you're going to be up against it. But Bob Paisley came down to the dug-out from his seat in the director's box, as he did quite often, to discuss options with Joe Fagan and generally assess the situation. During that time, I was told to have a run up and down the line. The orders were always very simple to me: "Just get up there and see if you can get a piece of something."

'Just as I was completing my warm-up, Ray Kennedy scored our second goal. We were now back in with a shout. So for me it was a case of just going on, getting a feel of the game and hoping. But by then all my nerves had disappeared. When I took off the old jumper I used to wear on the bench and adjusted my shorts, I was ready. Any worries had gone and the great welcome I always got from the supporters gave me a lift. I thought that maybe I could turn things.'

Only six minutes remained on the watch when Fairclough chested down and controlled a Kennedy through ball following a Clemence clearance. Even though he was 40 yards from goal, Fairclough showed an ice coolness more akin to stepping out of a fridge than emerging from an anxious Liverpool dug-out in a frenzied atmosphere. On and on he ran, swaying first one way then the other, like a field of corn caressed by the breeze, to bemuse the St Etienne defence. He evaded an attempted physical block by Christian Lopez as he sped ever closer to goal.

Liverpool fans held their breath before exploding with delight as the ball flashed from Fairclough's foot and past Curkovic to

Above: If the cap fits ... a young Paisley already with his eye on the trophies.

Below: Bob Paisley, in hooped top on the aircraft steps, with the rest of the Liverpool players and officials as they prepare to fly out for a 1948 United States tour.

*Stepping out for action as
Liverpool captain in
March 1952.*
(Copyright: Hulton Getty)

Above: *Paisley, the white-coated trainer and physiotherapist, with the Liverpool team in 1962.*

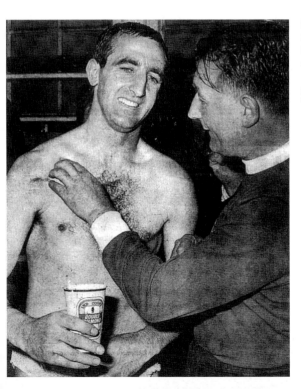

Left: *Sore point...
Bob Paisley inspects
Gerry Byrne's broken
collar bone after the
1965 Cup final.*
*(Copyright: Liverpool Daily Post
and Echo Ltd)*

Above: *Paisley strides across the Melwood training ground, a few days after succeeding Bill Shankly as manager in 1974.*

Above: *Liverpool players and Bob Paisley salute the Kop – 26 April 1975.*
(Copyright: Liverpool Daily Post and Echo Ltd)

Right: *Bob Bond's caricature of Bob Paisley.*

BOB PAISLEY

Left & Above: Bob Paisley's second
Manager of the Year award presented
in 1977.
(Copyright: Bell's Whisky)

Right: A triumphant Bob Paisley holds
aloft the European Cup in 1981.
(Copyright: Colorsport)

Kings of Europe: Paisley, sitting with the European Cup, and his Liverpool squad in 1981.

Above: Two legends share an after-dinner joke: Bob Paisley with Sir Matt Busby.

Below: Bob Paisley – and lucky mascot – at his desk in his Anfield office.
(Copyright: Liverpool Daily Post & Echo Ltd)

Bob Paisley proudly shows off the Division 1 Championships Trophy won by the club for the first time in 1982.
(Copyright: Popperfoto)

Above: Bob Paisley in his Anfield Kingdom. *(Copyright: Liverpool Daily Post & Echo Ltd)*

Below: Bob Paisley with his massive haul of trophies and medals. *(Copyright: Daily Express)*

Bob Paisley waves farewell to Anfield after the Liverpool – Aston Villa game, 7 May, 1983.
(Copyright: Popperfoto)

Jessie Paisley officially opens Anfield's 'Paisley Gateway' in April 1999.

Jessie Paisley with some of her family at Anfield after officially opening the 'Paisley Gateway' in April 1999.

bulge the Kop net. Within seconds, the match-winner who had secured a European Cup semi-final place for Liverpool disappeared under a mound of ecstatic team-mates.

Fairclough recounted his wondrous strike: 'While many people joked that I never knew what I was doing when I had the ball, I can assure everyone that I knew exactly what I was doing on that occasion. I was fully in control. It had become a bit of a trait of mine to run on to the ball in open spaces. Ray Kennedy said on more than one occasion that if he was ever in doubt, he would just lump the ball into the inside-right or inside-left positions for me to chase. It was an area I used to look to exploit and that night it worked to perfection. I don't know whether people always appreciated the fact that I was quick. Perhaps I was deceptive. But I had a good reputation as a sprinter at school. I knew I could run. So I relished that type of pass from Ray.

'Their player Christian Lopez was out to my left but once I'd shrugged him off I had little in front of me. I remember thinking, "Get the ball under control, don't be too clever and make sure you get your shot on target." If you do that there's always the chance the keeper will dive over it or throw it in. I made good, clean contact with the ball and hit it with reasonable force without going for all-out power. Thankfully it went in and I remember all the other lads piling on top of me, absolutely delighted. And the crowd went wild. It was a great moment for me – the moment of my career that most people recollect.'

Skipper Hughes exclaimed afterwards: 'We have to thank super sub Dave once again. We call him Charlie Chaplin because sometimes we think he wears different boots! He's scored some important goals for us, but none more so than this one.'

A jubilant Paisley declared: 'St Etienne played better than they did on their own ground in the first leg, but Davie has the pace, ability and skill that I was looking for to take the game to the French defenders, who were tiring. There's not another player I would prefer than him in such a situation. I know he doesn't like being called a super sub. But it's as though he was made for the job he did tonight, because we needed to change the pattern and make the French think a bit. I'm always an optimist and I was banking on the fact that Liverpool never give in. It was a game in which you needed heart, guts, stamina and determination. Liverpool players have these in abundance. That's what won us the match.'

But in that moment of elation for Liverpool, there were thoughts, too, for their highly respected opponents who had restored French football's pride. Even though St Etienne were later to be embroiled in corruption and decline, their displays heralded a renaissance for French football at club and international level. The French national side were crowned European champions in 1984 and achieved the ultimate feat of lifting the World Cup as hosts in 1998. And a bond was forged between Liverpool and St Etienne. The Kop, in flattering imitation, gained a new eulogy for their heroes – 'Allez Les Rouges' – while French supporters 'adopted' Liverpool. Indeed, the banners of the Greens were to march with Paisley and his players all the way to glory.

The semi-final draw pitted Liverpool against Swiss champions Zurich, with the other tie pairing Borussia Moenchengladbach with Dynamo Kiev. The draw brought relief and a warning from Paisley, who admitted: 'I'm pleased we haven't been drawn against Kiev. It means we've avoided all the problems of travelling to the Soviet Union. But I saw Zurich play Rangers in the first round and said then they were no easy touches. They've proved it by also knocking out opposition of the stature of Dynamo Dresden. Zurich are a useful side. We'll have to be on our mettle.'

Liverpool were on the threshold of something special, but in an era when the arrival of some managers was heralded by the sound of clanking jewellery as they eagerly stepped in front of the cameras and microphones, Paisley was a man alone, shying away from the media whenever possible. As comedian and lifelong Liverpool fan Jimmy Tarbuck said of him: 'I knew Bob since I was a kid and my pal Bobby Campbell was captain of Liverpool reserves. Phil Taylor was manager then and Bob was the trainer. Despite all his undreamed of success he remained the same Bob Paisley. Not for him the spouting and the shouting after games like so many of these Fancy Dan managers with their bouffant hair dos and gold rings and bracelets. They make me laugh.

'Bob gave his players a rollicking when he felt their performance merited it or when they were beginning to think they were film stars. But, generally, he was just a quiet, modest man who let his team's football do the talking. And, by God, how they talked!

'Paisley also had little time for the jargon of the game. Asked by a newspaper colleague for his definition of a flair player he replied: "It's something on the bottom of his trousers." And one pundit's tactical reference to his players "getting round the back" drew the response from Bob: "What do you think they are . . . burglars?!" '

Paisley's outward calm on match days made an impact on Ray Kennedy, a deep admirer of his fellow son of the North East. 'Most of our talking and preparation for a match is done in training, long before we arrive in the dressing room, so we don't get any complicated team talks from the boss,' said Kennedy. 'In fact, on Saturdays, with the kick-off only an hour or so away, you'll find the boss and Terry McDermott talking about horses, with the winner of the 2.30 at Kempton being the main topic of conversation. Eventually the boss will say: "Now come on, lads, it's time to concentrate on the game. As always, it's important to play as a team and support each other." '

But if the standard of performance was below Paisley's expected level it prompted, in his assistant Joe Fagan's words, 'a quite sharp reminder to the team and any individuals not doing their stuff'. One of Paisley's barbs to errant players was: 'What do you think you're doing out there, selling programmes?' But Fagan stressed: 'Whatever Bob said was always plain, straightforward stuff. He wasn't a flamboyant man. You didn't find Bob joking with the opposition, as Bill Shankly did. The extraordinary thing about him was his ordinariness. There were no gimmicks with Bob.'

Liverpool had no time to dwell on the European draw or the fact that while they were toppling St Etienne, their closest title rivals Ipswich were crashing to a shock 4-0 defeat at West Brom. Next up was a home FA Cup sixth round engagement with Middlesbrough, who paraded in their midfield a certain Graeme Souness. Ian Callaghan and John Toshack were ruled out, to begin a lengthy spell on the sidelines. Callaghan, suffering from a damaged left heel, would return in early May at QPR. But Toshack, whose Anfield career was blighted by a succession of enforced injury absences, missed the rest of the season with his Achilles tendon problem and eventually entered hospital for a summer operation. So the heroic Fairclough and Terry McDermott were drafted into Paisley's starting line-up. McDermott was to stay in the side for the rest of the season, while Fairclough's call-up heralded half a dozen successive starts.

It was the super sub who again came up trumps by breaking the stalemate with a goal ten minutes into the second half, and seven minutes later Keegan clinched Liverpool's second victory over Middlesbrough in eight days to secure a place in another semi-final, in which they were drawn against city rivals Everton. As well as battling against relegation, Gordon Lee's Goodison side were in the midst of a League Cup Final marathon against Aston Villa, which meetings at Wembley and Hillsborough had failed to settle and which was heading for a third meeting at Old Trafford, a game Everton were to lose 3-2 after extra time. The all-Mersey FA Cup semi-final collision would be staged at Maine Road, while Leeds and Manchester United contested the other tie at Hillsborough.

By one of those fixture list ironies, the next game for both Merseyside clubs was the League derby at Goodison, which finished goalless and extended Liverpool's unbeaten run against their oldest foes to 11 matches home and away, in which they had conceded just one goal. But the draw cost Liverpool the First Division leadership to Ipswich, who slammed West Ham 4–1 that same evening to go top on goal difference. Both clubs were on 43 points from 32 games, with Manchester City three points adrift with a game in hand. Paisley, though, was not despondent and dug into his horseracing parlance to announce: 'As long as we keep going, I don't concern myself with other teams. I'm not talking about a treble. If I back three horses, I don't think about a treble unless and until the first two have come in.'

The manager revealed his concern about the next hurdle facing his side, a home League meeting with Leeds United staged on Saturday morning, 2 April, to avoid a clash with that afternoon's Grand National at nearby Aintree. 'This is one of those fixtures that worries me,' he admitted. 'For a start, there is an unreal atmosphere about a morning kick-off. And Leeds are the type of team who can lull you into their own tempo if you give them time to settle down. We mustn't allow that to happen.'

The wisdom behind his apprehension was patently obvious as Leeds, managed by Jimmy Armfield, moved to within sight of half-time without a goal being scored. But with nine first-half minutes remaining, the stage again belonged to Fairclough as he engineered the breakthrough, then scored himself. First he swept past Trevor Cherry, Gordon McQueen and Paul Madeley before the latter's push conceded a penalty dispatched by Phil Neal. And two minutes later, Fairclough stooped to put his head in the path of Jimmy Case's well-struck cross and divert the ball past helpless Dave Stewart. A third Liverpool goal struck by Steve Heighway wrapped up the points for a 3–1 win – Leeds claiming a consolation strike by McQueen – and the performance gave the watching Zurich spies plenty to think about.

A few hours later, the legendary Red Rum won at Aintree and it was the second Grand National day in succession that Fairclough had scored, following his mesmerising winner against Everton the previous year. 'I might enter Davie for the next National because he'd probably win it!' joked Paisley.

Having overcome Leeds, it was back into Euro mode for Liverpool. The following Wednesday they travelled to Zurich for the first leg of the European Cup semi-final. The trip was handled in the usual business-like Anfield manner, with travel, accommodation and training plans made studiously in advance by general secretary Peter Robinson after consultation with Paisley and his staff. Paisley named an unchanged side for a game Liverpool were strong favourites to win. Even Zurich's German manager Friedhlem 'Timo' Konietzka claimed: 'We will work wonders even to draw against Liverpool at home.'

Paisley was having none of it. 'I'm not falling for that,' he responded. 'I'm not being lulled into any kind of complacency. Underdogs can sometimes bite.'

The Swiss side, as expected in their own Letzigrund Stadium crammed with a capacity 30,000 crowd, opened with a determined assault on the visiting defence and quickly drew blood. Within five minutes Tommy Smith was lectured by Turkish referee Anatoli Babacan for a foul on the flying Rene Botteron, around whose swift breaks from midfield much of Zurich's ambitions hinged in the absence of their banned Sicilian striker Franco Cucinotta. Smith was then adjudged to have felled Fredy Scheiwiler to concede a penalty, though he vehemently insisted his tackle had been fair. Ray Clemence was left beating the turf in frustration after getting an unavailing hand to Peter Risi's spot kick, which gave Zurich an early breakthrough. Six minutes later, Smith's challenge on Botteron brought him a booking and Liverpool were looking decidedly rocky.

They were level, however, with the game just 15 minutes old. Phil Neal, taking over Chris Lawler's mantle as the Liverpool full-back with scoring touch, was at the far post to meet Ray Kennedy's free kick from the left and sweep the equaliser past Swiss international goalkeeper Karl Grob. The goal was a triumph for Paisley's tactical planning at Melwood, as revealed up in the stadium radio box by the watching John Toshack, sitting next to me in the commentary position. As the free kick was about to be taken, Toshack said: 'Just watch for Phil Neal coming in at the far post. This is a move we've practised in training.'

How Zurich must have wished for such prior warning, because Liverpool's equaliser turned the game on its head. Nobody was more commanding in a red shirt than Smith, 32 the day before the game and showing great professionalism and composure despite being on a knife edge after his early booking. Smith's display was complete vindication of Paisley's decision to recall him the previous month. It might even have surprised Bill Shankly, as Paisley revealed: 'Just before he retired, Bill thought that Tommy and Ian Callaghan were finished. Fortunately, he was wrong and I got a few more years out of them.'

Liverpool should have taken the lead before the interval. But three minutes into the second half, Terry McDermott and Steve Heighway, an outstanding pair on the night, combined for the explosive Heighway to bewilder Zurich with a run that took him past Jacob Kuhn and Hilmar Zigerlig before he drew Grob and scored with a left-foot shot. Heighway then helped set up a third goal for Liverpool after 67 minutes. A delightful first-time flick by David Fairclough from Jimmy Case's long through ball looped up into Heighway's path. All defender Max Heer could do to stop him was to send him plunging to the turf. Penalty specialist Neal beat Grob from the spot to give Liverpool a 3-1 win and one foot in the European Cup Final.

It was further emphatic evidence of Liverpool's supreme confidence and motivation, qualities that Heighway believed were self-generated. 'We were driven from within,' he said. 'There was a wide range of personalities amongst the players in the squad, but a tremendous camaraderie and a feeling that we couldn't be beaten.'

'I think we must have a chance now,' said Paisley, master of the understatement, as he and the Liverpool party flew home from Zurich. 'A few of our players found themselves struggling for breath during the game because of the altitude. But once we solved one or two problems, we settled down to a nice rhythm. Zurich have one or two good players and Botteron troubled us at times. Once we got that sorted out, I was confident we'd give a good performance.'

The Zurich match was a notable milestone in the career of a young player who would go on to become an acclaimed midfielder for Liverpool and England. Sammy Lee, 18 two months earlier, was named by Paisley as one of the five substitutes, joining David Johnson, Brian Kettle, Alan Waddle and Peter McDonnell on the bench. Liverpool-born Lee filled only a spectator's role in Switzerland, just as he had done in his only previous stint on the bench in the home League game with Derby earlier that season. But it was significant progress for the chunky 5ft 4in youngster, who compensated in tenacity and effort for what he lacked in height. He was a player after Paisley's heart, embodying his own exemplary qualities on the field, and Lee went on to earn a fulsome salute from his manager. 'If Sammy was a little taller they'd make him Lord Mayor,' Paisley enthused.

While Liverpool were moving closer towards landing a fabled treble, the speculation over Kevin Keegan's future was bubbling. Every week the media claimed a new twist in the saga, ignited by the player's insistence that he was standing by his pre-season announcement that he would be moving abroad at the end of the 1976-77 campaign. Madrid, Munich and Barcelona were among a welter of predicted destinations and Paisley accepted the inevitability of Keegan's departure. The manager had no choice. He was well aware that determination, single-mindedness and a strong stubborn streak were bedrocks of Keegan's character. But he was unhappy about the impending exit, and not only because Liverpool would be losing an extraordinary talent. He also felt it was a gamble that could rebound on Keegan.

'Kevin is a determined boy with his head screwed on,' Paisley conceded. 'But you wonder what he is planning to do with his career. You point out the difficulties there can be for stars in Europe. Kevin knows that at Liverpool we have a system which makes it virtually impossible for one particular player to struggle with his form for any length of time. If someone is suffering there are people around him who will draw the fire and take up the pressure. One of the things I keep reminding the players is that when you're in a fog, you must stick together. Then you don't get lost. If there's a secret about Liverpool, that's it. But I have pointed out to Kevin that top football in Europe can be a very lonely place and the pitch can be the loneliest place of all. We do not encourage loneliness at Anfield. It just doesn't work. As I keep saying, it's communism with a small 'c' here.

'Kevin is motivated by a remarkable determination. He'll take on noted players head-on to prove he is better than them. In fact, he could destroy them by keeping his balance. But he's so combative. I'm sure that one of the reasons for his desire to move abroad is to prove something to himself, as well as other people.'

Keegan, who lived with his wife Jean, and their Old English Sheepdogs and horses in a retreat on top of a hill near Mold, North Wales, admitted that he would be leaving an ideal football home at Anfield.

'I know that in a thousand years I might not find a situation so perfect for me as this one,' he said. 'Our system at Liverpool, our willingness to work for each other, is astonishing, and probably I'll never have a set-up to suit my game so completely as this one. I am thinking about it constantly. I know Liverpool could win the treble and I could sign a new long-term contract to make life lovely and very uncomplicated. But I believe it is at such a stage that anyone in sport, or life generally, can lose something inside. I've made my mind up as a footballer and a man. By moving abroad I'll be taking on a new challenge and opening up a new chapter. It will refresh and stimulate me. It could also herald something new and stimulating for Liverpool.' How accurate Keegan's last sentiment would prove to be. Reflecting on it some 20 years later, his deep respect and admiration for Paisley shone through.

'Somebody else might have followed Shanks and wanted to make drastic changes. But Bob let the ship sail on, making adjustments as he went along. He was a much cleverer man than people thought. He wasn't as eloquent as others but he had his own terrific sense of humour and a million sayings. He once said of Tony Currie, for instance: "He hits a far-flung one" which meant he hit a good long ball! His use of the word "doins" earned him the nickname "Duggie Doins" and Terry McDermott actually did a "Duggie Doins Dance". He was also nicknamed "The Rat" but this was totally misconstrued. It was because he'd fought in the war as a Desert Rat, which also prompted yet another nickname of "The Gunner".

'But Bob could be hard when he had to be. He wasn't exactly Shanks's hatchet man, but when it came to people being dropped when Shanks was in charge, it was Bob who would speak to the players. He also spoke to the players at their worst time, when they were injured and ruled out. He earned the total respect of all of us.'

Backroom man Tom Saunders, later elected to the Liverpool board after being appointed Liverpool's youth development officer by Shankly, following spells managing England's youth and schoolboy teams, said of Paisley: 'As a former headmaster, I thought I was pretty hot at weighing up people and situations. But you have to be quick and alert to keep up with this fellow! I've watched many matches with him not involving Liverpool and very little escapes him. When a goal's scored he'll have the complete move analysed in a flash and he'll often emphasise the contribution of players running off the ball who were not directly involved. You might not even have been fully aware of them yourself.

'Every scrap of information is stored in his memory. He astounds me by recalling detailed incidents of matches we saw a long time ago. He's not given to idle chatter, and after we've watched a match together, often he'll hardly say a word for long periods on the journey home. That's probably when he's concentrating and reflecting on what he's seen at the game, which he can instantly recall.'

The return from Zurich saw Keegan embark on an important scoring run of five goals in eight games. He was on target when an unchanged side scored a crucial 2–1 home win over rivals Manchester City at Anfield – Heighway was the other scorer – before the same team played out a goalless draw at Stoke. The following Saturday, Liverpool shot back to the top of the First Division and dispelled their home jinx against Arsenal, who had been unbeaten at Anfield since November 1971 and had plundered seven points from their previous four visits. David Johnson, sent on by Paisley as a substitute for Fairclough at Stoke, started against Arsenal – and Paisley admitted his relief that Alan Ball had departed the London club.

Ball had been a thorn in Liverpool's side since his early days at Blackpool and through his memorable period at Everton, when his goal on a wind-tossed Saturday night at Goodison in March 1967 sent the Anfield club plunging out of the FA Cup. His penchant for sabotaging Liverpool continued during his time at Highbury. It was the perfect, prolonged riposte by the dynamic red-head to one of the classic Bill Shankly jibes. Ball, one of Sir Alf Ramsey's World Cup winners, was telephoned by Shankly following his record-breaking £110,000 move to Goodison shortly after the glorious 1966 Wembley conquest of West Germany.

'Congratulations, son,' said Shankly, 'you'll be playing *near* a great team.'

But Shankly never disguised his admiration of Ball's talents and his Anfield successor Paisley was no less aware of his ability, admitting: 'I'm glad he's gone to Southampton and that we don't have to face him in the Arsenal team. Bally has been one of the chief reasons for Arsenal's results at Anfield in the past few seasons. He has the ability to get the best out of his team-mates and make them play. His influence is a great one. I know when we've got a competitor playing against us, and he's one of them.'

Whether Ball's absence was significant or not, Liverpool won 2–0 with goals from Neal and Keegan in a contest they dominated, forcing 18 corners. With Ipswich losing at Leeds, it meant that Liverpool were now a point ahead of them at the top with a game in hand, and two ahead of third-placed Manchester City, who had also played 36 matches.

It sent Paisley and his players bouncing into the European Cup return with Zurich the following Wednesday. The Swiss side's top scorer Cucinotta returned to action after suspension but prefaced Zurich's mission by announcing: 'We have come to our own funeral. We have no chance. It was good to get this far and meet a team like Liverpool. But now it is all over for us.' An honest appraisal by the Italian striker or a desperate psychological ploy? It mattered not. Paisley's unchanged side, armed with a 3–1 first-leg lead, cantered to a 3–0 victory on the night and a 6–1 aggregate triumph, the biggest semi-final victory by any team since Zurich had been overwhelmed 8–1 by Real Madrid in 1964. Jimmy Case, whose spectacular display of fierce shooting power had gone unrewarded against Arsenal, struck twice with a goal in each half, while Keegan completed the demolition job ten minutes from the end.

Paisley also had praise for Steve Heighway, now an established Republic of Ireland international and a highly impressive front-running performer for Liverpool. 'There's no doubt that Steve is having his best season since his first one here when he burst on to the scene after university and caught opponents unawares,' he said. 'He joined professional football later than most and he just went out and took players on, oblivious to who they were. At one time he would race to take up a position, particularly a defensive one, but now he'll walk into it. He's showing maturity and a broader knowledge of the game. This has also helped his stamina.'

Liverpool's elimination of Zurich made them only the third English club to reach the European Cup Final, following Manchester United, led by Paisley's long-time friend Sir Matt Busby, who beat Benfica at Wembley in 1968, and Leeds United, who had lost to Bayern Munich in Paris in 1975. But for Liverpool and Paisley, instead of contemplating throwing three coins in the fountain and wishing for success against Borussia Moenchengladbach in Rome, it was back to the grinding schedule of pursuing a treble.

'To be honest, the games against St Etienne felt more like a semi-final than the Zurich matches,' Paisley admitted. 'But we're in the final and no Liverpool team has been there before. I consider that an honour in itself, but we've a lot of work to do before that.'

Keegan observed: 'It's a great feeling to reach the European Cup Final but our celebrations will be quiet and brief. We've got to get ready for Saturday's FA Cup semi-final against Everton and then the remaining championship games.' He was right. Everton would test them all the way.

Paisley's counterpart Gordon Lee had left Newcastle to succeed Billy Bingham at relegation-threatened Everton earlier that year. He was a man who wore his feelings on his sleeve; a straight shooter who was disarming in his black and white views which allowed few shades of grey. Lee left you in no doubt that Paisley was a man he deeply admired. During one press conference at Everton's training ground, he told the assembled media representatives in his distinctive Black Country tones: 'Listen, scribes, I've written an article saying Bob should be England manager. I've sent him a copy.' Paisley duly confirmed the fact and opened his Anfield office drawer to produce the publication carrying Lee's salute – the house magazine of the National Coal Board! Obscure it might have been, but no less sincere on Lee's part.

He was not the only person to suggest that Paisley's knowledge and wisdom was worthy of the international stage. But the man himself was less than eager to fuel such talk in a conversation with Bob Azurdia of BBC Radio Merseyside:

Azurdia: Bob, as the most successful manager in Britain, why have you never been asked to manage England?

Paisley: Well, I've got my own problems at Liverpool without being saddled with England's. There's no way of telling if I could do the England job.

Azurdia: No, but there was no way of telling whether you could do the Liverpool job and you certainly could! The odds

Paisley: Not really, not really. In younger days, maybe. But it just doesn't cross my mind. If I had gone to England, I'd have gone on the same tack as I have at Liverpool, knowing the players and balancing the team's strengths and weaknesses.

are you would have been able to do the England job. Wouldn't you have liked to have a crack?

If Lee admired Paisley, his feelings towards one of his own players, Duncan McKenzie, could not have been more different. McKenzie was a member of the squad Lee had inherited from Bingham and he was one of that breed of forwards called either a crowd pleaser or a clown, depending on your point of view. He did not please Lee, who once said: 'Duncan's a nice type of lad, someone you'd like to have living next door to you. But he's not the kind of player I'd go out and sign for my team.' Lee even refused to recognise the winning goal McKenzie scored in the FA Cup fifth-round tie at Cardiff en route to the semi-final, because of what he claimed was the striker's over-elaboration before putting the ball in the net. 'I don't count it,' he said bluntly, underlining that his football appreciation was more artisan than artist.

It was supremely ironic, therefore, that McKenzie gave one of his most influential Everton displays in the semi-final against Liverpool at Maine Road, the venue where Paisley had scored against the same opponents in the 1950 semi-final which Liverpool won 2–0. McKenzie, who might not have been selected at all but for Bob Latchford's absence with ankle damage, was involved in the move which Everton and their supporters were convinced had crowned a stirring fightback and taken their team into the final after a game draped in drama from beginning to end.

David Johnson has an intriguing memory of that semi-final, although it was an agonising experience at the time. 'We stayed overnight at the Lord Daresbury Hotel between Liverpool and Manchester and I was rooming with Kevin Keegan,' he recalled. 'You can imagine how much it meant to me to play in a semi-final for Liverpool against my first club, Everton. I couldn't wait. It was so exciting.

'At a quarter to eleven on the Saturday, Kevin and I were going down for our meal when Bob came towards us along the corridor. "Good morning, boss," said Kevin. "Morning, son," said Bob. Then he turned to me, said, "You'll be sub," and carried on walking.

'He didn't say any more. I was gobsmacked, riveted to the spot. I was so disappointed. But that was Bob, and I have to say that there were times as a player when you really didn't like him. But that was only because you never knew if you were going to play or not. He could change a successful side and rotate players around. You might even find yourself dropped when you'd been playing well. On those occasions you didn't like Bob. But you always respected him and he took the pressure off us. In that season of 1976-77 when we were going for a treble, we never talked about it. We were always told we'd won nothing yet. He was a fantastic manager and in the modern era Sir Alex Ferguson is the man who comes closest to him.'

When the semi-final action began, Fairclough, swapping places with Johnson, set off on an electrifying early run down the right flank. He cut in but as he was about to unleash his shot, the ball stuck in the mud, forcing him to miskick.

'I thought I was home and dry,' was how Fairclough bemoaned his fate on the rain-sodden pitch, with no irony intended.

Terry McDermott did break the deadlock, quite brilliantly, with only 11 minutes on the clock. Collecting a Keegan pass on the edge of the box, he 'lost' his marker and midfield rival Mick Buckley with a superb feint and, after a brief glance ahead of him, delivered a magnificent chipped shot over the stranded Everton keeper David Lawson. It was an exquisite goal in any game but especially so in the frantic, frenetic atmosphere of an all-Merseyside FA Cup semi-final. But Everton fought back and McKenzie, whose talent rose above the quagmire conditions, equalised in the 34th minute after Emlyn Hughes had slipped when attempting to prevent Jim Pearson's cross.

Liverpool regained the lead in the 73rd minute when Jimmy Case's header punished Lawson's failure to gather a free kick. Still Everton were not finished. McKenzie set up the opportunity for Bruce Rioch to fire them level a second time with only seven minutes left. But the next 90 seconds or so will be recalled by those who were present – and related in derby legend to those who were not – as long as Liverpool and Everton meet.

Everton winger Ronnie Goodlass crossed from the left and McKenzie helped the ball on for Bryan Hamilton, who had replaced Martin Dobson two minutes earlier, to control and fire past Ray Clemence. Bedlam broke out. Everton players went wild with delight and their fans were ecstatic, while Clemence's agonised prone position in the goalmouth told its own story of

Liverpool's utter dejection. But suddenly, emotions in the 52,000 crowd did a crazy somersault as referee Clive Thomas signalled a free kick to Liverpool. He had disallowed Hamilton's strike, although he took a while to explain exactly why. His only comment to the media before leaving Maine Road was, 'An infringement occurred.' The following day the Treorchy official put some flesh on the bone of his decision by telling the *Daily Express*: 'There was never any doubt in my mind that Bryan Hamilton was offside, and I'm delighted that the cameras proved me right.'

Years later, Thomas enlarged on that in his autobiography *By the Book*, in which he wrote: 'I was satisfied looking at Hamilton when the ball was passed to him that he was offside. I blew accordingly but the Everton players had drowned Hamilton in their celebration and, even more unfortunately, linesman Colin Seel was on his way back to the halfway line, also satisfied with the goal. I am also convinced that Bryan Hamilton handled the ball, too. If I had not blown for the offside, you Everton fans, I would still have disallowed the "goal" for handball.'

To this day the incident still burns in Everton hearts as one of the great derby injustices and for Hamilton it was a case of Thomas lightning uncannily striking twice.

'It's fair to say that Mr Thomas is not my favourite person,' said Hamilton. 'He also controversially disallowed another "goal" of mine in another FA Cup semi-final two years earlier, when I was playing for Ipswich against West Ham. We drew 0–0 and lost the replay! At Maine Road I don't think there was any doubt in anyone's mind except the referee's that I had scored a perfectly good goal. I wasn't offside and I certainly didn't handle the ball – it caught me on the hip bone.'

The replay meant another game added to Liverpool's demanding programme, but they were grateful for the chance. However, if Liverpool had fortune and Clive Thomas to thank for their escape, the Everton display held no surprises for Paisley. He had winced in the days before the game when the pundits virtually dismissed the Goodison side's chances, and he said after the 2–2 draw: 'Everton might have surprised our players but they didn't surprise me. Nothing is easy in football. Everton were bound to fight hard because everyone was making them the underdogs. That can motivate teams.'

Paisley was acutely aware of the psychological impact public statements could have on opponents, both negatively and positively. He would often laud opposition teams and players to the skies, or in his words, 'give them a bit of toffee' in the hope that they would come unstuck trying to live up to his praise. Conversely, he knew that criticism could inspire players to prove themselves. So he certainly did not relish John Toshack's remarks as the clubs prepared to renew battle in the following Wednesday's replay back at Maine Road. The injured striker, who had observed the first game from the sidelines, commented: 'Henry Cooper had Ali down for eight but he couldn't finish him off. Everton have just had the same experience. They won't get a second chance.'

They were brave words – or foolish ones – before any derby duel, but as it transpired, in this case utterly accurate. Liverpool, with David Johnson replacing the injured Heighway, broke through on the half hour after another crucial decision from Mr Thomas, who judged that Mike Pejie had pushed Johnson and awarded a penalty. Phil Neal duly sent his spot kick past David Lawson. Thomas rejected two more penalty appeals – by Everton when they claimed Clemence had caught McKenzie with his foot, and by Liverpool when Mick Buckley appeared to handle.

Everton, still without the injured Latchford and with Andy King as substitute to allow Hamilton to travel with Northern Ireland to West Germany, pegged Liverpool to a single-goal lead with only four minutes left. But late strikes from Jimmy Case and Ray Kennedy applied an emphatic gloss to the scoreline as Liverpool emerged worthy 3-0 winners to book a Wembley date with Manchester United, who had beaten Leeds 2-1 at the first attempt in the other semi-final.

Liverpool, watched by Udo Lattek, manager of their European Cup Final opponents Borussia Moenchengladbach, had moved into a position no English club in history had so far occupied, as finalists in both the FA and European Cups and leaders and favourites for the League championship.

'The only games we can afford to lose now are in the Central League, because our reserves have already won that!' Paisley quipped, adding more seriously, 'We've got eight games left and at this moment they're all cup finals. And as far as injuries are concerned, we're down to the bare boards. I made Ian Callaghan substitute in the replay more for psychological reasons than anything else, because he's still not fully fit. We can't afford to lose any more players.'

It may sound trite and impractical in a fast-flowing physical game, but Paisley advised his players on minimizing the chance of injury, especially his forwards. For a man whose own commitment in the tackle as a player was total, it was ironic that he told the attack members of his squad not to take big risks by making foolish challenges. Paisley and his squad were aware that their next engagement would be one of the toughest and most critical of the entire season. But they never visualised just how bruising the home duel with championship rivals Ipswich would be, nor that the events and atmosphere would prompt Paisley to declare Anfield close to a riot.

Ipswich arrived in third place with 49 points from 38 games. Manchester City were second with 50 points from 37 matches, and Liverpool top, having amassed 50 points from 36 games. The game was only three minutes old when Ipswich striker Paul Mariner clashed with Tommy Smith, the forerunner of further hostilities between them in a remarkable game. Although referee Peter Willis spoke to the feuding pair, neither was among five bookings by the official, who was a police road safety officer in Paisley's native County Durham.

Liverpool's supporters were incensed. One furious fan ran on to the pitch and reached the referee to offer him a pair of spectacles before being bundled away. Then Willis stopped the game after objects were hurled on to the pitch. A public address appeal urged fans to stop the barrage into the Kop goalmouth. But the crowd's mood was back to boiling point in first-half injury time when Willis booked substitute David Fairclough for entering the field without permission to replace Steve Heighway, who had prematurely departed on a stretcher after a challenge by Mick Mills in which the Irish star sustained an ugly gash that required six stitches above his right eye. Jimmy Case and Brian Talbot were the first to be cautioned for a touchline flare-up before Kevin Keegan was shown the yellow card for encroaching at a free kick. Johnson was also booked, his offence being dissent at Ray Clemence's booking for taking too many steps!

The brighter moments of a powder-keg contest were reserved for the final stages. With 20 minutes left, Smith and Case combined for Ray Kennedy to shoot Liverpool in front and four minutes later Keegan met Johnson's cross at the far post to head a superb second. John Wark, later to join Liverpool, replied with an 85th-minute penalty. But Liverpool's 2–1 win as Manchester City were crashing 4–0 at Derby was a watershed result and the kiss of death for Ipswich's title aspirations.

Their manager Bobby Robson conceded: 'I've got a broken heart. We're right out of the championship now. Liverpool want smacking if they don't win it.'

But his fellow North Easterner Paisley, while delighted at the result, was concerned at the frenzied atmosphere in which the contest had been staged. 'That was the closest Anfield has been to a riot, the worst I've ever seen at this ground,' he said. 'The referee spoiled what was going to be a great game through being nervous. You know for a start you're not going to have a cricket match atmosphere for a game of this importance, but some of his decisions incited the crowd. Kevin was booked for not being ten yards from a free kick. But if he was nine or nine-and-a-half yards away, you don't stop a game of such tension for something like that. And when Steve Heighway was stretchered off, the referee knew we were going to put our sub on. If there's anyone to blame, it's us for sending Davie Fairclough on. It wasn't his fault. Davie's booking certainly shouldn't be allowed to stand.'

Paisley added: 'I would like to see a referee and two linesmen kept together as a team for matches right through the season. Working as a unit would help create better understanding and liaison. Points could be awarded for their performances, with the best three-man teams handling the big games. We've seen from our games in Europe how impressive officials working in harness and with good communication can be.'

Willis revealed after that tempestuous Anfield contest that a broken bottle had been found in the goalmouth – which he reported to the FA – and that he had appealed to both teams to cool down and act responsibly. 'Obviously there was tension,' he said. 'I told the two captains that players were starting to do things without thinking. I asked them to give more thought to their actions.' Willis, a widely respected official who handled many major matches and was later appointed a Football League Referee Assessor, became the first referee ever to dismiss a player in an FA Cup Final when he sent off Manchester United's Kevin Moran in 1985 against Everton. But United went on to win 1-0 through an extra-time Norman Whiteside goal, which prevented Everton completing a treble following their success in landing the championship and European Cup-Winners' Cup.

Liverpool's amazing hunt for three trophies made Paisley a magnet for all branches of the media. But as Jessie Paisley emphasised, it was the part of the role of manager he found least attractive. She recalled: 'Dealing with the press was the worst aspect of the job for Bob. He'd been thrown into it and he wasn't good at it. He said it was a much more onerous task than looking after the team, which is why he didn't do a lot of television interviews.' Reading the newspaper sports pages was not an easy experience for Paisley, either. 'Things you say can get totally the wrong meaning in print,' he said. 'It's so different in black and white.'

Victory over Ipswich firmly installed Liverpool in the championship driving seat, with 52 points from 37 games and a goal difference of 29, the best in the First Division. Manchester City were two points behind having played a game more, while Ipswich, in third place, were on 49 points from 39 games. By now even the cautious Paisley warmed to the prospect of the title coming to Anfield as he prepared his players for their next challenge, a home collision with Manchester United in what was a League rehearsal of the FA Cup Final looming on 21 May.

'We are in the favourites' position for the championship on points, games and goal difference, and if we can beat United to collect another two points it will really put the pressure on,' he declared. Then, with typical understatement, he added: 'We're not in a bad position but we've got to soldier on. This game will be a cup final for us but it won't be for United, who are out of the running in the League. That's why I don't think there'll be any psychological advantage for Wembley for either side. United will be relaxed and this is the type of game you can slip up in if you're not careful.'

The game was one of the most placid and uneventful in the long series between the fierce rivals, a contest strangely lacking passion and fire. Paisley provided an apt summing up when he said: 'We wanted to get at it but there was nothing to get at. United were never going to make it teethy. They took it easy and our lads had too much space and time.' Keegan's 17th-minute headed goal was sufficient to earn the points for a Liverpool side which had Fairclough taking over from Heighway and Alan Waddle having a rare stint on the bench as an unused substitute. Waddle made only 22 first-team appearances in his Anfield career, but his single goal to give Liverpool victory at Everton in December 1973 assures him of a niche in history.

'It's amazing,' said Waddle, 'that even now, more than a quarter of a century later, people still talk about that goal. I only scored one for Liverpool but it's nice to know that people remember it!'

Liverpool were now four points clear, and captain Emlyn Hughes said: 'We're getting nearer to the title. Four points from our last four games will do us.' But Hughes and Liverpool did come out second best on the night in one respect. Lou Macari, acting United skipper in the absence of the injured Martin Buchan, won the toss for Tommy Docherty's team to wear their familiar red at Wembley, where, Paisley and Docherty both insisted, the meeting of their clubs would be a totally different encounter.

'I think it could be one of the best finals in a long time,' said Paisley, while Docherty pledged: 'You will see a different Manchester United at Wembley than you saw tonight.'

A 1–1 draw at Queens Park Rangers, thanks to a Jimmy Case goal, kept Liverpool on course for the title in a game that was significant for the return of Ian Callaghan after a seven-week absence. The 35-year-old midfielder eased back into senior action as a 61st-minute substitute for David Fairclough and stayed on the bench for the goalless midweek draw at Coventry, which saw Heighway's comeback. For Callaghan it was to set up a bitter-sweet climax to the most remarkable season in his Liverpool career, which stretched back to before Shankly's arrival in 1959. He would also figure in a tactical FA Cup Final jigsaw which Paisley, showing characteristic frankness and honesty, admitted he got wrong.

There was nothing wrong with the outcome of Liverpool's next outing, despite the fact that it proved to be a goalless home stalemate with relegation-battling West Ham. It secured the club's record tenth championship, with Paisley involved in six in his varying roles as player, coach and manager, one more than Sir Matt Busby had won managing Manchester United. Liverpool became the first club since Wolves in 1959 to retain the title, and this was the 4-3-3 line-up Paisley paraded for his club's coronation as champions: Ray Clemence; Phil Neal, Tommy Smith, Emlyn Hughes, Joey Jones; Jimmy Case, Terry McDermott, Ray Kennedy; Kevin Keegan, David Johnson (substitute David Fairclough, 70), Steve Heighway.

The game was Kevin Keegan's farewell to the Kop prior to his move abroad, although for which destination was still to be determined. It was also set to be a parting shot for Tommy Smith prior to his end-of-season testimonial, although the Anfield Iron subsequently reconsidered his future. Callaghan was also in action, by request, in a Central League match at Burnley, while the first team were securing him his fifth championship medal as a player, equalling the record at that time set before the Second World War by Arsenal's Cliff Bastin.

'After being out of the team for the longest period since my cartilage operation in 1970, the more games I can get in the better, because there is tremendous competition for places,' Callaghan explained. 'It will be a bit strange not being at Anfield on the big day, but I feel another reserve game will benefit me.'

A 55,000-plus crowd acclaimed Liverpool as champions, although Paisley reflected: 'I've never known a team win the championship amid such relatively quiet and unemotional scenes. It was quite unlike last year when we won it at Wolves and the fans were singing and dancing in the middle of a motorway during a traffic jam on the M6! This time it was almost as though the supporters had taken a title triumph for granted and they were almost preoccupied with the FA Cup Final coming up. Even in our dressing room there was no champagne. Everyone sensed, without saying anything, that winning the title was just the first round of a three-round contest. That really puts into perspective the position we've reached.

'But that must not take anything away from the players for retaining the title. They've deserved it for the football they've played. We lost key players like Phil Thompson, John Toshack and Ian Callaghan for long periods. Yet it's a tribute to the squad that they overcame setbacks and got on with the job.'

It was a reflection, too, of the qualities of leadership Paisley had shown. To use his own parlance, he had generally kept reins tight as treble talk heightened, but now his team were galloping into the finishing straight with two games to shape their destiny – at Wembley the following Saturday and in Rome four days later.

Keegan, presented with a heady climax to his Liverpool career, examined the qualities of the two Anfield managers he had served. 'Shankly the greater motivator, Paisley the better tactician – I think that's fair comment,' he said.

In the aftermath of the title win, Paisley confided: 'One of the reasons I never got involved in talk of the treble was because I just didn't think it was on. But winning the championship means that the impossible now seems a faint possibility. It's still a tall order, though.'

But a Football Association announcement infuriated Paisley and, by his own admission, affected him so deeply that it influenced his Wembley team selection and, he believed, cost Liverpool the treble.

The FA lobbed the equivalent of a Molotov cocktail into the Wembley build-up by announcing that if the Cup Final was drawn the reply would be staged on Monday 27 June – after the first cricket Test against Australia, halfway through Wimbledon fortnight and five days before the Tour de France! The FA claimed: 'With Liverpool's European Cup Final on 25 May followed by the home internationals and then tours of South America by England and Scotland, plus important meetings, we could not find an earlier replay date. This is an exceptional year.'

An incensed Paisley stormed: 'I'll tell you the score now – 6–0 for somebody! I'm not intellectual enough to find words to express my disgust at this stupidity. It's cruelty. The FA are taking blood from the fans and the players, though obviously we in football don't matter to them. They don't think we're human. It's ridiculous and I don't think an ounce of thought has gone into it. Not many of the people who've come up with this can have kicked a ball in their lives. The final should be finished there and then, with either extra time or penalties or both. But it should be a one-off thing. Let's get it over with.'

Anfield general secretary Peter Robinson revealed that Liverpool had suggested reaching a decider on the day, with the alternative of a replay during the home internationals, adding: 'We are astonished and almost speechless at this decision.'

Manchester United boss Docherty also attacked the FA decision. 'We'll have to take our holidays on the Costa del Stretford,' he quipped. 'If there is to be a replay, why not have us back at Wembley the following week? After all, the home internationals are a bit of a joke, really.

'If they insist on leaving things so late, why not let Liverpool and us return to Wembley on Charity Shield day, 14 August, and we could play each other for both trophies. I suppose the FA think that 27 June is something of a bonus for the players. They can win the Cup and then go to Wimbledon for the tennis!'

With the FA announcement gnawing away at Paisley, his newly confirmed champions completed their League programme five days before Wembley, at relegation-fighting Bristol City on the Monday night. It was Liverpool's 60th game of a momentous season and the first one in which, for them, the pressure was off. Paisley gave Callaghan 90 minutes of senior action in place of Keegan and handed defender Alec Lindsay his only League outing of the season in place of Joey Jones, who was one booking away from a suspension.

Paisley, who also drafted in Fairclough and rested Heighway, explained: 'No player wants to get injured five days before a Cup Final, yet ironically it's when they try to keep out of trouble that they're at their most vulnerable. Loss of concentration is the reason for most injuries, not for the player who makes the mistake but for the one put in trouble by a lackadaisical pass.

'We were already without John Toshack and Phil Thompson while Cally was only just coming back. So we couldn't afford any more injuries. I left out Kevin for two reasons. He had a slight groin strain, which I didn't want him to aggravate, and it would also give him a break at a time when he was charging around everywhere with his commercial activities and his forthcoming move abroad.'

David Johnson put Liverpool ahead on the half hour in front of a bumper Ashton Gate crowd of more that 38,000, but two goals from Chris Garland gave the home team a 2-1 win in their penultimate game to bolster their eventually successful battle against the drop.

'The important thing is that we came through with no new injuries and when we returned from Bristol we kept the routine as normal as possible,' Paisley recalled. 'The players were given their usual post-match day off, but I didn't impose any curfews. At a time like that you expect players in their position to have self-control, and, in any case we have always believed at Liverpool in treating our players like men. It was business as usual on Wednesday and Thursday, training at Melwood in the mornings. But on Thursday afternoon we set off for an historic week when we left Lime Street Station by train for London.'

And as the Anfield squad, a 14-man party including cover defender Alec Lindsay, travelled to Liverpool's base at Sopwell House Hotel in the Hertfordshire countryside near St Albans, Paisley kept a massive secret. He had already decided on his Wembley line-up, a decision he later admitted was hugely influenced by the late June replay date which haunted his subconscious. But he decided not to reveal his selection until the day before the game.

'There was nothing to be gained by announcing it before the

Friday,' he later recalled. 'The days of announcing your Cup Final side at the beginning of the week are long gone. You have to try to keep your entire squad on their toes for as long as possible. Those who are left out can lose their self-discipline and start to take it easy. You find that players in a similar boat tend to pair off together and lead each other into trouble. You can't afford that, in case you have a last-minute training injury or accident and you have to call on one of those players whose attitude is all wrong.'

Paisley had to decide on both formation and personnel for Wembley. Despite being stripped of Toshack and Thompson, the return to fitness of Ian Callaghan left him grappling with several options. He knew that two players with hopes of being in the team were going to be bitterly disappointed; one of them would not even make the bench, because it was still the era of single substitutes in domestic competitions.

'Breaking the news to the players I'd left out was a moment I dreaded,' Paisley admitted. 'I knew from bitter experience just what it was like because I'd been dropped from our 1950 FA Cup Final team against Arsenal after scoring in our semi-final win over Everton. I felt numb when I found out. I coulsn't even look at our manager George Kay, even though it was the directors who picked the team, not him! I'm sure George got no pleasure from the situation, either. So when I said I understood how players felt I really did. I was not cold blooded and unfeeling about it. I'd been through it myself and it was horrible.

Picking the 1977 Cup Final team I was concerned in my mind with three players but I had about five permutations. It was a case of choosing what I thought were the best men for the game. On the Friday morning we trained at Arsenal's training ground, near to our hotel, before I broke the news to the players then announced the team to the press.'

This was Paisley's Wembley line-up in 4-3-3 formation: Ray Clemence; Phil Neal, Tommy Smith, Emlyn Hughes (captain), Joey Jones; Jimmy Case, Terry McDermott, Ray Kennedy; Kevin Keegan, David Johnson, Steve Heighway. Substitute: Ian Callaghan.

An age gap of fifteen years separated Callaghan and 20-year-old David Fairclough, but they shared the heartbreak of missing out on a Cup Final place. 'I've got to accept it but there's no consolation for being the odd one out at Wembley,' said Fairclough. 'It's deeply disappointing. The same thing happened to me at school. I was the youngest player in the side when we reached a cup final. The teacher told me to stand down to allow a lad who was leaving school to play in the match. He said I had plenty of time. But it was three years before we reached another final.'

Callaghan, consigned to the bench in his fourth FA Cup Final, said: 'I'm disappointed, obviously. But I'm trying hard not to feel too upset. The manager's got a difficult job.'

In contrast, David Johnson, whose two previous Wembley appearances with England had brought him three goals against Wales and Scotland in 1975, was beaming. 'I'm well pleased,' he declared. 'That's the understatement of the year! It's been a worrying time for three of us. Although I'm delighted to be picked, I feel sorry for Davie and Cally.'

But it was a decision Paisley later admitted he regretted. 'The announcement of that ridiculous June replay date got to me,' he said candidly. 'It drastically altered my entire attitude to the game because it made it a win-or-bust affair. That, in turn, drastically affected my team selection. It made me opt for a more adventurous three-man attack instead of a four-man midfield, which I knew was our best formation. There was no way we could be involved in a replay in late June. It would have meant keeping players in training through the summer and robbing them of a break. We were due to start pre-season training on 12 July, anyway! The whole situation was outrageous.

'When we arrived at Wembley and got into our dressing room, the theme of my pre-match talk was about us rather than Manchester United. As we were playing three front runners, I had to make slight adjustments. I also mentioned set pieces, both ours and United's. I told the players it was important for us to impose our pattern on the game. In the tunnel before we walked out on to the pitch, I shook hands with Tommy Docherty and said I hoped it would be a good game. I didn't wish him good luck. That would have been hypocritical.

'Leading out a team at Wembley is the most pleasing and proud thing you can do, a career highlight many managers would give their right arm for. But as you walk out, your mind is in turmoil. You're playing the game yourself. You're anticipating moves and destroying them. That was so much the case in 1977 that I didn't even wave to my wife and family in the stadium! My mind was so full of the match to come.'

United's 4-4-2 line up was: Alex Stepney; Jimmy Nicholl, Brian Greenhoff, Martin Buchan (captain), Arthur Albiston; Steve

Coppell, Sammy McIlroy, Lou Macari, Gordon Hill, Jimmy Greenhoff, Stuart Pearson. Substitute: David McCreery.

If fate frowned on Liverpool's superiority in the first half – when Ray Kennedy's header from a Jimmy Case cross smashed against Stepney's right-hand post – it snarled at them after the interval. Pearson drove United into the lead in the 50th minute only for man-of-the match Case to strike a superb half-volleyed equaliser two minutes later. Then, completing a scoring burst of three goals in five minutes, came one for which no team can, or ever will, be able to legislate. It not only shattered Liverpool's dream of an unprecedented treble, it also prevented them becoming only the third team at that stage of the 20th century to capture the League championship and FA Cup double. After a tussle between Tommy Smith and Jimmy Greenhoff, the ball fell to Macari, whose shot appeared to be going wide until it cannoned off Greenhoff's chest and diverted into the net, with Clemence committed and helpless.

Paisley sent on Callaghan as a 63rd-minute substitute for Johnson as Liverpool mounted a determined rally, with United sending on McCreery in place of Hill to bolster their ranks. Kennedy went close to equalising but not close enough and for all Liverpool's toil and effort in the cauldron of Wembley, their FA Cup dream died. When referee Bob Matthewson blew the final whistle to end a superbly sporting contest, the centre of the pitch was covered with the prostrate white and black clad figures of the Liverpool players, who had slumped to the turf in sheer frustration and dejection. Paisley, Joe Fagan and Ronnie Moran, after congratulating United, urged their men off the floor. 'You've got nothing to be ashamed of and you can be proud of your performance,' Paisley told them. But the physical drain had been enormous, the mental one massive. It showed on the agonised face of the skipper Emlyn Hughes as he led his men up to the Royal Box to receive their losers' medals. Hughes had won an England recall earlier in the season and been voted Footballer of the Year, the third Liverpool player to earn that accolade from the Football Writers' Association following Callaghan and Keegan in 1974 and 1976 respectively. But all he felt now was an emptiness which showed, too, in the sad, stony silence of the Liverpool dressing room as the United supporters acclaimed their team out in the sunlight.

'For once, United were the underdogs and I think it helped us,' said Macari. For winning manager Docherty it was Wembley success at the seventh attempt. He failed to taste victory in three attempts there as a player for Scotland against England, and as a Preston player he conceded a penalty to West Brom who went on to win the 1954 FA Cup final.

Later he was boss of Chelsea when they lost to Tottenham in 1967 and a year before his United side met Liverpool they were sensationally beaten by rank outsiders Southampton, thanks to a goal by Bobby Stokes. As his opposite number Paisley pondered on Liverpool's defeat, he concluded that he had picked the wrong team and system: 'I was haunted by that replay date,' he confessed. 'I just couldn't bear the thought of it and it affected me psychologically. It swayed me into playing David Johnson up front with Keegan and Heighway. It was my worst ever tactical decision and I regret not playing Ian Callaghan from the start as a fourth man in midfield. If I'd done that I think we would have won at Wembley.'

Paisley added: 'We'd been the better side in the first half but hadn't taken our chances. There wasn't much I could say to the players at half-time, apart from reminding them to concentrate more when opportunities arose. Ray Clemence should have saved Pearson's shot at the near post for the opening goal, even though it was well placed and not easy to deal with. It was the sort of shot you usually use your foot to stop. But what can you say to a great goalkeeper? Even the greatest people make mistakes and you can't criticise someone for a moment of human error, least of all at Wembley.

'When Jimmy Case equalised so quickly I thought we would go on to win. It was the best goal of the game. United's winner was a pure fluke, because Macari's shot was going yards wide when it hit Greenhoff and deflected in. But even though we lost, we performed with credit and had nothing to be ashamed of.'

My colleague David Miller was moved to a comment in the *Daily Express* that one would find it impossible to make in today's increasingly bitter rivalry between Liverpool and United followers. 'Like modern Corinthians, Liverpool yielded with a pride and dignity which was matched by their remarkable supporters,' Miller wrote. 'The passion on the terraces could not have been more committed, but there was tolerance and humour from both red armies.'

While Liverpool licked their wounds and departed Wembley,

their European Cup Final opponents in Rome four days hence, Borussia Moenchengladbach, were celebrating a hat-trick of West German championships, clinched with a 2-2 draw at outgoing European champions Bayern Munich. They were watched by Tom Saunders, who provided Paisley with the latest information on the German threat.

The transformation from abject disappointment to an upbeat, positive mood for the challenge of Rome began inside Wembley. 'We sat in the dressing room after losing to United absolutely gutted. We were as dead as dodos,' said Emlyn Hughes. 'We'd had a chance of doing the treble and it had gone. As captain I was thinking desperately of something to do, something to say, to lift the lads. Everyone was shattered. Suddenly, Ray Clemence stood up, picked up his boots, threw them in the bath and shouted: "I don't know about you lot, but I'm going to get absolutely legless!" Except he didn't say legless. That changed the entire atmosphere. From that moment I knew we were going to win the European Cup.'

There was no post-Wembley banquet. One had not been planned, win or lose, because of the looming European final. Instead, the Liverpool squad boarded a coach to Watford station to catch the 7.45pm club chartered train back to Liverpool. Paisley stood on the platform deep in thought and observed: 'It was incredible that we went into the Wembley game bidding to achieve a double that had been done only twice before in modern times. Yet it was hardly mentioned. Everyone just kept talking about the treble. That's gone now. But we do have the chance to win a double that has never been achieved. I will never forget my last visit to Rome, with the army during the war. It was an open city by then, after the liberation. We just walked in. I hope it's as open for us this time. I know one thing for sure. We won't let the country down. We'll be doing our best.'

The manager, players, families, directors and other members of the official club party duly boarded the train. Then fate, courtesy of British Rail, stepped in to aid the Liverpool cause.

Paisley recalled: 'One of the football specials ahead of us had broken down and we were stuck on a stationary train for almost two hours. Normally, you'd be very angry about that kind of delay to your journey. But in our case it was a positive thing. The players let their hair down and by the time we got off at Lime Street they had well and truly got Wembley out of their system. There was alcohol on the train and the players were drinking. Not to excess, but to help drown their disappointment. In that state of mind you don't need much.

'That extra couple of hours or so on the train was all they needed to switch from depression to defiance and by the time we drew into Lime Street station that Saturday night, they were ready to take on Borussia Moenchengladbach there and then. Top professional footballers are like thoroughbred racehorses, highly strung and very susceptible to atmosphere. If the players' heads had stayed down, there was no way they would have won in Rome – and if that train had been on time they would probably have gone home in the wrong frame of mind. Those extra drinks got it out of their system and nobody stepped out of line. There might have been one or two clowns in the team but we treated them like men and expected them to behave likewise.

'People who sit in the stand perhaps don't realise the extra pressure exerted by the emotional side of the game. It's not easy to cope with and it's quite possible to become drunk on four ounces of wine gums! But I knew as I left Lime Street and headed for home that the players' attitude was all right. They knew they still had a job to do.'

Phil Neal recalled: 'We had a few glasses of wine on the train and we got really merry. We put Wembley out of our minds and began to enjoy ourselves. Steve Heighway started the proceedings by throwing sugar about!

'It sounds like the antics of St Trinians, it sounds daft. But it did us the world of good. Clem was unofficial master of ceremonies and I remember we had a few choruses of 'Yes, We Can Do It'. It was the song we'd recorded weeks earlier in the build-up to the two finals and our bid for the treble. I was told it reached number 15 in the charts. They got the lads into a recording studio, somebody threw in a crate of lager and we were happy to sing our heads off. The lads all thought they were Pavarotti! We didn't make *Top of the Pops* but I've still got a copy of the vinyl record.'

Heighway, the exciting Republic of Ireland forward who was to earn a whole new impressive reputation later in life as overlord of Liverpool's youth development programme, crowned by a £10 million ground-breaking academy, has his own memories of that psychologically restorative train journey. 'We had a mammoth sugar fight, using wrapped cubes, in the train compartment,' he recalled. 'It was a riot! Players, wives, everyone was involved. It wasn't the traditional reaction to losing an FA Cup Final, but very beneficial.'

Kevin Keegan is another who believes that the glory of Rome might never have happened for Liverpool but for their defeat at Wembley. 'Don't get me wrong, Wembley was very disappointing,' he said. 'But I honestly feel if we hadn't lost the FA Cup Final we might not have won in Rome, because we reacted to Wembley in such a positive manner.'

If the train journey had provided an unexpected and unusual mental uplift for the players, Paisley also continued his month-long mind game revolving around John Toshack's chance of playing in Rome, a prospect he knew would keep Moenchengladbach guessing and on edge. The aerial power of the big striker had demolished the German club in the 1973 UEFA Cup Final first leg at Anfield, and Paisley fuelled their apprehension about facing him again by saying that Toshack could come into contention for Rome. In truth, he had no chance of playing, something Paisley had been aware of for a while, but the psychological advantage of publicly keeping him in the frame was something Paisley seized on. Although Udo Lattek had succeeded Hennes Weisweiler as Moenchengladbach manager, he shared a general German unease about the air-raid menace of traditional British centre-forwards.

'I knew about their fear of John's height, so I kept him in the squad,' Paisley revealed. 'Tosh frightened them to death, but I knew he wouldn't play because he wasn't fit. But I almost convinced John that he'd be in the side! I wanted to keep the Germans thinking that way so they would adapt their tactics to counter the threat of his height. The Germans are so disciplined that even if they find a mistake in their planning, their thinking is too rigid to allow them to change. And to fox them even more, and convince them that I was ready to cash in on their fear of height, I also included big Alan Waddle in the squad.'

Paisley enjoyed a drop of Scotch when he got home that Saturday night after the FA Cup Final. 'I had a quick drink to help me relax because the post-match reaction is probably worse after a cup final than at any other time, because you constantly replay the game in your mind,' he said. 'But I had already begun to make plans for Rome and I had already reached a conclusion about the formation I would play. I picked the team then, on Saturday night. It was business as usual on Sunday and I went to Anfield as I always did, in case players reported in with any injuries. Fortunately, there were none.

'The players reported back for training on the Monday and went through the normal routine prior to a midweek match. They didn't seem to be suffering any adverse reaction from Wembley and were reasonably relaxed. We trained again on Tuesday morning and then it was time for the off.'

9

The Glory of Rome

A huge exodus of around 27,000 Liverpool supporters headed for the Eternal City by road, rail and air. Naturally, irreverent Scouse humour was much to the fore. A classic example was captured by BBC Radio Merseyside, who reported this dialogue between two fans:

> *First fan*: 'I'll see you in the Vatican.'
> *Second fan*: 'Where will you be, in the bar or the lounge?'

Among the thousands who travelled to Rome were Paisley's sons Robert and Graham. Jessie Paisley recalled: 'The boys and one of my daughters-in-law went to Rome and they travelled with the rest of the fans by train. I remember taking them down to Lime Street station and seeing all the excitement. My daughter-in-law said later that it was an arduous journey and that she never wanted to eat another cracker and cheese in her life! I couldn't go because I was teaching and Bob hadn't asked me to go. He knew that I was as committed to teaching as he was to football. So I stayed at home and watched the game on television with my other daughter-in-law.'

Only a late appeal to provide an aircraft, made to the top brass of British Airways by their northern commercial manager and lifelong Liverpool fan Frank Bowskill, allowed the Anfield club to fly the flag and travel to Rome with the national carrier. It was in stark contrast to Manchester United's journey to Barcelona for their dramatic, treble-clinching 1999 European Cup Final against Bayern Munich, when the club were flown by British Airways on Concorde.

Liverpool's aircraft jetted out from Speke airport on Tuesday lunchtime, little more than 24 hours before the biggest game in their history, and somewhere over the English Channel Paisley announced his line-up to the accompanying media. It was to be the team that finished the game at Wembley, with Toshack, Johnson, Fairclough, Alec Lindsay and reserve goalkeeper Peter McDonnell on the substitutes' bench.

'This was the side I should have started with against Manchester United,' admitted Paisley. 'If I had done, I'm convinced we wouldn't have lost. On the other hand, if Cally had played at Wembley it's doubtful if he would be as fresh for Rome. What's more, if we'd done the double, would we be so determined to win the greatest prize of all? We know this is the chance of a lifetime and we are determined that if we don't take it then it won't be for the want of trying. We never needed telling we were not invincible, and after Wembley we know we're not. That should have provided all the geeing-up the team needs. They'll run until they drop if they have to. We know Borussia are a great side, with a half a dozen great players. But they know we are, too. They also know we have a reputation for picking ourselves up and bouncing back better than ever. Our FA Cup defeat might have done us a European Cup favour.'

Paisley and his coaching staff were armed to the teeth with information on Moenchengladbach. They had watched their semi-final in Kiev on television in the hours leading up to their own semi-final first leg in Zurich, and Tom Saunders had seen them in the flesh on six occasions. 'They are a typical German side, skilful and disciplined,' said Paisley. Their captain Berti Vogts was a world-class defender with more than 70 West German caps, 22-year-old midfielder Uli Stielike was preparing to move to Real Madrid for £400,000 – a massive sum at that time – while the versatile Rainer Bonhof was a powerful influence. They also had dashing Danish raider Allan Simonsen, but Paisley confided to his backroom colleagues: 'While we must be aware of the threat of Simonsen and his lethal finishing, I think we've got a couple of things going for us. Jupp Heynckes, who put us on the rack and scored twice in the second leg of the 1973 UEFA Cup Final, has had a knee problem and their elder statesman Herbert Wimmer is getting on and has had muscle trouble.'

Within hours of Liverpool arriving at Rome's Leonardo da Vinci airport and checking into the Holiday Inn St Peter's Hotel, news came through from England that Callaghan, preparing for his 83rd and most important European appearance, was wanted by West Bromwich Albion to succeed Johnny Giles as player-manager. The invitation was politely declined by Callaghan, who said: 'I'm flattered but I want to go on playing for Liverpool. A European Cup medal is the one I've been waiting for. After such a long career, it's something you dream about. I know what it's like to win the championship and I've also won medals in the FA Cup and the UEFA Cup. But the European Cup is something special and I have to admit I didn't think I'd be playing after being only a substitute at Wembley. It was a lovely surprise when the boss told me I was in the team.'

The morning of Wednesday 25 May dawned bright and warm over Rome. It was to be what Paisley would forever describe as 'my perfect day', one that would be etched into English football's annals of achievement. After breakfast he and his players travelled a short distance from the hotel to an all-weather pitch which had been put at their disposal by a local semi-professional club. Even then the temperature had climbed into the high 80s and Paisley reported: 'We didn't do much in the heat apart from just loosen up. The sense of occasion, the weather and the culmination of ten months of football dictated that the players should keep as much strength as possible for the game itself.'

But the morning session did prove decisive for Toshack, who broke down with his lingering Achilles damage and was ruled out of a seat on the bench. It meant a place instead for 6ft 4in Alan Waddle while Toshack was left to face summer surgery.

Whatever Paisley's feelings about Bill Shankly's shock declaration that the best team in Europe were not even in Rome, he kept his own counsel. His predecessor, who had travelled to Italy as a guest of the club, told Jeff Powell in the *Daily Mail* on the day of the final that Juventus were the Continent's finest team. 'The best team in Europe were not in this competition,' said Shankly. 'Juventus are very, very fit. They're alive and urgent. Good minds, balanced and hard. By Christ, they're hard. Giving nothing away. And the discipline of the Italian clubs keeps them in phenomenal condition. Borussia Moenchengladbach will have a lot of that Continental attitude about them – and the Liverpool lads are drained, make no mistake about that. They've never been so tired. Don't underestimate them, though, even after a season like this.' A few hours later, Shankly was proclaiming the quality of

Liverpool as a yardstick of football excellence.

Rome had witnessed many sights in its long, colourful and eventful history, but surely nothing quite like the massive Scouse invasion that swelled the streets of the ancient city, swamping the comparatively few German supporters. 'There were plenty of tickets available to us because Moenchengladbach wanted only a relatively small number,' recalled Peter Robinson, then Liverpool's general secretary but later to become chief executive and executive vice-chairman. 'Where it was an administrative nightmare was that the European final followed straight after the FA Cup Final, so we had two major finals to deal with in four days. At the time our office staff totalled about six people, so I don't understand now how we handled it all. But we obviously did.'

Thousands of Liverpool fans made their presence felt inside the Olympic Stadium hours before kick-off, the legends on their banners reaching new heights of ingenuity. One of them, inspired by terrace hero Joey Jones and the opponents Liverpool had overcome en route to Rome, was truly unforgettable. It read: 'Joey Ate The Frogs' Legs, Made The Swiss Roll, Now He's Munching Gladbach.'

As the official Liverpool party were about to leave their hotel for the stadium, my friend and colleague Stuart Hall and his BBC TV crew were indebted to Paisley, who sliced right through Italian red tape on their behalf by employing his native cunning in an ingenious manner.

The obstacle was Gigi Peronace, a former goalkeeper who made his name as an adviser and link man in the deals that took a succession of British stars into Italian football, including John Charles, Tony Marchi, Joe Baker, Denis Law and Gerry Hitchens. He was now working as a media officer for the Italian Football Federation and Hall revealed how Peronace was outwitted by Paisley: 'The door opened and in came Peronace, looking like the heart and soul, the embodiment, of the Mafioso, a dark overcoat draped over his shoulders, wearing a wan smile and his hair slicked back.

'He walked over, picked up my broadcasting passes and said: "Impossible - solo Italiano." Then he ripped up my tickets, which fluttered to the floor like confetti. So I went to Bob Paisley and explained our predicament.

'Bob said: "All you've got to do is leave it to me. I'll fix it for you."

'This, remember, is just before his greatest match. This is how wonderful the man was. Anyway, the next thing we know, Bob is telling Kevin Keegan to carry the camera to the team bus, Emlyn Hughes to carry the lights, Tommy Smith to carry something else, and so on! Then myself and the film crew donned Liverpool tracksuits and boarded the team bus which drove off. Eventually, there we were driving down Olympic Way and into the stadium.

'The players then carried our gear in just before they were to go out and play the most important match in the club's history! It was fantastic. Can you imagine anything like that happening with Arsenal or Manchester United? No, it could only have happened with Liverpool, the greatest club in the world.'

Inside the dressing room, Paisley prepared his players for their task by wasting little time on tactical jargon or the strengths and weaknesses of Moenchengladbach. Phil Neal, who had experienced the cold, cautious and crushingly extreme planning of Don Revie when he was on England duty, believed the Paisley approach was exhilarating and liberating.

'It was quite amazing, really, that there we were in Liverpool's first ever European Cup Final and all Bob talked about pre-match was that the last time he'd been in Rome he drove in on the back of a tank during the war!' said Neal. 'That didn't do us any harm. In fact, it was typical of the man and the club not to harp on about the opposition and worry the players unduly. Never once did Bob tell me how I must play. I was allowed to be an individual, as we all were. But he would have something to say if we ever forgot we were individuals within a team. Teamwork was paramount.'

The reception the Liverpool players received when they first emerged from the tunnel for a stroll around the stadium was breathtaking. 'I knew then there was no way we could lose,' said skipper Hughes. 'You could hardly hear the Moenchengladbach fans. It was our supporters who were singing and chanting.'

For the Liverpool players there was a distinct family atmosphere. 'As well as our wives being present, the parents of all the players were in Rome, too, the only time I can remember that happening,' recalled Steve Heighway. 'They had flown on a special charter flight. It was the first time my mother and father had travelled to an away game.' But for some it was a case of thumbing a lift rather than enjoying the luxury of air travel to reach Rome. 'My brothers got there any way they could,' said Terry McDermott. 'They weren't paid very well in those days and I couldn't afford to pay for them. But they made it! Walking on to the pitch an hour or so before the game and seeing a mass of red and white gave me an incredible feeling. Then, when we went out for the kick-off, the sights and the sound was something I'd never experienced before and probably never will again. It was just fabulous.'

As kick-off loomed, there were many personal incentives for victory swirling amidst the collective will in the Liverpool dressing room. For the departing Keegan, the dream was to end his Anfield career with Europe's greatest prize. 'I could have got away last year but this is what I stayed for. To lose now would be like going out in the first round,' he said. Days before the Rome final it was revealed that West German club Hamburg was to be Keegan's destination, with agreement ultimately reached on a record-breaking £500,000 fee, which was then the biggest deal ever involving a British club. The previous summer Real Madrid had been ready to pay £650,000 for him, but Keegan's desire to help Liverpool land the European Cup and the club's wish to keep him meant that he stayed for another season of intense speculation and personal heartbreak. Keegan's father Joe died in the middle of the campaign, in December 1976, and Paisley commented: 'Kevin and his father were very close and Joe's death deeply upset him. So with all his personal turmoil it was not surprising that we didn't see the best of him that season. Yet he still finished our top scorer in the League, with 12 goals, two more than John Toshack, to help us win the championship.'

Rome was to provide Keegan with a marvellous farewell performance and a launch pad for the next stage of his career. To provide an extra spur, it was at the same stadium in which Keegan, Hughes and Clemence had been on the losing England side against Italy in a World Cup qualifier six months earlier, while for veterans like Callaghan and Smith, youngsters at Liverpool when the club was in the old Second Division meeting the likes of Scunthorpe and Lincoln City in the early 1960s, the prize before them provided amazing testimony to Liverpool's incredible journey.

The glory in Liverpool's grasp hugely outweighed their financial incentive to win the trophy – £1,600 each. The Moenchengladbach players had been promised a much more substantial £3,750 a man if they could take the European Cup back to West Germany for the fourth successive year, following a hat-trick of triumphs by Bayern Munich. This is how the teams lined up, both in 4-4-2 formation.

Liverpool: Ray Clemence; Phil Neal, Tommy Smith, Emlyn

Hughes (captain), Joey Jones; Jimmy Case, Terry McDermott, Ray Kennedy, Ian Callaghan; Kevin Keegan, Steve Heighway. Substitutes: David Fairclough, David Johnson, Alec Lindsay, Alan Waddle, Peter McDonnell (goalkeeper).

Borussia Moenchengladbach: Wolfgang Kneib; Berti Vogts (captain), Frank Shaefer, Hans-Jurgen Witkamp, Hans Klinkhammer; Horst Wohlers, Herbert Wimmer, Uli Stielike, Rainer Bonhof; Allan Simonsen, Jupp Heynckes. Substitutes: Wilfried Hannes, Herbert Heidenreich, Christian Kulik, Horst Koppell, Wolfgang Kleff (goalkeeper).

Referee: Robert Wurtz (France).

Paisley said of his players: 'I have never seen a team so relaxed before a match. It was as if a great weight had been lifted from everyone's shoulders and that they realised they just had to make one last effort; that they just had to go out there and do their best and if that wasn't good enough, well, so be it.'

Just as they had done at Wembley four days earlier, Liverpool quickly dictated the course of the game, adopting a calm and patient approach and building their moves with assurance. But after 20 minutes Bonhof, the player then hailed as 'the new Beckenbauer', broke through and unleashed a ferocious 20-yard shot which left Clemence groping. This time, however, fate was with Liverpool as the ball smashed against the base of the goalkeeper's right-hand post and was scrambled back safely into his clutches. Two minutes later Wimmer, the experienced 32-year-old West German international with almost 40 caps, limped out of Moenchengladbach's midfield to be replaced by Christian Kulik. Liverpool, visibly growing in confidence in the Rome heat and roared on by their followers in the 57,000 crowd, tightened their grip on the game and deservedly forced a breakthrough in the 28th minute. Callaghan dispossessed Bonhof to send Heighway away down the right flank. As McDermott raced into space, Heighway slipped a superb pass into the midfielder's path and his brilliant right-foot shot flashed across the advancing Kneib and into the net.

McDermott, who amazed everyone inside the club with his seemingly boundless energy and hard runs from midfield but was a modest almost self-deprecating player, described his goal in characteristic terms: 'I was supposed to be famous for my blind-side runs, mainly to the bar! But this time I thought I better run into space and Steve Heighway cut inside and gave me a smashing pass. It was just a question of hitting the target. I saw the giant keeper Kneib, who was about six foot nine, coming towards me, and I thought: "There's no way I'm going to try to control this. I'm just going to kick it and hope for the best." Fortunately, it ended up in the corner of the net. Scoring a goal in a European Cup Final is any lad's dream, especially for a lad like me from Merseyside, a Scouser who never dreamed I'd ever play for Liverpool. It was a tremendous feeling, not just for me but for my family and friends. Even now I tend to get emotional when I think about it.'

Said Heighway: 'That goal looked simple but it was down to the willingness of Terry to run from midfield, something that perhaps is lacking in some teams today. After I got the ball I cut in, probably because I didn't know where else to go. Terry's run encouraged me to slot the ball into space to the right and I think Terry hit it as it came across him. It looked simple and people used to say our game was based on simplicity. But it was a bit more sophisticated than that.

'I used to enjoy the European games because Bob Paisley would say to me: "Just go and play up front. Run, move, keep mobile. Take people off Kevin and come back and help a bit when you need to." I enjoyed not having a direct confrontation with a full-back which, through a League season as a winger, you do have. There's a bit of pressure in that. But playing up front you can try to find a soft centre somewhere and keep probing until you find a bit of success.'

Paisley hailed his side's opening goal in glowing terms. 'I can only describe it as a coaching showpiece,' he said. 'Borussia were spreadeagled as Cally won the ball in midfield and pushed it out to Steve Heighway on the right. Cally followed on down the flank, pulling the Germans even wider and allowing Steve to cut inside and play the ball into Terry McDermott's path. It was a perfect example of Terry's awareness, anticipation and running at their best, and he scored a magnificent goal.'

By half-time Liverpool were well in control, with Paisley thrilled by Keegan's display. 'He was giving that great professional Berti Vogts a dog's life,' he remarked. 'For the goal, he had the German selling programmes to the crowd, so far had he pulled him away from the build-up. Vogts didn't realise what was happening until it was too late.'

It pleased Keegan too. He declared: 'I quite enjoyed man-to-man marking and Berti's attentions. It gave me an even greater challenge – as if I needed one! I'd played against Berti before and scored two goals against him at Anfield in the UEFA Cup four years earlier. I think he had a lot of respect for me, probably too much that night. He followed me everywhere.

'The game had been going only four minutes when he tried to pull my shirt off. I said to him: "No, Berti. In England we change shirts after the game!" At half-time when he was walking up the tunnel, I said to him: "Are you going into our dressing room or yours?"

'During half-time Bob urged us on. "We won't be here again and just look at that support we've got," he told us. To be honest, there were so many of our fans there I thought the city of Liverpool must have been empty. I'll never forget those supporters and their song: 'Tell Me Ma And Pa I'm Not Coming Home For Tea, I'm Going To Italy.' It made me feel we were playing at home instead of in Rome.'

But Liverpool had not climbed the mountain yet. Moenchengladbach, drawing on some inner inspiration and responding to a half-time pep talk from Lattek, launched a full-scale assault at the start of the second half and struck swiftly and lethally. A misplaced 51st-minute pass by Jimmy Case let in the flying winger Simonsen, who cut in from the left and drove a magnificent equaliser beyond Clemence high into the far corner of the net.

'Jimmy didn't deserve to be punished for his mistake as severely as he was,' said Keegan. 'It was one of the great goals. To beat Clem from that distance you had to hit the top corner, and that's exactly what Simonsen did.'

Said Paisley: 'I warned them against complacency at half-time because they were so comfortably in control. But Jimmy's intended back-pass to Phil Neal let in Simonsen. He was on it in a flash and demonstrated the lethal finishing we knew he had. It put us back to square one. The game was wide open.'

For the first time on that sultry Roman evening, Borussia's fans made their presence felt as their team threatened. For Liverpool, the haunting thought was inescapable. Was this going to be Wembley all over again? Was the prize going to be denied them once more? Summoning all their reserves of character and courage, they clawed their way back into the game. Vogts, still finding Keegan a devilishly elusive target for his marking mission, appeared to bring down the England star in the 59th minute only for referee Wurtz to wave play on. But three minutes later, at the other end of the field, Clemence produced a save that was to turn the tide of the final. Stielike seized on a Simonsen pass and headed towards the Liverpool keeper in a straight face-to-face duel. The Germans, it seemed, were about to take the lead. But Clemence displayed his great England class by reducing Stielike's options and then blocking his shot.

'When people ask me what was my best save, I tend to rate them for their importance, for what they meant,' said Clemence. 'On that basis, the save from Stielike is on a par with a penalty save I made from Peter Kotte at Dynamo Dresden in the previous season's UEFA Cup. In Rome, Stielike broke through on to a ball played over the top. It was one against one, a situation I'd been brought up and trained to deal with at Liverpool, and I blocked his shot with my knees. No save I've ever made was more critical than that one.'

Paisley was in full agreement. 'Ray might have made more spectacular saves but I doubt he has made a more important one,' he said. 'It was the turning point of the game. The Germans never recovered from it.' Two minutes later Liverpool were back in front, with a goal straight from the pages of comic-strip fiction. Heighway took a corner on the left and Tommy Smith moved in at the near post to head past Kneib. It was a wonderful way for Smith to celebrate his 600th senior appearance, prior to his planned retirement, and crown his recall by Paisley earlier in the season after the injury to Phil Thompson.

'I've changed my name to Roy of the Rovers,' exclaimed Smith, who had joined Liverpool as a 14-year-old. 'Before the corner was taken, Kevin told me to just stay back a bit and then shouted, "Go!" It was a great corner by Steve and I just met it, although I thought it was going to take ten minutes to go in! The goalkeeper was six foot five tall, but he must have felt like a mouse.'

Said Heighway: 'I'd like to say that goal was planned. But nobody ever knew where my corners were going. I just whipped the ball in and Tommy got to the front post. It was as simple as that. I wasn't aiming for anyone in particular. I just put the ball into the front space. Tommy had taken a gamble and just made a run. We knew then that the European Cup was ours and I had so much energy I could have run all night.'

Paisley remarked: 'I can't remember Tommy scoring with his

head before, but that was a goal Dixie Dean would have been proud of. It stemmed once again from Borussia's fear of high crosses. Larry Lloyd had scored a similar goal against them in the 1973 UEFA Cup Final. The Germans were so rigidly disciplined that they followed the big men like Ray Kennedy, who were acting as decoys at a corner, and were dragged away from the danger area. They were vulnerable to a man arriving late into a space and that's exactly what Tommy did as Steve's corner came over. 'It was a perfect header – in fact, just one perfect part of a perfect night – and magnificent for Tommy. He was one of those rare personalities who could not only cope with tension but actually improve as the tension increased, qualities he demonstrated superbly in Zurich in the semi-final.'

The fulfilment of Paisley's cherished ambition, the dream he had helped build for the club in earlier days alongside Bill Shankly, an enthralled spectator in the Olympic Stadium, was imminent. Paisley and Liverpool were just minutes away from conquering Europe. Moenchengladbach visibly wilted, with Keegan and Heighway tormenting their defence. Yet another penalty claim was rejected when Heighway went crashing in a duel with Bonhof. The Germans roused themselves for one last effort to get back into the game but they were foiled by Clemence, who made a brave save on the edge of the penalty area as Heynckes and Simonsen challenged him for Stielike's cross. It was the signal for Lattek to send on his second substitute, Wilfried Hannes taking over from Horst Wohlers after 79 minutes, but it made no difference.

Keegan, now teasing and torturing Vogts, embarked on a menacing run into the Borussia box. Another couple of strides and he would have unleashed a shot aimed at taking his career goal total for Liverpool to 101. But Vogts ensured his haul stayed at a round century in 323 appearances for the club. The great West German defender had no option but to send Keegan tumbling and concede a blatant penalty. This time referee Wurtz had no doubts.

'Berti seemed to be chasing me forever and the big German keeper never moved, which made it even more difficult for me because if he'd started to come out I'd have tried to clip the ball round him,' Keegan reflected. 'I remember thinking if I run much further I'll go straight through the net, I was getting so close to the goal. Then Berti caught up with me, although I'm not absolutely sure it was a penalty.'

However, his team-mate Neal, like Mr Wurtz, was certain. 'It was an obvious penalty,' he said. 'Berti committed himself and slid in on the floor.' So to Neal, who had successfully dispatched ten penalties through the season, fell the responsibility of scoring once more from the spot to secure the European Cup for Liverpool and for England.

'I assumed that as my previous penalties had been televised around Europe, the Borussia keeper had done his homework,' said Neal. 'So I decided to put my kick in the opposite corner to the one I'd scored against Zurich, and with Kneib being so big I thought I'd keep it low. He went the wrong way and in it went! The game was over. It was only when I saw clips on television later that I learned that Ian Callaghan was standing with his hands together on the edge of the box, praying I wouldn't miss. That brought home to me how much winning the European Cup meant to Liverpool. I'd had less than three years at the club, but people like Cally and Smithy had been there almost 20 years and this was the ultimate achievement.'

Callaghan was suitably appreciative of his team-mate's composure and precision. 'Phil had this lovely attitude to taking penalties,' he said. 'He just went up, put the ball down and picked his spot. People don't realise how much pressure is on a penalty taker in big games. Phil was always willing to take that on and handle the pressure. It must have taken a bit of doing that night. The whole experience of Rome, the stadium, the atmosphere, everything, was unbelievable. It was on a par for me with being in the Liverpool team at Wembley that won the FA Cup for the first time in 1965. Occasions like that live with you forever.'

Among the millions watching on television were, of course, Jessie Paisley and one of her daughters-in-law. 'I remember the unusual sight of Bob jumping up off the bench and waving his arms in the air when the penalty went in,' said Jessie. 'He rarely did things like that because he wasn't an outwardly emotional person. But deep down he was very, very proud of being the first English-born manager to win the European Cup. Needless to say, so were we. We kept shouting at the television set.'

Paisley, never a man to wear his heart on his sleeve, could not contain his joy when referee Wurtz blew the final whistle, as he leaped up to embrace Keegan. Ronnie Moran hugged Tommy Smith before bursting his water-filled sponge bag in sheer delight, while Callaghan and Keegan, each having fulfilled their own personal missions, draped their arms across each other's shoulders. The five Liverpool substitutes, denied action because of the magnificent performances of the other 11 jumped high in celebration, their white tracksuit tops giving them the appearance of animated snowmen. Joey Jones congratulated everything that moved before leading the charge to salute the supporters chanting his name, and falling foul, briefly, of the Italian police.

'I got hold of a Union Jack, wrapped it round me and jumped over the boards towards the Liverpool fans,' said Jones. 'The police set their dogs on me because they thought I was a supporter. I had to unwrap myself from the flag to show them I was a player. But I felt a closeness to the fans. If I hadn't been playing I'd have been with them. A couple of supporters presented me with the "Munching Gladbach" banner when I left Liverpool to rejoin Wrexham in September of the following year. I've still got it and I think as much of that banner as I do my European Cup medal.'

There was a tear in the eyes, too, of Manchester United legend Denis Law, who had witnessed from the stadium's radio box the first European Cup triumph by an English club since United beat Benfica at Wembley nine years earlier, a game he missed through injury. 'That was a fantastic performance by Liverpool,' he exclaimed. Shankly, Law's fellow Scot and former manager at Huddersfield, had seen the dream he nurtured at Liverpool become reality under his successor Paisley and declared: 'Liverpool have been working towards this for years. The players were tremendous and so were the crowd. This is what football is all about and England should take note at national level.'

Paisley glowed in the emotion of the evening as he filled with pride in his players, the club and a sense of achievement for English football. 'Wasn't that just tremendous!' he declared amidst the tumult of Liverpool's dressing room. 'Words fail me and I've got no voice, anyway. To come away from Wembley and play like that was a feat in itself. Then our spirit was further tested when we made a mistake and gave away a brilliantly taken goal. Their response speaks volumes for the players and shows just what great professionals they are.

'We did our work from midfield. That is the strategy we've worked on and employed in Europe.

'We concentrate on getting the front players to pull their markers away and that leaves space for our midfield men to come through. Tonight we slowed the game down to our pace, which allows greater expression of skills. It would be a good thing, also, for the game at national level. English football is always being knocked but we have the players and we have the skill and we shouldn't be frightened of anyone. The one department we do need to improve on in England is our finishing but there's so much to be proud of in our football. The secret is that our Liverpool team never know when to stop running and working. At Anfield we have always believed in players supporting each other and concentrating on not giving the ball away. Sometimes it's difficult because crowds create pressure. But you can't go charging forward all the time, willy-nilly. You must have patience, and this is where we can play the Continentals at their own game.'

Then he added with a twinkle in his eye: 'We've done the country proud and this is my greatest moment – apart from when my team won a five-a-side game in training at Melwood a couple of weeks ago!'

Captain Emlyn Hughes received the huge urn of a trophy and lifted it high into the Roman air. He recalled: 'I had to walk up only about eight steps for the presentation and when I picked up the cup, I said: "There you are, lads, that's for us." By us I meant the players, the fans and the boss, because we all thoroughly deserved it. Liverpool had joined the great teams of Europe and we had some bloody good players. We had an aura about us in Europe and everyone was frightened to death of us, just as they were of other great teams such as Ajax, Real Madrid and Bayern Munich.

'During the 1970s I was privileged to play in great Liverpool teams who did magnificently in Europe. My only regret is that I never took a single photograph of all those places I visited in more than 12 years with Liverpool. I never saw the sights of a city and never visited a monument or a church which tourists travel thousands of miles to see. But that was because of Liverpool's professional attitude. All that Bob and Shanks were interested in was the job we there to do, to win that particular match.'

For Keegan, the final whistle in Rome personified the sentiments of that haunting, thought-provoking Peggy Lee song, 'Is That All There Is?' He said: 'A lot of people talk of Rome 1977 as one of the great finals and rightly so. It was a credit to European and world football and it is probably the game most people remember when they talk about Liverpool FC in Europe. We had dominated one of the world's best sides. But at the end I just felt flat. It was the end of my Liverpool career and already it was in the past. I had taken a bit of stick about leaving but I'd tried to be honest from the start.

'My greatest memory of Rome is of Berti Vogts coming over from the Moenchengladbach hotel to ours and sitting with my wife Jean and I at our banquet. He said to me: "You were fantastic tonight. I want to buy you a drink." It was a magnificent gesture and one I don't think I could have done if the roles were reversed. I built up a great rapport with Berti which, to this day, is still there. I consider him one of my great friends in football.'

Although Paisley was loathe to lose Keegan to Hamburg, he saluted the departing hero's massive contribution to the night of triumph in Rome. 'Our win was a great team effort but Kevin stood out,' he said. 'He played his finest game for Liverpool in his last match for the club and his performance proved that he's worth every mark the Germans are paying for him. Kevin had a wanderlust and during the season he played really well in only about half a dozen games, because of his frustration and desire to move on. In turn, the crowd became frustrated with him, which was understandable. They knew he was a good player and didn't want to lose him. I'm sure if Kevin had turned in a performance against Manchester United like the one he gave in Rome we'd have won the FA Cup, too. But the big question is: could he have run like that twice in a few days?'

But the misery of Wembley and the end of the treble quest was drowned in the celebration of European Cup glory. Liverpool were champions of Europe and had achieved it with style and courage. In the year of the Queen's Silver Jubilee, they had struck a massive blow for Britain, reflected in the subsequent awards of the OBE for Paisley – when surely it should have been a knighthood – and an MBE for Tommy Smith, to follow a similar honour two years earlier to his room-mate Callaghan. The reaction of Joey Jones after the game was boundless and uninhibited. His room-mate Heighway recalled: 'Joey's joy after the game was just uncontrollable. He jumped and ran about like a spring lamb. All the energy of euphoria was there. I also remember that after the game in Rome was the only time in my life I ever saw my father drunk!' Not so Paisley, who refused a drink right through a riotous night of celebration, beginning in the Liverpool dressing room at the Olympic Stadium. The BBC cameras rolled and captured the exuberance of the players as they sang in the showers. 'Yes, We Can Do It' was the refrain. Then goalkeeper Ray Clemence popped his head out and shouted: 'Hey, lads, we HAVE bloody done it!'

For Stuart Hall, having got himself and his film crew into the stadium only through Paisley's ingenuity, there was a final act in the soap opera involving him and the Italian official Peronace, as he relates: 'Into the Liverpool dressing room he came, still wearing his faint smile, his greasy hair and his overcoat draped over his shoulders. He looked at the scene. It was like a theatre with all the lights, clouds of steam, players cavorting. He couldn't believe what he was seeing. His mouth literally dropped open and he took a step back. He couldn't understand what was happening. Then he spun on his heel. With no congratulations, no hand shakes, Peronace was gone. A beaten man.

'Eventually, the players left and I sat on an upturned kit skip with Bob, Joe Fagan, Ronnie Moran, Tom Saunders and Roy Evans. It was the Boot Room on location! And, like the Boot Room, there was no champagne. Mind you, there was no beer or whisky either! We drank warm Coca-Cola out of polystyrene cups. And Bob turned to me and said: "Are you happy?"

'I said: "Bob, I owe it all to you. This is the most amazing day of my life. I've had some amazing ones but this has topped them all."'

Later, Paisley put Liverpool's triumph into his own personal context. 'I was the first English-born manager to win the European Cup and I couldn't have picked a better time or place to do it,' he said. 'I suppose this will make it difficult for whoever has this job after me! Everything was perfect. Even now I can feel the emotion welling up inside me whenever I watch the film, centred around our game in Rome, called *Hope In Their Hearts*. Memories flooded back for me as the team bus left the stadium after the game and threaded its way through those ancient streets back to the hotel. I had driven into Rome on a tank back in 1944. I was part of another conquering force then and came back as manager of another conquering force, thankfully in football not war.'

The partying and revelling at the team hotel lasted until dawn, the official guests supplemented by an invasion of supporters. 'We had about 27,000 fans in Rome and I think half of them must have turned up at our banquet!' recalled Peter Robinson. One of the highlights of the celebrations was Keegan, stripped to the waist after presenting his shirt to a supporter, singing the sailors' lament 'The Leaving Of Liverpool', thus demonstrating an equally fine sense of timing off the pitch as he had shown on it.

Through it all, Paisley sat quietly and teetotally, explaining: 'I like a drink and, in common with most people, I enjoy celebrating a great victory. This, though, was different. It was no ordinary triumph. The buffet at the banquet was magnificent enough to have fed my regiment throughout the war, with enough champagne to have sunk Noah's Ark. But I wanted to remain sober. I was drinking it all in – the atmosphere, the sense of pride, of achievement, of joy and reward for ten months' hard labour. I wanted to savour every moment.'

Those who made breakfast later that morning witnessed a disarming sight. Phil Neal will never forget it. 'Bob came into the breakfast room carrying the European Cup, wearing a cardigan and carpet slippers with a paper tucked under his arm,' Neal recalled. 'It was a reminder to everyone, even if it wasn't meant that way, that we had to keep our feet on the ground. We'd won it once and he wanted to make sure we won it again. Hard work was Bob's ethic. He believed nobody had a right to win anything they hadn't earned.'

Paisley's entry in his daily log read: 'After Saturday's defeat at Wembley we wondered what effect it would have on the players. We needn't have worried because right from the start we dominated the game and turned in the best performance in the history of the club.'

Liverpool flew home the following day to make an amazing tour of the city when more than half a million people, including many Evertonians, turned out to salute Paisley's conquering heroes. Skipper Hughes blotted his copybook by rewording the Kop's triumphant chant to 'Liverpool Are Magic, Everton Are Tragic', a remark he regretted and for which he publicly apologised. 'It was the biggest boob I ever made,' he admitted later.

Jessie Paisley joined her husband on the victory tour and recalled: 'Going round the city on the open-top bus was a wonderful experience. There were great scenes outside Picton Library, where Bob and the players stood on the balcony, and when it was all over we came home, had a cup of tea and went to bed.'

Liverpool's triumph made a massive impact on new England manager Ron Greenwood. Only hours after succeeding Don Revie, Greenwood arranged a meeting with Paisley, his players and the Anfield backroom staff. 'Ron said he liked our approach to the game. It's the only way if you're going to combat the Europeans,' said Paisley.

'The top European teams showed us how to break out of defence effectively. The pace of their movement was dictated by the first pass. We had to learn how to be patient like that and think about the next two or three moves ahead when we had the ball.

'Ron suggested that one of our staff attend England training sessions, not to run the place but to observe and offer constructive ideas.

'We welcome that. We've always been a bit concerned when players have gone away with England because changes of exercise in training are likely to cause stiffness and lose you half a yard in a game.

'I've got a different impression of Ron now. I thought he was a theorist with a blackboard but he told us he'd never used a blackboard in his life! He's like us and after talking to him I realise he's more practical than I first thought.'

Greenwood reflected in his autobiography *Yours Sincerely:*

'There was only one starting point. Liverpool were the standard setters. They had just won the European Cup and had a strong, exciting backbone of English players. I realised they were as keen to get a new slant on me as I was to get one on them. No blindingly new truths emerged from our chat but it still proved immensely valuable.

'There was no swank or side at all and I felt that if they were typical of England's footballing people then there wasn't much wrong with our game. The measured rhythm of the Liverpool team comes from understanding the good technique.

'They vary their pace and point of attack. They build from the back and they use the whole width of the field. One moment they are playing within themselves, creating space and passing beautifully, the next they put their foot down and go looking for a kill.'

Destiny had rewarded Liverpool. They had missed out on the treble but had superbly completed what was then a unique double. Paisley, though, was convinced that winning all three trophies was not an impossible dream. 'We had come so close to winning the FA Cup as well that it is foolish for people to say the treble will never be won,' he said. 'We damned nearly proved it could.'

His prophecy proved correct. 22 years and a day after Liverpool's victory in Rome an English club completed the fabled treble when Alex Ferguson's Manchester United scored twice in injury time to shatter Bayern Munich in Barcelona.

But by then Paisley was assured of his own pre-eminent place in the annals of English managerial achievement.

10

The Capture of Dalglish

A copy of the *Daily Express* of Saturday, 6 August 1977, landed with a thud on the hotel lounge table at which I was sitting with Ian Callaghan, Tommy Smith and my sportswriter colleague Colin Wood of the *Daily Mail*. The paper had been thrown down by a clearly irate Bob Paisley, who barked: 'You've got Johnson in trouble now. He's for the high jump.' Then he stormed off into the lift and was gone, leaving me totally and utterly baffled. But it was the prelude to a remarkable revelation by Paisley which was to hugely influence the course of Liverpool and European football history.

It was Saturday night in Amsterdam, where Liverpool were involved in a pre-season tournament. The copy of that day's *Express* had been brought out to Holland by Paisley's close friend Ray Peers, a corpulent, avuncular former boxing promoter and sandwich bar proprietor, who shared Paisley's passion for horseracing and followed his beloved Liverpool at home and abroad. The back-page lead story in the paper was my report about England striker David Johnson's disclosure that he wanted to leave Liverpool because he felt he could not command a regular place, a year after his club record £200,000 signing from Ipswich. He had played the previous evening in Liverpool's 2–1 defeat by Ajax and also in their opening pre-season match against Hamburg – and Kevin Keegan – which Paisley's side lost 3–2, but felt he was figuring only because of the absence of injured Steve Heighway.

'Manager Bob Paisley has the task of picking 11 men from 14 and I have gained the clear impression that unless someone is injured, I shall not be one of the 11,' Johnson told the press representatives on tour with the club. 'I have found myself in the unenviable position of having to think about asking for a move from a club with which, only 12 months ago, I was quite happy to finish my playing career. Liverpool are the best team in England, the best in the world, but you have to have a playing part. The manager and myself, for some unknown reason, have never really been able to communicate and so a feeling of unrest has affected me. I have been to him to discuss this and to try to find a reason, but he assures me he bears me no malice. I must stress that the reason I am considering action is that Liverpool can do without David Johnson, because they did it last year.'

Johnson's comments were reported in several national and regional papers, so the story itself was not the reason for Paisley's anger. But one word in my report – a word I had not used and which I later learned had been inserted by a sub-editor in the Manchester office – had sparked his fury. The *Express* article carrying my name claimed Johnson had issued a 'written' statement. To do so without permission was then a breach of club rules. But Johnson had done no such thing.

My own anger at seeing the rogue word 'written' inserted in my report was as great as Paisley's. I went to my hotel room, picked up my typewritten article which I had telephoned to the *Express*, and then knocked on Paisley's room door to show him exactly what I had filed to the paper. He accepted this without a quibble and a few minutes later there was another knock on Paisley's door. It was my colleague Colin Wood, inquiring whether Bob and I had ironed out the problem, which, by then, we had.

Paisley then kicked off his shoes, relaxed in a bedside armchair and said to both of us: 'Do you boys want a drink?' He produced a bottle of Cognac and poured some into three glasses. His next words had the force of a bombshell. 'Where do you think Kenny Dalglish is going?'

His question hung in the air for several seconds as we took in its impact. There had been summer-long speculation about who Liverpool would sign to replace Keegan. Trevor Francis and Liam Brady, as well as Dalglish, had been named as possible Paisley transfer targets, but no indication had yet emerged about which, if any of that trio, it would be.

It soon became clear that Dalglish was the player Paisley wanted. He was not planning moves for Arsenal's Brady or Francis of

Birmingham, especially with the latter's unfortunate injury tendency which severely reduced his number of appearances. 'I wasn't interested in Francis because you have to rely on your key men playing in most of the games,' he said. This was a factor that weighed heavily with Paisley and Liverpool, a club noted for their number of 'marathon men', long-serving players who missed few games over a sustained period. Players like Lawler, Callaghan, Smith, Hughes, Clemence and Neal and, before that, Hunt and Liddell.

After a short discussion, Paisley revealed: 'There's only one player for a passing team like ours. Dalglish is coming to us.' It was a revelation so disarming that Wood and I gulped on our sips of brandy. There was little more than a week to the European Cup transfer deadline of 15 August, so clearly Liverpool would have to move quickly to get their man in time for him to be eligible to begin the defence of their prized crown won so gloriously in Rome. But Paisley, having taken us into his confidence, insisted that we could not run the story as a done deal, as it might adversely affect the final pieces of the negotiations between Liverpool, Celtic and Dalglish. We reached agreement with him that we would run a story in Tuesday's papers identifying four potential Liverpool targets – naming Cardiff's Peter Sayer as well as Francis and Brady – but heavily emphasising the likelihood that Dalglish was the man they were set to sign. The stories duly appeared and 48 hours later Dalglish put pen to paper at Anfield to join Liverpool.

The £440,000 fee was a record between British clubs but having banked £500,000 from Keegan's sale to Hamburg, Liverpool were still £60,000 to the good. 'The best bit of business we've ever done,' was chairman John Smith's verdict. The huge fee raised some eyebrows and some criticism, but Smith was right. The capture of Dalglish was a master stroke by Paisley. If you judge a man by his friends, then the evaluation of a football manager, apart from his trophy collection, must surely revolve around his signings.

Keegan's departure had many pundits fearing that Liverpool would struggle to replace him. The move abroad was certainly not applauded by Paisley, who let his feelings be known after receiving his second successive Manager of the Year award and attending Keegan's official signing for Hamburg in a London hotel which secured the player a deal reportedly worth £100,000 a year. Giving vent to views that seem ironic given today's cosmopolitan, polyglot state of English football, Paisley insisted that Keegan should not now be selected for England while he played overseas, declaring: 'I'm not being vindictive but I'm not in agreement with anyone going abroad and then coming back to play for the country. I think the England shirt is belittled a bit. Foreign clubs can come here and take what they want for financial reasons and we have got to protect our own interests. We've certainly got to do something about it, because other players are being tapped by agents right, left and centre. I am the first manager in this decade to suffer by losing a great player abroad. I don't want the money – I want a team.'

His views were echoed by Smith, who said: 'Our best brains are leaving the country. Our people should be able to keep more of the money they earn. I feel very strongly about it and successive governments are to blame, not just this one.'

Later, after Keegan had responded to Paisley's views, the Liverpool manager reflected: 'Kevin has said that he could never forgive me for saying what I did. But my comments were not aimed personally at Kevin, because I have the utmost admiration for him. He's courageous, as well as skilled, and he's made of the same village stuff as me. I said it because I was concerned at losing our best players abroad. It was the British football public I was concerned about, because it is they who suffer if they are deprived of seeing our star players in action week after week. Kevin repeatedly stressed his desire to play for England and he insisted on a release clause in his Hamburg contract. What I said was not meant to be detrimental to him.

'I did have some difficulties with him, more than Bill Shankly had when he was manager, because under Shanks I saw a major part of my job as keeping trouble out of his office and nipping any problems in the bud. I'm talking about situations such as the one caused by Kevin's mystery injury shortly after his arrival at Liverpool. That called for the utmost tact, diplomacy and psychology on my part, gained from a lifetime in football. Kevin had played outstandingly in his opening seven or eight games for us at the start of the 1971–72 season before complaining of a foot problem which remained a mystery. Bill Shankly, who was then manager, had no time for injured players and Kevin got wind of the fact that Bill had called him a "malingerer" after he had reported his foot injury. It was not said with malice aforethought. It was just Bill being Bill. But Kevin took offence at it and his strong determined nature was evident even then. I think he was ready to pack up football on the spot.

'I realised how delicate the situation was. Thankfully Kevin didn't walk out and I examined his foot and the side of his leg which was also affected. I was baffled over the cause. Joe Fagan had a look in Kevin's car and discovered that the pad on the clutch pedal, which was also very stiff, had worn away, leaving a very sharp edge. We suspected that could have been responsible. But when Kevin had missed a total of seven games I took him to a specialist who gave him an injection. It did the trick and Kevin played again the following Saturday. But I never discovered exactly what the reason was. After that, apart from a muscle-splitting whack on the thigh he sustained in a game against Dynamo Berlin 18 months later, Kevin was remarkably free from injuries. He was one of the fittest lads I've ever seen in football.'

On another occasion when Keegan complained about a nagging ankle problem, Paisley's applied psychology acted as a placebo. Keegan had asked for an injection Paisley was loathe for him to have, but instead of refusing the England star he told him to go to the treatment room. 'Lie face down on the table,' Paisley told him, before wrapping his ankle in a towel and filling a hypodermic with water. Paisley then proceeded to give Keegan's ankle the merest pin-prick – and injected the water from the needle into the towel! The outcome was that Keegan played on, his problem 'cured', and Paisley's methods had once again triumphed. He said of Keegan: 'I think he thought of me as a father figure. But he was never impudent with me. He never overstepped the mark and I was proud of what he went on to achieve with England and Hamburg including the remarkable feat of being elected European Footballer of the Year in successive seasons.

'We had a good talk when I first took on the job of Liverpool manager. I refused a contract. I said I wanted to do the job and earn one. But Kevin told me that he thought I should have a contract for my own good. Kevin and I had some good, heart-to-heart talks. The chat we had after Kevin had walked out on England, for instance, helped heal the breach with Don Revie.

'Kevin was upset that after playing for England in Northern Ireland, despite receiving a death threat, he had been left out of the following Wednesday's Wembley game against Wales, without Don saying a word to him. I saw my job as lifting Kevin's spirits. Eventually, the axe was buried and Kevin went on eventually to captain his country as an automatic choice.

'In Kevin's early England appearances under Sir Alf Ramsey, I think his role in the team was too rigid. Kevin likes to fill attacking roles from wide on the left to the old inside-right berth. When he started his England career they wanted him tied down to a position wide on the right which didn't really suit him. After Ron Greenwood succeeded Revie as England manager, Kevin's stature as an international player became immense.'

The passing years clearly softened any ill-feeling Keegan might once have felt as he made clear to me during his period reviving Fulham's fortunes and guiding them to promotion from Division Two before taking charge of England. 'I played for Shanks and Bob at a key stage in my life between 20 and 26,' said Keegan. 'It was a privilege to play for them both. Without them I wouldn't have had the success I had. The great thing about Bob is that he had massive football knowledge but no football ego. He led Liverpool to great things and left behind a record of achievement that was a millstone round the neck of anyone who followed him. I just associate him with success.'

Keegan's departure prompted Paisley to offer up a silent prayer. 'I just hoped that after the trials and tribulations of my early years in management, someone on high would smile on me and guide my hand,' he admitted. 'My plea was answered when we got Kenny Dalglish. What a player. What a great professional! Just as Kevin had wanted a new challenge, so Kenny had let it be known to Celtic that he was unsettled and wanted to embark on a new chapter of his career.'

In Dalglish he signed a player who would prove to be generally accepted as the finest in the history of the Anfield club. He was the second of a trio of Scottish acquisitions in eight months by Paisley which rank as three of the greatest ever made by a manager in British football. The previous May, as Anfield was consumed with the championship and the FA and European Cup Finals, Paisley paid £100,000 for a 21-year-old from Partick Thistle. Alan Hansen was to become a central defender of such class and culture that even Joe Mercer, who for a lifetime had lauded his former Everton team-mate Tommy G. Jones as the best British centre-back he had ever seen, was moved to proclaim that Hansen was in the same exalted category, perhaps even shading the great Welshman. Then in January 1978 Paisley completed his 'treble Scotch' by signing midfielder Graeme Souness, a player he had long admired and who had suddenly been made available from Middlesbrough for £352,000.

Souness, memorably described by my journalist colleague David
Miller as 'a bear of a man with the touch of a violinist', was to have
a massive influence on Paisley's team, with his potent blend of skill
and steel.

The injection of the talents of Dalglish, Hansen and Souness
brought a new dimension to Liverpool, whose team over the years
had traditionally been ingrained with Scottish players but who
had become champions of Europe without a single Scot in the 16-
man squad on duty in Rome. Indeed, but for Joey Jones and Steve
Heighway, the squad was entirely English.

Liverpool's friendly relations with Celtic, the respect that
existed between Paisley and Parkhead boss Jock Stein and a
television documentary on the Anfield club were the instrumental
factors in Dalglish's arrival.

'I was on holiday in Majorca with Tom Saunders when Celtic
made contact to see if we'd be interested in signing Kenny should
he become available,' Paisley recalled. 'Of course I was interested
in Kenny, a fine player tailor-made for our passing style. I cut
short my holiday and came home, and told Jessie that I'd be
making myself scarce for a few days. But I didn't tell her where I
was going because I didn't want it to be public knowledge where
I was. Jessie will not tell lies. So if she didn't know where I was,
she wouldn't have to tell lies if anyone tried to find me.

'I promised I'd ring her each night while I was away. My secret
hideaway was a small hotel in North Wales and the only person
who knew about it was my good friend Ray Peers. It was Ray who
told me that Jock Stein had been trying to contact me at the club
and when I rang home, Jessie told me he had left his telephone
number. When I spoke to Jock he told me he was going to make
another attempt to persuade Kenny to stay at Parkhead. But he
asked me if Kenny was still adamant about leaving, would we be
in the market for him at around £440,000? The make-or-break in
the situation was Celtic's forthcoming Australian tour. If Kenny
preferred not to go on it, then Jock was resigned to losing him and
he was giving us first bite.

'I spoke to our board about it and they told me that if Kenny
was the player I wanted, I had the go-ahead to sign him. I rang
Jock to tell him and also made it clear that we wanted to sign
Kenny before the 15 August deadline for the opening rounds of
the European Cup, otherwise we'd have to look elsewhere to try
to replace Kevin. Celtic left for their Australian tour without

Kenny, but when I telephoned Jock in Singapore he told me he was still going to have another try at persuading him to stay at the club when he got back.

'Jock and I agreed that with the European deadline moving closer, the day of decision must be Tuesday, 9 August. Jock kept his word and contacted me on the Tuesday morning. He'd had another chat with Kenny but had failed to persuade him to stay at Celtic and, reluctantly, he was making him available. Jock asked us to meet him at Parkhead at ten o'clock that night after Celtic's friendly game at Dunfermline.

'I dashed up to Scotland with our chairman John Smith and in an attempt to avoid recognition and keep things quiet, we booked into a Moffat hotel as brothers under the names of John and Bill Smith. A few minutes after we'd checked in, a lad came up to me and asked: "Can I have your autograph, Mr Paisley?" Our cover had quickly been blown! When we arrived at Parkhead we talked with Jock and Kenny and the deal was done in about ten minutes. Kenny travelled down to sign at Anfield the next day. The £440,000 fee soon began to look ridiculously low. I said at the signing ceremony that we had bought probably the best player in Britain, a proven goalscorer with the skill to play anywhere. We went for the best without making too much fuss about it. We wanted to get on with the job.'

As they left Parkhead, Paisley turned to Smith and said: 'Let's get out of here before they realise what we've done.' What they had done was pull off one of the best deals football has seen anytime, anywhere. Dalglish was to spend almost 14 years as a player and manager of the club he was drawn to after seeing a BBC TV documentary on Liverpool's European Cup Final in Rome. Watching the programme at Scotland's hotel in Chester, prior to a home international against Wales at Wrexham, he was impressed not only by the quality of Liverpool's play but also the general demeanour of the club, ranging from Nina the telephonist and receptionist to chairman Smith.

'There was something very appealing about Liverpool Football Club,' said Dalglish. 'I had been there briefly as a fifteen-year-old when Shanks was manager and I knew there were similarities with Celtic. What really came across on television was how closely knit everyone was at Anfield. There was a real family atmosphere there. All in all, the programme portrayed Liverpool as a club I'd love to play for, especially as I knew they could give me the opportunity of success in Europe, something I was yearning for. There wasn't any other club I wanted to play for.'

If Keegan had been the dynamic mainspring of Liverpool during his six years there, Dalglish was its brainbox, a player oozing skill and vision but with a remarkable body strength to withstand physical challenges in the hostile area of the goalmouth.

Paisley recalled: 'Kenny had been at Anfield more than a decade earlier when he came down for trials as a youngster. He came twice, once playing in a junior game against Southport. He got a ticket to watch our 1966 Charity Shield game against Everton at Goodison Park. We'd won the championship and they'd won the FA Cup, but the occasion was made unique by the fact that the World Cup, which England had just won, was also on show. That was some occasion for young Kenny to experience and, apparently, Bill Shankly asked him to come down for a third trial. He'd also had trials with West Ham, but Kenny preferred to stay in Scotland and join Celtic. I was delighted we finally got him.

'I told Kenny when he arrived that I wished we still had Kevin, too. Then it would simply have been a question of choosing the other nine players and a substitute and I'd expect to win the Grand National as well as cups and championships! There is no doubt in my mind that Kevin and Kenny together would have formed a lethal blend. Great players can always play together. They had contrasting styles – Kevin a bustling, hustling player employing tremendous energy and physique to twist in all directions, Kenny having the anticipation to turn players in one smooth movement. Kevin's ability to run with the ball would have been complemented by Kenny's outstanding ability as a purveyor of it, his liking for people being around him enabling him to capitalize on his great vision. Kevin injected a racy tempo with his mobility whereas Kenny stroked the ball around. The judgement in his passing bore the hallmark of great golf shots along with the ability to read ground conditions the way cricketers can and this uncanny knack for knowing when a ball will bounce, carry or skid on a particular surface.

'A partnership of Kevin and Kenny would certainly have been quick – Kevin the physically faster with Kenny's first five yards in his head, the same as John Toshack had the first two yards in his head when he played alongside Kevin. Neither Kevin nor Kenny could boast outstanding heading ability but were more than competent in the air. Overall as players they had two different techniques: Kenny reading what team-mates and opponents do, Kevin reacting to them.

'But because of the differences between them, there was a change in Liverpool's style when we signed Kenny. With his subtlety, a 4-4-2 formation with the accent on passing was clearly our most effective line-up whereas in the past we had often employed 4-3-3 as well.'

Dalglish declared as he signed the transfer forms: 'I'm not trying to take over from Kevin. I just want to be my own man. I'm told Kevin wanted a new challenge. So did I, and that's what I've got. Liverpool were the first English club to come in for me and who needs persuading to join someone like them? The size of the fee doesn't worry me. I don't have to carry a price tag on my back. I just have to play to the best of my ability.'

Liverpool's new signing made his first appearance at Wembley, in a goalless Charity Shield contest with Manchester United, which marked Phil Thompson's return following injury, after comeback outings in three pre-season friendlies. But among the five players on Liverpool's bench at Wembley that day were two figures representing the past and future of the club. One of them was Tommy Smith, whose Anfield testimonial two days after his headed goal in Rome attracted a 35,000-plus crowd producing receipts of around £35,000. The European Cup triumph stirred new ambition in 32-year-old Smith and instead of retiring, he accepted the club's offer of a new contract. Alongside him on the bench at Wembley was a tall, slim Scot, ten years his junior, who was adept not only at playing football but also highly skilled at golf, squash and volleyball. Indeed, Alan Hansen had represented his country at all four sports and captained Scotland's Under-21 soccer team.

Curiously, like Dalglish, Hansen also had spent a trial period as a 15-year-old at Liverpool only to return home, eventually joining Partick. 'We have never claimed to be infallible and it has to be admitted that Alan was one of the youngsters whom we allowed to leave after a very brief period of time,' recalled Tom Saunders. 'Alan came down to Anfield with three or four other lads from Scotland but we didn't take matters any further and he returned home after a four-day trial. You have to remember that there are so many things to consider when it comes to signing a lad of that age, and obviously we couldn't have been sufficiently convinced. Alan admits that until he left school at 18 he enjoyed his golf more than football and had no thoughts of becoming a professional footballer. But after ten weeks of working in an insurance office, he realised that wasn't for him, and when Partick Thistle offered him part-time terms, he accepted.

'By the time he had shown he was good enough to play for the Scotland Under-23 and Under-21 sides, he was becoming ambitious about his career. Newcastle and Bolton both had ideas about signing him, but with Partick battling to avoid relegation they wanted to keep him. That was when we reappeared on the scene. We had been keeping an eye on Alan for the best part of two years. I remember our chief scout Geoff Twentyman watched him play in various roles, as a sweeper in defence and as a midfielder. He was a good reader of the game, possessed good control and passed the ball well. Geoff remarked that because Alan made everything look so easy, he was not an easy player to assess. So Alan came back to Anfield this time to sign on the dotted line. But even then he was one for the future.'

Hansen, in fact, had an early taste of first-team action because of a rare injury to Hughes, launching a Liverpool career in which he established himself as a defender of such class and composure that Paisley drew on the superlatives to salute him. 'Alan's the most skilful centre-half I've ever seen in British football,' he was moved to enthuse. 'He has such beautiful balance. When he carries the ball he never loses control and always looks so graceful. He's a joy to watch.'

But as Paisley led Liverpool into the new season he warned his squad – which saw the departure of former England left-back Alec Lindsay to Stoke for £20,000 in September – that the demands on them would be even greater. 'The challenge will be fiercer than ever,' he told his players. 'Now we are European champions, everyone will be out to topple us. They'll have even more incentive to "do" us. We must be ready for it.'

Dalglish scored on his League debut in a 1–1 draw at Middlesbrough and three days later delighted the Kop with another goal on his home debut as Liverpool beat Newcastle 2–0. He scored again in a 3–0 Anfield victory over West Brom, claimed another in a 2–0 League Cup defeat of Chelsea and bagged two more against Coventry and Ipswich. This blistering opening of six goals in seven games made him an instant hero with the Anfield faithful and a worthy successor to the great forwards of Liverpool history. Paisley, it was self-evident, had signed quality when he captured Dalglish.

Yet Liverpool were destined to miss out on a championship hat-trick. Never in the course of the campaign did they occupy top position and had to be content with the runners-up slot as the title fell to Nottingham Forest managed by Brian Clough. The former Middlesbrough, Sunderland and England centre-forward became the first manager since Herbert Chapman pre-war to win the championship with different clubs following his triumph with Derby in 1972. Forest signalled their intent and menace with a 3–1 win at Gordon Lee's Everton on the season's opening day, their first game back in the top flight after gaining promotion. New boys they might have been but novices they most certainly were not. They were a team assembled brilliantly by Clough and his assistant Peter Taylor, who achieved a highly effective, durable blend of discarded players and costly signings.

It was Clough who reignited the career of former Liverpool centre-back and title winner Larry Lloyd, paying Coventry just £60,000 for him in November 1976, and transformed Scottish winger John Robertson from an overweight reserve into a European Cup winner. Clough also made the inspired £270,000 acquisition from Stoke of England goalkeeper Peter Shilton, a player Everton had turned down the chance to sign several seasons earlier during the Billy Bingham era. Pungent, arrogant and opinionated, Clough was poles apart from Paisley in character and personality, but one day paid him an unexpected visit.

'It was late afternoon and I was getting ready to go home when there was a knock on my office door,' Paisley recounted. 'Brian was standing there in an old tracksuit holding a bottle of whisky. I think he'd already had some. He wanted us to talk football over a drink. I told him I couldn't because I was going home for my tea. Eventually, he got up and said he was going to watch Tranmere's match. I think he walked across the river!'

Clough, typically, had a barbed observation about Anfield. 'I remember playing here when Liverpool could have fitted their trophies in a biscuit tin,' he declared. Paisley's spartan office also came in for some Clough invective. 'It reminds me of a foreman's hut on a Wimpey site,' he said.

Jesting apart, Paisley had much respect for Clough. 'He and Peter Taylor typify the perfect partnership, with one acting as foil for the other,' he observed. 'I don't think it was an easy relationship for either of them and sometimes I think they did and said things between themselves to get the rebound off the other. They seemed like two people who would not sit in the same room. It was like an Agatha Christie mystery. But they sparked off each other and brought each other out. They had good tactical knowledge and the basis of their success, wherever it's been achieved, was teamwork. Like Liverpool, their requirements for a side were simple. There's nothing complicated about their type of game. I remember Brian as a player who simply loved to score goals. He had this self-confidence which has obviously been very important to him. Yet as a manager he's always insisted on the organisation of his teams. I wonder how Clough the manager would have got on with Clough the player? But there's something about Brian I've never been able to fathom out. He was a stickler for his players being smartly dressed, insisting they wore their club blazers and ties. Yet he was often seen in public in a tracksuit carrying a squash racket! The contradiction baffles me.'

Liverpool drew both League games against Forest that season – 1–1 at the City Ground on Boxing Day and a goalless home duel in May – and also confronted them in the League Cup after reaching the final of the once-maligned competition for the first time. Dalglish scored his first Liverpool hat-trick en route to Wembley in a 3–1 fifth-round win at Wrexham, and struck again in the two-leg semi-final to give Liverpool a 2–1 aggregate victory over Arsenal. In the final, Liverpool dominated but found their luck right out and cup-tied Shilton's deputy Chris Woods in inspired form. Terry McDermott had the ball in Forest's net only to find referee Pat Partridge refusing to allow a goal because of a linesman's offside flag. The referee also rejected penalty claims for a Kenny Burns challenge on Dalglish and the game ended goalless after extra time, much to Paisley's chagrin. 'I'm convinced that we were not only the better team but that we should have won,' he said. 'Terry's goal was a perfectly good one. Everyone in the stadium, Forest players included, accepted it was a good goal. Everyone, that is, with the exception of Pat Partridge and a linesman. Partridge disallowed it because of his inter-pretation of the rule relating to "interference with play". But nobody else was interfering. Add to that the blatant penalty offence when Dalglish was tripped by Burns, with the route to goal wide open, and you will begin to understand my feeling of injustice. Yet that was nothing compared with the way Partridge handled the replay at Old Trafford.'

Indeed, the second meeting in Manchester left Paisley and the entire Liverpool club furious. The final was still goalless when Partridge awarded a 54th-minute penalty for Phil Thompson's foul on John O'Hare, deeming it to have been committed inside the box while Thompson and Liverpool insisted it was well outside the area. John Robertson scored from the spot – Ray Clemence agonisingly touching the ball on its way in – and although Liverpool mounted sustained attacks, they failed to breach Forest's massed defence and their hopes of lifting the League Cup for the first time slipped away.

Thompson was adamant that Partridge had got it wrong and as he reflected on the incident, claimed a little piece of football history. 'I did bring down O'Hare but it was at least two yards outside the box and I was very angry about it,' he said. 'I called it a "professional foul". That was the first time that phrase had been used but it's been a part of the language of football ever since. The only way to stop O'Hare was to bring him down. As a centre-back the rest of the lads would have expected me to do so.'

Under later-introduced, stricter regulations, Thompson would have been sent off. But the Old Trafford incident did not just cost Liverpool a trophy. It led to a stiff fine for the player, who was found guilty on an FA charge of bringing the game into disrepute.

'The papers were full of my quotes about my feelings, so the FA charge was no surprise,' Thompson admitted. 'When I was travelling to London with Bob Paisley to appear at Lancaster Gate, he told me to tell the disclipinary commission how much I regretted it and that it would never happen again. I told them exactly that. But Bert Millichip produced a batch of press cuttings quoting me saying I'd do the same again if I had to! That was it. I was fined £300, no small sum in those days, and the club told me I had to pay it out of my own pocket.'

Paisley vented his wrath on Partridge, saying: 'There were three incidents in the replay when I'm certain he made wrong decisions. The first was the penalty awarded against Phil Thompson. I know you can claim that it was poetic justice because the professional foul is morally wrong, and the authorities have since tried to eradicate it by sending off the offender. But Partridge had been in the game long enough to know that Phil had a choice between the devil and the deep blue sea. Either he could have let O'Hare go, risking a goal and a tongue-lashing from me, or commit the foul and accept the inevitable booking.

'But what Phil would not do, and did not do, was bring down O'Hare in the penalty area. Television cameras proved clearly it happened outside the penalty area, so a penalty should not have been awarded. If the referee was in doubt about where the foul occurred, he should have consulted a linesman and if he thought the offence to be so bad then he should have sent off Phil. But not give a penalty.

'Pat Partridge put his own head in a noose by admitting afterwards that he was ten yards behind the play but was convinced it was a penalty. Because it was the decisive and most controversial moment of the game, Phil was hustled in front of microphones at the end when mentally he was in no condition to comment. Right after a game is the worst time of all to talk because your mind is racing. Consequently, Phil admitted publicly that he had committed a professional foul, which led to his appearance before the FA and cost him a fine.

'A few minutes after the penalty decision, the referee was caught again when we broke quickly and the ball was played forward to Terry McDermott. Terry controlled it with the top left-hand side of his chest and went on to put the ball in the net for what would have been the equaliser. But it was disallowed. The referee was in no position to judge whether Terry's arm played any part in controlling the ball, and he had to rely on a linesman's decision. Terry swore the ball didn't touch his arm. Be that as it may, the referee should have been in the right position to make a decision of his own. It is essential that referees keep up with play.'

McDermott was equally upset after having a 'goal' ruled out for the second time in the two games. 'I couldn't believe it when the referee disallowed it,' he said. 'Why he disallowed it I don't know. He's gone with the linesman again, which he did at Wembley. I'd swear on the Bible that there was no way the ball hit my hand or my arm. It hit my chest, bounced perfectly for me and I put it in the back of the net. I'm choked and all the lads in the dressing room are sick about it. It's another injustice.'

Paisley was also angry at another Partridge decision which ended a proud record for long-serving Ian Callaghan. 'It rubbed salt in our wounds that he found it necessary to book Ian for the first time in 849 games for Liverpool for what was a perfectly legitimate shoulder charge on Peter Withe,' he said. 'Withe himself told the referee the challenge had been fair, but he still went ahead and booked Ian.' Liverpool were seething at their 1–0 defeat and the events of that traumatic March night at Old Trafford. By then, though, they had already clinched their place in the European Cup semi-final, in which they were to face a swift renewal of combat with old adversaries Borussia Moenchengladbach.

After being given a bye in the first round, because there were only 31 entrants in the competition due to disciplinary sanctions against Albania, the holders began the defence of their crown against another set of familiar German foes, this time from the East. They were pitted against Dynamo Dresden and the omens were massive for Liverpool. In their previous meetings, in the 1973 and 1976 UEFA Cup tournaments, they had gone on to lift the trophy on each occasion.

'I told the players they had to forget Rome and they responded magnificently,' enthused Paisley, after his team toppled Dresden 5–1 in the home first leg. Jimmy Case struck twice and the other goals came from Hansen – on his European debut – Ray Kennedy and a Phil Neal penalty. The match was also notable for the return of John Toshack, who squeezed out McDermott for his first full senior game following his long-term Achilles problem which had required summer surgery. It was one of only five occasions that Toshack partnered Dalglish, before ending his Anfield career the following March. After scoring 96 goals in 246 Liverpool outings, he agreed to become player-manager of Swansea City. Within two months his new charges won promotion to Division Three to begin an amazing journey all the way to the top flight. For Toshack it was the launch of a managerial odyssey that took him around Europe, including two spells at Real Madrid, a whistle-stop spell in charge of Wales and three times being in the frame to return to Anfield as boss.

The emphatic first-leg conquest of Dresden prompted Paisley to enter in his diary: 'This was a very good win and our victory made the Germans look much worse than they are. We took our chances well and got the goals at the right time. It should stand us in good stead for the return, but we can take nothing for granted.' How wise his caution proved to be. Liverpool suffered more than a few jitters in the second leg as Dresden pulled back two goals with a fine, attacking performance and it was not until Heighway prodded in a 67th-minute goal that the apprehension of the visitors was relieved. Liverpool lost 2–1 but clinched a 6–3 aggregate triumph and a place in the quarter-finals the following March, for which Paisley was massively thankful.

'Dresden gave us anything but an easy ride in the return and played brilliantly,' he reflected. 'I don't think I've seen a team play as fast as they did and for so long. Only our 5–1 lead kept them at bay. I'd hoped the game would be a quiet one, given our big first-leg advantage. But they harried us over every yard of the pitch and it wasn't until I introduced David Fairclough, in place of Terry McDermott, to run at them in the second half that we got into the game a bit. The substitution worked and Steve's goal knocked the stuffing out of them, because they then needed three more goals even to force extra time.'

The satisfaction felt by Paisley and Liverpool at reaching the European Cup last eight was followed by concern at home as they plunged into a sequence of dismal results which ultimately cost them their chance of completing a championship hat-trick. They returned from East Germany to suffer a rare home defeat by Aston Villa, their first reverse in front of the Kop since Middlesbrough's win 46 games earlier in March 1976. Villa's goals were also the first Liverpool had conceded at Anfield in domestic competition for seven months, and even their reply was an own goal by Frank Carrodus.

The headlines screamed 'crisis' and Paisley responded by declaring: 'Hard work must now be the first order of the day. I've always said we have no divine right to win anything. Nor has anybody else. Whatever you get you have to earn. We always knew that after last season's successes, the challenge this time would be fiercer than ever. I've still got the best squad of players in the country once we get things sorted out. We'll not change our approach to the game and we're not going to relinquish what we've got. The fact that people are calling it a crisis only serves to emphasise the standard we've set.'

But Liverpool woes continued with a 2–0 defeat at Queens Park Rangers on what would have been a totally forgettable November afternoon for Paisley but for the turn of events he experienced as the team bus carrying the downhearted Anfield party left Loftus Road. The defeat was Liverpool's fourth in succession – they had gone down 3–1 at Manchester City prior to their trip to Dresden – which constituted their worst string of results for 12 years. So there was a subdued after-match atmosphere on board the team coach, in which Paisley sat at the front alongside chairman John Smith, believing they were heading for Euston Station and the train back to Liverpool. Suddenly, a figure rose from the back seat clutching a microphone and walked up the aisle of the coach before delivering that famous phrase: 'Bob Paisley, this is your life!'

Eamonn Andrews had been smuggled on board through the emergency door at the back of the coach posing as a member of a German TV crew shooting a football documentary. Paisley's instant reaction was one of disbelief as he recognised Andrews and exclaimed: 'Oh, no!' Smith, who had been in on the secret with the players, roared with laughter, which intensified as Paisley joked with Andrews: 'I thought at first you were the QPR centre-forward.' Instead of Euston Station, the coach headed to the nearby Thames TV studios in Euston Road for the recording of one of the most memorable *This Is Your Life* shows. But it had meant Jessie Paisley breaking one of the hard and fast rules of her life by being forced to tell a white lie.

'When Liverpool had an away game, Bob and I used to speak on the telephone on the Saturday morning,' said Jessie. 'But I told him I wouldn't be at home that Saturday because I'd be taking a group of my school children to a camp in North Wales. In fact, I was with the family travelling to London for the TV show. How Bob believed that I'd be taking primary school pupils to a camp in the middle of November I don't know! But he seemed to accept it.'

The show, launched by Andrews saluting the miner's son who had brought the European Cup back to England in the Queen's Jubilee Year and been awarded the OBE, was a heady cocktail of emotions for the Paisley family. Bob's brother Hughie, present with his wife Mary, recalled their boyhood in Hetton, as did his junior football team-mate Ned Blenkinsop, who revealed how Bob would use a trip to the fish and chip shop as a training exercise by running there and back. The guests, as well as a studio ensemble that included fans and players, heard how Paisley became a bricklayer, only for life to lead him into professional football after his spell with Bishop Auckland. Fulsome tributes came from such football luminaries as Sir Matt Busby, Kevin Keegan and Billy Liddell, and, of course, from Bill Shankly, who gave Paisley a hug after insisting: 'We never had time to fall out when we were together because we were too busy planning to win cups.' Jessie related the story of how she and Bob first met, as strangers on a train in the 1940s, while his love of horseracing was represented by his friend, the celebrated trainer Frank Carr.

By the time the show was screened to the nation, Liverpool's fortunes on the field had been restored. But a week after the QPR reverse, they could manage only a 1–1 home draw with struggling Bristol City, which was to be John Toshack's last Liverpool appearance. Alan Hansen's stomach upset a few hours before kick-off brought a first-team recall for Phil Thompson and with only two recognised midfielders in Ray Kennedy and Ian Callaghan operating behind a four-man attack of Dalglish, Toshack and wingers Heighway and Fairclough, it was an unusual Liverpool formation that sought an upturn in Anfield fortunes. However, even an early Dalglish strike failed to prise victory. Bristol, inspired by the resolute Norman Hunter, snatched a draw with a 25-yard shot from Gerry Gow that swept past Clemence in the blustery wind. So in mid-November, Liverpool were sixth in the First Division with 19 points from 16 games, five points behind Nottingham Forest.

Paisley's side turned the corner with another venture into Europe, this time to meet Hamburg and Kevin Keegan for the European Super Cup, competed for by the holders of the European and Cup-Winners' Cups. The commitment to a two-leg date with Keegan's new club had only fuelled Paisley's hostility to facing the South American champions for the World Club crown, which led to Liverpool declining FIFA's invitation to take part. Past encounters between the champions of the two continents had proved explosive and Paisley said: 'Football's just a war against the South Americans – we'll leave the world title with Ali. There's no way I want us involved against the South American champions because of the risk of injuries and aggravation that we've seen so often in the past in these games, plus the fatigue factor caused by travelling. We've got a new European challenge on our plate, anyway, to try to retain the European Cup, and we've got the two matches against Hamburg in the Super Cup. Our domestic programme is too fierce to fit in those as well as home and away World Club championship matches. For all those reasons I recommended to the board that we didn't take part.' Borussia Moenchengladbach took Liverpool's place and lost 5–2 on aggregate to Argentine foes Boca Juniors.

The much shorter trip to Hamburg that winter of 1977, though prolonged by a delayed flight, provided the launch pad for a Liverpool revival. A 16,000 crowd who braved the wintry elements in the Volkspark stadium saw Liverpool recover after conceding a first-half goal by Keller. Fairclough's 66th-minute equaliser gave them a draw and a much-needed confidence boost.

An injury to Joey Jones in Germany meant a five-match recall for Tommy Smith and his return at right-back, with Phil Neal switching to the left, coinciding with a thumping 4–0 win at Leicester, Liverpool's first victory in seven games, thanks to goals from Fairclough, Heighway, Dalglish and McDermott. It also provided a happy send-off for Paisley on his trip to Buckingham Palace three days later. Jessie and the family travelled south with him for the investiture ceremony at the Palace, and Paisley recounted this dialogue with Her Majesty when he stepped up to receive his OBE.

Queen: And you are?
Paisley: Bob Paisley, ma'am, manager of Liverpool.
Queen: You have been having a lot of success lately.
Paisley: I don't think, ma'am, you've been reading the papers over the past month.
Queen: Oh, well, we all have our ups and downs.
Paisley (*later at Anfield*): If she has ups and downs then we're all entitled to have them!

Although the award provided official recognition of Paisley's achievements there is little doubt that the prevailing football climate during his managerial career cost him a knighthood. He was, in that sense, a victim of his time. The cloud of hooliganism and crowd violence still hung over the national game, and would do so until the disasters or Bradford, Heysel and Hillsborough signalled a new dawn for football. The Taylor Report was the catalyst for the construction of new and renovated stadia on a scale that could not have been envisaged in the 1970s and early 1980s. The formation of the Premier League in 1992, its bank-rolling by Sky Television and the sky-rocketing surge in players' earnings completed a football revolution that took less than a decade.

The sport is now a chic commodity, a sport with a showbiz glow in which politicians and celebrities like to bathe. Bob Paisley was pre-bonanza. If he had performed his feats in a similar environment to the existing one, in which football is the fashion, surely 10 Downing Street would have been swift to approve the monarch tapping him on the shoulder with a ceremonial sword and saying, 'Arise, Sir Robert.' Witness the announcement within three weeks of Manchester United's completion of the treble in

1999 that Alex Ferguson had gained the prefix 'Sir', the eighth
football manager or player to be awarded a knighthood and the
third from Old Trafford, following Sir Matt Busby and Sir Bobby
Charlton. Ferguson's accolade went down like a lead balloon on
Merseyside, where the media demanded fair and due recognition
of Paisley's unprecedented feats. 'Where was the hype when Bob
was in his pomp?' asked *Liverpool Echo* sports editor Ken Rogers
in an opinion column. 'The gritty Paisley was not just the most
successful boss of all time but also the most modest. Why not a
posthumous knighthood for Bob Paisley, based on his remarkable
achievements? Such an honour for Bob and his family would be
richly deserved.' Paisley's brother Hughie echoed the belief that
Bob was short-changed. 'He definitely deserved a knighthood
because what he did was unbelievable,' he said. 'If anyone earned
a tap on the shoulder, Bob did.'

The only honours Bob Paisley ever mentioned, of course, were
those he wanted Liverpool to win. He was delighted if he could
meet the personal target he revealed when he succeeded Shankly:
'I said when I took over that I would settle for a drop of Bell's
once a month, a big bottle at the end of the season and a ride
round the city in an open-top bus!'

In September 1977, Liverpool's status at least had been
recognised by new England manager Ron Greenwood when he
picked six Anfield players – plus Kevin Keegan – for his first
match in charge, a goalless duel with Switzerland. Ian Callaghan
collected his first cap for 11 years in a Wembley team that also
included Ray Clemence, Phil Neal, skipper Emlyn Hughes, Ray
Kennedy and Terry McDermott, who was making his debut.

Paisley, though, had to negotiate several testing phases during
the 1977–78 season before he and Liverpool registered another
notable and historic triumph. Unlike their League Cup experience
in the replayed final against Forest, the team's fate in the FA Cup
was largely self-inflicted. They crashed 4–2 at Chelsea, where their
goals came from David Johnson, still battling to command regular
first-team football after revealing his summer discontent, and
Dalglish. It was a dismal display by Liverpool, their first exit at the
third-round stage for 12 years and one which felt the lash of
Paisley's tongue. 'I couldn't recognise our players out there today
– their heads were full of sawdust,' was his acerbic verdict, which
had a dramatic sequel three days later when he pulled off the
signing of Souness, one of the most crucial in the club's history.

Once Middlesbrough decided to part with their unsettled star, the deal took just minutes to finalise and agreement was reached in the empty ballroom of a Leeds hotel.

'There are not many players who come up to our standard and because they're in such short supply, you have to try to get them when they become available,' said Paisley, whose first bid, made prior to the 15 December deadline for the European Cup quarter-finals, had been rejected by Middlesbrough. 'Graeme can pass a ball, he's got vision and he's got strength. He'll play in central midfield, which is his position, and we'll sort the rest out from there.'

The day before the ignominious Cup exit at Chelsea, Scottish centre forward Joe Jordan of Leeds announced that he had rejected a chance to join Liverpool and had chosen to sign instead for Manchester United in a £350,000 move. Paisley's success in landing Souness, though, proved to be a master stroke.

Souness, raised in a pre-fab on an Edinburgh council estate and educated at the same secondary school as Dave Mackay, had just finished a week's suspension imposed by Middlesbrough manager John Neal because of the growing rift between the player and the club. Indeed, on the night he joined Liverpool, Souness had been due to play for Middlesbrough reserves in a North Midland League game against Lincoln. Instead he arrived at Anfield to pose for photographs with Paisley and the European Cup and enthused: 'Liverpool have got to be the top club in the country. Any player would give his right arm to play for them. I'm delighted to be here. I didn't think Boro would ever be another Liverpool in my playing career, and I wanted to join a club where I had a chance of winning something.'

The capture of 24-year-old Souness meant that Liverpool had set three transfer records in seven months: the top deal between a British and foreign club (£500,000 from Hamburg for Keegan), the highest between British clubs (£440,000 for Dalglish) and the record cash deal between English clubs for Souness (£352,000). The latest arrival swiftly earned the nickname of 'Champagne Charlie' after his drinks bill at the Liverpool hotel in which he was living hit £200 for the first fortnight. He soon discovered that life at Paisley's Liverpool meant having your feet on the ground rather than your head in the clouds. The club frowned on the drinks expenditure and tales of extravagant activities, and Souness revealed that his compatriot and fellow hotel resident Dalglish helped curb such excesses.

'If Kenny had not been staying in the hotel with his family at the same time, I would have gone completely crazy,' Souness admitted in his book *No Half Measures*. 'He was in the room opposite and would always make his point with a joke, saying I could bring in his breakfast on my way back to my room. I have a lot to thank him for. Kenny's quiet jibes helped pull me round. I'm certain if they hadn't have done, Liverpool would have transferred me.'

Communication between the pair was not always so productive. Fellow Scots and Liverpool room-mates they might have been, but the Glaswegian tones of Dalglish sometimes caused problems for Souness. That was demonstrated perfectly on a club trip abroad during the period I was writing Dalglish's weekly *Daily Express* column. Souness, aware of my penchant for translating some of the more difficult Dalglishisms, knocked at my hotel room door wearing a baffled expression.

'Kenny's just said something to me and I haven't got a clue what he's saying,' announced Souness before imploring: 'Please go and ask him what he's on about!'

Souness also brought with him a disciplinary record that alarmed Paisley, whose players were annually in contention for the Fair Play Award. He had a carry-over of three bookings from Middlesbrough, and two more collected with Liverpool took him to 20 penalty points and a three-match ban ruling him out of games against Wolves, Aston Villa and Everton. He had suffered a similar fate with Middlesbrough the previous year and now became the first Liverpool player to be suspended under the disciplinary totting-up system which the FA had introduced three years earlier. Because of his suspension, plus his ineligibility for both the League Cup and the European Cup quarter-final, he started only seven of Liverpool's first 18 games following his signing, spanning mid-January to early April, and figured in another as substitute.

Souness's propensity for falling foul of referees was a priority issue with Paisley, who reminded his new recruit that he had bought him to play, not to serve suspensions. The message was echoed by Joe Fagan and Ronnie Moran and driven home at Paisley's request by Tom Saunders, who would stand at the top of the tunnel on match days and remind Souness as he ran out not to collect avoidable bookings.

'Graeme gets these cautions because of the way he tackles,' said

Paisley. 'If he can change that part of his game, he wouldn't get into trouble with referees. We realise he's been extra keen to do well after joining us. But he's been told about the way he goes into these tackles.

'The last player we had suspended was Joey Jones, who was sent off at Middlesbrough two seasons ago. He received a one-game ban but we've never had a player get so many cautions in a season that he's reached 20 points.'

Souness's arrival, to link up with Dalglish, left an indelible impression on their fellow Scot, Alan Hansen, who said: 'The great thing about Souness and Dalglish is that they never lost an argument in their lives . . . even when they argued with each other! The most outstanding of all their many qualities was their sheer will to win.'

Liverpool's efforts at honing Souness's tackling and curbing his on-field excesses richly bore fruit as he established himself as a midfielder of style and sophistication pervaded with a menacing touch of steel. 'I want to justify the money Liverpool have paid for me,' Souness said. 'I know I won't have done that until I have achieved what players like Ian Callaghan and Tommy Smith have done at Anfield. They did the most difficult thing in football – getting to the top and staying there.' Souness was to develop a productive, harmonious relationship with Paisley, about whom he observed: 'He may be regarded by supporters and the public as a fatherly figure, but I can tell you one thing: he rules Anfield with a rod of iron. If we looked as if we were becoming a little bit complacent or if we were not performing up to standard, Bob would say: "If you have all had enough of winning, come and see me. I will sell the lot of you and buy 11 new players." Another time he warned: "I am only a modest Geordie – but get me cornered and I am a mean bastard." But it would be wrong to give the impression that we all walked round in fear and trepidation. He always kept a velvet glove on.'

Souness's arrival at Anfield was cheered by Paisley's friend Bob Rawcliffe. He had got to know the Scot through former Liverpool player Phil Boersma, who shared digs with Souness at Middlesbrough. Garage proprietor Rawcliffe had supplied cars to Paisley and his family as well as servicing Liverpool FC vehicles. On his way to training each morning, Paisley would call in to see Rawcliffe at the nearby Wheatsheaf Garage for a cup of tea and a study of the newspaper racecards before placing a bet. When Souness signed, he too joined the morning ritual in the garage office.

'I'd been singing Graeme's praises as a player for some time and pleading with Bob to sign him,' said Rawcliffe. 'He used to smile and say: "You look after your garage and I'll look after the football!" Then one morning he said to me: "I'm telling you this because it's going to happen today – we're signing Souness." I was over the moon. Graeme called in almost every day and he, Bob and I chatted about all sorts of things, even tactics! Bob would come into the office, sit behind the desk and even answer the phone. If I wasn't there, he'd let himself in. Even when I was on holiday he was there! In fact, people used to think it was his garage.

'Bob loved a bet. He had a flutter every day but he was very careful. Even though he carried a wad of money, he would never gamble more than £3 a day. Once at Chester races we got four out of six winners and we each collected about £500.'

If Souness represented a key part of Liverpool's future, one of their old boys, Kevin Keegan, had a chastening experience on his return to Anfield with Hamburg in December of that 1977–78 season. The occasion was the second leg of the European Super Cup, following the 1–1 draw in Germany. It was the cue for Liverpool to run riot with Terry McDermott, playing in a central midfield role in the absence of flu victim Ian Callaghan, firing the first hat-trick of his career two days before his 26th birthday. Hamburg were overpowered and overwhelmed 6–0, with Phil Thompson, David Fairclough and Dalglish also on target, leaving Keegan to walk off the pitch at the end and reflect ruefully: 'I'd heard Liverpool hadn't been doing too well but from where I was stood watching there didn't seem to be much wrong with them! There were no cracks and they look as strong, if not stronger, than they ever were.'

It was indeed a season in which much of Liverpool's finest form was evident on the European stage, not least when they encountered Benfica in the European Cup quarter-final. The first leg was in Lisbon on a rain-lashed night in March when the famous Stadium of Light could have been renamed the Bowl of Water. Virtually everyone in the 75,000 crowd, barring the loyal band of Merersyside fans who had made the trip, held up an umbrella to the weeping skies, giving the stadium an eerie look. 'It was like a tropical storm and all the umbrellas made it look as if there were thousands of black beetles watching the match,' said

Paisley. 'It was weird and I can't remember conditions like it.'

In this torrential downpour, Liverpool were facing a side who had not lost for 46 matches under their English coach John Mortimore. A test of stamina also became a test of character for Liverpool when they went behind after 15 minutes to a breakaway goal by Nene. But eight minutes before half-time they pulled level with a Jimmy Case free kick, which he smashed past goalkeeper Bento after McDermott had run over the ball. A minute later Alan Hansen replaced the injured Thompson but Liverpool grew in stature as the game progressed and collected an impressive victory through a rare strike by Emlyn Hughes after 73 minutes. The Liverpool skipper received the ball from Case out on the left flank and checked before curling a shot over Bento and into the far side of the net. It proved to be the only goal of the season for Hughes in his 58 appearances. 'My annual one,' as he described it.

Paisley wrote in his diary: 'There was so much rain that perhaps we were fortunate the match was completed. It was a tremendous result, more than we had dared to dream of, and it should put us in good heart for the return.'

The second leg became a mere formality with less than twenty minutes on the clock as Callaghan scored his only goal of his final season with Liverpool, with a shot intended as a cross, and Dalglish also struck. Nene scored again for Benfica before half-time, but further goals from McDermott and Phil Neal took Liverpool through to the semi-finals on a 6–2 aggregate. 'Two early goals just about put paid to Benfica's chances,' Paisley entered in his diary. 'We played well in that early period, but later, individuals took over and we lost a bit of our rhythm. Benfica got a goal back from a Jimmy Case back pass but it was the same old story – they can only play as well as you let them.'

The victory sent Liverpool into a semi-final clash with familiar adversaries Borussia Moenchengladbach, against whom, Paisley believed, they had won the 'mind game' before a ball was kicked. 'We knew we had a psychological advantage,' he said. 'Not only had we beaten them in Rome the previous May but also in the 1973 UEFA Cup Final. We also had a great record against German teams. In fact, no West German club had even scored at Anfield in the various European competitions, and that included Bayern Munich, Cologne and Eintracht Brunswick, as well as Moenchengladbach. Added to that, we were drawn away in the first leg, just as we preferred it.'

Souness was at last eligible for European combat with Liverpool, although Paisley named him among the five substitutes at Dusseldorf's horseshoe-shaped Rheinstadion, delaying his introduction until the 71st minute when he replaced Steve Heighway. It was Souness's first taste of European football for almost seven years since he had been sent on in Keflavik, Iceland as an 18-year-old Tottenham substitute for Alan Mullery in a UEFA Cup tie in 1971. Liverpool were trailing to a first-half Hannes goal when he made his entrance but it was Paisley's first substitute, David Johnson, who struck a crucial blow. He had taken over from McDermott just after the hour mark and with two minutes left headed an equaliser. Even though dead-ball expert Rainer Bonhof snatched a second Borussia goal from a free kick in the dying seconds, the 2–1 reverse still left Liverpool in a strong position for the second leg.

Paisley, however, reflected: 'We felt aggrieved that we'd not drawn. Bonhof's free kick swerved, dipped, took a deflection, and it should never have been awarded in the first place. Phil Thompson was pushed on to the ball for what the Spanish referee decided was a deliberate handling offence and gave the free-kick. Even Borussia's first goal came from a corner which should have been a goal kick. They probably had the better of the first half, but we never lost our composure and had the better chances. The tie is still wide open and it's up to us to force the pace in the return.'

Johnson's contribution in Germany earned him a starting place in Liverpool's next three games. He teamed up with two-goal Dalglish and Heighway in a three-man attack in an emphatic 3–0 win at Aston Villa, with Ray Kennedy also on the mark, and then struck the only goal of the Merseyside derby at Goodison Park with a shot that rebounded off goalkeeper George Wood's left upright. The irony was supreme, for when Everton had last claimed victory over Liverpool, back in November 1971, Johnson was their scorer at the same Gwladys Street end of Goodison.

Johnson's derby joy turned to heartbreak in his next outing, against Leicester at Anfield. The game was only six minutes old when the bearded striker sank to the turf in agony, his right knee ligaments torn. 'My shot was blocked but my knee carried on,' was his rueful description of the incident. Teenager Sammy Lee not only replaced the injured Johnson but celebrated his debut by scoring. He drove a shot through the legs of Leicester keeper Mark Wallington, his goal sandwiched between a brace by Tommy Smith in a 3–2 win.

Having had a taste of the big time, Lee stepped down to make way for Heighway's return for the second leg against Moenchengladbach, which was also Souness's first start in a European game. Liverpool produced a stirring display and took just six minutes to wipe out Borussia's first-leg advantage thanks to a glorious header from Ray Kennedy. Dalglish and Case were also on target to clinch a convincing 3–0 win and a 4–2 aggregate victory. It took Liverpool through to a second successive European Cup Final, this time on English soil at Wembley where their opponents would be Bruges, also old adversaries. The Belgians, beaten by Liverpool in the UEFA Cup Final two years earlier, had overcome fancied Juventus in their semi-final.

'We got the early goal we needed against Moenchengladbach and then took complete control,' said Paisley. 'It was a real team effort and we've made history by becoming the first British club to reach the European Cup Final in successive years.'

Souness, who gave a masterful performance, savoured the moment so much that he refused to part with his jersey when the players swapped at the end. 'I kept it because I felt so proud just being a Liverpool player,' he explained. He gave his number 11 shirt instead to his parents Jim and Bette, who were at Anfield to see him play for the club for the first time.

Liverpool had seven more League fixtures prior to the European final and their impressive form prompted thoughts of what might have been if they had produced more consistency earlier in the domestic campaign. Draws at Bristol City and at home to Ipswich were followed by four straight wins over Norwich, Arsenal, West Ham and Manchester City. The Maine Road club, who had been heavily involved in the championship battle, were demolished 4–0 at Anfield, with Dalglish firing his second Liverpool hat-trick. The team completed their First Division programme with a goalless home draw against new champions Nottingham Forest to finish runners-up, seven points behind Clough's side but two ahead of Everton. The visitors avoided defeat thanks largely to a fine goalkeeping performance from Peter Shilton, the great rival of Ray Clemence for the role of England's number one.

If Shilton had proved an inspired signing by Clough, then Clemence was continuing to enhance his reputation as one of the best keepers in the history of Liverpool. His durability, as well as his talent, was remarkable, and that was underlined earlier in the season when his amazing 333-game ever-present run stretching back to September 1972 was ended by a shoulder injury which meant a two-game blooding for Steve Ogrizovic, Paisley's giant £70,000 November recruit from Chesterfield. Clemence's unbroken sequence set an English record for a goalkeeper and was only 17 games short of Brian Lloyd's British goalkeeping record of 350 successive appearances for Wrexham.

When former police constable Ogrizovic arrived for duties at Anfield, he described his task understudying Clemence as 'the hardest job in the world'. At least he tasted first-team action, five times in all. (The previous reserve keeper, Peter McDonnell, was denied even a single senior appearance, although he did collect a European Cup medal for sitting on the bench in Rome). Ogrizovic, who picked up two such European medals himself before moving on to Shrewsbury in 1982, was plunged into his debut in Clemence's absence at Derby. He found himself beaten four times in 66 minutes, with only late goals from Fairclough and Dalglish restoring a sliver of respectability to the scoreline. Clemence, though, was generous to his understudy. 'Steve was in no way to blame for our defeat,' he said. 'He made some great saves and did as well if not better than I could have done, the way we played at Derby.' At 20, Ogrizovic put it down to experience and more than two decades later at Coventry he was still playing in his forties, to set remarkable records of his own.

However, during his period at Liverpool, Oggy, as he was known, fell victim to Paisley's sometimes sardonic humour. Chatting to Terry McDermott one day the reserve keeper revealed that he felt he should have a wage rise. 'Go and see the boss,' said McDermott, always ready for a bit of mischief. 'Tell him to pay you what you're worth.'

Suitably persuaded, Oggy went to see Paisley in his office and said: 'Boss, I really do feel you should pay me what I'm worth.' Paisley, with a twinkle in his eye, replied: 'I can't do that, Oggy. I'd never forgive myself if I paid you LESS than you're getting already!' Exit Oggy, having conceded an own goal.

Paisley, naturally, was delighted to have Clemence as his last line of defence. But he revealed how he used a psychological ploy to cover a rare weakness in the England's goalkeeper's range of talents. He devised a series of gymnasium goalkeeping exercises at Melwood to increase Clemence's body strength, and explained: 'Soon after I became manager I had an idea I felt could eradicate one of the few weak points in Ray. Very few people noticed what I did – but it worked.

'At Anfield we used to fly flags from the top of the Kemlyn Road Stand on match days and as the players ran out on to the pitch they had a good view of them. In particular, they could tell from the flags when it was windy. When there's a wind, Anfield is one of the trickiest grounds in the country especially when it's blowing from the Kop end. Ray hated the wind. His biggest problem was his deadball kicking, and it was worse when he tried to kick into the wind. If he worried about his kicking it could also affect other parts of his game. I decided it was no good making him worry about how bad the wind was when he saw the way the flags were blowing as he came out of the tunnel. So I had the flags removed and Ray's kicking improved. I'm sure he felt easier in himself because he wasn't constantly being reminded that there was a wind blowing. You have to sift these things out with players who can be hit by all sorts of anxieties stemming from problems at home as well as those connected with football. Experience tells you when there's something wrong mentally as well as physically.'

Clemence took his familiar place between the posts at Wembley in May 1978 as Liverpool confronted Bruges with the aim of retaining the European Cup. They had lost their previous year's hero, Tommy Smith, who had been forced out of the last three League games following an accident in his garage at home when a pick-axe fell on his foot. But it meant an opportunity instead for Alan Hansen, who at 22 found himself propelled into the biggest club occasion on the European calendar in his first season at Liverpool.

It was a graduation not without jangling nerve ends for Hansen, who admitted: 'I always appeared cool, calm and collected to my team-mates in the dressing room before big matches. But inside I was churning up, just as I was before that European final against Bruges. The last 45 minutes or so before kick-off was never a good time for me, but that night waiting to play at Wembley was really bad. All I remember is being on the toilet for the last 20 minutes before we went out on to the pitch. As we got out there, the importance of the occasion really hit me. I felt alright after that, although I can't remember a thing about the match itself.'

Such pre-match anxieties were nothing new to Paisley, who recalled: 'Kevin Lewis, a Liverpool winger when we came out of the Second Division in 1962, looked as if he didn't have a care in the world. But he was so anxious he was physically sick before going on the field. Alan was similarly highly strung, even though he looked to be the coolest customer around.'

While the choice of Hansen was virtually dictated by Smith's misfortune, Paisley had a decision to make between David Fairclough and Steve Heighway for a place in attack. Heighway had been out of senior action since receiving a blow to the ribs in the April home clash with Ipswich. In his absence, Fairclough scored twice on his recall against Norwich, hit another goal in the home game with Arsenal and yet another in the win at West Ham. It was enough to sway Paisley into giving him a place in the Wembley team, with Heighway, having had a reserve-team outing the previous Friday, on the bench.

The Liverpool line-up, in 4-4-2 formation, was: Clemence; Neal, Thompson, Hansen, Hughes (captain); Case, McDermott, Souness, Kennedy; Dalglish, Fairclough. Substitutes: Heighway, Callaghan, Jones, Ogrizovic, Irwin.

The occasion and Liverpool's achievement proved more memorable than the game, which was spoiled by the sterile, negative tactics of Bruges, still guided by Paisley's old adversary Ernst Happel, who had also become the Dutch team coach. In the first half Liverpool's superiority went unrewarded because of a defiant display by Bruges goalkeeper Birger Jensen, the Danish international. Their dour resistance continued after the interval until the moment when sheer genius shattered the stalemate, as Kenny Dalglish offered absolute confirmation that Paisley had acquired a player who had given Liverpool's game a new dimension.

Almost immediately after replacing Fairclough in the 64th minute, Heighway linked with Terry McDermott, who continued the move down the right. It gave Graeme Souness the opportunity to deliver a delightful pass to Dalglish on the right of the Bruges box. All of a sudden, nothing happened! Dalglish just took possession and froze the game as he waited for Jensen to make his move. And as the Dane did so, Dalglish lofted the ball over him into the far corner of the net. The Liverpool supporters were ecstatic but none more so than Dalglish, who leaped over the perimeter advertising hoardings in sheer jubilation. 'I wanted to run to our fans and give them a salute,' said Dalglish. 'I don't remember jumping over the boards but I do know I couldn't leap over them on the way back because the emotion made my legs weak. Seeing that goal go in was the greatest moment of my football life. Getting a European Cup winner's medal is every player's dream.'

The ice-cool audacity of Dalglish's strike struck a chord with goalkeeper Ray Clemence, who applauded from the opposite end of Wembley. 'Very few players would or could score a goal like that,' he enthused, 'but typical of Dalglish. He invited the goalkeeper to do what he wanted him to do and then he punished him for it.'

Liverpool had to endure one heart-stopping moment ten minutes before the end when Hansen directed an under-hit backpass which gifted possession to Jan Simoen. But as he dribbled round Clemence and shot towards an empty net, Phil Thompson arrived out of nowhere and, stretching every muscle and sinew, cleared it from inside the post for a corner. 'I remember running back and thinking to myself that I just had to reach it,' said Thompson. 'I'd missed the previous year's European Cup Final through injury so I was desperate to help us keep hold of the trophy and collect a winner's medal. Clearing that shot was a great moment for me.'

'I'm proud of the players. We've won for Britain,' proclaimed Paisley afterwards. 'We needed a spark of individualism to give us victory and it was provided by Graeme and Kenny, two players comparatively new to our set-up. Graeme's sense of awareness allowed him to spot the opening and put Kenny in a one-to-one situation with the keeper that he thrives on. When Kenny scored I sensed that would be enough to win the game because of the Belgians' attitude. They were without their centre-forward Raoul Lambert and midfielder Paul Courant but they never tried to play. I think they'd come with a plan to hold out for a penalty decider. Mind you, my heart was in my mouth when Alan Hansen's mistake could so easily have led to an equaliser and extra time. It was far and away a poorer game than the final in Rome and our two matches against Bruges in the 1976 UEFA Cup Final. But we dominated and we were worthy winners.'

The impact and influence of Dalglish on Liverpool was underlined by Phil Thompson when he said: 'Right away we all sussed out, the players and training staff, that you must give Kenny the ball to his feet in the box. We'd played with John Toshack in the team for quite a few years when we would get crosses in to capitalise on his heading ability, but Kenny's arrival changed things. Now we were drilling balls to Kenny on the deck and we knew right from his first game with us how good he was going to be with his skill, his strength and his aggression.'

Dalglish, having proved he could solve problems on the pitch, was equally successful off it. A UEFA edict banning media representatives from the Wembley dressing room area jeopardised my chances of interviewing him and filing his *Daily Express* column for a special European Cup edition. When I told him about this threat to meeting the paper's deadline, Dalglish soon came up with the answer. 'Meet me by the tunnel,' he said. 'When the players come off the pitch after we've done a lap of honour, I'll give you the European Cup and you carry it back to our dressing room. Nobody will stop you when you're carrying that!'

So a short time after captain Emlyn Hughes had thrust the prized trophy into the night sky, there was I walking with it through the bowels of Wembley and straight into the Liverpool dressing room. Dalglish's column made the edition just as his goal had made history.

11

Genius in a Flat Cap

Less than four years after he had reluctantly succeeded Bill Shankly, Bob Paisley had the club's supporters pinching themselves to ensure that the cascading success under his stewardship was real.

It was real enough – and so was Paisley. Realism was ingrained in him like lettering in a stick of rock. Like the club whose attitudes and mores he helped fashion in his lifetime at Anfield, there was no arrogance in Paisley. Neither, as Kevin Keegan observed, was there any evident ego.

'If the floor needs sweeping, I'll pick up a brush and do it,' Paisley would say. 'You'll find that goes, too, for Joe Fagan, Ronnie Moran and the rest of the backroom staff. It's the way this club is. The only titles that concern us are those we try to win on the field.' (Never was this egalitarian ethic better illustrated, incidentally, than during Fagan's first season after succeeding Paisley. Within minutes of Liverpool clinching the championship at Notts County, he was busy with a broom sweeping the dressing room.)

Sitting in his windowless office at Anfield, Paisley's trademark was a woollen cardigan. On match days, he took to wearing a flat cap. 'My dad started to wear a flat cap only after he became manager,' recalled his school-teacher daughter Christine. 'Probably it was a bit more draughty sitting in the directors' box than it had been when he used to sit in the dug-out.' But a flat cap became so closely associated with Paisley that one now has a place of honour as an exhibit in the Liverpool FC museum at Anfield, while Jessie Paisley keeps another in her car glove compartment.

Away from football, too, Bob Paisley lived an uncomplicated

lifestyle. His choice of cars was hardly glitzy, comprising several Ford models followed by an Audi. He loved the company of his family, including seven grandchildren, and talking about football with his sons Robert, a Littlewoods computer operator, and Graham, a bank clerk, both of whom played football for Quarry Bank School Old Boys.

While Liverpool's pursuit of domestic honours in 1977–78 had proved as frustrating for Paisley as the European campaign had been satisfying, the following two seasons saw those fortunes reversed. It was in Europe that Liverpool experienced deep disappointment while at home they rewrote the record books with searing displays of poised yet potent football. Paisley's warning of the inherent perils of resting on laurels was incessant and the policy of building from strength not weakness was evident in his transfer market activities. He said farewell to two of the greatest players in Liverpool history. Ian Callaghan left Anfield with his friend, room-mate and distinguished former captain Tommy Smith, and as they joined up with John Toshack at Swansea following Alec Lindsay's exit to Stoke and Alan Waddle's departure to Leicester, Paisley brought in new blood. Midfielder Kevin Sheedy cost £80,000 from Hereford but in four years at Liverpool made only five appearances before making the short move to Goodison Park where his career belatedly blossomed.

But Paisley's second acquisition during the summer of 1978 was to become a major figure in Liverpool's continuing success. In the process, Alan Kennedy also fulfilled a bold prediction by Paisley after he had paid Newcastle United £330,000 for the left-back who had been on the losing side against Liverpool in the 1974 FA Cup Final. 'If we don't make this boy an England player they can throw me into the Mersey when the tide's out,' Paisley declared at Kennedy's signing press conference. The player had been on the shopping list of a batch of clubs including Leeds United but the lure of Liverpool took Kennedy to Anfield and his transfer completed a remarkable family circle. It was Kennedy's mother who, as we have seen, used to serve the teenage Paisley with fish and chips back in his native pre-war Hetton. 'Bob knew me and my family,' Kennedy recalled. 'I think he wanted another North Easterner in his team!

'But he knew what he was buying and the kind of person I was. He'd seen me playing often enough and the Liverpool chief scout Geoff Twentyman watched me specifically on a couple of occasions. Joining Liverpool was like a homecoming and Bob was like a father figure to me. My own father Gordon also knew Bob and we'd talked about how nice it would be for me to play for him. I know my mother would have been very proud at seeing me sign for Liverpool managed by Bob Paisley. Bob looked beyond what sort of a player you were. He looked at the character of the person first. I think he saw something of my mother in me. I fulfilled what he wanted as a full-back in being strong, passionate and aware of situations. The creed at Liverpool for a full-back was: "You're a defender first of all but, if you have the chance, go forward and enjoy yourself." I was a wholehearted player who would never give up and always gave 100 per cent. I think Bob appreciated those qualities. I also added an extra North East ingredient which I think Bob was very comfortable with. There was only Ray Kennedy, no relation, keeping the Geordie flag flying at Anfield when I signed! When I first met Bob I was very impressed with him. He was like I'd anticipated he'd be, a typical North Easterner who had worked very hard and always had time to speak to people. My mother had always talked about Bob, especially after he had succeeded Bill Shankly. I felt I knew him already, so even though an offer came in from Leeds, there was only one place I wanted to go and that was Liverpool.

'In 1978 not many people in the part of Durham I lived had telephones. You had to rely on public telephone boxes. It was from one of those, in Penshore, a little mining village a few miles from Sunderland and Newcastle, that I rang Peter Robinson at Anfield after the two clubs had agreed a fee. From where I lived it was the only phone box for about a mile. But when I got there I found a queue of people waiting to use it so I just had to be patient. I had the number written on a piece of paper and I was dying to make the call. I was so excited and finally when it came to my turn, I got through to Peter and he told me that Liverpool would like to sign me. He said we had to arrange a meeting. There I was in a phone box being told that Liverpool wanted me as people were knocking on the window asking how long I'd be in there! I felt like jumping for joy when I left that box!

'But Liverpool didn't tell me what the next step would be and I had to contact a local journalist to find out what was going on. I reported for training at Newcastle next day. Bill McGarry was manager and all the time I was just thinking of joining Liverpool.'

Paisley moved in for Kennedy while he was away on Liverpool's pre-season tour of Switzerland, West Germany and Austria. The player flew out with Robinson to meet Paisley and watch the final tour match in Vienna before returning home to discuss the move with his father before confirming his decision to join Liverpool. His arrival spelled the end of the three-year Anfield career of Joey Jones, whose final first-team appearance came in that tour game against FK Austria in the Prater Stadium, watched by Kennedy, when he collected a last-minute booking. Jones, who had lost his Liverpool place the previous season through hamstring damage, returned to Wrexham in October 1978, with the Welsh club paying twice the £110,000 they had received from Liverpool in 1975. He later joined Chelsea and Huddersfield before returning to Wrexham and becoming a coach. But he has never lost his love for Liverpool, retaining a burning enthusiasm for the club that was a hallmark of his playing days at Anfield.

Enthusiasm was a quality Kennedy also displayed in abundance, although his arrival at Liverpool was not without last-minute anxieties. 'I was at least two hours late meeting Bob Paisley at Burtonwood motorway services because it was raining so heavily on the journey down from the North East that my car windscreen wipers packed in,' Kennedy revealed. 'When I finally got there, Bob met me and said: "Hello, son, what happened?" I explained to him and he said: "Well, alright. We've got you here now." And he put his arm round me. I thought that was nice and from then on I felt at home.'

The bearded Kennedy made a scoring debut in a 3–2 win at Celtic in Jock Stein's testimonial match, Liverpool's final pre-season game, and even though it took almost six years, Paisley's prediction that he would play for England came true when Bobby Robson capped him twice in 1984. Kennedy was water ski-ing in the Lake District when Chris James of the *Daily Mirror* tracked him down and broke the news of his England call-up.

He smiles when he recalls his league debut for Liverpool: 'My first game was against Queens Park Rangers at Anfield and early on I miskicked with my right foot, the one I use for standing on, and knocked a policeman's helmet off. I also conceded a couple of corners and made a few errors. I just wanted half-time to come to get some reassurance from the manager. But when I got back to the dressing room, Bob said to me: "I think they shot the wrong Kennedy!"'

There was little time for Kennedy to adjust to Liverpool life before plunging into an exhilarating record-breaking season of championship football. But the 1978–79 campaign was one that Paisley preceded with a perceptive European warning about Nottingham Forest, who had been drawn against Liverpool in the first round of the Champions' Cup.

'I told the players that Brian Clough and his team could be the biggest stumbling block to our ambitions of retaining the trophy,' said Paisley. 'Whether UEFA or the rest of Europe wanted two English clubs in the European Cup, I wouldn't know. But the odds against us drawing Forest in the first round were long even though we were seeded and they weren't. That's what happened though and I can still feel the utter dejection I suffered when we were knocked out by them. Apart from the great five-times winners Real Madrid in the opening years of the tournament we had seen Ajax and Bayern Munich win the European Cup three years in succession and we really felt we could follow suit. It was a bitter blow to go out at the first hurdle.

'We lost the first leg at Nottingham 2–0, partly because when you play a team from your own country the players tend to treat it as a League match. We were a goal down at half-time. If the game had been abroad we'd have settled for that rather than become too keen looking for an equaliser. We left ourselves exposed and the result or our over-adventure was a second Forest goal. We let Forest disturb us and what makes it worse is that we knew that's what they'd try to do. They harassed us out of our game and we had players who didn't compete. Forest marked our midfield tightly and when they were in possession, they didn't ask for any build-up from their own midfield. Instead, they bypassed them with long balls up the middle and we had difficulty mastering their front men.'

Despite Liverpool's domination of the second leg they found the tie irretrievable thanks largely to resolute performances from former Anfield centre-back Larry Lloyd alongside Kenny Burns in front of Peter Shilton. The match ended goalless to send Forest through on a 2–0 aggregate. Said Paisley: 'I was very depressed in my office the next morning and wrote in my diary: "Once again we were unable to score against a side which we completely outplayed from start to finish. The first half was as well as we'd played but in the frenzied atmosphere we hurried our best chances. We were very disappointed to go out in the first round of a competition which I honestly believed we could win for a third time."

'But as soon as I closed my diary I picked up the telephone and rang my bookie to place a bet on Forest for the European Cup. That's how confident I'd been that we would win it. So I was doubly delighted when they beat Malmo in the final, both as an Englishman and as a punter!'

The European defeat by Forest followed another cup exit, a surprise 1–0 League Cup reverse at Second Division Sheffield United on August Bank Holiday Monday. The shock of that result, through a goal by Gary Hamson, was compounded by the Yorkshire club's relegation to Division Three at the end of that season. In the FA Cup there was semi-final despair for Paisley and his players when they lost 1–0 to Jimmy Greenhoff's 78th-minute goal for Manchester United in a Goodison Park replay, following a 2–2 draw at Maine Road. Liverpool had swept into the semi without conceding a goal, beating Southend, Blackburn, Burnley and Ipswich. But that old FA Cup jinx against United, whom they had not beaten in the competition since 1921, struck again and would continue into the new millennium.

Liverpool's fate in the three cups, however, contrasted starkly with their fortunes in the League championship, which they recaptured from Forest in swashbuckling style. The sheer quality of their performances was such that many pundits and supporters believe it was the best Liverpool side ever. Alan Hansen rates it as the finest team he ever played in over a 14-year span. Paisley's men stormed to the title with 68 points, a record under the two points-for-a-win system, conceded an all-time low of only 16 goals from their 42 games with only four let in at home, and scored 85 goals, to collect a £50,000 prize from *The Sun* newspaper for topping 84. They also set a new goal average peak of 5.31, shattering the previous best of 2.88 set by Forest a year earlier, and equalled Arsenal's 1935 record with a goal difference of plus 69. In addition, they equalled the all-time records for home points (40) and home wins (19). Overall, they won 30 games and drew eight.

'That team was superb at both ends of the field, scoring 85 and conceding only 16, which will never be beaten,' says Hansen, who went on to win eight championships among a total of 17 medals he amassed with Liverpool. 'I played in other Liverpool sides that won doubles and a treble, yet I rate that team the best.'

Hansen, though, had to wait until late September to win a regular place in the team in what became his familiar number six jersey. Liverpool began the season at a sun-drenched Anfield with a 2–1 home win over QPR on 19 August with this line-up: Clemence; Neal, Thompson, Hughes (captain), Alan Kennedy; Case, McDermott, Souness, Ray Kennedy; Dalglish, Heighway. Substitute: Fairclough.

Convincing away conquests of Ipswich (3–0) and Manchester City (4–1) followed, to take Dalglish's early-season goal haul to four from the opening three matches, after two pre-season strikes against his former club Celtic. But even that Maine Road win could not mask the daunting standards Paisley demanded. 'We got a rocket from him because we lost possession a bit too much and gave City chances after we'd scored our fourth goal,' said Alan Kennedy.

There were no complaints from Paisley about Liverpool's next League display, one of the most emphatic by any Anfield team in the club's history and crowned by probably the finest team goal they have ever scored. The date was 2 September 1978, the third Saturday of the new season, when Anfield saw the visit of ambitious Tottenham, managed by Keith Burkinshaw, who, as we have seen, played under Paisley when Bob was Liverpool's reserve-team coach in the 1950s. Although the London club had not won in front of the Kop since 1912, their hopes of ending that sequence and making an impact in the championship were sky high after their audacious signings of Osvaldo Ardiles and Ricardo Villa. The Argentinian duo had been members of their country's World Cup winning team on their home soil that summer, a tournament that the highly respected Yugoslavian coach Milan Miljanic had said Liverpool would have been favourites to win had they been allowed to enter! Such was the pinnacle Liverpool had reached under Paisley, although such flattering comments were met with a straight bat by the Anfield manager, who treated praise as a potential psychological disturbance of his team's mental equilibrium.

He certainly had to contend with eulogies to his players after they put Tottenham through the mincer, winning 7–0 after an awesome performance. Two Dalglish goals – his sixth in the first four League games – were followed by a couple from substitute David Johnson, who had replaced the injured Emlyn Hughes. A Ray Kennedy strike and a Phil Neal penalty ensured that Tottenham goalkeeper Barry Daines fished the ball out of his net for the sixth time. And when he had to do it yet again 14 minutes from the end, the Kop were in seventh heaven and Tottenham in tatters. In a few spellbinding seconds, the ball flowed from one end to the other with Tottenham mesmerized by a move that was at once lethal and poetic. Ray Clemence started it by giving the ball to Ray Kennedy, who in turn found Dalglish with a header. The Scot passed to his right to David Johnson, who clipped it out to the left flank for Steve Heighway. He went on a few strides before delivering a cross that was headed in by the hard-running Terry McDermott, who had been behind Johnson but sprinted sixty yards to score a goal hailed by Paisley as 'probably the finest ever seen on this ground'. For Dalglish, who dropped deeper in the reshuffle following the departure of Hughes and Souness, the victory over a team including the two Argentinians was made even sweeter after the huge anti-climax of Scotland's over-trumpeted World Cup mission under Ally MacLeod. Tottenham, even with Passarella, Luque and Kempes in their ranks as well as Villa and Ardiles would have struggled to contain Liverpool, whose fluency was unaffected by Jimmy Case's switch to right-back and Neal's move to the heart of defence after the Hughes injury.

'What can you say?' asked Paisley. 'That performance was frightening. We've started well but we've got to keep our feet on the floor.' Then, with a comment that fuelled the misguided external view that Liverpool never enjoyed their success to the extent they should, he added: 'This result won't help us next week. In fact, we'd rather have brickbats than praise. We seem to thrive on that sort of thing.'

There were no brickbats from Tottenham, just a stream of salutes to the players who had overwhelmed them. 'This Liverpool side is the best team I've ever played against,' said winger Peter Taylor.

Dalglish, an intoxicating blend of deftness and toughness with a marvellous talent for making and taking goals, was again proving a massive asset. 'He's one of the strongest players we've ever had, especially when he's in possession,' said Paisley. 'When he's got the ball, not many people can take it off him.' Souness's ability to spray passes as if he had a homing device in his boots and McDermott's ability to cruise into open spaces were complemented in midfield by Ray Kennedy, a hugely influential player whose career had been reshaped and reignited by Paisley. The player who used to run up front for Arsenal often seemed as if he was out for a stroll with Liverpool, but ensnared opponents with his vision and bewitching left foot.

If there was an absence of cartwheels of joy around Anfield when the team performed at its peak, there was no lack of pleasure. It was evident in an almost unspoken professional satisfaction felt by Paisley and his backroom staff when they met for a beer or a whisky in the Boot Room on Sunday mornings. Paisley, Joe Fagan, Ronnie Moran, Tom Saunders, Reuben Bennett, Roy Evans, youth coach John Bennison and chief scout Geoff Twentyman would meet to chew the football cud in a frank but convivial wide-ranging chat when brilliant, mediocre and poor performances would be considered and analysed. The general verdict of Paisley and the Boot Room was that the team's League form in 1978–79 was a triumph for the corporate response of the players and staff to crushing European disappointment.

'After going out of the European Cup to Forest we could have stayed on the canvas but instead we got up and regained the championship,' said Paisley. 'We stood up and turned a negative experience into something positive.'

The injury Hughes received against Tottenham forced him out of the game at Birmingham a week later. His appearance record, as one of the great marathon men Liverpool paraded more than any other club, was startling. In the 11 seasons since he became a first-team regular in 1967–68, it was only the 15th League game he had missed in Liverpool's 466 matches. His absence meant another outing for Hansen, who stepped in for a one-match taste of first-team football before Hughes returned for four games. Then when Hughes again succumbed to knee damage for the home clash with Bolton, opportunity knocked for Hansen, who was called up by Paisley on a regular basis. When Hughes regained fitness, there was no automatic return.

The same fate befell Terry McDermott, ruled out through illness from the 4–1 win at Norwich in October, when David Johnson returned and scored to secure a run in the team. McDermott, relegated to substitute after the Carrow Road triumph, had to wait almost two months before injury to Johnson provided his ticket back into the side. Hughes, who made his first ever appearance in the reserves, did not taste senior action again until December. Yet even though the pair were out of Liverpool's team, they were still called up by England manager Ron Greenwood, with Hughes remaining captain for the European Championship draw in the Republic of Ireland. Such a situation would be unthinkable today but Paisley saw no conflict in the players' contrasting fortunes at club and international level.

'I've spoken to Ron and told him the score,' he said. 'It's unfortunate that Emlyn and Terry had to drop out through injury or illness, but I owe it to the men in possession. It doesn't necessarily mean that because they can't get into our team that they can't get into England's.'

Paisley recalled Hughes in place of the injured Phil Thompson in a 3–1 first-leg European Super Cup defeat by Anderlecht in Brussels, dropped him for the next three games after Thompson's return and then brought him back for the second leg against the Belgians, who won 4–3 on aggregate despite losing 2–1 at Anfield. This time Hughes displaced Alan Kennedy at left-back, for what was to prove the last stand of his magnificent Anfield career. He had a 20-game run from December to April appearing at left-back in place of Kennedy and at centre-back during a period when Phil Thompson missed matches after suffering knee damage. Paisley added to the battle for places by using both 4–3–3 and 4–4–2 formations.

A week after his testimonial match against Borussia Moenchengladbach attracted a 25,000-plus Anfield crowd generating receipts of almost £40,000, Hughes made what was to be his 665th and last Liverpool appearance in the FA Cup semi-final replay defeat by Manchester United at Goodison Park. Paisley recalled Alan Kennedy for the next game, the home clash with Arsenal, for which he also brought back Jimmy Case in place of Steve Heighway and reverted to 4–4–2 as Liverpool powered to a 3–0 win, with Case, Dalglish and McDermott on target. Paisley explained his decision to drop Hughes by saying: 'Emlyn and I have talked things over and in fairness to him, I was trying to cash in on his experience recently. He was doing us a favour by playing at full-back which is not his best position. Emlyn was doing a job for us while Alan Kennedy was gaining experience of our ways. We have a simple way of playing but ours is not the easiest side to settle into quickly. Now I hope Alan can do it.'

Hughes said philosophically: 'I could not really expect anything else because I've not been playing well. But I've not become a bad player overnight. I still feel I can do a job in the First Division playing in the middle of the back four, where Alan Hansen and Phil Thompson are doing so well for Liverpool.' Later, he revealed: 'After the replay defeat by United, Bob came to me and said: "Emlyn, I'm going to have to leave you out." I said: "OK, boss. I've had great years here, that's fair enough. But I can't play in the reserves every week." To be honest, I couldn't have handled it and Bob, to his great credit, fully understood. The lads went on to clinch the championship, bringing me my fourth title medal, after playing some superb stuff. My only regret was that we didn't win the European Cup for the third successive season. It was a bitter disappointment to be knocked out by Forest. I was coming to the end of my career and I had a nightmare in both games against them.'

Within four months of losing his Liverpool place, Hughes, one of the most successful captains of all time, moved to Wolves for £90,000 and was immediately installed as skipper at Molineux. During his time there he won a further three England caps to add to the 59 he collected at Liverpool, along with two European Cup medals, four League championships, an FA Cup and two UEFA Cup winner's medals.

Less than a year after leaving Anfield he received an OBE and added a League Cup winner's medal to his collection, captaining Wolves to a 1–0 win over Nottingham Forest at Wembley. With a significant insight into the Anfield creed fostered by Shankly and Paisley, Hughes reflected: 'I can honestly say that in all my years at Liverpool I never once backed out of a tackle. There were a bloody lot of tackles I never went into! But if you can't win a tackle, why go in for it? Bob and Shanks constantly used to preach to us not to pursue lost causes. They said it was the quickest way to get injured. Bryan Robson and Andy Gray, two magnificent players, are classic examples of what I'm talking about. Bryan seemed to be injured every other week because he went in for things that were impossible to get. Andy, my team-mate at Wolves, was the same. He loved to walk off the pitch with a few stitches, not happy unless he'd headed a boot! Then he'd be out for weeks. Bob and Shanks made a point of stressing to us that rather than dive in with no hope of getting the ball, we should jockey the opponent, try to shepherd them where you wanted them to go. They said the ball had to come your way eventually. When you think of it, it's just common sense.'

Hughes' last act as a Liverpool player will remain indelible in his memory. 'I went to collect my boots from Anfield before going to Wolves when Graeme Souness came over to me,' he recalled. 'He wished me the best of luck, then said: "If I can achieve a tenth of what you have at this club, I'll be a proud man." That's the nicest thing anyone has ever said to me.'

His departure was a key factor in the careers of both Phil Thompson and Alan Kennedy. During the absence of Hughes earlier in the season, Dalglish and Clemence had skippered the side, but in the wake of Liverpool's FA Cup exit, Paisley appointed Thompson as the new club captain. Kirkby-born Thompson, another who once stood on the Kop cheering Liverpool, was handed the armband before the Arsenal game and exclaimed: 'I could hardly believe it when the boss told me. The greatest ambition of my life has been to captain Liverpool and now it's come true.'

Kennedy, who took up the challenge thrown by Paisley to make the left-back berth his own, said: 'When I arrived at Liverpool I was in awe of the players around me, with that great Scottish backbone of Dalglish, Souness and Hansen and England's Ray Clemence in goal. Ray was a great leader from the back. He was like a fifth defender, a fine reader of the game who liked to play outfield in training, a marvellous shot-stopper and a great talker. All in all, a superb professional. I eventually settled in with these players and it was a pleasure to play in one of the best teams Liverpool have ever had.'

Liverpool, shouldering the title 'Best Team In The World', as voted by the International Sportswriters' Association among a welter of awards, surged to the championship as if to prove their worthiness of the accolade. It was stirring consolation for their premature exit from the European Cup, the trophy which had been taken proudly by Paisley back to his roots in Hetton-le-Hole, where the little mining town's most famous son was rapturously received. Liverpool's 11th championship also provided a glorious celebration of his 40th anniversary of joining the club. An opening six straight League wins signalled their intent, although Forest and city neighbours Everton had their own designs on the championship.

During the season Forest completed a new record of 42 First Division games unbeaten, while Everton inflicted Liverpool's first League defeat of the season with a 1–0 win in the Goodison derby at the end of October.

When the trip to Everton loomed, statisticians were quick to point out that it had been seven years since Liverpool had last lost to their arch rivals. In that time there had been three Popes, three British Prime Ministers and three United States Presidents, but it all left Paisley unmoved and warning: 'If you toss a penny in the air 20 times and it comes down heads on every occasion, there's still an even chance it will come down tails next time. The past means nothing and has no bearing on this game.' His cautionary words were significant as Liverpool's 15-match unbeaten derby run was ended in the 58th minute when Andy King hit Everton's winner The midfielder also scored Everton's goal in a 1–1 draw at Anfield the following March to become the only player in the 1978–79 season to score twice against Ray Clemence.

Everton's win moved Gordon Lee's side on to 19 points, just two behind leaders Liverpool after 12 games, with unbeaten Forest a further two points adrift. But Liverpool lost only another three First Division games which, allied to their scorching launch to the season, burned off the opposition. One of their most significant scalps was Forest, who arrived at Anfield in December having been undefeated in the League for more than a year, amassing 21 wins and 21 draws since November 1977. In addition, they had become a jinx to Liverpool since returning to English football's top flight. In six meetings with Brian Clough's side, Liverpool had not won once, a sequence that comprised a League Cup Final and replay, two League matches and the two-leg European Cup encounter three months earlier.

This time, with Phil Thompson returning after injury in place of Hughes, Liverpool threatened to overrun them. Their deserved breakthrough came on the half hour when McDermott, 27 the previous day, beat Peter Shilton from the penalty spot after Dalglish had been upended by Archie Gemmill. Four minutes after the interval McDermott snapped up a second goal following Shilton's brilliant save from Alan Kennedy. Even Clough admitted: 'They murdered us. We didn't get a kick from three o'clock onwards.'

Liverpool inflicted similar treatment on many opponents, although they surprisingly lost by the game's only goal at Bristol City before walloping Manchester United 3–0 at Old Trafford on Boxing Day, where an early strike from Ray Kennedy set them on their way. Further goals from Case and Fairclough completed the convincing victory to send them into the New Year at the First Division summit with 33 points from 21 games, a point ahead of Everton and four ahead of West Brom, who had two games in hand. Then the severe weather, which played havoc with fixtures, causing a mass of postponements, saw Liverpool deposed as leaders for the first time that season. They were out of League action from late December until early February, in the process losing the leadership to West Brom on 13 January. The Midlands side's draw at Norwich took them to the top – the first time they had reached the summit since 1954 – and set a new club record for Ron Atkinson's team of 18 games unbeaten. By a twist of fate and the vagaries of the weather, Liverpool's next League engagement was a home duel with West Brom on 3 February, by which time Albion had extended their undefeated sequence to 19 games. Like Forest before them, though, they had no answer to Liverpool. Goals from Dalglish and Fairclough clinched a 2–1 win that flattered the visitors. They were outplayed by Paisley's side, who leapfrogged their opponents to go back to the top of the table.

They followed that with another three straight wins, 1–0 over Birmingham through a Souness strike, a 6–0 thrashing of Norwich in which Dalglish and Johnson hit two apiece with the two Kennedys also scoring, and a 2–0 triumph at Derby where Ray Kennedy and Dalglish were on target. During that period they were briefly deposed as leaders by Everton, who beat Bristol City on the day Liverpool's match at Bolton was postponed due to another wintry blast. But Liverpool were back on top four days later and stayed there to the end of a season they finished in style.

Paisley, though, remained typically guarded. After his side's fourth and last League reverse, a 3–1 crash at Aston Villa in April, he declared: 'We were absolute rubbish and the championship's still wide open.' At the time Liverpool were six points ahead of West Brom and Everton and seven ahead of Forest. Even though the pursuers all had games in hand, few pundits agreed with Paisley that the race was wide open. His comments, though, were aimed as much at reigniting his team as an observation on the championship struggle and, as such, had the desired effect as they won six and drew two of their remaining eight games, including a goalless duel at eventual runners-up Forest. Their 2–0 home win over Southampton was one of such flowing Liverpool power that visiting manager Lawrie McMenemy was moved to reflect: 'For us it was like trying to baptize a baby in Niagara Falls!'

The title was secured with a 3–0 decision of Aston Villa on a heady and emotional Tuesday night at Anfield on 8 May, 40 years to the day since Paisley had first arrived at the club. Fittingly, his prize signing Dalglish was on target to register his 25th goal of the season and his 56th for the club on his 113th senior appearance, statistics which helped earn him the Footballer of the Year award from members of the Football Writers' Association. Dalglish struck following a first-minute opener from Alan Kennedy, with McDermott adding a third early in the second half. At the end, the vociferous demands of the Kop prevailed over Paisley's natural modesty as he walked on to the pitch in front of a 50,000 crowd to take a salute, and his sixth major trophy in five seasons of management.

'I don't want to take anything away from the players,' he insisted. 'They did it, not me. The atmosphere here tonight was just incredible. It was overpowering and I was concerned that all the publicity about my anniversary would affect the concentration of the players. But I needn't have worried. They were very professional. In fact, the quality and consistency of our football this season has been the best I've ever known. We've got two away games left and to concede only four goals at home in an entire League season is almost beyond belief.'

The championship win, though, did not by any means indicate that Liverpool players would now contemplate donning flip-flops on the beach rather than football boots. The £50,000 *Sun*–Corals prize for hitting the 84-goal jackpot and a new overall defensive record were still to be attained. 'It was the fact that we still had targets to go for, rather than the money, that maintained our concentration level and made us determined to finish in real style,' said Ray Clemence, who was again unbeaten in his next outing, a 1–0 win at Middlesbrough through a spectacular headed goal from David Johnson.

So Liverpool moved on to their final League game, a Thursday evening trip to Leeds United, knowing that only a calamitous collapse could rob them of several new records. In their 41 games they had conceded only 16 goals with the top-flight record standing at 24, shared by Liverpool and Nottingham Forest. The record 42-match low for any division stood at 21, set by Southampton in the Third Division South in 1921–22 under the old offside law. They also needed to score twice to qualify for the 84-goal prize. In the event, they went one better on a night when they gloriously confirmed their status as champions.

With 21 minutes on the clock, Johnson challenged Paul Hart and the ball ran loose for Dalglish to float in a cross from the right. Although Leeds goalkeeper David Harvey got a hand to it,

Terry McDermott pounced on the loose ball and when his shot was blocked, Johnson stabbed in the breakthrough goal. Four minutes before half-time, a sweeping, characteristic run from defence by Alan Hansen set Dalglish on a winding path across the pitch before he turned to lay on a chance for Jimmy Case. The opportunity was powerfully accepted as Case blasted a fierce shot into the roof of the Leeds net for the team's 84th league goal. Fittingly, within seconds of Case's strike, a rainbow painted the sky above Elland Road as if in tribute to the Anfield masters. The pot of gold, in the form of the £50,000 jackpot, was now assured and Liverpool were closing in on the victory they needed for a new all-time points peak of 68.

Liverpool were even more dominant in the second half, with Leeds rarely granted a chance to even threaten Clemence's remarkable 27th clean sheet. Indeed, the total of 16 goals he did concede over the season – which included own goals by Thompson and Souness – was just one more than the Invincibles of Preston North End conceded in a mere 15 First Division matches back in 1888–89. 'If we won a game 3–1 or 4–1 it was the goal we'd let in that we'd talk about rather than those we'd scored,' said Clemence. 'The team was that good.'

They had no such goals against to concern them that night at Elland Road, where the issue was put beyond all doubt when Johnson scored his second goal of the game, off a headed flick by Dalglish, to make it 3–0 and ensure that Leeds' previous record of 67 points would be surpassed. It was Johnson's 18th goal of the season in 37 senior appearances, underlining how the once-unsettled forward had revamped his Anfield career as an effective strike partner to Dalglish, still an ever present since his arrival two years earlier.

Liverpool had set the records tumbling despite Paisley using only 15 players, two of whom, David Fairclough and Sammy Lee, made only half a dozen appearances between them. It also revealed Paisley's tactical genius in the deployment of substitutes, still restricted to one in domestic matches. He deployed his 12th man less than any other manager but with brilliant effectiveness. During the season Paisley sent on his substitute in only 11 League games – Fairclough being used just once – and the impact of his substitutions over his seasons in charge was remarkable. In four seasons to the end of 1978-79, Liverpool scored more than 80 goals after Paisley had made a substitution, a record unequalled by any other manager.

Paisley's new captain Phil Thompson had no doubt then, and certainly none with the advantage of hindsight, that Liverpool's 1979 vintage was one of rare quality. 'People talk about the double- and treble-winning Liverpool teams but you ask anyone who played in them, such as Alan Hansen, and they will tell you that the 1978–79 team was probably the finest,' said Thompson. 'We went up and down the country that season and played some magnificent stuff. You look at a team throughout a campaign and that was something really special. We beat teams by three and four goals and more, incredibly conceding only 16, including only four at home, and had such confidence wherever we went. We felt nobody was going to beat us. That team really did have everything, with great players like Dalglish and Souness, and we all played for each other. I think we all must have peaked at the same time.'

Thompson is clear, too, about the qualities in Paisley that allowed his managerial skills to manifest themselves with such massive impact: 'He bought players and moulded them together to create great teams. People talked about him as "Uncle Bob", but he was as ruthless as they come. Anyone who worked under him, as I did, knows that. He could be hard but he went about it in the right way and was quite gentlemanly about it, for all his rough edges. He had a genius for creating teams.

'You've only got to look back to his first couple of signings, Phil Neal and Terry McDermott. Phil, signed from Northampton, was one of the best Liverpool servants ever. Just look at the number of successive games he played and the England caps he won. That was one hell of a spot by Bob. Terry Mac was another great buy. He had a few teething problems but he scored some of the finest goals you'll ever see, which any league in the world would have been proud of. He seemed to save them for the television cameras, too! Terry was one of the best strikers of a ball in the game. Then you look at Bob's switch of Ray Kennedy from striker to midfielder. That brought him England caps, too, and won us many a game.'

Liverpool had stormed to the title as the League's best supported club, their First Division average of 46,504 shading Manchester United's 46,430, as Paisley's team proved to be box-office gold wherever they played. And Dalglish's choice as Footballer of the Year by the writers provided a firm riposte to his fellow professionals of the PFA, who had snubbed the great Scot in their Player of the Year Award announced in March. A majority of votes in the players' poll, which closed midway through the season, went to Arsenal's Liam Brady. 'The whole thing is cockeyed and judged at a time when the real competition is only starting,' rapped Paisley, who was voted Bell's Manager of the Year for the third time in four seasons. 'For some reason very few Liverpool players are rated as individuals in the PFA awards. When Kevin Keegan was here, he didn't win it either. But I bet a few centre-backs voted for Kenny!'

Future PFA awards, however, did recognise Anfield players, which was hardly surprising as they triumphantly fulfilled Paisley's high expectations. With the roars of celebration for Liverpool's 11th title barely over, Paisley declared: 'The depth of ability in this squad, their approach and attitude, their skill and teamwork convince me that 12 months from now they will win Liverpool's 12th championship.' For Paisley, a cautious professional not given to hyperbole, it was a bold prediction, underlining his faith in the group of players he had assembled.

Only two of the 11 who clinched Paisley's anniversary championship against Aston Villa, Ray Clemence and Phil Thompson, had appeared under Shankly. This was very much a Paisley team, one that gloriously achieved his forecast that they would retain the title in 1979–80. The squad gathered two new faces. Defender or midfielder Avi Cohen was signed for £200,000 from Maccabi Tel Aviv, following a trial period and after playing 45 minutes for each side in a summer friendly between Liverpool and an Israel Select side in Tel Aviv. The other arrival was striker Frank McGarvey, who cost £300,000 from St Mirren but left ten months later without even making a senior substitute appearance, after losing patience in the queue for places. The striker, who went on to win seven Scotland caps, returned north to join Celtic for £275,000, but only after figuring in a puzzling picture submitted to national newspapers by a freelance photographer. As the Liverpool squad left Liverpool's Lime Street station for their impressive 3–1 Charity Shield win over Arsenal, for which Paisley had already announced McGarvey would be denied even a place among the five substitutes, the photographer staged a shot of the Scot beaming from the train window with his thumbs up. The mind boggles at what McGarvey would have done if he had been in the Wembley team!

Not even a run of scoring in 16 consecutive reserve games could prise McGarvey a senior breakthrough and a week after telling Paisley he wanted to leave he was heading for Parkhead. 'Bob told me he wanted me to stay and that when I did get in it wouldn't be just for one game, but for a run of matches,' McGarvey reflected. 'I should have taken the advice and stayed – but I couldn't wait.'

Cohen stayed at Liverpool for little more than two seasons before returning to Maccabi for £100,000, having only fleeting opportunities to demonstrate the style that earned him the rather grandiose soubriquet of the 'Beckenbauer of the Middle East'! But he was a landmark signing as the club's first foreign import since 1954, when Doug Rudham was the last of a batch of South Africans who joined the club over a 30-year period. Two decades after Cohen's arrival, Liverpool could parade two teams of foreign players, plus a foreign manager and coach, throwing into stark focus the collapse of restrictive barriers and the growth of massive financial rewards which revolutionised the game. The problems of foreign players adjusting, however, were recognised by Paisley and his comments remain bitingly apposite today.

'When we signed Avi we had no doubts about his skill,' he said. 'But then we had to build on that by developing his stamina and getting him used to the contrasting conditions and pace of English football. Unfortunately, he never quite made it with us and returned to Israel. I was disappointed things didn't work out for him because there are worse players than Avi in the First Division. But apart from anything else, his wife was feeling homesick. In addition to language difficulties, the effect on family life is another big factor when you talk about signing foreign players. At the end of the day, everyone likes his own environment. It requires a lot of character and determination to overcome all the social, cultural, climatic and football problems associated with competing at top level in a foreign country.'

Cohen, as well as being Liverpool's first foreign capture of the modern era, would secure another niche in Anfield history at the end of his first season. His arrival prompted a memorably humorous exchange between Paisley and the *Jewish Chronicle*. In a story Paisley loved to recount, he said: 'The phone rang in my office and a chap said he was from the *Jewish Chronicle*. I asked him how I could help him and he said he wanted to know if Avi Cohen was orthodox.

'I said: "Orthodox what? Do you mean defender or midfielder?"

'He replied: "No, Orthodox Jewish. If he is, he cannot play on Saturdays."

'I replied: "I've got half a dozen like that already!"'

12

Title Deeds for a New Decade

Liverpool were in the vanguard of another revolution in the summer of 1979 when they became the first League club to carry a sponsor's name on their jerseys, after agreeing an initial one-year package deal with the Japanese electronics company Hitachi. The firm's name was featured in a two-and-a-half-inch-deep strip across the players' shirts. Regulations in force at the time, which seem almost antediluvian now, banned shirt advertising in televised matches, FA Cup ties and European games, rules which Liverpool vowed to change.

'We are talking about an industry that is desperately short of money and we are fighting for our existence,' said chairman John Smith. 'In terms of commerce and industry we, at Liverpool, are broke. But in football terms we are wealthy. From a turnover of £2.4 million last year Liverpool's profit at the end of the day was a meagre £71,000 – this for one of the leading clubs in Europe. The overheads in our game are colossal and we have got to generate more remunerative activity off the field.

'The days are gone when a club like ours can control its destiny on the money coming through the turnstiles. I think other clubs will follow our lead. We are taking up the cudgels and I believe we will see the day when shirt advertising is allowed in televised games and in UEFA competitions. Only two European countries, England and Italy, outlaw TV shirt advertising, but if that ban was lifted English clubs could collect £250,000 a season and upwards, in common with their European counterparts.'

Even in this area, Paisley was amazingly accurate in his vision of the future. His backroom colleague Ronnie Moran, who retired in 1998 after almost half a century of Anfield service as player, captain, coach and caretaker manager, revealed: 'Bob was 20 to 30 years ahead of his time. As well as knowing the game and players inside out, with the great ability to blend them into a team, his predictions were spot on. Back in the 1970s he said that advertising and sponsorship would become massive. He said that not only would players have advertising on their shirts but that they would all have their own agents. People laughed. But he was right. It's all come true.'

The 1979–80 season was remarkably similar to the previous campaign for Paisley and Liverpool: agony in the cup competitions but ecstasy in the League. Although their FA Cup and League Cup runs both lasted until the semi-finals, their European fate was painfully reminiscent of a year earlier when they had gone out at the opening stage to Nottingham Forest.

Once again, despite being seeded, they were pitted against a powerful side, the Georgians of Dynamo Tbilisi, with the first leg at Anfield. Liverpool's task was made even more demanding by a batch of injuries. They were without thigh casualties Ray Kennedy, whose left-side midfield contribution had always been a crucial part of their European armoury, and Alan Hansen. Kevin Sheedy, signed as cover for Kennedy, was in hospital recovering from back surgery, and Sammy Lee was out with a stress fracture. Reserve forwards Howard Gayle and Bobby Savage were also injured, prompting Paisley to declare: 'This is what makes football the uncertain game it is and renders forecasting ridiculous. Fortune hasn't smiled on us, particularly in losing Ray Kennedy, because he's shown in the past that he can score goals when the pressure is on. But it's no good beefing about it. We've just got to get on with the job.'

Paisley's response was to draft in local boy Colin Irwin for his European debut in place of Hansen, the 22-year-old having had his senior baptism in the second League fixture of the season, a 3–1 win at West Brom.

A 20th-minute headed goal by David Johnson from Terry McDermott's cross put Liverpool ahead in their 104th European match, but little more than ten minutes later the menacing, counter-attacking Dynamo equalised when centre-back Chivadze set off on a run, exchanged passes with Daraseliya and shot past

Clemence. A typically driven free kick from Jimmy Case on the stroke of half-time flew past Otar Gabeliya to put Liverpool ahead again, but despite fierce second-half pressure, the massed ranks of the visitors, backed by the brilliance of Gabeliya, Liverpool could not increase their slender lead.

Paisley's post-match diary read: 'This was a tremendous battle against a very confident and skilful side who have highly talented players like Kipiani, Chivadze, Shengalia and Gutsaev. Now only a tremendous performance will get us a result over there. Our three men in midfield never got to grips with their opponents and although we dominated the second half, we could not get a decisive lead in the tie.'

The 3,500-mile journey for the second leg in the Georgian capital, in the outer regions of what was then the Soviet empire between the Black and Caspian Seas, opened one of the most dramatic chapters in Liverpool's long European story. Paisley, angered by the experience, insisted: 'Anyone who thinks Communism is the answer to our political problems would quickly think again if he had experienced the trip we had to make.

'For a start we were not allowed to charter a plane from the airline of our choice. The Russian authorities would allow in only a national carrier, British Airways, and even then only as far as Moscow. The rest of the journey would then have to be made with their own airline, Aeroflot. Nor were we allowed to fly direct to Tbilisi.

'To try to reduce the problems, we chartered Aeroflot for the full flight from Liverpool's Speke Airport to Tbilisi and back. But the Russians still insisted on the dog-leg flight via Moscow, where we had to put down and disembark for seemingly interminable immigration procedures. We had to leave our hand luggage on the plane while they searched it. We were told later they were looking for "subversive" literature. One of the party going through a checkpoint was told that a Liverpool FC match programme was "propaganda"!'

This hassle-filled stage of the journey would have been worse and longer but for the fact that the club had included in their party George Scanlan, former head of languages at Liverpool Polytechnic and an expert in Russian, to help overcome problems and cut through the red tape.

But on arrival in Tbilisi the headaches continued. The media found communications with Britain a nightmare, heightened by the fact that all the rooms had their own telephone numbers, quite separate from the main hotel number, which were unknown in advance. We also belatedly discovered that some kind soul had turned down the bell volume control on the base of the phones, so that even if there was a call it was inaudible! Those fortunate enough to make contact with their offices back home were then interrupted by a female voice saying: 'You have only another 30 seconds.' An angry response to this meant the call being instantly cut.

The food, too, was of lamentable quality, calling for supreme vigilance by Liverpool's travelling food tasters, hoteliers Harry Wight and Alan Glynn, whose task it was to ensure that the playing and coaching staff were served the most wholesome meals possible. That was not easy, as Paisley conceded. 'The food would be rejected in a soup kitchen,' he rapped, drawing on his own boyhood experience in the deprived North East.

Liverpool's discomfort was complete when, at around 4am on the day of the match, the team hotel was surrounded by a mass of demonstrators holding torches of blazing newspapers and chanting 'Dynamo, Dynamo,' which awakened virtually everybody and ruined the players' sleep. What made it even more infuriating was that it seemed to have at least the tacit support of the Tbilisi authorities, if not a greater degree of official complicity. The square outside the hotel was suddenly cleared until a few minutes later it was filled by several hundred demonstrators, escorted by police

Paisley, Peter Robinson and other members of the Liverpool party, some wearing dressing gowns, others having hastily dressed when the marchers arrived, went down to the hotel lobby, but despite their angry protests that it had all been stage-managed, the demonstration ran its course.

If it was planned to help Dynamo capture victory, then it succeeded. Liverpool, with Ray Kennedy and Hansen back in the team, but now without groin casualty Alan Kennedy, crashed 3–0 to go out on a 4–2 aggregate in a torrential downpour in front of 80,000 passionate Georgians.

'The preparations were all wrong for a match so finely balanced,' said Paisley. 'We just had to grin and bear it and try to give our answer where it counts – on the field. This time we weren't able to do so. We kept the game goalless until the interval but then lost to three second-half goals to go out in the first round for the second year running, which was bitterly disappointing.'

Dynamo levelled on aggregate through Gutsaev, Shengalia added another and when West German referee Heinz Aldinger awarded a penalty for Phil Thompson's challenge on Gutsaev, Chivadze scored from the spot to complete Dynamo's victory.

'We played well enough in the first half but didn't take our chances,' added Paisley. 'We knew a 2–1 first-leg lead would be difficult to defend, but for 50 minutes or so we controlled the game. Just when Dynamo heads were about to go down, they got the breakthrough. If we had taken a similar chance just before the interval we would probably still have been in the European Cup. In the end, though, Tbilisi deserved to win. There are no excuses, and I include the early-morning demonstration when I say that. But it was still hard to take.'

There was, however, an element of revenge for Liverpool, whose experiences were passed on to Kevin Keegan's Hamburg, Dynamo's next European opponents. 'Get the players to bed very early the night before the match,' was the Anfield message. The German club acted on the advice and even though Dynamo fans staged another demonstration, the Hamburg players had already spent hours sleeping and were well rested for the game. The outcome was that Hamburg won 3–2 in Tbilisi following a 3–1 home victory in the first leg, Keegan scoring in both games, and went on to reach the final, where they lost 1–0 to Nottingham Forest. That duel in Madrid, for which Brian Clough packed the Forest midfield to counter the threat of Keegan, signalled the end of the former Liverpool star's reign at Hamburg. At a time when transfer fees between European Union nations were pegged at £500,000, Southampton boss Lawrie McMenemy struck a £420,000 deal to take Keegan to The Dell.

Liverpool had first option on Keegan's return to English football and Peter Robinson revealed that they did make overtures to him to return to team up with Dalglish in a mouth-watering attacking combination. 'Our chairman John Smith and I went to Hamburg a couple of years after Kevin had gone there, when we knew he might be moving,' said Robinson. 'We had dinner with him and tried to persuade him to come back to Liverpool as a player-coach, with the intention of Kevin eventually succeeding Bob Paisley as manager. Bob was fully aware and supportive of the idea. Kevin said he was very flattered but that he didn't think he would go into management when he finished playing. At the time I'm sure that is how he felt, but I was always disappointed that we never saw Keegan and Dalglish play together for Liverpool.'

The England star, however, warmed to the prospect of moving to Southampton to team up with his closest football friend, Mick Channon. 'If I'd wanted to go back to Liverpool I would never have left in the first place,' said Keegan. 'I suppose if things hadn't worked out it was a possibility. But I'm not one for looking back and, after all, Liverpool had signed Kenny, who was proving very successful.'

Paisley had his own pithy reflection on what might have been when he said: 'When they come to write my epitaph, they might say this: "Bob Paisley was a successful manager but he was probably the most unfortunate of all because he never had Dalglish and Keegan in the same Liverpool team."'

The frenzied spiral in transfer fees had been heralded in 1979 when Brian Clough smashed the £1 million barrier in English football to sign Trevor Francis from Birmingham, followed by Steve Daley moving from Wolves to Manchester City and Andy Gray from Aston Villa to Wolves, each for close on £1.5 million. The madness of the market had begun. Meanwhile, Liverpool were left languishing in ninth place, having won only two of their opening seven First Division games, and with the European exit in Tbilisi compounding the agony, Paisley offered his diagnosis of the malaise affecting his team.

'Great teams score goals,' he declared. 'It's no use looking impressive and then not producing the goods at the end. We're making six or seven moves in build-ups but then we get carried away with the music of them. The music soothes us when we should be exploding. We're knocking the ball around but when we get up there, where it counts, we're powder-puffs. I'm not just talking about the men at the front, although I'm not exonerating them either. Everyone in the team has a responsibility. Players of the quality we have at this club, and on their kind of wages, should motivate themselves. But if complacency exists in some players, it must be snuffed out immediately.

'I think this is a bigger test of character than we faced in Rome to win the European Cup in 1977 after losing to Manchester United in the FA Cup Final. It's going to need a lot of hard work now, and I don't just mean from the players. It's going to take everybody, including our supporters, to give us the encouragement that's needed. The whole crux of this season so far has been the way Kenny [Dalglish] has been playing. He's not been at his best and could have had a few more goals. He's so important to us and if he starts attacking in the way I know he can, then I can't see any lasting problems.'

Liverpool had excelled in the Charity Shield at Wembley, demolishing Arsenal 3-1 with a brace of goals from McDermott and one from Dalglish, which meant that Phil Thompson was climbing the 39 steps to receive the trophy before his first full season as captain was even underway. The plaudits rained down on his team for their Wembley wonder show, which put canny Paisley instantly on guard.

'If we play like this and people manage to beat us then it can only be good for the game,' he said. 'But the welter of praise we've received is not always welcome. Praise has to be withstood and handled by the players, and that's not easy.'

Liverpool's start to the League campaign was delayed because of reconstruction work at Molineux, which forced a postponement of their opening game against Wolves, and when they did get underway, safety-first Bolton prevented them scoring in a home League game for the first time in 15 months, the match ending goalless. Injuries to Hansen and Alan Kennedy meant debuts early in the campaign for Avi Cohen and Colin Irwin, while a rare first-team absence for Ray Clemence, only his seventh in almost a decade, gave Steve Ogrizovic his only senior appearance of the season in a 1–0 defeat at Forest.

Hansen's injury provided him with one of his enduring memories of Paisley, as he recounts: 'Bob was great at the one-liners. I was in the gym at Melwood one day after being out injured for a few weeks with a bad knee, and he came in and said: "How's that one, then?" I said: "Seems to be getting better. I should be playing in a week. But I'm struggling running upstairs at home." Quick as a flash, he said: "Son, you should have bought a bloody bungalow."

'Another player, Brian Kettle, went to see Bob and said: "Boss, exactly what is my future at Liverpool?" Bob replied: "Who do you think I am. Old Moore?" '

Dalglish had scored only one League goal as the alarm bells rang, but he, and the team in general, responded to Paisley's call magnificently in a devastating run that took them unbeaten – and virtually unchanged – through 19 successive games in League and League Cup, stretching from early October to mid-January. The line-up generally on parade through that sequence was, in 4-4-2 formation: Clemence; Neal, Thompson (captain), Hansen, Alan Kennedy; Case, McDermott, Souness, Ray Kennedy; Dalglish, Johnson. Substitute: Heighway or Fairclough.

It was such a rich seam of form that Paisley, as glowing as previously he had been critical, hailed it as 'the best football I have ever seen from a Liverpool team'. The run included a quartet of four-goal performances, comprising a 4–0 home trouncing of Bristol City in the club's 3,000th League game, with Dalglish among the scorers, a similar win at Manchester City, where the Scot scored twice, as he did in a 4–1 romp at Brighton, and a 4–0 Anfield conquest of Middlesbrough. The 121st Mersey derby ended in a 2–2 draw at Anfield, a game etched in the record books for anything but its football. A mass mêlée between the players in the second half ended with referee David Richardson sending McDermott and Everton's Garry Stanley on a short walk into history by ordering them off. They were the first players to be dismissed since the all-Mersey meetings began in 1894, and the game also chalked up another 'first' when a female streaker ran across the Anfield Road end of the pitch before being led away by police.

But the naked truth for Liverpool's opponents was that Anfield was almost a barren wasteland when it came to plundering points. Paisley's team, who climbed to the top of the First Division and stayed there after a scintillating 3–1 win at Aston Villa on 8 December, turned on the style in Anfield's last game of the calendar year and the decade.

Only goal difference separated Liverpool and Manchester United at kick-off on Boxing Day, with the two clubs locked on 30 points, six ahead of the chasing pack headed by Arsenal, although Paisley's team were armed with a match in hand on their visitors from Old Trafford. At the end, though, the gulf in class between Liverpool and United was yawning, as Dave Sexton's side were outplayed and fortunate to lose only 2–0. Liverpool swept through the first-half wind and rain with devastating passing moves and ripped United apart with an unforgettable 14th-minute goal, the build-up for which began with Clemence, whose throw was steered on by Phil Neal to Phil Thompson. The captain passed to Souness for the midfielder to find his fellow Scot, Hansen, who started a run 20 yards inside his own half. He then exchanged passes with Ray Kennedy before shooting past Gary Bailey. The ball had been ferried from one end of the field to the other and planted in the United net without one of their players so much as touching it.

Liverpool richly deserved their second goal six minutes from the end when Johnson's thunderous volley from Dalglish's gently flicked header crashed through Bailey's arms and legs into the net to ensure that Liverpool were unbeaten at home in all competitions during a calendar year for the first time in the post-war period. It was a magnificent way for the Kop to say farewell to the 70s, a decade which had seen Liverpool storm to four League titles, two European Cup triumphs, two UEFA Cup successes and an FA Cup win as well as a Super Cup and various Charity Shield wins.

Little wonder their home had become known as 'Fortress Anfield'. The statistics of their virtual impregnability are amazing. During the decade from January 1970 to the win over Manchester United on 26 December 1979, a period which embraced both the Shankly and Paisley eras, Liverpool lost only 11 League games out of 208 at Anfield. The full, remarkable record was: Played 208, won 154, drawn 43, lost 11, goals for 413, goals against 129. In the five and a half seasons since Paisley became manager they had lost a mere six home League matches. Liverpool's overall home record in the 1970s for games in all senior competitions was equally impressive: Played 279, won 205, drawn 58, lost 16, goals for 571, goals against 159. Indeed, they went into the 1980s not having lost a home game in any senior competition since 21 January 1978 when Birmingham, managed by Sir Alf Ramsey, snatched a surprise 3–2 victory. That run would continue and shatter all previous records.

Paisley ushered in the 80s in typically reflective manner, repeating one of the tenets of his football philosophy. 'We've been the team of the 70s and I'll be happy if we can play the same type of football in the next decade,' he said. 'Then if anyone beats us it can only be for the good of the game.'

Liverpool followed their defeat of United with a 2–0 win at West Brom before their first action of 1980 was a 5–0 FA Cup drubbing of Grimsby, with Johnson collecting his first Liverpool hat-trick and Souness celebrating his 100th appearance for the club, and Case also scoring. 'I followed the referee around the pitch for the last few minutes because I wanted the match ball as a souvenir,' said Johnson. 'I managed to get the ball when I scored a hat-trick for Ipswich but I missed it when I hit three for Everton because Joe Royle got it for scoring four in the same match against Southampton.' The win over Grimsby was Liverpool's biggest in the FA Cup since a similar nap hand against Derby back in 1964 and it maintained the club's unique achievement of scoring in the third round every season since 1953–54.

Liverpool's 19-game unbeaten home and away run ended with a 1–0 defeat at Coventry, but they were still on course for a domestic treble until the first of a flurry of meetings with Nottingham Forest. After they had seen off Tranmere, Chesterfield, Exeter and Norwich, the first leg of the League Cup semi-final sent Liverpool to the City Ground for their tenth meeting with Brian Clough's side since they returned to the First Division in 1977. Liverpool had won only one of those games with Forest winning three and five drawn.

Paisley's side were within sight of their second League Cup Final appearance in three years when the electronic scoreboard clock registered 90 minutes with the tie at 0–0. Then the Forest curse struck again. A misunderstanding between Hansen and Clemence forced the England goalkeeper to bring down Garry Birtles and with just 15 seconds left, John Robertson scored from the penalty to give Forest a crucial 1–0 win. Another Forest spot kick in the Anfield second leg – Robertson again on target after Clemence had upended Martin O'Neill – was too much for Liverpool. A 90th-minute equaliser on the night from substitute David Fairclough preserved their long unbeaten home record, but could not prevent them going out on a 2–1 aggregate. It extended Forest's unbeaten League Cup run to 24 games and took them to Wembley for the third consecutive year. 'We had to make all the play against difficult tactics,' said Paisley. 'It was just unfortunate that Forest didn't carve out two moves yet got a penalty in each leg to win the tie.'

In between the two League Cup clashes, there was at least some overdue revenge for Liverpool, who also had to travel to Forest in the FA Cup fourth round and won 2–0 through goals from Dalglish and a McDermott penalty. And in the fourth meeting of the clubs in three competitions in under a month, Liverpool also enjoyed the sweet taste of victory over Clough's side with a 2–0 First Division win at Anfield. With 12 minutes left, that game was set in a familiar, goalless pattern with Liverpool attacking in waves and Forest defending desperately. Then McDermott latched on to a chance set up by some cool thinking by Dalglish and broke the deadlock on his 200th Liverpool appearance. Ray Kennedy added a second goal to clinch a crucial victory but Liverpool's march was checked with their next two results. The first of these was a 1–1 home draw with Ipswich, when McDermott's late penalty was saved by Paul Cooper. David Fairclough, standing in for injured David Johnson, had given Liverpool the lead with his sixth goal in four outings. It followed his hat-trick in a thrilling 5–3 win at Norwich – a game in which Sammy Lee stood in for Souness, who served a one-match ban for accumulating five bookings – and a brace as substitute to clinch a 2–0 FA Cup fifth round win over Bury. Eric Gates equalised for Ipswich but Terry Butcher's challenge on Dalglish gave Liverpool a chance of victory. However, as McDermott ran up to take the contested spot-kick, Frans Thijssen threw a dollop of mud at the ball and Cooper saved. Referee Bert Newsome, remarkably, refused a retake and allowed the Dutch international to escape unpunished for his mudlark. 'I saw the mud being thrown but it didn't interfere with the action of taking the kick,' said the Shropshire official.

Even Thijssen admitted: 'I was lucky not to be booked. I didn't think Terry Butcher's challenge on Dalglish was a penalty. Throwing the mud was just a reaction. But it didn't put McDermott off. It was a good save.'

McDermott, creditably, refused to use the incident as an excuse, saying: 'I saw the mud coming across on my run-up but, whether it put me off or not, it was a bad penalty. Cooper was just waiting for it. He had time to eat his sandwiches. I think it's time that Phil Neal and I started sharing the penalty job. If it's down to one man all the time, goalkeepers can get to know too much about how you take them.'

With the mud-hurling affair still reverberating, Paisley offered another down-to-earth reason for his side's sudden stutter, which was again evident in a 1–0 defeat in the rearranged match at Wolves three days later. 'The holding state of the pitches at the moment are not doing us any favours,' he said. 'We're not playing at our best, but the grounds at present don't lend themselves to our type of football.'

Liverpool resumed winning ways with a 2–1 Mersey derby win at Everton on what was a sad day for the whole of football. Overshadowing a bad-tempered game, in which Neal successfully took on the penalty-taking task and David Johnson also scored, was the death of one of the 53,000-plus spectators. The legendary

Bill 'Dixie' Dean went to the match as my guest, following a book launch also attended by Bill Shankly. Near the end of the game, Britain's greatest ever centre-forward felt unwell and died inside his beloved Goodison Park, drawing warm tributes from Paisley and the rest of football.

The derby victory was the first of six straight wins in the League and FA Cup at a time when the pitches were now hardening and Liverpool were able to fully express their passing game. The run ended with a 2–0 defeat at Tottenham on 29 March through a penalty from a certain Glenn Hoddle and a goal from John Pratt. It was the London club's revenge for their sixth-round FA Cup exit at White Hart Lane when McDermott scored the game's only goal with a magnificent, swerving shot into the far top corner of the net, to book a semi-final collision with Arsenal. Significantly, the League defeat came at the end of a week when Liverpool had a club record 12 players away on international duty. Clemence, Neal, Thompson, McDermott, Johnson and Ray Kennedy were with England in Spain, Scotland called on Dalglish, Souness and Hansen, the Republic of Ireland selected Steve Heighway, Avi Cohen flew to Israel for the World Cup qualifier with Northern Ireland, while Alan Kennedy was called up for the England B squad. It left Jimmy Case in lonely isolation at Melwood as the only first-team regular not to receive an international call. He had scored for the England Under-23 side on his only representative appearance four years earlier but was destined never to win a full cap.

'I suppose I should be singing a variation of that old wartime song, "Wish Them Luck As You Wave Them Goodbye"', said 25-year-old Case, putting a brave face on being ignored by Ron Greenwood. Paisley, though, had far more serious observations on his midfielder's fate.

'Ron Greenwood should have gone the whole hog and picked Case as well,' said Paisley. 'He's a key man in our midfield and links up well with McDermott and Ray Kennedy. Case gets through a lot of work, a job he could also perform for England.

'From the time Ron took charge of England he quite rightly plumped for the club system by taking more than half our team, six players in all, for his first game against Switzerland. At that time he picked three of our midfield men, McDermott, Callaghan and Ray Kennedy, yet ignored Case. The strength of our midfield was based on the collective efforts of four men, not three. Case's absence threw extra work on the other three. I also believe Ray Kennedy has been wrongly used by England. He's asked to do a marking job and "pick people up". That's something he's never done at Liverpool. His positional play is outstanding, but you should never give him the job of chasing after somebody or doing a defensive chore. He can close people down with his superb positional play, but that's quite different.

'A lot of things baffle me at England level. Last season Emlyn Hughes was selected for England when he was in our reserves, yet the man who had taken his place, Phil Thompson, was overlooked. Later in the season Phil was injured and Emlyn came back into our first team, but it was Phil who was picked to play for England! If you find that hard to follow, you're not alone.

'Having a lot of players away for internationals can be a big handicap for us at club level but, from a patriotic point of view, I think having players together who understand each other and know their roles is the correct approach. Many international players are too interested in safeguarding their own positions, even at the expense of the side. Managers can contribute to this by saying things like: "Just go out and play your normal game." That's a classic case of a manager avoiding his responsibility. If 11 internationals from half a dozen clubs went out at Wembley and did just that, I shudder to think what the outcome would be. Chaos, for certain.

'I believe a top club side will always be more effective than the national one until the wrinkles are ironed out, but there are players in the game today more interested in representing their countries than their clubs. Some players will protect themselves in League matches to avoid injury if an international game is imminent. It may be human nature, but it doesn't mean we must accept it.

'It's not easy to adopt that attitude if you're a Liverpool player because our game is based on teamwork with everyone pulling his weight. Any shirker would stand out like a sore thumb, because almost all our matches have something at stake. Most clubs may have 20 truly competitive games in a season, but virtually every one of ours is like a cup tie.'

Despite losing at Tottenham, Liverpool, with 50 points, were still top, four clear of Manchester United, both having played 34 games, with Ipswich and Arsenal a further two points adrift. A Dalglish goal gave Liverpool a 1–0 home win over Stoke and when Manchester United lost at Nottingham Forest the following evening, it meant that Paisley's side went into the Easter period with a six-point lead over their closest pursuers. Old Trafford was their next destination but even though Dalglish's goal gave Liverpool a deserved early breakthrough, it was not their day. Goals from Mickey Thomas and Jimmy Greenhoff gave United a 2–1 win, cutting the gap to four points, with both clubs having played 36 games. However, Liverpool's goal difference was a massive 44 against United's 23.

The result, though, was not Liverpool's only blow at Old Trafford. Alan Kennedy pulled up with hamstring damage, the first of a crop of casualties as a tense stamina-sapping climax to the season in League and FA Cup became a demanding test of endurance. Colin Irwin was recalled for a five-game run in Kennedy's left-back berth and celebrated by heading Liverpool ahead against Derby County at Anfield and helping to make another goal for David Johnson. A Keith Osgood own goal completed a 3–0 win.

That brought Liverpool to the opening of a chapter unique in FA Cup history. When they faced Arsenal at Hillsborough it was to be the start of the longest semi-final battle ever in the world's oldest knock-out competition. The struggle encompassed four matches with two periods of extra time, and surpassed the previous record which also involved Liverpool, when they met Sheffield United in 1898–99.

It was Paisley's 18th major semi-final in his various roles at Liverpool and one he had to go into not only without Alan Kennedy but also McDermott, who was forced off against Derby after a kick on his right fibula. Although David Fairclough had replaced McDermott as substitute in the Derby match, for the semi-final Paisley handed a starting place to Sammy Lee with Fairclough again on the bench.

'Sammy's been going like a bomb in training and been faster than anyone,' said Paisley. 'I've got no worries about him. But I think we're in for a dour game. When we beat Arsenal 3–1 in the Charity Shield at Wembley last August, I was surprised how open they were. They won't be as open this time. Because of the styles of the teams I expect the game will be very tight and a battle all the way similar to our goalless draw at Highbury in November.'

He was uncannily accurate in his forecast. In a tense, taut contest, there were no goals and Liverpool were struck again by the injury jinx when a first-half collision between Case and Arsenal's Sammy Nelson forced the Liverpool midfielder to withdraw ten minutes after the interval suffering from shoulder damage. Liverpool penalty appeals for a challenge on Dalglish were rejected by referee Keith Hackett, while at the other end Ray Clemence, on his 600th appearance and after being dazed in a clash with Frank Stapleton, twice raced off his line to clear from the Arsenal striker.

Four minutes from the end, fate did afford Liverpool a little smile when Brian Talbot's shot hit the bar. 'I was blowing the ball up in the air,' Paisley joked. 'It was obvious from the reaction of our defenders that it was not going over the bar. It was either going to hit it or go in.'

When Liverpool travelled to Villa Park for the replay the following Wednesday, their hopes of landing the Double were on the line at the start of an intensive programme of seven crucial matches in 18 days between 16 April and 3 May. Paisley conceded the pressure was on and observed: 'It's a pity you can't get tax relief for it!' With Case ruled out of the replay, he relied on the side that had finished at Hillsborough, with Avi Cohen taking over as substitute.

Again it ended in deadlock, despite extra time. Fairclough's goal five minutes after the interval was cancelled out by Alan Sunderland and it meant a second replay, almost a fortnight later, back at Villa Park. By a quirk of the fixture list, Liverpool's next engagement was a home League collision with Arsenal, their third meeting in a week, and was once again without a winner. Dalglish's early goal put Liverpool ahead but Talbot equalised near the end. Manchester United's 2–0 win at Norwich the same afternoon pushed them to within one point of Liverpool although they had played one more game. The midweek match at Stoke therefore assumed even more importance for Liverpool, but a goal in each half from Johnson and Fairclough sealed a 2–0 win. During the match Colin Irwin was hit by ankle damage that ruled him out of the season's remaining matches. It gave substitute Cohen only his second taste of League football but the following Saturday saw Alan Kennedy's return in a goalless draw at Crystal Palace. The heat at the top was now increasing. Manchester United's home win over Coventry took them level with Liverpool although they had played a game more with a goal difference inferior to the Anfield side by 17.

The League had to take a temporary backseat as Liverpool resumed battle with Arsenal in their semi-final second replay.

Fittingly, the match saw the return of McDermott, who had completed a spring double of his own by being elected Footballer of the Year by the football writers. He had earlier been named Player of the Year by the Professional Footballers Association, and so became the first man to win both awards in the same season. 'He's been well worth the double honour,' said Paisley. 'He's had a good season and I'm delighted for him.'

McDermott, who became the fifth Anfield player in seven seasons to become Footballer of the Year after Ian Callaghan (1974), Kevin Keegan (1976), Emlyn Hughes (1977) and Kenny Dalglish (1978), was typically self-deprecating. 'I can't get over it,' he exclaimed. 'When I think of all the fantastic players who have won it before, and now it's going to a rag-bag like me.' As Liverpool prepared for the next stage of the Arsenal saga, Paisley refuted a London newspaper claim that he had told certain players to man-mark some of the Highbury team. 'I've read that in our recent games against Arsenal we detailed players to mark men like Liam Brady and David Price,' he said. 'My answer to that is that over the years Liverpool have deliberately man-to-man marked only two players – Alan Ball at Everton and Franz Beckenbauer of Bayern Munich.'

McDermott's return pushed Fairclough on to the substitute's bench, with Lee keeping his place. Since the clubs had last tussled, Arsenal had scored a stunning Cup-Winners' Cup win over Juventus in Turin, and now they had a swift shock for Liverpool. Just 20 seconds after the kick-off Alan Sunderland fired Arsenal ahead, and with 30 seconds of the game left and Liverpool down to ten men, through injury to David Johnson, that scoreline stood. Then, at the last gasp, Dalglish beat Pat Jennings to send the tie into another half-hour period of extra time.

Alan Kennedy had already limped off with a recurrence of hamstring trouble in the 66th minute to be replaced by Fairclough. Ironically, it was the Liverpool substitute who was involved in a collision with team-mate Johnson as they challenged Arsenal goalkeeper Pat Jennings late in the game. Johnson was carried off on a stretcher with blood pumping from deep gashes above and below his right eye, wounds which needed five stitches. It was a setback to the Liverpool cause that provided a classic example of Paisley's unique qualities; of his genius in a situation where the pressure was intense. As extra time began, the Liverpool coaching staff, in consultation with the club doctor, pondered whether stitched-up Johnson could return to action.

The fear was that he might be concussed. Among the members of the backroom staff at Villa Park that night, along with Joe Fagan, Ronnie Moran and company, was Tommy Smith, who had returned to the club as a youth coach the previous autumn and would spend almost a year in the role before leaving to concentrate on business activities.

In the frenzied atmosphere, Paisley took a decision. He told Smith: 'Tom, I want you to tell Johnson to go back on and play wide on the right. But don't show him where to play. If he can tell the right side from left then he's not concussed. If he doesn't know where to go then he is dazed and he'll have to come off again right away.'

Johnson went back on, immediately took up his emergency right flank role and almost won the game for Liverpool with a shot that brought the magnificent best out of the great Northern Ireland star Jennings. So, after a 1–1 deadlock, the marathon moved into a fourth game three days later at Coventry, where Cohen took over at left-back from injured Alan Kennedy, with Fairclough substitute. By now the prospect of the first all-Merseyside FA Cup Final had disappeared with Everton's semi-final replay defeat by West Ham. The FA, though, were drawing up contingency plans to settle Liverpool's semi-final if the latest instalment of the marathon was still deadlocked.

Both Liverpool and Arsenal angrily denounced FA plans for a penalty decider if the teams could still not be separated after a fourth replay – and fifth match – scheduled for Bramall Lane the following Monday. Liverpool had threatened to walk off the pitch rather than participate in a penalty shoot-out in the third replay. The issue of football and television, still a burning one, was a factor in the equation, with the FA summarily rejecting Arsenal's request for the final to be put back, because of TV arrangements and pre-booked satellite time.

'Television has become too important,' said Arsenal chairman Dennis Hill-Wood. 'I don't believe the FA are entitled, or have the power, to change the regulations in the middle of a competition.'

Paisley backed him, saying: 'You could accept penalty deciders if they were in the rules, as they are in European football. But to introduce them now that this semi-final has gone on for so long is like locking the stable door after the horse has bolted.'

The supporters were certainly prepared for the hardship of paying for the experience of watching the marathon battle. One of the thousands of Liverpool fans, car delivery night shift worker Richie Clarke, revealed that the four games in less than three weeks had cost him £180 in tickets, travel and lost wages, a substantial amount in 1980. 'When I go off to watch an evening match it costs me £30 in earnings but it's worth it to watch the lads,' he declared. 'I even go to Wembley to watch the Liverpool players turn out for England.'

In the event, the Highfield Road duel was decisive, with the thirteenth minute proving unlucky for Liverpool in general and Ray Kennedy in particular. A rare mistake by the player hailed by Paisley as 'a pillar of consistency' allowed Frank Stapleton to cross for Brian Talbot to head the only goal of the game. 'Something like that was always going to settle it,' said Paisley, philosophically. 'I would have put my life on Ray's left foot. It's the most trusted in football. He'd got the ball but lost his footing and went completely off balance.'

Not only did Kennedy's slip against his former club cost Liverpool the chance of the classic double of League title and FA Cup, it also robbed him of the opportunity of becoming the first player to win the double with two different clubs. 'I feel I've let down a lot of people,' Kennedy admitted. 'Just one mistake and I made it. It's sickening. I've been to Wembley before but I feel sorry for people like Sammy Lee and Avi Cohen, who played so well.'

The four-match epic had proved a box-office bonanza, grossing more than £620,000 in gate receipts from a total attendance exceeding 170,000. But Liverpool's remaining objective was priceless – the retention of their League title. They had two games left, a Saturday home duel with Aston Villa less than 48 hours after the crushing disappointment of their Cup exit to Arsenal, and a trip to Middlesbrough the following Tuesday evening. But Liverpool knew that victory over Villa – also their Anfield opponents when they clinched the title the previous season – would secure the championship, regardless of what Manchester United did in their final game at Leeds.

The impact of the Cup defeat took its toll on Paisley's squad. 'After losing to Arsenal on the Thursday night we went straight back to a Cheshire hotel to get ready for the Villa game and it was terrible,' revealed Phil Neal. 'The hotel seemed like a big black hole, with hardly any of the players knowing what to do with themselves.'

His colleague Alan Hansen recalled: 'I remember vividly after the huge disappointment of losing to Arsenal that the following morning's training session consisted of a walk and a short one at that! We couldn't have managed a long one. We were almost on our knees after the intensive programme of massive matches, and less than two days later we had a potential championship decider to play in.'

Paisley, destined like Brian Clough never to win the FA Cup, swiftly began the task of restoring his players psychologically, of recharging their mental batteries. 'The FA Cup might be the showpiece competition but the League is the big one,' he told them. 'Anyone in football worth his salt wants a championship medal. It's always been more important to me and it's at the top of this club's list, too.'

The championship also provided the single, golden key to the European Cup, unlike today's perversely titled Champions' League which is also open to non-champions and, thus, in many people's eyes devalued. The 1999 final in Barcelona, for instance, when Manchester United dramatically beat Bayern Munich, was a dubious 'first' in football history – a contest between the League runners-up of England and Germany.

Paisley's only team change for Liverpool's attempt to transform their FA Cup gloom into title glory was at substitute, where Howard Gayle, the striker who would play an unforgettable role in Europe the following season, had his first stint on the bench following a loan period at Fulham.

David Johnson, still bearing the scars of his head injury less than a week earlier, took just three minutes to put Liverpool in front and transport most of the 51,000-plus crowd into raptures. Midway through the first half Avi Cohen brought them back down to earth with a bump. The Israeli, making his home debut in place of injured absentees Alan Kennedy and Colin Irwin, diverted the ball past Ray Clemence and into his own net, to present Villa with an equaliser in front of the Kop.

'I just wanted the ground to swallow me up,' Cohen admitted, although half-time information that Manchester United were losing raised Liverpool spirits. Amazingly, Cohen then had the fans singing by scoring for Liverpool in the same Kop net as his own goal. He steamed into the attack and his shot flew past Jimmy Rimmer six minutes into the second half to restore Liverpool's advantage with what proved the only goal of his 23-game Anfield career. This time the lead was for real and another strike from the impressive Johnson, his 27th of an eventful season, and an own goal by Noel Blake, carved out a stylish 4–1 win to bring Liverpool's championships to a round dozen.

The strain of the season affected some of the team long before the final whistle. 'Midway through the second half the events of the past few weeks caught up with me and I started to cry,' revealed Phil Neal. 'The game was going on and tears just started rolling down my cheeks. I'll tell you something, that semi-final marathon against Arsenal and the hectic run-in to the championship affected even experienced players like me, let alone youngsters like Sammy Lee. I'm delighted for Sammy that we've won the title because there was no consoling him when we went out of the Cup. The strain and tension of the past few weeks have been enormous. This has made it all worthwhile.'

The glittering trophy was carried on to the pitch by non-participants David Fairclough and Alan Kennedy as they joined their victorious colleagues and Paisley on a lap of honour, the Kop chanting the manager's name. When the trophy was taken back inside, Kenny Dalglish put the prized pot on a table and sat his three-year-old son Paul, destined to become a professional player himself, next to it to pose for a picture.

The first player Paisley went to was Cohen. 'I patted him on the back,' said Paisley. 'His own goal made us sweat a bit. But then he scored one for us and I suppose that proves just what a good utility player he is and how versatile he can be!'

Said Cohen: 'After putting through my own goal it was just fantastic to score for Liverpool on such a fantastic day as this.' It was a memory that will stay with Cohen always, just as I will keep recalling his involvement in the wonderful anecdote featuring him and Kenny Dalglish, a player and manager the Israeli idolises to this day.

Cohen, trying to conquer a new language when he first arrived at Liverpool, found his peg for training next to Dalglish's. The new signing repeatedly told the great Scot: 'Me, you, same.'

Dalglish, his curiosity at breaking point, could contain himself no longer and asked in his heavy Glaswegian: 'What do you mean by that?'

To which Cohen replied: 'Kenny – you, me, same – both learn English!'

With the title won and the pressure off, Cohen played in an unchanged side that lost 1–0 in Liverpool's closing League fixture at Middlesbrough to give them a final record of: Played 42, won 25, drawn 10, lost 7, goals for 81, goals against 29, points 60. They finished two points clear of Manchester United and seven ahead of third-placed Ipswich. Arsenal, who lost the FA Cup Final to West Ham and the Cup-Winners' Cup Final to Valencia on penalties, were a further point adrift.

A week after the game at Ayresome Park, the championship trophy was brought out of its glass case at Anfield and officially re-presented to Liverpool on the pitch by the League's senior vice-president Bob Lord, as a curtain raiser to Ray Clemence's testimonial match against Anderlecht.

'It's been a very demanding season and with the problems we had to overcome it's been a good one,' was the Paisley verdict. 'The football we played in the middle of the season has not been bettered by any Liverpool team in my experience. When you're involved in a marathon series of matches as we were against Nottingham Forest and Arsenal, it's a tremendous mental drain and it affects players. Despite the fact that we lost in the semi-finals of both the FA Cup and League Cup, we can look back on the season with satisfaction. It was pleasing to see lads like Sammy Lee, Colin Irwin and Avi Cohen respond when they were thrown into the team.

'At the end of the day, we have won the League in the right manner – winning more matches than anyone else, scoring more goals and conceding the fewest. We've got near to total football, even though the majority of opponents have been trying to cancel us out. Instead of trying to be constructive, most teams have been concerned with stopping Liverpool rather than attempting to exploit us. We have carried that burden all the way through.

'Critics can crucify Malcolm Allison at Manchester City (who finished 17th) as much as they like, but he's one of the few positive coaches in the game. At least he's looking in the right direction at Maine Road and, despite the club's problems, gates have stayed high. Malcolm is constructive in his outlook when too many are not. There are exceptions, like Ipswich and Manchester United, but most teams are looking simply to cancel us out by closing players down.'

Liverpool's title triumph matched Arsenal's achievement of five championships in eight years between 1930 and 1938, and Paisley was named Bell's Manager of the Year for the fourth time in five seasons, receiving a gallon bottle of whisky and a cheque for £2,500. Yet he was still intent on paying out cheques to reinforce his squad, in what he considered was a continuous process. He had experienced six blank seasons during the Bill Shankly era, spanning the end of the 1960s and start of the 1970s, when Liverpool failed to win a single trophy. That was due, Paisley believed, to Shankly remaining loyal to spent stars when new blood should have been introduced. It was a harsh lesson he had absorbed, and something he had no intention of repeating.

During the season, a talented teenager from Dublin amateur club Home Farm arrived at Anfield. Ronnie Whelan would go on to become one of the great midfielders of the post-war era and a natural successor to Ray Kennedy on Liverpool's left flank. His room-mate would be another 18-year-old, recruited by Paisley in April 1980, although while Whelan was signed for the donation of a nominal sum, Ian Rush cost £330,000 from Chester, a British record for a player of his age. Rush had scored 17 times in only 38 outings for his Third Division club when Paisley decided to move in. The young Welsh striker's progress had been carefully monitored by Liverpool's chief scout and former player Geoff Twentyman.

When Paisley cast his own eye on the Chester prodigy, he recognised his raw talent. 'I could see there was tremendous promise and potential in Ian so we decided to make our move,' he recalled. 'Mind you, not long after he came to us the football world was full of people saying how they "nearly" bought him and scouts telling of how they recommended Ian to this or that club. I don't know how Chester got them all in their ground to watch him!' The judgement of Paisley and Twentyman in spotting the youngster's talent and investing in it was proved in subsequent years to be masterful, as Rush became synonymous with goals, trophies and success. Given the scale of players' earnings today, it is intriguing to record Rush's reaction to the £300 a week salary offered by Paisley when they first met in his Anfield office. 'It just took my breath away and I couldn't speak,' he admitted. 'My dad was with me and he was overwhelmed like me.'

Another Paisley signing in 1980 was Richard Money, a versatile 24-year-old defender or midfielder from Fulham. He had begun his career at Scunthorpe, the club that produced

Kevin Keegan and Ray Clemence. Money, like Rush, cost £330,000, but was destined to make only 17 appearances before moving on to Luton two years later. One of those outings, however, would be on a marvellous night in Europe when Liverpool defied the odds – and the Germans.

13

Munich Magic, Paris Triumph

With little more than an hour to kick-off, the tension and atmosphere is building in Munich's magnificent Olympic Stadium for the second leg of Liverpool's European Cup semi-final against Bayern. The Germans are hot favourites to reach the final after holding out for a goalless draw at Anfield and armed now with home advantage against injury-ravaged opponents. Suddenly there is a knock on Liverpool's dressing-room door.

'It's the UEFA observer, boss,' Ronnie Moran shouts to Bob Paisley.

'Can I help you?' Paisley asks as he walks across to the doorway to meet the Austrian official, whose job as the emissary of European football's ruling body is to ensure that no regulations are flouted and to report any misbehaviour on or off the field.

'Can you tell me about this Howard Gayle?' he asks.

'He's a registered player with Liverpool Football Club,' replies Paisley in deadpan tones, repeating his reply to ensure that UEFA's man is left in no doubt that further information on Liverpool's largely unknown black forward will not be forthcoming.

The official shuffles uncomfortably, offers a thin smile and is gone, heading down the stadium corridor hardly any the wiser.

In that cameo the seeds of a majestic Liverpool feat were sown, then germinated with another classic illustration of Paisley's genius in the intense heat of football battle.

It was a moment instrumental in Liverpool lifting the European

Cup for the third time, thus ensuring Paisley a place in managerial legend.

It was the climax of an intriguing 1980–81 season in which Liverpool reversed their fortunes of the two previous campaigns. Although they finished a disappointing fifth in the First Division – the club's lowest position in ten seasons as they trailed nine points behind champions Aston Villa – they still had a double celebration. In addition to getting their hands on the European Cup for the third time, Paisley's men also landed the League Cup for the first time in the club's history, beginning a four-season monopoly of the competition which the following year became sponsored as the Milk Cup.

Paisley, by now a proud 61-year-old grandfather, still enjoyed the thrill of a new season, his appetite for the challenge undimmed. After travelling to Italy to comment on the European Championships for a national newspaper during the summer of 1980, he recharged his batteries in customary fashion. He spent an invigorating week at Frankie Durr's Newmarket stables and enthused: 'I was out on the Downs at six o'clock in the morning and it was like throwing a bag of cement off my back. Now I'm ready to get back and compete. My view is that if you can't stick the pace then leave the game. There's no alternative.'

Even though a feature of Paisley's Anfield office was a joke clock that went backwards – presented to him when he officially opened an insurance company's new offices – he refused to dwell on the past. 'It's no good moaning about close seasons getting shorter,' he insisted. 'You have to move with the times. Everyone in life seems to be in a hurry now and there are lots of pressure jobs outside football. Having said that, relaxation in football when it can be taken, is crucial. That's why I had to tell Ronnie Moran to leave the training ground this summer and take a break. He would have been out there every day if we'd let him. But mental and physical rest is invaluable.

'The younger players today, mind you, don't know anything other than the high-speed life. They've been brought up with faster and faster cars, easy overseas travel and modern facilities. In the old days there was only the championship and FA Cup and the close season lasted three months. If the club could fix up a foreign tour you might be away for five weeks! Or you could play a whole summer's cricket to get away from football and relax. When I was a player, it took me longer to drive home to Hetton than it now takes to fly to Russia! But today's players have never known that lifestyle, so we have to find ways of relaxing and unwinding them during the season. But every time a new season starts, those of us who love the game just have to get up and go again.'

As the curtain went up on the new campaign in August 1980, Paisley was not shy in setting out his targets even though to most clubs they would have seemed mere flights of fantasy. 'I'd like us to complete a championship hat-trick, to equal the pre-war feats of Arsenal and Huddersfield, and I'd love a crack at bringing the European Cup to Anfield for the third time,' he said.

The first of those aspirations eluded Paisley, whose side's 17 draws, the third highest in the First Division, cost them any hope of a third successive title triumph, even though their total of eight defeats was matched only by champions Villa and third-placed Arsenal. But as well as the League Cup, Europe beckoned Liverpool again in a season they opened in style by winning the Charity Shield against West Ham. Terry McDermott's only goal of the Wembley contest meant that Liverpool became the first club to lift the Shield outright in successive seasons since Tottenham in 1961 and 1962.

Paisley was delighted at his side's initial European pairing with Oulun Palloseura, the Finnish club with the distinction of being the most northerly in UEFA competitions. Oulu, a small port on the fringe of Lapland at the north of the Gulf of Bothnia, fewer than 100 miles south of the Arctic Circle, was the setting for the first leg in mid-September, just a few weeks before the onset of the Arctic winter. After the first-round collisions with Nottingham Forest and Dynamo Tbilisi in the previous two seasons, the draw had at last been kind to Liverpool. 'We finally got the luck which had deserted us,' Paisley conceded.

Liverpool warmed up for their mission to reindeer country with a 4–0 home League drubbing of West Brom on the Saturday, when two-goal David Fairclough, defender Avi Cohen and midfielder Sammy Lee slotted in like jigsaw pieces to replace injured trio David Johnson, Alan Kennedy and Jimmy Case. Paisley's only complaint concerned the racetrack rather than the football field. He had failed to invest in Light Cavalry, a 3–1 winner of the St Leger, despite being urged to by his friend Ray Peers, who duly collected.

'I backed it last time out but, unfortunately, I didn't put anything on it this time,' said Paisley. 'But the team made up for that.'

An unchanged team failed to transport that scintillating weekend League form into midweek European action, although the biggest shock for the Liverpool party came even before a ball was kicked. 'In some of the remote parts of Europe, like Oulu, you have to fall in with local customs, and our directors fell in alright!' Paisley chuckled. 'They were a bit taken aback when, after being entertained hospitably by their hosts, they were driven to have a sauna, where the cold plunge afterwards consisted of jumping into the near-freezing waters of a lake!'

Lukewarm was a fitting label for the team's performance in only drawing 1–1 with their part-time Finnish opponents, who were making their debut in Europe. A rare header from McDermott put Liverpool ahead but a combination of spectacular goalkeeping by army officer Jukka Rantanen, dour defence by the Finns and a treacherous, uneven playing surface conspired against the visitors, who missed a batch of opportunities. Ten minutes from the end, Soini Puotiniemi, a welder by trade, spotted a gap at Liverpool's near post and fired an equaliser.

'How can you blame your team when they have to play on a pitch like that?' asked Paisley. 'It was tight and bumpy and one touchline had a kink in it where there was a long-jump pit. Nevertheless, we did miss many chances.'

Oulun rated that result the greatest in their history. A fortnight later at Anfield, though, they were on the wrong end of Liverpool's biggest ever single match victory in the European Cup. The same line-up that had been on duty in Finland raced to a 4–0 lead by half-time, with two goals apiece from Souness and McDermott. Two minutes after the interval Oulun snatched a sliver of consolation when Keith Armstrong – a Geordie who, with Scot Hugh Smith, was one of two British players in the Finnish ranks – beat the offside trap to score. It was a brief suspension of Liverpool hostilities. Souness completed his hat-trick – for his seventh goal in six games – from the penalty spot. Then Sammy Lee and Ray Kennedy, the other members of Liverpool's midfield quartet, were on target before two headers from David Fairclough put Liverpool 9–1 in front on the night. Six minutes from the end McDermott completed his hat-trick for a 10–1 win and an 11–2 aggregate triumph. 'As the score suggests, this was a cruise,' Paisley drily noted in his daily log.

Another significant feature of the evening was the news from Nottingham that holders Forest had bowed out of the European

Cup to the Bulgarian champions CSKA Sofia, opposition with whom Liverpool were to make their own acquaintance in the forthcoming months.

The second-round draw plunged Liverpool into a 'Battle of Britain' collision with Aberdeen, the Scottish club managed by Alex Ferguson, who had broken through the Rangers-Celtic stranglehold on Scottish honours. The European tie was to be the only time Paisley and Ferguson would pit their wits against each other as rival managers. Paisley emerged the emphatic winner but the lesson was a valuable one for the man who would later lead Manchester United to glory and join Paisley among the legends of management.

The first leg in Aberdeen provided the stage for Paisley to indulge his brilliant psychology by showering praise on the opposition, or, as he called it, 'giving them a bit of toffee'. His target for a fulsome salute this time was midfielder Gordon Strachan, one of the stars of an Aberdeen team that also included other notable Scotland internationals in Willie Miller and Alex McLeish.

'If Aberdeen ever relent and decide to sell Gordon, he'll become Scotland's first £2 million player,' Paisley told the media. 'He impresses me greatly, as do Aberdeen as a team. They don't give much away and with a few wins under their belt they'll face us with confidence.'

The confidence trick, though, was Paisley's. The 24,000 all-seated fans at a sell-out Pittodrie witnessed an efficient, victorious display by Liverpool, for whom Alan Kennedy returned after a ten-match absence. Their 1–0 win was secured with a superb strike from McDermott, whose 12th goal of the season came from a brilliantly chipped fifth-minute shot from an acute angle.

'That goal must rate as one of my best ever and the funny thing is that whenever I score them like this the television cameras always seem to be around,' said McDermott. 'The Aberdeen goalkeeper Jim Leighton made my mind up for me. I saw him advancing as I was going to hit the ball. Then he started to go back and I knew he wouldn't reach my shot. It's something we used to practise in training when I was with Bury ten years ago, but this was the first time I've tried it since.'

Of Strachan, though, little was seen. Paisley's salute had clearly detrimentally affected the red-headed player, whose displays were usually so dynamic. His battery looked flat. 'That was probably the greatest example of Bob giving out his toffee,' said Alan

Hansen. 'When we got to Aberdeen it was unbelievable, because the paper up there had a 28-page pull out, 27 pages of which were about what they were going to do to us! Bob saw this and decided to add a bit of spice to things by hailing Gordon Strachan as the best player in Britain and saying that he was worth £2 million. We all knew why he'd said it. It was to put Strachan off, to give him the heebie-jeebies when he read it. It worked like a dream because Strachan never kicked a ball in the two legs against us.

'Bob used to come out with lines like that to the press every seven or eight weeks. I think that Kenny [Dalglish] and Alex Ferguson learned a lot from that. Both of them use the press to incredible effect. Whenever they come out with lines in the paper on a Saturday morning, it's to influence someone or something. I must say, it usually works. They've become experts. But Bob Paisley was the master at it.'

Paisley wrote in his diary after the win at Aberdeen: 'It was one of our most efficient away performances. Aberdeen proved a useful side with lots of enthusiasm and the second leg should be another hard game.'

It was, in fact, much easier than Paisley anticipated or could have hoped for. The date was 5 November and although Liverpool's fireworks were delayed, once the touch paper was lit Aberdeen's ambitions just fizzled out. It took Liverpool 38 minutes to add to their first-leg advantage. Ironically, the substitution of Avi Cohen for hamstring casualty Alan Kennedy two minutes earlier set up the breakthrough. Cohen's first touch brought a corner which ended with Miller slicing the ball into his own net. Then Phil Neal hit a second just before the interval to put the tie beyond Aberdeen's reach. Dalglish headed a third goal before his compatriot Hansen climaxed a seven-man move to make it 4–0 on the night – Aberdeen's heaviest single match deficit in Europe – and 5–0 on aggregate.

'If it had been a late kick-off I would say we played brilliantly,' quipped Paisley. 'Early on I don't know whether we were too excited or too tense but in the first 25 minutes we played into their hands. Once the own goal went in, though, we began playing. Everyone started doing their stuff and we strung the passing movements together superbly. Aberdeen had no answer.'

Ferguson, reflecting on that meeting with Paisley, described him as 'full of cunning'. He labelled that Anfield defeat "annihilation' and admitted he learned that night the value of using the ball and keeping possession: 'After that Anfield episode I knew I didn't have to say another bloody word to my players about keeping the ball, particularly in European games. That was part of my education and it's always been part of my strategy. Hold on to the ball, keep passing it, let the other teams do the chasing.'

Paisley, picking up one of his favourite themes and one which is still a burning, relevant issue today, had special praise for the East German referee Adolf Prokop, saying: 'I'd nominate him as man of the match. He's super fit and so quick that players don't have the chance to retaliate or cause trouble. I'd like to see people of his calibre deployed in checking the fitness levels of referees.

'In the future we may or may not see professional referees. Whether we do or we don't, they'll have to be fit, and I don't just mean the ability to run up and down a pitch for 90 minutes. Mental fitness is just as important. Anticipation – and I don't mean prejudging things – comes from the alertness of mind. It helps a referee keep up with play and find better positions from which to make decisions.

'When the game was more individual and players held the ball for longer, a referee could have the occasional breather. Now, movement of the ball is important. The referee has to widen his field of vision by anticipating counter-attacks and keep up with them. A poor referee will be caught out and left behind. He knows it, too, and will blow his whistle at the first sign of an infringement so that he can catch up.

'Consistency in applying the regulations is essential. So is psychology and understanding. Despite what we in the game and the fans sometimes think, referees are only human, so they have different personalities. A man who was a perfect example of a good referee was Arthur Ellis, who controlled a number of Liverpool games during my playing days. I had the greatest respect for him, probably stemming from an incident in a game against Middlesbrough when I was playing against Lindy Delaphena, a tricky West Indian winger with a fair goalscoring record.

'He beat me on one occasion and I said to him: "Do that again and I'll part your hair." It was a deliberate attempt on my part to frighten him. If I'd done it today in earshot of the referee, no doubt I'd be booked for ungentlemanly conduct. But Arthur Ellis heard me and let play continue. He decided not to interrupt the flow, which would have deprived Middlesbrough of the advantage Delaphena had given them.

'A couple of minutes later I found Arthur running beside me and offering me a comb. "Do you want to borrow this?" he said. It put me in my place and I didn't need another warning. I'd like to see more referees using a bit of subtlety and humour in awkward moments.'

Liverpool's elimination of Aberdeen sent them into a quarter-final tussle with CSKA Sofia the following March, the first time they had faced Bulgarian opposition. But the win over Ferguson's side proved a defining moment in Liverpool's season in more ways than one. The recognised first choice line-up who kicked off the return with Aberdeen – which was; Clemence, Neal, Thompson, Hansen, Alan Kennedy; Lee, McDermott, Souness, Ray Kennedy; Dalglish and Johnson – was fated not to play another full game together for more than six months. That was in Liverpool's last game of the season, against Real Madrid in the European Cup Final on 27 May. The club was rocked by an amazing flow of injuries, with Paisley admitting: 'Anfield is more like a casualty station than a football club.'

In addition to Alan Kennedy's hamstring problem, David Fairclough had already been the victim of cartilage trouble that required surgery, captain Phil Thompson broke his collar-bone at Crystal Palace, and reserve striker Gayle had his injured back encased in plaster. The Scottish contingent were also hit, with Kenny Dalglish's remarkable run of 147 consecutive League appearances ending when a damaged right ankle ruled him out of the visit to Ipswich in December, a fateful month also for his compatriots Graeme Souness and Alan Hansen. An infection in a leg wound forced Souness to miss three games at the turn of the year, while Hansen's knee injury at Manchester United on Boxing Day meant an operation that kept him out of a total of nine games. Then Paisley had to contend with Alan Kennedy receiving another setback, this time a knee injury at Norwich in January that ruled him out of six games, with Avi Cohen and Richard Money sharing the job of deputising in the number three shirt.

This wave of misfortune inevitably took its toll on Liverpool and by the time they went into their League game with Southampton at Anfield on 28 February, their last outing before their European date with CSKA, they had been knocked out of the FA Cup in the fourth round at Everton and were trailing First

Division leaders Ipswich by eight points.

It was also a period that saw the end of the longest unbeaten home run in the history of British football. Paisley's Liverpool had marched through 85 Anfield games undefeated in League, FA Cup, League Cup, European Cup and European Super Cup since their surprise 3–2 reverse against Birmingham on Souness's home debut in January 1978. Then on 31 January 1981, in Liverpool's first home match of the year, the First Division's bottom club Leicester arrived and pulled off a stunning 2–1 win. What made the result even more remarkable was that Liverpool led 1–0 at half-time, through an Alan Young own goal. However, second-half goals from Pat Byrne and Jim Melrose clinched an astonishing win for Leicester, who were relegated at the end of the season. It ended an unbeaten home sequence that included 63 League games, which smashed the previous top-flight record of 49 set by Nottingham Forest between 1977 and 1980, and the all-divisions best of 59 established by Millwall between 1964 and 1967.

Curiously, the end of the run was foreseen by Ray Kennedy, who said before the game: 'We're playing so erratically that I wouldn't be surprised if our home record went today.'

Paisley reacted to the defeat by saying: 'Some people said that the unbeaten home run was getting to be a weight round our shoulders and it might be a good thing that it's gone. Well, the weight wasn't bothering me!'

The Leicester defeat came a week after their FA Cup defeat at Goodison Park. The manner of the Cup exit riled Paisley, who also believed the game provided firm evidence that the FA decision to abolish red and yellow cards in mid season (which seems incredible today) was foolish and misguided. The game, handled impressively by referee Clive Thomas, began with a flurry of questionable challenges and Paisley declared: 'It was a tricky start and I believe if the referee had been able to show a yellow card it would have settled things down. If he's got to stop play to get his notebook out he's slowing things down and nobody's really sure what's happening.'

Paisley, though, had stern words for his players after Everton's 2–1 victory, in which substitute Jimmy Case's 76th-minute goal was insufficient to rescue Liverpool after strikes from Peter Eastoe and Imre Varadi. It was only their second defeat in 21 derbies but Paisley said: 'In my 42 years with Liverpool, I cannot recall an Everton team that's been stronger than us. But they were stronger than us in the first half and hurried and harried us out of it. Some of our players were strolling around as if to say they would get into the game eventually. We were playing into the hands of Everton, who were like vultures. Almost every time we've been beaten this season (this was their fifth defeat in all competitions) we've lost like this. We were going on the attack without even having the ball. If we keep playing like that we'll have nothing left to go for.'

His injury-hit team atoned for their FA Cup demise by reaching the League Cup Final ahead of the resumption of their European Cup campaign. Despite a shock 1–0 defeat at Fourth Division Bradford City in the first leg of their second round opener, in which a knee ligament injury ended Dalglish's 180-game ever-present run in all competitions, they romped to a 4–0 win in the return. Dalglish was on target twice, with Ray Kennedy and Johnson also scoring, and in the next round Liverpool thrashed Swindon 5–0 at Anfield thanks to a brace from Sammy Lee and other strikes from Dalglish, Fairclough and an own goal from Glenn Cockerill. Dalglish maintained his sequence of scoring in every round by hitting the target again in a 4–1 home rout of Portsmouth – with Johnson scoring twice and Souness also on the mark – and collected another in a 3–1 quarter-final home conquest of Birmingham, when Johnson and McDermott also struck. A late goal from Ray Kennedy at Maine Road secured a 1–0 win over Manchester City in the first leg of the semi-final, and Dalglish extended his run of scoring in every round by firing Liverpool's goal in a 1–1 draw in the Anfield return to send Liverpool into the final.

When Paisley was, at last, able to parade his recognised, full-strength line-up for the first time in the calendar year of 1981, to face Southampton on the last day of February, it was together for only 45 minutes. David Johnson had to withdraw at half-time with hamstring damage, which meant that substitute Colin Irwin, previously a defensive deputy for Thompson and Hansen, had to take over as an emergency striker as Liverpool pursued their first win in seven games. The loss of Johnson did not, however, prevent Liverpool collecting a morale-lifting success before their European mission, with a Terry McDermott goal adding to a first-half strike by Ray Kennedy for a 2–0 win. Anfield 'old boy' Kevin Keegan, on the losing side for the Saints against his former club, and a Bulgarian 'spy' reached a similar conclusion: Liverpool were still formidable.

'I didn't see much wrong with them,' said Keegan. 'They've had a bit of a sticky patch but they've been without several players and people have been a bit unfair to them. Can they win the European Cup? Well, I wouldn't bet against them.'

Boris Stankov, described as 'observer and tactician' of a three-man CSKA delegation, enthused: 'We eliminated Nottingham Forest but they are a firework. Liverpool are a tradition of many years. Liverpool are stronger. They play football, tackle hard and do a lot of work. They will be difficult for us and they have obviously improved by having many of their injured players back.'

Forest boss Brian Clough, whose side had gone out after single-goal defeats home and away against the powerful Bulgarian army side, had come to the aid of Liverpool. 'Brian's told us a thing or two about them,' said Paisley. 'He's given us information about their work and pattern of play, without singling anyone out. These sides are all right if everything is going well for them. I want to give them something to think about and they might have a problem when they get out there. Losing Johnson is a disadvantage because he's the type who could cause panic. But we've got other people.'

They included Jimmy Case, displaced on the right flank of midfield by Lee but at the time the leading European marksman at Anfield with 13 goals, and Ian Rush, who had made his debut, and his only senior appearance up to that stage, in a December draw with Ipswich at Portman Road. Yet Paisley passed over their claims and opted instead for 33-year-old Steve Heighway, in the midst of his testimonial season, which he would end by drawing the curtain on his Liverpool career and moving to American club Minnesota Kicks the following summer.

It was Heighway's first European action since a substitute stint in the home clash with Dynamo Tbilisi in September 1979, and once again, a Paisley decision was kissed with success as Heighway played his part in a resounding 5–1 mauling of Forest's conquerors. If it was a happy return for Heighway on his 65th European appearance, it was many happy returns for his strike partner Dalglish, whose 30th birthday coincided with the demolition of CSKA.

Happiest of all, though, was Dalglish's room-mate Souness, who blitzed the Bulgars with a hat-trick, his second of the season in the European Cup, with other goals from Lee and McDermott virtually booking Liverpool a semi-final slot.

'A lot of people have been giving us stick recently but we won't be written off,' Souness asserted. 'We wanted to win this game so much and right from the start we were going hammer and tongs. The encouraging thing was that even after the Bulgarians pulled a goal back [through Yonchev to make it 3–1 after 58 minutes] we just kept going and they knew they'd never get back once we scored our fourth. I scored a hat-trick against Oulun in October but tonight's has given me more pleasure. Last year I got only a couple of goals all season but I said then that it doesn't matter who scores as long as they go in.'

Paisley even found a positive note from the one blot on Liverpool's evening, the first-half withdrawal of Phil Thompson with thigh damage which meant another substitute call for Colin Irwin. 'It was a very good display and result and the most pleasing thing was the way the side kept playing after losing Phil,' said Paisley. 'Graeme's long-range shooting was lethal and it was a great hat-trick. We won well but the Bulgarians are still a good side and we will need the cushion we gave ourselves.'

Because of Liverpool's exit from the FA Cup, Paisley had a ten-day wait for the club's next engagement, the League Cup Final against West Ham at Wembley. With skipper Thompson ruled out, Paisley kept faith with the team that finished the job against CSKA.

Once again the competition brought frustration for Paisley and his players after three semi-final appearances in four seasons and the controversial penalty defeat by Nottingham Forest in the replayed 1978 final at Old Trafford. The contest once more went into extra time when Alan Kennedy's 117th-minute goal appeared to have given Liverpool victory after a goalless 90 minutes. The trophy had even been bedecked with red-and-white ribbons ready for acting captain Ray Kennedy to hold aloft on the club's 11th Wembley appearance in ten years, a visiting frequency that prompted chairman John Smith to dub the stadium 'Anfield South'.

Fate, though, had other plans. Referee Clive Thomas instantly awarded a penalty after McDermott had fisted away an Alvin Martin header, and Ray Stewart steered the spot kick past Ray Clemence to force Liverpool to start all over again in their pursuit of the one domestic honour the club had never won.

It also completed an unwanted League Cup Final 'hat-trick' for McDermott, who had had a 'goal' ruled out at Wembley in 1978 and another disallowed in the replay. His team-mates, though, stressed: 'Terry had no option but to handle the ball because it was almost certainly going in.'

The Villa Park replay was not for another two and a half weeks and Paisley and his players just had time to travel home from London, have a training stint and then pack their bags again to head for Sofia and the second leg against CSKA. Paisley was not fooled by his side's four-goal first-leg lead and warned: 'We've still got a job on our hands. We must not leave any loopholes because the Bulgarians can play a bit. They have a lot of skill and as soon as one of their men gets possession, he has support all along the line. I was impressed by their centre-forward Djevizov, who can dig the ball with his left foot. And Yonchev, who scored their goal at Anfield, also looks a good player.

'We can't lie back totally. We did that in the away leg against Dynamo Dresden in the 1977–78 European Cup, after winning the first game 5–1, and we were pounded so much we couldn't get off the ropes. They went 2–0 up and could have knocked us out until Steve Heighway scored for us and we managed to get through on a 6–3 aggregate. I'm sure CSKA will also have a go at us right from the start, so we've got to try to do something on the break. We'd like to get a goal so that they would have to score six. That's what we'll be looking for. We don't deserve to be in the competition if we lose this now.'

His words were echoed by goalkeeper Ray Clemence, who said: 'We need to keep them out in the first half hour or they could cause us problems. When I played here in England's 3–0 win two years ago and the Bulgarians hadn't scored, the crowd were on their backs long before half-time.'

Clemence added to his litany of distinguished deeds for Liverpool with a late penalty save, moving to his left to keep out Markov's spot kick, which was awarded for Alan Kennedy's challenge on Yonchev. Long before that, though, Liverpool had secured their passage into the semi-final when Johnson, restored to the attack after injury and illness, struck in the tenth minute after Lee's angled shot had smacked against an upright. That gave Liverpool the 6–1 aggregate advantage Paisley had set them as their target at the Levski Stadium, imposingly set against the backcloth of Mount Vitosha. CSKA must have felt their task was even more mountainous, with Clemence's heroics denying them even a goal on their own ground as the piercing whistles of 65,000 disenchanted Bulgarian fans rent the night air of Sofia.

It was a solidly impressive Liverpool performance, especially after losing goalscorer Johnson with hamstring damage during the first half to add to the absence of McDermott and Thompson, in addition to Fairclough and Sheedy. They also had Dalglish limping heavily after a ferocious first-minute tackle by Iliev, and Ray Kennedy and Steve Heighway emerging with knocks. 'At this rate the tea lady might have to play for us in the Mersey derby against Everton on Saturday,' quipped Paisley, adding more seriously: 'We gave a magnificent disciplined display and our early goal finished them off. The Bulgarians looked a better side in the first leg. They were too hectic tonight. They had to try to put the pressure on. They had to force their game to try to get goals and didn't look nearly the side they did at Anfield.'

A year later in the same stadium at the same quarter-final stage, Paisley would fully realise the accuracy of his judgement. But now the semi-final beckoned and it was to prove one of the most thrilling and stirring episodes in Liverpool's long European odyssey.

Without Johnson, Alan Kennedy, Thompson and McDermott, and with Richard Money, Irwin, Case and Heighway in the side, they scrambled a 1–0 win over Everton – thanks to a John Bailey own goal – before losing by a similar score at Arsenal as a prelude to their League Cup Final replay with West Ham. Skipper Thompson was fit to return but Liverpool suffered the massive blow of being without Souness, suffering a reaction to a back injury, as well as Johnson and Heighway. It meant a midfield return for Case and a dramatic call-up for Ian Rush in attack alongside Dalglish at Villa Park.

We were not to know it that Wednesday night, April Fool's Day 1981, in Birmingham, but we were witnessing the birth of a partnership that would become the stuff of legend, a Scottish-Welsh combination that would make fools of the finest defences.

'I've no worries about my temperament and all I hope is that I can show my best form,' said 19-year-old Rush as he braced himself for his second senior outing since his arrival from Chester a year earlier. Rush's first taste of life at Anfield had been frustrating for him and for Paisley, with his impressive play in the reserves lacking a cutting edge. His opening season at Liverpool brought him 12 goals in 30 Central League appearances and Paisley was desperate for his new acquisition to be meaner in front of goal.

But for a coat of paint at Villa Park, his route to a regular first-team place might have been swifter and smoother. But just when he and everyone else were about to acclaim a Rush equaliser, after Paul Goddard had given West Ham an early lead, his shot crashed against the bar, with Phil Parkes beaten. It did not deter Liverpool, though, and their poised, irresistible football, in which Rush played his part, brought a richly deserved 25th-minute equaliser, a triumph for the genius of Dalglish. A magnificently measured McDermott pass fell to the Scot and, as Parkes came out, Dalglish steered the ball into the net for his 18th goal of the season. 'The goal and the move were brilliant,' Paisley enthused. 'Kenny was reading the situation even when the ball was being knocked around. When I talk about the first few yards being in your head, this is exactly what I mean.'

Within four minutes of Dalglish's cool, classic strike, Alan Hansen connected with a Jimmy Case corner for a goal that clinched victory, his header spinning off the knee of Billy Bonds on its way in. Only the defiance of Parkes denied Liverpool further goals and their 2–1 win was kind to West Ham, who had been vanquished by style and skill. 'The whole approach and attitude of the team was superb,' said Paisley, proud that the elusive trophy had at last been captured. 'What really pleased me was the way they persevered playing their football even after West Ham had scored. Kenny Dalglish and Ian Rush did a lot of hard running, which was not easy at the pace the game was played at.'

The end of Liverpool's long quest for the League Cup coincided with the presentation of the first winners' medals instead of the traditional tankards, while Phil Thompson's timely return to fitness allowed him the honour of being the first Liverpool captain to receive the trophy.

'We've waited a long time for this,' Thompson declared. 'The League Cup has been going for a good few years without Liverpool's name on it, and now we've put that right in the best possible way. The lads showed typical Liverpool character and mettle to win it.'

The competition Liverpool did not even enter in the early days, and whose fans had dubbed it the "Mickey Mouse Cup', had proved to be the mouse that roared, with victory ensuring Liverpool of European qualification for the 18th consecutive season with a guaranteed UEFA Cup place. However, they still had ambitious designs on the European Cup, and they went into the home leg of their semi-final against Bayern Munich on the back of a 3–0 home win over Stoke, a game notable for Ronnie Whelan's impressive goalscoring debut in place of knee casualty Ray Kennedy. Kennedy was back to face the Germans, though, after a pain-killing injection – his importance to the team for once outweighing Paisley's reluctance for players to have pain-masking jabs. Souness and Johnson were still ruled out, which meant that Case and Rush were named in the line-up to take on opponents carefully assessed by Paisley and European 'spy' Tom Saunders. They had flown out to watch Bayern win 3–1 at Bochum in a Bundesliga fixture and Paisley's verdict was: 'Bayern won exactly the way they wanted to, with the minimum of effort and at their own pace. On their own ground they would have crucified Bochum, and this is what you have to bear in mind when you're planning for two legs.'

Bayern were equally worried about Liverpool. 'Nothing will help us, only the strength of our team,' declared manager Uli Hoeness, the distinguished former West German international who had played against Liverpool four times a decade earlier. Reflecting on Liverpool's development under Paisley since those 1970 duels, when the Anfield club knocked out Bayern in the Fairs Cup with the Germans gaining revenge in the Cup-Winners' Cup, Hoeness observed: 'Compared with their style then, Liverpool are more like a Continental side today. Now the two best teams in Europe are coming together. The winner of our two games will lift the European Cup.'

Despite glib pledges to attack, Bayern clung to a rigid containing game at Anfield and prised a goalless draw which made them favourites to reach the final in Paris on 27 May. But Liverpool breathed defiance. 'If Bayern think it's all over bar the shouting they've got another think coming,' proclaimed Phil Thompson, while Paisley told the media afterwards: 'It's not over yet. Bayern played well to contain us tonight, but they'll have to come out and attack us in the second leg.'

In his daily log, he recorded: 'We knew we had one helluva match on our hands and so it proved. It was a very disappointing result. Bayern closed the game down and we didn't have the experience in the side to break through. With Ray Kennedy needing an injection in his knee and Graeme Souness and David Johnson out, it was asking a lot from youngsters at this level, especially when Terry McDermott dislocated his thumb in the first five minutes and was in such pain that he had to be substituted by Steve Heighway at half-time. Now we have a tremendous task on our hands, so let's hope we can get our full squad fit in time. We're due a bit of luck.'

Fate, though, continued to frown on Paisley and Liverpool. After Bayern's visit, they played out goalless draws at Nottingham Forest and Leeds, with a 1–0 home defeat by Manchester United sandwiched between. It meant they would make their daunting journey to Munich after failing to score in four consecutive games and with their forces still depleted. Although Souness and Johnson were fit again, squeezing Case and Rush on to the substitutes' bench, Liverpool were stripped of the defensive talents of captain Thompson, a knee casualty at Leeds, and Alan Kennedy, who broke his wrist in the first leg against Bayern. It meant Richard Money filling Kennedy's number three slot and Colin Irwin replacing Thompson in a Liverpool side that walked out on to the Olympic Stadium stage with their chances of progress virtually written off.

They did, though, have a couple of weapons at their disposal, both of them psychological and both the product of German over-confidence bordering on arrogance. It was like manna from heaven for Paisley. If he was a master at handing the opposition 'toffee', he was equally adroit at boomerang tactics, of making remarks from the opposite camp fly back in their faces. Accordingly, newspaper cuttings of Bayern captain Paul Breitner's comment that Liverpool had shown no intelligence in the first leg had been pinned up on the dressing-room noticeboard. Motivational factor number two for Liverpool came on their arrival at the stadium in Munich, as Alan Hansen recounted: 'There were leaflets all over the ground and we wondered what they were. When we got out on to the pitch for a warm-up, a Liverpool supporter gave us one of these leaflets. Printed on it were directions for Bayern fans to travel to Paris for the final. That really put our backs up.'

Just to remind Bayern that Liverpool were no soft touches, Souness affirmed the team's qualities. 'Opponents know that whether they want to face us by playing football or if they want to fight, we'll be more than a match for them,' declared the powerful midfielder, the fire stoked in his belly.

Nevertheless, Liverpool's task became even more difficult with the game only five minutes old when a wild challenge by Calle

Del'Haye sent Kenny Dalglish plunging to the turf in agony with major ankle ligament damage. As the Scot was being helped off the field, his evening's action prematurely ended, it was widely expected that Paisley would send on Rush in his place. The Liverpool manager, though, had other ideas, largely inspired by his brief pre-match encounter with the Austrian observer quizzing him about Howard Gayle.

'I thought to myself that if he knew nothing about Gayle, then the Germans wouldn't know very much about him either,' Paisley revealed. 'For all I knew, Bayern might have asked him to get some information about the player. They like to do things by the book. The unknown can unnerve them. It was just a hunch that Gayle would be the one to send on.'

So Paisley left Rush on the bench and tossed the fleetfooted black raider into the fray after only one previous senior appearance, as a substitute at Manchester City six months earlier, following which he had been hit by back trouble. It proved an inspired move. Gayle's swift attacks stretched Bayern's defence almost to breaking point and there were fervent penalty appeals when Wolfgang Dremmler appeared to send him sprawling. Portuguese referee Antonio Garrido was unmoved and at half-time the tie was still goalless.

Gayle's response to the challenge thrown down to him, though, only underlined Paisley's wisdom in the art of substitutions, a trait evident in Alex Ferguson in the 1990s. Paisley was never profligate in using substitutes but when he did it was often with telling effect, illustrated by David Fairclough's various dramatic entries, including the games against St Etienne and Everton, Case's introduction in the first leg of the 1976 UEFA Cup Final, when Liverpool came back from 2–0 down to win, and the almost immediate Dalglish goal that followed Steve Heighway's replacement of Case in the 1978 European Cup Final. Incredibly, Liverpool scored more than a century of goals after substitutions had been made by Paisley during his period as manager, and on that European semi-final night in Munich his distinguished record took another twist when he substituted the substitute.

After the interval Liverpool, displaying all their character and drawing on their vast treasure chest of European experience, took command and remained resilient despite mounting fitness and injury worries, with Souness and Johnson limping heavily. Gayle had run himself into the ground and his booking for a 66th-minute foul was the signal for Paisley to withdraw him and send on Case. 'Howie was tired and was starting to retaliate to the physical buffeting he was taking, and the last thing we wanted was to be down to ten men if he got sent off,' Paisley explained.

Johnson relates a wonderful anecdote of Paisley during the tense, odds-defying battle: 'To add to all our injury and fitness problems, I did my hamstring after Bob had used the two subs. I signalled to the boss that it had gone. Roy Evans, who was sitting next to Bob on the bench, told me that Bob shouted to one of the armed guards patrolling the running track with dogs: "Give us your gun – I'll shoot the bastard!"'

With eight minutes left, Liverpool's defiance of the odds ranged against them was rewarded. A long clearance from Ray Clemence was hit first time by 'crocked' Johnson, out on the right, square into Ray Kennedy's path. The former Arsenal centre-forward, pushed up from midfield into attack, showed he had lost none of those ice-cool striking skills from his Highbury days by calmly controlling the bouncing ball before blasting it with his 'wrong' right foot beyond the reach of Bayern goalkeeper Walter Junghans. Paisley, Fagan, Moran and the rest of the Liverpool backroom team leapt off the bench in sheer delight as Kennedy was mobbed by ecstatic team-mates and the Merseyside contingent in the 78,000 crowd celebrated. But there were a few tense, nail-biting minutes still to endure and Karl-Heinz Rummenigge, Europe's Player of the Year, heightened the mental pressure by hitting an 87th-minute equaliser. Liverpool, though, held out superbly to reach the final on the away-goals rule.

'What can words say to describe this performance?' asked an exuberant Paisley after striding from the bench to congratulate each heroic member of his team as they walked off the pitch, having clinched the club's tenth major final appearance in ten years and their third European Cup Final in five seasons. He added: 'This was the club's 113th European game and I'm the only person who has been involved in all of them. This was certainly the greatest ever, because we had so many injuries. It was almost like our Central League side that toppled the West German champions. We couldn't have afforded extra time because we'd used our two substitutes, several players were limping and we wouldn't have had anyone to send on. Everything was going wrong for us but the players did everything right.'

Graeme Souness could not resist briefly cocking a snoop at

Liverpool's defeated and deflated Teutonic foes at the end. 'I put my head in their dressing room and shouted a few things because they'd been rather arrogant about the whole thing right from the first leg,' he said.

Paisley added: 'I certainly didn't have to motivate the lads. Paul Breitner did that for me when he said we didn't play with intelligence at Anfield. I think we played with intelligence tonight.' It was a particularly forgettable experience for Breitner. Such was his influence and importance to Bayern that Sammy Lee was deputed by Paisley to perform the rarely employed Liverpool task of man-marking the German star. Not only did tenacious Lee blot out the bearded Breitner, he was involved in an after-match cameo that caused Paisley to smile whenever he recalled it. Said Paisley: 'It was very rare for Liverpool to single out individual opponents for special attention. You can count the occasions on the fingers of one hand. But I asked Sammy to do a specific marking job on Breitner. He did it superbly and I'll never forget the scene in the dressing room corridor at the Olympic Stadium. Breitner was being interviewed by the press and as Sammy walked past the German sportingly said: "Well played." Sammy replied: "Thank you, Mr Breitner!"'

Paisley's admiration of Lee went beyond a manager's delight in a player's ability. There was a deeper significance. Paisley's sons Robert and Graham believe their father saw in Lee the qualities he had possessed during his own playing days. 'They played in similar positions and did similar jobs in their respective Liverpool teams,' said Robert. 'They were also both very committed players and had similar playing physiques, although my dad was slightly taller than Sammy. My dad never said it in so many words but the whole family feels certain that in Sammy he saw a reflection of himself as a player.'

Another player in whom Paisley had great pride was Ray Kennedy, and I had the pleasure of accompanying Liverpool's match winner together with Anfield press box steward Malcolm McEwan to a Munich beer cellar after the game, where, it must be recorded, Kennedy was hailed as a conquering hero by the sporting and hospitable burghers of the Bavarian capital.

'We'd been doing well enough and we knew a goal would come if we just stayed patient,' said Kennedy. 'I'd been up front only a few minutes when David Johnson played a great ball to me. The only difficult part was controlling the bounce.' Kennedy was at the forefront of Paisley's thoughts when he reflected: 'Apart from that night in Rome four years ago, I don't think I've ever been so proud of a team as I was in Munich. They did me, Merseyside and England proud. That bit of luck I'd wanted was there in Ray Kennedy, a man whose ability is appreciated far more in Europe than in England. Ray kept his cool to get us into the final. He saw the opportunity to get forward and when David Johnson's centre came over he took his time, turned and tucked the ball deliberately into the net. Many top-class strikers would have whacked the ball first time and probably wasted the opportunity.

'We got the result because we contained Bayern and were thoughtful in everything we did, even though everything was stacked against us, especially Kenny being kicked out of it in the first few minutes. Everyone responded. Let's hope we can do it in Paris.'

In the final they would meet Real Madrid, 2–1 aggregate semi-final victors over Inter Milan and six times winners of the trophy, the legendary club with the tradition of old masters Puskas, Gento and Di Stefano. Liverpool, though, faced a desperately worrying five weeks before meeting the Spanish club at the Parc des Princes. Dalglish, whose damaged ankle was put in plaster, headed a list of casualties that also included Phil Thompson, Alan Kennedy, David Johnson and David Fairclough, whose persistent knee trouble had provided him with a nightmare season. All of them missed the next three League games, but Liverpool's closing fixture against Manchester City at Anfield, a week before the European Cup final, assumed crucial importance to Paisley's hopes of parading his full-strength line-up in Paris.

Alan Kennedy, who had come through a run-out in Steve Heighway's testimonial match with his broken wrist in plaster, returned still wearing the cast to face City, who had lost the replayed FA Cup Final to Tottenham the previous week. Thompson and Johnson also resumed action in a game Lee was forced to miss with groin trouble. Ray Kennedy's third goal in five games gave Liverpool a 1–0 win to clinch fifth place in the First Division, a disappointing finishing position but secondary in significance to the fact that Alan Kennedy, Thompson and Johnson emerged unscathed and on course for Paris. Then Paisley delivered the best news of all when he announced: 'Kenny Dalglish will play in Paris and Sammy Lee will be fit as well. With the exception of David Fairclough, I will have a full squad to choose from.'

Paisley's planning for Paris included a trip to Madrid with Tom Saunders to watch Real's misnamed 'friendly' against Nottingham Forest at the Bernabeu Stadium, which the Spanish club won 2–0. Saunders saw Real three times and a welter of other information ensured Paisley and his aides were well briefed on the threat from a squad including the roving forward Juanito, defender Camacho – both in Spain's team that beat England at Wembley two months earlier – midfielder Uli Stielike and striker and skipper Santillana. Liverpool would be renewing acquaintance with Stielike, the West German international who had been on the losing Moenchengladbach side in the 1977 European Cup Final in Rome. There was also a guessing game in the build-up over whether England international winger Laurie Cunningham would face Liverpool in his first competitive game for six months, after crushing his right big toe. That speculation was also ended when Real's Yugoslav coach Vujadin Boskov declared: 'Laurie has worked hard in training and will play.'

The Aer Lingus aircraft that took the Liverpool party to Paris encountered a thunderstorm and was struck by lightning as it approached Orly Airport, but nobody in the Anfield squad was any the worse for the experience as they settled into their pre-final headquarters. Their hotel at Versailles was close to the world-renowned palace where the treaty terms that ended the First World War were presented to the German Government. While Paisley pondered the forthcoming football battle, his wife Jessie, a confirmed non-flier, was literally getting lost in France.

'I went on one of the coaches organised by Ken Addison, who ran the club's development association,' Jessie recalled. 'I travelled with my daughter Christine and her husband Ian, my son Graham and his wife Sandy, and a friend of mine who, very fortunately, spoke French. I say that because after we'd crossed the Channel by hovercraft, the coach driver got lost. My friend had to sort things out and get us on the right road to our hotel. But we had a great time – better, it seemed, than my other son Robert and his wife Irene, who flew to Paris.'

Europe was captivated by what many pundits saw as a mouth-watering confrontation between the disciplined skill of Liverpool and the temperamental talents of Real. Not Paisley, who admitted later: 'I was under no illusions about how the game would go. I never thought it would be the classic everyone was predicting.'

Not quite everyone. Paisley's familiar adversary Brian Clough said with uncanny accuracy: 'Don't expect a flowing game. Bob won't be concerned if Liverpool win 1–0, and good luck to them. If Liverpool do win the trophy for the third time, they will deserve to be ranked alongside Real as one of the all-time great teams of European football. Five of Real's six European Cups came in the late 50s when the tournament did not have the same quality of competition that it has now.'

Real's coach Boskov tried the old trick of trying to disturb Liverpool with a war of words, for which Paisley was far too long in the tooth. 'Liverpool are veterans – we will outrun them,' he claimed. Paul Breitner chipped in, too, with a prediction that his former club would succeed where his Bayern side had failed in the semi.

'The more they say about us, the better we like it,' said Paisley. 'Real have got some so-called veterans of their own. Boskov is entitled to say what he likes but it really doesn't mean a carrot. When foreign managers start making claims like that, it shows tension. And I hope Breitner's forecasting is as accurate as it was for the semi-final!' There was, in fact, little difference in the average age of the two teams – Liverpool's just under 28, Real's a little over 27.

A figure from Liverpool's past, from their first season in Europe, offered his verdict on the outcome. Helenio Herrera, manager of the Inter Milan side which had eliminated Liverpool in the 1965 European Cup semi-final – amid bitterly controversial circumstances in the second leg in Italy, which outraged Bill Shankly – opted for the Latins. 'Real will win,' said Herrera. 'They will do so not necessarily because they are the better team. Over two legs they would probably lose to a team like Liverpool. No, I think they will win because their ability to raise their game for a single occasion like this is remarkable.'

So much for Herrera the forecaster! Paisley, having ensured that the plaster was removed from Alan Kennedy's broken wrist specially for the final, was at last able to name his strongest team. It lined up in 4-4-2-formation: Clemence; Neal, Thompson (captain), Hansen, A Kennedy; Lee, McDermott, Souness, R Kennedy; Dalglish, Johnson. Paisley's five substitutes were Case, Irwin, Money, Gayle and reserve goalkeeper Steve Ogrizovic. There was no place on the bench for either Ian Rush or Avi Cohen, a bitter disappointment to both players and one which would lead to a showdown between Rush and the Liverpool manager at the start of the following season. But that face-to-face meeting would be instrumental in Rush becoming one of the world's great strikers.

The team news for the final was broken to the players during a loosening-up session on the morning of the match. After naming his starting 11, Paisley added: 'When it comes to the subs, I'm going to have to disappoint two of you. Avi Cohen and Ian Rush won't be included.' For Rush the news was crushing.

'I was dumbstruck,' he admitted. 'I thought I'd be on the bench with a chance of getting on at some stage in the final. The manager had said I'd be in the squad and I took that to mean I'd be one of the 16. After all, I'd played in the first leg of the semi-final against Bayern, been on the bench in Munich and played in eight of the previous 11 Liverpool games. I was just devastated when the manager announced I wouldn't even be a substitute. It was the lowest point of my life and only the fact that it was such a big game prevented me doing something stupid. I just felt sick.'

Rush's place on the bench had gone to Gayle, a brave decision by Paisley given the winger's lack of big-match experience, but earned by his key contribution to the semi-final performance in Munich. In the event, Paisley used only one substitute, sending on Case for Dalglish for the last four minutes as Liverpool counted down to glory.

One of Paisley's and Liverpool's concerns over the venue for the final, some 17 years before Paris built its 80,000-capacity Stade de France for the 1998 World Cup Finals, was that the Parc des Princes had a capacity of only 50,000. 'We could have filled the stadium with our own fans and I know a lot were disappointed that they were unable to get tickets to support us,' said Paisley, whose wife Jessie found herself with a cash demand inside the stadium that was definitely not included in the official gate receipts of 3,040,458 francs, converting to around £275,000, or a couple of months' wages for some of today's Premiership players.

'When we arrived at the ground, black-skirted stewardesses descended upon us insisting on showing us to our seats, whether we wanted them to or not,' said Jessie. 'They kept repeating something. Eventually, I realised they were saying, "Tip, tip, tip." Then I spotted that these women had pockets full of francs!'

As the players walked out on to the pitch, one particular banner did nothing to calm Alan Hansen's jangling nerves. 'I was even more nervous in Paris than I'd been in the 1978 final against Bruges at Wembley,' he recalled. 'Usually when I got out on to the pitch I felt better. But not that night. As we ran towards the fans we were stunned by seeing the biggest banner I've ever clapped eyes on. It covered one entire end of the stadium and in letters as big as houses said starkly, "Real Madrid". Bloody hell, I thought. I tried to ignore it but I couldn't. Intimidating? It was terrifying.'

There were, of course, eye-catching Liverpool banners. One huge red and white one, thrust into the air when Hungarian referee Karoly Palotai blew his whistle to start the game, proclaimed: 'Liverpool Score De Gaulles!'

Yet neither side managed to score goals in a testy, tedious opening 45 minutes, one which Paisley reflected on in his diary with the entry: 'It was a very physical first half and some of the Real Madrid tackling was outrageous, to say the least. But at the same time, they had players of real quality. We started quite well but we were upset, probably, by some of the tackles.'

Compounding Liverpool worries at half-time was an injury to Graeme Souness, who spent the interval with ice-packs on his leg. Yet Souness, typically, went out for the second half to play a major part in Liverpool's performance. They took command of the game and as Real became more and more rattled, Stielike was booked for an illegal challenge on David Johnson and the striker was chopped down again by Sabido on the edge of the Real box.

Eight minutes from the end, Alan Kennedy, the man whose Paris build-up had been filled with anxieties over his broken wrist, broke the back of Real resistance. Sammy Lee tossed the ball down to Ray Kennedy to take a Liverpool throw-in on the left. The midfielder threw the ball into the path of his namesake Alan, who chested the ball down as he raced in through the Real ranks. Shrugging off a final challenge by Cortes, the left-back steamed on and blasted an angled shot beyond goalkeeper Agustin and into the net. It was Liverpool's 50th Cup goal of the season – an English club record – and Kennedy's first ever in Europe, to secure the coveted Champions' Cup for Liverpool for the third time in Paisley's amazing reign.

After the ball had hit the net, Kennedy ran on ecstatically all the way to the railings behind the goal to celebrate with the supporters. 'It took me a few seconds to realise that I'd got the goal that won the European Cup,' said Kennedy, who would assure himself of a unique place in football history three years later by repeating the feat in the penalty shoot-out against Roma. His nickname of 'Barney Rubble', inspired by the television character in *The*

Flintstones, was chanted by delighted Liverpool fans. The hero, however, almost found his own celebrations doused. Kennedy explained:

'There was a moat filled with water around the pitch and after I'd run to the supporters, the first players to get to me were Terry McDermott and David Johnson and they tried to push me in. I only just managed to struggle free!' Amidst the jubilation the big question was whether Kennedy had meant his majestic strike as a shot or a cross.

'If I'm very honest, it was one of those cross-shots,' he revealed. 'If the goalkeeper had stayed where he was he would have saved it, without doubt. But in the back of my mind I knew the keeper was going to go for the cross, maybe because David Johnson was at the far post. So I drilled it in near post after one of their players had nearly cut me in two with a tackle. I decided to have a go and, although I say it myself, it was a great shot from a difficult angle. It flew into the top corner.

'To score a goal like that whether it's in the first minute or the last was a tremendous feeling in itself. It wasn't a great game and one of the reasons for that was that they played rugby on the pitch and it wasn't in the best state. We thought the surface was poor. But it was a great occasion with a wonderful atmosphere. Because of my broken wrist, I'd been sweating on whether I would play in the final. When Bob told me I'd be in the team, I remember thinking to myself: "I just can't let him down." The other lads like Richard Money and Colin Irwin had done extremely well without me to reach the final and he could have played one of them or Avi Cohen in my place. But Bob took a chance on me, probably because he knew I was a natural left-footed player who could defend and get forward and support the attack. When my goal went in, I'm sure Bob's thoughts were: "I've made the right decision.' My late mother, who had known Bob all those years earlier as youngsters in the North East, would have been overjoyed that I had not only played for him but scored the goal that won the European Cup.'

Case's introduction for Dalglish for the last few minutes meant that he became one of five players to have appeared in all three of Liverpool's European Cup Finals, joining Ray Clemence, Phil Neal, Ray Kennedy and Terry McDermott. When the final whistle sounded, the Parc des Princes became a sea of red and white. There were empty spaces which only a little earlier had been filled with passionate Real followers, chanting to the beat of a drum which had been muffled by Kennedy's golden shot.

'I'm so proud to be the manager of the first British club to win the European Cup three times,' Paisley announced. 'It was a triumph for our character once again. We started with three players – Dalglish, Thompson and Alan Kennedy – short of match practice, and Souness was hurt shortly after kick-off. We were too hurried and lost possession too often in the first half, but we corrected that and controlled most of the second half. I'm sure Real don't begrudge us our victory.'

Later he reflected: 'It was a remarkable goal from Alan. I'll never forget him collecting that throw-in from Ray Kennedy and blasting the ball in from what seemed an impossible angle. It was Alan at his unpredictable best, for I'd swear that half the time he doesn't even know himself what he's going to do next. Without any disrespect, I'm sure he'd know what I mean if I say he's not a typical Liverpool player. While he has enthusiasm and heart in abundance, and is totally committed to the team's cause, he's not the type who sees a move three or four passes in advance. Alan's the instinctive rather than the calculating type. He reacts to situations rather than creates them, which is exactly what he did to score the goal that won us the European Cup. I'm glad I signed him!

'The fans, of course, took to Alan like a duck to water. In fact, he and Ray Kennedy are perfect examples of the types of player the Kop do and don't respond to. Our crowd's been like that ever since I joined Liverpool. Ray's got good control and distribution, he's got vision, he's very economical in using up energy and rarely gives the ball away. But when things go wrong, he's never been a big favourite with the crowd. Alan, on the other hand, is a crowd hero. They want the Barney Rubble type, they respond if they see someone sweating blood and showing natural enthusiasm, almost as if they're getting more for their money. When I played there was a similar contrast between Phil Taylor and I. Phil was articulate in everything he did, an immaculate, sophisticated player. But the effort he undoubtedly put in was not apparent to the fans. They responded more to me, a rough and ready player. The fans went for my tigerish nature. It's the same with Alan and Ray, both great lads from the North East but very different types of players. You've got to have contrasts like that in a team if you're going to have balance.'

Alan Kennedy's 'Barney Rubble' tag had a humorous spin-off a short time after Paris when a national newspaper staged a picture of him dressed in a caveman's outfit, complete with loin cloth and club, in the Kop goalmouth one afternoon. As Kennedy was walking back to change in the dressing room he encountered Paisley in the Anfield corridor.

'Hello, boss,' said Kennedy. 'Do you think I look like a caveman?'

'I don't know about that,' came the reply, 'but you bloody well play like one!'

Kennedy took such banter in his stride, his enthusiasm undimmed, and when he sat with skipper Phil Thompson at a pavement cafe on a Paris boulevard the morning after his European Cup spectacular, the massive trophy on the table between them, he could take pride in the achievement. One Scouse supporter, spotting the two players and their glittering capture, came over, stared at the cup with its protruding handles, and exclaimed: 'It's great to have old Big Ears back!'

The lyrics of Frank Sinatra's famous song embraced the triple European glory of Liverpool – Paris, London and Rome. For the Anfield legions, it certainly had been nice to go travelling. Thompson was acutely aware of the significance of Liverpool's feat in joining Real, Bayern Munich and Ajax as the only clubs in history to win the European Cup on three or more occasions.

'We've joined the immortals now,' he proclaimed. So had Bob Paisley.

14

The Ruthless Quest

If ever one phase in Paisley's managerial career crystallised his ruthless quest for success, it was his response to a third European Cup triumph and lifting the League Cup for the first time. Football, in awe of the man Manchester United's jewellery-wearing manager Ron Atkinson affectionately and ironically dubbed 'Mr Glitter', sat up in astonishment as Paisley dismantled his team and built another.

While his new-look side would see out his last two years in charge by disappointing in the European arena and the FA Cup, it brought him glorious success with consecutive doubles of League championship and League Cup. Paisley's Paris triumph in the European Cup a few months earlier had, if anything, sharpened his appetite to maintain Liverpool's pre-eminence as English football's ship of state, a status achieved through his startling sweep of trophies since succeeding Bill Shankly seven years earlier. During that period he had won ten major trophies, comprising four League titles, the European Cup three times, the UEFA Cup, the League Cup and the European Super Cup. That orgy of success had surpassed the achievements of his early mentor and lifelong friend Sir Matt Busby, who had led Manchester United to eight trophies.

Yet, incredibly, shortly before Liverpool's European triumph in Paris the previous season, there had been criticism of Paisley and his team in the letters column of the *Liverpool Echo*, the local evening newspaper. Paisley reacted to that with a smile and typical philosophy: 'All I can say is that the next manager who comes here will have to win a dozen trophies in seven years or they'll be calling for his head,' he chuckled.

While he had by now reduced the size of the cigars he smoked on celebratory occasions – 'I've knocked off the big ones because they're wasted on me' – his yearning for success was as great as ever, even though he still indulged his passion for racing whenever possible. In 1981 he made his first visit to the Derby, travelling by train to Epsom station then walking more than two miles over the Downs to the course with his friend Ray Peers. Their friendship had begun in the early 1960s when Paisley, a boxing fan, went to watch fights at Liverpool Stadium, where Peers promoted. As well as being racing and boxing buddies, they also holidayed together, with Jessie unable to take time off from her teaching duties during football's close season.

Peers, who died in 1995 at the age of 69, was a warm, friendly character who spoke with a lisp. He recalled a close-season break in Majorca when Paisley's presence in the apartment block provided a holiday bonus for a group of Irish tourists. 'Bob made their holiday for them,' he said. 'Every day he signed autographs and posed for photographs. Nothing was too much trouble and they loved it. When we went out for a drink – I had a pint and Bob had his glass of lager and lime – I told him to wear a cap and sunglasses as a disguise. We'd no sooner sat down when a chap coming up the road with his wife and child shouted excitedly: "Hello, Bob, having a good holiday?" Bob took off the cap and glasses, gave them to me and said he wouldn't be needing them any more. But we had a good arrangement on holiday – I cooked the breakfast and he did the washing up.'

Peers lived at the Central Hotel in Birkenhead, across the Mersey from Liverpool, a welcoming but unpretentious establishment where Bob would often go for a quiet drink and a meal after big games. Said Peers: 'After one Wembley win, Bob and I and a few friends ended up at the Central and he drank his usual half of lager and lime. A lot of his fellow managers would be knocking back champagne in some London nightspot. That's just not Bob's style. He calls in to the hotel after games most Saturday nights after matches for a drink, and often we have a bite to eat at a local Chinese restaurant or a chippy. He's a smashing guy without any kind of airs and graces.'

Paisley simply wanted to win more silverware, even though at his age many men would be contemplating the slow lane of life rather than the maelstrom of managing England's most successful club. Nobody was more aware of the pitfalls than Paisley. On the wall of his office, like the fabled Boot Room a windowless place situated under Anfield's main stand, he stuck a large coloured picture of a litter of piglets, with the caption: 'It isn't easy to stay on top.' He also had a framed copy of Kipling's famous poem 'If', bought for him by his family as a Christmas present and which his widow Jessie still has as a cherished memento. The poem's message of maintaining an equilibrium in life became one of Paisley's creeds, and on many occasions he would quote the enduring lines: 'If you can meet with Triumph and Disaster/And treat those two impostors just the same . . .'

He had a powerful belief in always looking forward, never back, or at least only fleetingly. It was a credo that typified the whole club, personified by coach Ronnie Moran telling the players as he handed out championship medals in the dressing room: 'You get nothing for those next season. We're back in training on 10 July!'

Goalkeeper Ray Clemence, who chose to end his illustrious Anfield career that watershed summer of 1981, provides a perfect illustration of Paisley's drive for new achievements and his refusal to rest on any laurels.

'Bob hated looking back,' said Clemence. 'Shortly after we'd won the European Cup for the first time, we were on the team coach crossing London when Bob overheard Steve Heighway saying the 1977 team should have an annual reunion, because the Rome win had been so special. Bob went absolutely bananas. "Never mind bloody reunions," he shouted. "We've got to look forward to winning something this year, next year and the year after that." He would always look forward. He was a tremendous manager and he influenced each and every one of us who played for him. We all owe him so much.'

Clemence, one of the greatest last lines of defence in the entire history of a club whose quality of goalkeepers was reflected in its telegraphic address of 'Goalkeeper, Anfield', knocked on Paisley's door on 8 June 1981 and dropped the bombshell that he wanted to leave Anfield after 14 years at the club. In the latter stages of the previous season, Paisley had launched his team rebuilding job by making a double swoop for two South African-born players. One of them was forward or midfielder Craig Johnston who cost £650,000 from Middlesbrough. The other was goalkeeper Bruce Grobbelaar, a £250,000 recruit from Vancouver Whitecaps, whose abilities were saluted by the Canadian club's general manager Tony Waiters, the former England and Blackpool goalkeeper once on Liverpool's staff. Former Rhodesian jungle fighter Grobbelaar breezed into Anfield like a vaudeville act, with a reputation for acrobatics and eccentricity and announcing that he had envious eyes on Clemence's place.

'The demands of constantly striving for success at Liverpool can take its toll on players and Ray was no exception,' said Paisley. 'Our signing of Grobbelaar was probably the last straw that pushed Ray to ask for a move. Sometimes players don't realise the pressures they're under and Ray was under plenty. Apart from the challenge of constantly trying to win things with us, he had the rivalry with Peter Shilton for the England job and the limelight trained on him because of his regular appearances on radio and television.

'My plan in signing Bruce was the tried and trusted one at Liverpool of grooming him in the reserves for a couple of years as a gradual successor to Ray, who was about to reach his 33rd birthday. But Bruce, never short on confidence, told Ray that he'd have his place before the end of the season. It meant that Ray faced a battle he'd never had before. Ever since he'd succeeded Tommy Lawrence, Ray was undisputed number one. Now, suddenly, he had someone breathing down his neck. Ray said to me about Bruce: "Who does this fellow think he is?"

'When he came to me and asked for a transfer, I tried to change his mind. He was the greatest goalkeeper I've seen. He had the edge on Shilton. But in the end we agreed to Ray's request and at a bargain price. If it hadn't been for his great service the fee would have been not a penny under £450,000 rather than the £300,000 Keith Burkinshaw paid to take him to Tottenham. That was "washers" for the best goalkeeper in the country who, even well into 30s, could go on playing until he's 40.'

Clemence explained that the reason for his decision stretched back to the scenes of celebration in the Parc des Princes, where his 335th clean sheet on his 665th Liverpool appearance helped land the European Cup and his 12th major prize with the club. 'I sat in our dressing-room with a paper cup full of champagne yet felt strangely flat,' he revealed. 'I was usually one for having a sing song and a great night out. So I thought to myself: "If you're not on the ceiling after winning the European Cup, there's something wrong." I decided in that moment I needed to move on to a new challenge. Before the match in Paris I'd never thought anything of the sort. Bruce Grobbelaar had just been signed so there was plenty of incentive for me.

'Over the years, though, I'd seen players stay so long at Liverpool that when they left they had little or no chance of winning anything. Steve Heighway left for America, Roger Hunt went to Bolton and there were many others. I didn't want that.'

Clemence had become the first goalkeeper to captain England since Frank Swift in 1948 when Ron Greenwood gave him the honour for the Wembley friendly that year against Brazil. In wearing the armband he followed in the path of Eph Longworth in the 1920s and Emlyn Hughes, Kevin Keegan and Phil Thompson as Liverpool players to lead their country. Phil Neal and Peter Beardsley would also have the honour.

Paisley's sympathetic acceptance of Clemence's request to leave allowed the Skegness-born keeper to satisfy his desire of reigniting his career elsewhere. He helped Tottenham lift the FA Cup in his first season at White Hart Lane, his 13th major prize in a career that began at Scunthorpe in the 1960s and ran, as Paisley had predicted, until close to his 40th birthday, spanning more than 1,000 senior games.

His departure meant Grobbelaar being thrown into action as Liverpool number one far earlier than Paisley had planned, even though he had been tracked by Liverpool for more than two years since Tom Saunders saw him play during a loan spell at Crewe in 1978-79. The 6ft 1in Durban-born goalkeeper was made for the job. His father was capped in that position by Rhodesia – to where the family moved when Bruce was only two months old – and his mother was a hockey goalkeeper. Bruce, already capped for the newly established Zimbabwe, had also kept wicket at representative level at cricket, played baseball for the former Rhodesia and won state recognition at basketball.

Paisley and Saunders flew to Canada to watch him play for Vancouver and, in true Mounties tradition, finally got their man after a protracted wait for a British work permit. 'He's the most natural goalkeeper I've ever seen,' was the verdict of Tony Waddington, who had had Grobbelaar under his wing for 24 matches when he was in charge at Crewe. 'He's a born keeper and his handling is beautiful. He also scored a penalty for us!'

Grobbelaar was succeeding to one of English football's great dynasties. Since Tommy Lawrence made his debut as Liverpool goalkeeper in October 1962, followed by Clemence at the start of the 1970s, the two keepers between them had missed only 11 of Liverpool's 1,066 matches over a 19-year span. 'Now Ray's left, Bruce is being flung in at the deep end,' Paisley warned. 'I hope he'll be judged on what he is and not against what Ray is now. I feel he's as good as Ray was at his age.'

The contrast between Grobbelaar and Clemence could not have been more stark and on his first Liverpool appearance between the posts, a pre-season friendly in Zurich, the 23-year-old's antics had Paisley, Fagan, Moran and company leaping off the bench in shock! Swinging on the bar, ball juggling and acrobatics were second nature to Grobbelaar but frowned on by ultra-professional Liverpool. This clash of football cultures, however, managed to blend. Despite the occasional costly lapse which earned Grobbelaar the undeserved title of the 'Clown Prince', he made the position his own, rarely missed a game and eventually matched Clemence's haul of 13 major winners' medals, which made him more prince than clown.

When Grobbelaar did have a rush of blood and make one of his characteristic charges off his line, Paisley would adopt the 'softly, softly' approach rather than the big stick to try to curb such goalkeeping excesses. At one team meeting he looked Grobbelaar straight in the eye and said: 'Listen, son, if you have nothing to do in a match you still get paid the same money. If you don't have a save to make, that's fine.'

The pre-season also brought a first team call-up for Johnston, who bore a remarkable resemblance to Kevin Keegan in looks, personality and dynamic football style. Like Grobbelaar he had South African roots, being born in Johannesburg and moving with his Australian parents to New South Wales when he was five. There was a strong football influence from his father, who had a brief spell with Dundee United, and when Johnston was 15 he received a reply from Middlesbrough to a series of letters he had sent to English clubs. He had a trial at Ayresome Park and duly joined the North East club, making a memorable debut as a 17-year-old against Everton in the FA Cup in January 1978, a match preceded by both clubs spending a week toning up in Jersey. During Middlesbrough's stay on the island, Johnston decided to go for a swim in the sea. As he emerged from the waves and began to walk across the promenade back to the team hotel, he passed a woman walking her dog.

'Where have you come from?' she exclaimed.

'Australia,' he replied, leaving a dumbfounded resident in his wake.

Johnston brought a new energy into the side and Paisley said of him: 'He's like one of those toys with long-life batteries. You just switch him on, put him down on the pitch and watch him go. He's still going strong when the other batteries have run out.'

Paisley returned from the Swiss tour to pull off a transfer masterstroke by beating Manchester United and Arsenal for the signature of versatile Mark Lawrenson from Brighton. The Preston-born Republic of Ireland defender or midfielder cost Liverpool a club record £900,000 and was worth every penny. Said Paisley: 'Sometimes the problem with players who can fill a number of roles is that while they're useful jacks of all trades, they're masters of none. But wherever Mark plays, he does it brilliantly. He was my three-in-one signing because he can go in at centre-back, left-back or midfield and perform with equal quality. He's probably the best tackler in the box I've ever seen. A mistimed challenge in the penalty area can be costly but Mark nicks the ball off people as clean as a whistle. Like a thief in the night, he's in and got the ball before his opponent even realises it.'

Lawrenson simply oozed class and eventually succeeded Phil Thompson at the heart of defence, forging another brilliant centre-back partnership with Alan Hansen. He will never forget his first meeting with Paisley. 'I signed for Liverpool late on the Friday night and was dropped off at the Atlantic Tower Hotel prior to my medical at Anfield next day,' he recalled. 'Bob said he would pick me up so I was up two hours earlier than I needed to be next morning, ready to meet this great guy who'd just won the European Cup again. I was as nervous as a kitten, with my best suit, shirt and tie on, best bib and tucker. I went down to reception and the doorman told me: "Mr Paisley is waiting for you in his car outside."

'When I got in the car I saw that Bob was wearing slippers and a cardigan. I was waiting for Jeremy Beadle to pop up! I couldn't believe it. That was my first encounter with Bob Paisley and I knew I'd come to the right place. They'd just won the European Cup and there was this fellow, who everyone in football thought was an absolute god, driving me to the ground in his slippers and cardigan! I thought: "You'll do for me!"'

'He's not just the greatest manager. He was also one of the most humble of people. I quickly worked out, as the other players had done, that if Bob didn't talk to you about football it was a backhanded compliment. It meant he was happy at the way you were playing. Occasionally he would ask: "Have you played against this fellow before?" I'd say I had and he'd say: "That's alright then." But I remember a game at Arsenal which we won comfortably and which was the main game on *Match of the Day*. I did a little trick – I think I stumbled and fell over but it looked as if I meant it! – and Bob pulled me on the Monday morning. He said: "You realise a lot of people saw what you did on Saturday?"

'I couldn't understand what he was getting at.

'Then he explained: "A lot of football people will have seen it, so don't forget if you try it again, next time it might not work. Playing for Liverpool everything is highlighted and people are always watching you.' He was very clever at making you aware of such things.

'Bob's great ability was in putting players together. When you assemble players like Dalglish, Souness, Rush and Hansen, you don't need to be a great tactician! He went out, with his staff, and found the players to fit the jigsaw. It was very rare they didn't fit the jigsaw. But if they didn't fit, the player was quickly moved on at a profit. On some occasions he signed square pegs for round holes but was able to shave the edges of those square pegs and make them fit. In one of Craig Johnston's early games in pre-season he was playing on the right and Bob, Joe and Ronnie were shouting at him from the dug-out to do this and do that. At half-time, Craig said to them: "If you wanted a right winger you should have gone out and bought one." But eventually the penny dropped with Craig and he adjusted to Liverpool's needs.

'When I first met Bob, he said to me: "You can play in a few positions." He was telling me rather than asking. He said: "You'll go straight into the team but you might not play in the position you want to play in."

'If we'd beaten a team by a big score and the press were lauding us to the skies, Bob would walk into the dressing room at the end and say: "That team we played wouldn't win in the Zingari League!" It was his way of knocking you down and keeping your feet on the ground. But by the same token, if you got beat and you were expecting a roasting, sometimes Bob, Joe or Ronnie wouldn't say very much at all. Or they might say: "We didn't play well today but you know who didn't play well." They wouldn't point the finger. It meant that you'd walk out wondering if they meant you. It was designed to make you question your own game and make you determined to play well next time.'

Lawrenson's club record arrival was more than paid for by Paisley's sales of Jimmy Case, who moved in the opposite direction to Brighton for £350,000, Colin Irwin to Swansea, who had risen from Fourth to First Division under Anfield old boy, John Toshack also for £350,000, and Clemence's £300,000 transfer to Tottenham. In October Paisley bought again, this time recruiting Steve Nicol from Ayr United for £300,000, another inspired acquisition. Nicol's size 14 boots would carry him through more than 400 Liverpool games in a variety of roles and earn him a fistful of honours as well as 27 Scotland appearances and the Footballer of the Year award in 1989.

Paisley's rebuilding process also saw a further batch of departures before the end of the season. Avi Cohen returned to Macabbi Tel Aviv for £100,000, Richard Money was sold to Luton for £100,000, while Kevin Sheedy, whose prospects on the left flank were blocked by the rise of his Republic of Ireland colleague Ronnie Whelan, made the short journey across Stanley Park to join Everton and taste glory at home and abroad during Howard Kendall's golden Goodison era. There was another massively significant departure when Ray Kennedy, the player whose career was rescued and wonderfully revived by Paisley, became the latest Anfield player to join Toshack at Swansea in January 1982, for £160,000.

Said Paisley: 'Ray and I came from the same neck of the woods and we could talk to each other. It's not always easy for a manager and player to do that but Ray and I had a great understanding and anything said at a team meeting was never lost on him. We respected each other.

'Knowing the type of man and player he was, I realised something was not as it should be with Ray. His close friend and room-mate Jimmy Case had been transferred at the start of the season and maybe that had affected him. But somewhere there seemed to be an element of frustration in him. He was sent off twice in three months early in the season, first for reacting to an incident with Aston Villa's Allan Evans at Anfield and then for clashing with Arsenal's Peter Nicholas in a League Cup tie at Highbury. That was not like Ray. He had so much ball control and was such a good shielder of it that an opponent almost had to knock him down to get the ball. Yet Ray would never abuse his physical strength. If an opponent had a go at him he was the type who would just brush him off or push him aside in a legitimate manner. I doubt if he'd totted up two bookings at Liverpool before that, never mind two dismissals. So clearly there was something wrong. I am a firm believer that if a player suddenly starts retaliating, he's got something on his mind. Something is bothering him. Ray and I had a good heart-to-heart talk. He admitted something was affecting him but couldn't put his finger on it. He said he didn't feel the same kind of urge in his game any more, there was some kind of frustration nagging at him. Perhaps the incessant pressures to win things at Liverpool had become too much for him. He'd been unable to get back into our first team after his second suspension and young Ronnie Whelan had been blooded in his place. The upshot of our talk was that we both agreed it would be better for Ray and the club if he tried to rekindle his career elsewhere. At first he had his eyes and his heart set on moving to his native North East and he had talks with Sunderland. Stoke also showed an interest but Ray finally opted to join Tosh at Swansea.

'The fact that we understood each other so well and could communicate made his departure far less painful than it might have been. The most unpopular job in management is having to tell great players that they're past their best or it's time to move on. Ray was one of Liverpool's greatest players and probably the most underrated.

'I've also been in that situation with men like Tommy Smith, Ian Callaghan, Chris Lawler, Emlyn Hughes, Larry Lloyd, Alec Lindsay, Brian Hall, Steve Heighway, Peter Cormack and many others. There's no pleasure in having to do it. It's almost being cruel to yourself. But it's a big part of what football is all about. The one consolation is that those of them who have stayed in the game realise that it's part and parcel of being a manager and they have to do the same.'

Was the change in Kennedy, still only 30, the first effects of the Parkinson's Disease he had unknowingly contracted, according to later medical assessment, when he was a 21-year-old at Arsenal? That must remain in the realm of speculation.

While Paisley had been busy buying and selling, he also had the task of jump-starting the career of one of the young players already at Anfield. Ian Rush's omission from the European Cup Final had eaten away at him throughout the summer. Not even an assurance from reserve-team trainer Roy Evans that he had a glittering future at Anfield could dispel Rush's simmering anger at being passed over by Paisley in Paris. 'I bore a grudge,' he admitted. Finally, at the dawn of the new season, he summoned the courage to knock on Paisley's office door and demand to know why he wasn't in the team.

'Because you don't score goals, you're not worth a place,' came Paisley's withering reply. 'You want to lay the ball off, whereas I want you to be more selfish.' The showdown meeting followed Rush's request for a pay rise and after several minutes of heated argument, he told Paisley he wanted a transfer. Paisley, who revealed later he never had any intention of letting Rush go, told him he could leave. But as he went through the door, Paisley shouted after him: 'You'll have to pay your way by scoring goals.'

Paisley later disclosed: 'There were even some people at Anfield who thought we should sell Ian because he wasn't scoring goals. His confidence was being affected. In scoring situations he would look to see if a team-mate was better placed instead of having a go himself. That might have been partly due to a training exercise we had in which a player had to get rid of the ball after touching it twice. But in an actual match, I wasn't bothered how many times he touched it if it helped him put the ball in the net! If he'd have been a racehorse I'd have blinkered him!

'I knew he could score goals – he'd done it for Chester – and I had faith in him. When he got his next first-team chance early in the season, he took it by scoring his first senior goal. After that he never looked back. He couldn't stop scoring.'

Opportunity knocked for Rush in the European Cup first round second leg against Oulun Palloseura, the Finnish side drawn against Liverpool for the second successive season. Replacing David Johnson in the second half, Rush scored within four minutes of going on to help Liverpool cruise to a 7–0 win, 8–0 on aggregate. Although he sat out the following League game – a 2–2 home draw with Swansea – he started the following midweek's League Cup clash with Exeter and scored twice in a 5–0 win. He had arrived and the goal flood had started. Before Christmas, Paisley granted him his pay rise!

15

Sadness and Success

The 1981–82 season heralded significant changes in English football. Three points for a win, criticised in some quarters, was introduced. Artificial surfaces also arrived in the Football League, with Second Division Queens Park Rangers unveiling their plastic pitch at Loftus Road, a trend later continued by Luton, Oldham and Preston, before synthetic surfaces were officially outlawed.

The season was only a month old when a giant shadow was cast over Merseyside and the whole of British football. Bill Shankly died after a second heart attack in hospital on 29 September, a few weeks after his 68th birthday. The news saddened and shocked the nation, not least Bob Paisley, the man who had been at Shankly's shoulder from the moment the extrovert, charismatic Scot had breezed across the Pennines to resurrect Liverpool in December 1959 through to his bombshell decision to quit in July 1974.

'I heard the news in the early hours of the morning and I was just stunned, said Paisley. 'I had thought Bill was indestructible, that he would go on forever. He was always so fit. I couldn't believe that only a few days after being taken into hospital he had suddenly gone from us. The only time I really knew him to be ill was when he missed much of the pre-season training in 1970 with an infected foot. He was in Walton Hospital and had to take it easy for a while. Through his life, I don't think he ever had a serious illness. He was such a fitness fanatic that he once told the press: "I'm going to die a healthy man!" He had knocks while he was playing, of course, and he did his ankle once during training at Liverpool and was laid off for about three weeks – what upset the rest of us was that we had to miss our five-a-sides until he was fit again and ready to play!

'The news of his death was awful. We worked together for almost 15 years and I got to know his every whim and fancy; what upset him and what pleased him. Bill went on record, as I do, in saying that in all the time we worked together, we never had an argument. Discussions and different opinions, yes. But we never fell out. I knew from the moment he arrived at Liverpool that the people would respond to him. There was never any doubt about that. They showed what they thought of him when he died. The flag flew at half mast on the town hall, the church at West Derby was packed for his funeral and a week later Liverpool's Anglican Cathedral was full for a service in memory of Bill. I'm just glad that I was around to team up with him and get to know a unique character. Bill was what football is all about. It was a privilege and an honour to have been allowed to work with him.'

Liverpool's first League game after Shankly's death ironically saw the return to Anfield of one of his signings, John Toshack, with his Swansea side. It proved to be an occasion of high emotion, bad temper and what some felt was bad taste. Four other former Anfield players were also with Swansea – defenders Colin Irwin and Max Thompson and backroom men Phil Boersma and Doug Livermore.

Toshack, who had formed a celebrated attacking partnership with Kevin Keegan, had been hailed by Shankly earlier in the year as 'the world's best manager' after crowning Swansea's amazing odyssey through the divisions with promotion to the top flight. Paisley, too, joined in the praise for Toshack, saying: 'It's amazing what John has done. He's doing for Swansea what Bill did for Liverpool when he first came here.'

As the two teams lined up in the centre circle for a minute's silence in Shankly's memory, Toshack peeled off his tracksuit top to reveal a Liverpool jersey. Toshack's salute to the man who took him to Liverpool sadly backfired, with Liverpool officials, including chairman John Smith, believing it was an attempt to ingratiate himself with the club.

'When I saw John take off his Swansea top with the Liverpool strip underneath I thought nothing of it at the time but I understand it didn't go down too well with some of the people who mattered at Anfield,' recalled Graeme Souness. Toshack insisted: 'To go back to Anfield at that time made it a sadly special day for me.'

The minute's silence was broken by a group of whistling and chanting Swansea fans, with some Kop supporters responding with threats. Police said that 17 people were arrested for disorderly behaviour after the match.

The game itself, which included five Swansea bookings and an unseemly clash between Swansea's former Everton goalkeeper Dai Davies and Terry McDermott, saw Liverpool escape defeat after being 2–0 down, to a Leighton James penalty and a Bob Latchford strike. But it needed two penalties, both dispatched by McDermott, to salvage a point. At the end Toshack, unable to hold back tears, walked on to the pitch and saluted the Kop. 'They've been so great to me and they mean so much,' he declared.

Liverpool continued to splutter in the League, their woes compounded by a 2–1 home defeat by Manchester United, although in the European Cup they booked a quarter-final place by seeing off Holland's AZ Alkmaar on a 5–4 aggregate, after the first-round romp against Oulun. Paisley tried to rally his troops with a touch of boxing parlance. He watched Sugar Ray Leonard become undisputed world welterweight champion by stopping Tommy Hearns in 14 rounds, then told his players: 'Leonard showed total concentration. He had to, or he could have had his head knocked off his shoulders. You have to have the physical qualities in any sport, but if you have skill and concentration you're halfway there.

'If we think like that then we won't get lax. We must push on regardless of the critics. We've set such high standards that if we concede a corner, all hell is let loose.'

December, though, brought a new experience for Paisley and Liverpool when they flew to Tokyo to meet Flamengo of Brazil for the World Club Championship. As we have seen, Paisley had resisted such inter-continental involvement previously after the battles encountered by Manchester United and Celtic in the 1960s, when it was staged over two legs. But a sponsored one-off occasion in Japan finally lured Liverpool into confronting the South American champions. The debate over such competitions has reached fever pitch with the FA's decision to allow Manchester United not to defend the FA Cup in 1999–2000 so that they could participate in the World Team Championship in Brazil. Paisley explained Liverpool's stance back in 1981. 'The reasons we accepted were two-fold,' he said. 'First, we obtained the co-operation of the League and Birmingham City in rearranging a First Division fixture, scheduled for the Saturday, so that we could fly to Tokyo for the game on the Sunday. Without that co-operation we couldn't have accepted because we would not have been able to fly out in the middle of the previous week and have a couple of days to counter the effects of jet lag. Nottingham Forest found this a problem last year when, after losing to Nacional, they returned only the day before an FA Cup tie with Bristol City and almost lost it.

'The second reason we accepted was sponsorship. The fact that it was a one-off match in front of a 62,000 crowd meant that the financial inducements were far too great to ignore. It was wrong of the media to criticise us for not playing previously, because the real culprits were the fixture planners. Allowances for such things as the World Club Championship should be made before the season starts and then we would be able to compete on equal terms with the rest of the world. The fixture planners could help by postponing the whole programme for a fortnight. By doing that they would also prevent other teams stealing a psychological march by arranging a game and possibly opening up a lead at the top of the table.'

Liverpool's trip, while financially worthwhile through Toyota's sponsorship, was forgettable from a football viewpoint and, Paisley believed, left a legacy which could have had a catastrophic effect on their aspirations at home. They lost 3–0 to a Zico-inspired Flamengo in a game played at the stadium, in the shadow of Mount Fuji, that had staged the 1964 Olympics. Craig Johnston, having had time to adjust to Anfield demands, made his first senior Liverpool start while McDermott chalked up his 300th senior outing for the club. Liverpool, though, were totally out of sorts and crashed to a brace of goals from Nunes and another from Adilio, all in the first half. Flamengo captain Zico, earning £20,000 a month at a time when top English managers like Paisley were paid around £50,000 a year, won the game's 'outstanding player' award. It comprised a car and a trophy of a silver football mounted on a three-foot coil, which was bigger than the cup itself! While Flamengo headed for a holiday in Honolulu after their 77th match of the season, Paisley led his players back to an English winter, dubious about the wisdom of such a clash of football cultures.

'There's no doubt Flamengo are a great side and they're movement was so good,' he conceded. 'We were trying to play the ball on the floor but they were flicking one-touch accurate passes with the ball two or three feet off the ground. In Europe, if you challenge for a ball that high you are penalised and, with that type of game, I can understand how violence flares in South American matches. It was real beach football by Flamengo and the pitch certainly favoured them. Their style and the conditions were totally foreign to us. But we were dulled and our thought was so slow. We told our players not to get involved in a physical battle and perhaps they took us too literally. We lost the game through mistakes in the first half. There is no doubt, though, that on dry surfaces the Brazilians are a handful.'

The elements did Liverpool a favour when their next game, scheduled at Tottenham, fell victim to the English weather and was postponed. However, when they did resume League action, at home to Manchester City on Boxing Day, Paisley believed they were suffering a Tokyo hangover still. 'City beat us 3–1 and I'm sure the players were still feeling the after-effects,' he said. 'I knew that I, for one, still wasn't right. I didn't feel sharp and the players didn't look sharp, although I never told them that, because that would have given them a ready-made excuse for our poor performance against City.' Without dropped Terry McDermott and suspended Ray Kennedy and David Johnson, Liverpool fell behind to an early Asa Hartford goal. A Kevin Bond penalty, awarded after Phil Thompson had punched a Steve Kinsey shot over the bar following a Bruce Grobbelaar mistake, and a Kevin Reeves goal gave City victory. Ronnie Whelan's late reply was merely academic.

It seemed that not only had the last vestige of Liverpool's title hopes been wiped away but that the team was sliding alarmingly from the pinnacle of achievement so magnificently attained during the Paisley era. They were languishing 12th in the First Division, nine points behind leaders Swansea, and had won only six of their 17 League games. 'The start we made to our League programme was not the best in the world and we had an absolutely torrid time in that game against City,' Alan Hansen recalled. 'They scored three and, with Bruce coming for things and missing, City could have scored five or six. It looked at that stage as if it was the end of an era'.

His team-mate Mark Lawrenson remembers the after-match mood in the dressing room: 'For the first time since I'd been at the club, Joe Fagan raised his voice. I glanced at some of the others and you could see the realisation in the players' eyes. We knew we were not doing justice to ourselves or the club. Joe peeled the paint off the walls that afternoon. He made us think whether we could improve our own performances for the good of the team.'

The measure of a brilliant general, they say, is to examine his response to setbacks rather than success. After that Boxing Day debacle, Paisley once again demonstrated his genius at leadership and crisis management. He reacted dramatically and decisively, first by appealing to the Anfield fans to give the team greater backing and support and, second, by stripping Phil Thompson of the captaincy and handing it to Graeme Souness.

'Phil's job now is to get his own game in order, so I'm relieving him of the captaincy to see if it helps him and the team,' said Paisley. 'He's been having a bad time and I hope he call pull through it. Whatever your own form, you still have to be a captain and it should not be governed by your own performance. Phil feels the captaincy hasn't bothered him but I said it should have bothered him one way or the other – performance wise, it has not been there.'

Thompson admitted: 'I'm not happy about it but the boss and I have come to an agreement over it. Without wanting to sound big-headed, I still think I'm the best man for the job. But if it's best for me and the club, that's the main thing.' By a strange quirk of fate, more than a decade later Souness, then Liverpool manager, was to sack Thompson as reserve-team coach prior to the former England international returning to Anfield as new manager Gerard Houllier's assistant in 1998. Long before that, though, Thompson accepted Paisley's wisdom over the captaincy decision. 'I was having a very difficult time and wasn't playing too well and Bob in his wisdom thought it was time for a change,' he reflected. 'I was very hurt and disappointed. Being a Liverpool fan all my life, the captaincy was very precious to me. But his decision made me even more determined to show Bob Paisley what I could do. What Bob did had the desired effect on me. He saw that my game needed a lift. It helped me and I can only thank him for what he did for Liverpool and for me. He could be ruthless but he was a wonderful man and a great manager.'

Paisley believed that Souness had that touch of arrogance essential to captaincy. 'It wouldn't surprise me if Graeme tossed up before the game with a gold-plated credit card rather than a coin,' he drily remarked.

Liverpool's next outing after their collapse to Manchester City was a New Year's Day third round FA Cup trip to League leaders Swansea. The transformation was stunning. As well as installing Souness as captain, Paisley recalled Alan Kennedy, switched Lawrenson to midfield, brought back McDermott and returned Kenny Dalglish to the attack after his spell in a deeper role. The team powered to a 4–0 win – a scoreline that was merciful to Toshack's outplayed side – and proceeded to reduce the pundits' gloomy predictions to rubble by rattling up a club record of 11 straight League wins. Their next FA Cup engagement, a fourth-round trip to Paisley's boyhood favourites Sunderland, coincided with the manager's 63rd birthday. He was given a happy birthday result, with two Dalglish goals and another from Rush securing a 3–0 win at Roker Park. The club, though, had another present for him.

'On the way back we stopped at Ripon for something to eat and Peter Robinson and the directors had arranged for a birthday cake to be brought out for Bob,' recalled Mark Lawrenson. 'The cake was put in front of Bob and all the lads started shouting, "Speech, speech, speech," knowing how much Bob disliked making speeches. Bob stood up, picked up the cake and, with a tear in his eye, looked at us and said: "If you play like that every day it will be my birthday every day." It was one of my nicest memories of him.'

Liverpool's FA Cup ambitions, though, ended dismally with a 2–0 fifth-round defeat at Second Division Chelsea in February, and Paisley's anger turned to abject frustration three days later when his side crashed 2–0 at Swansea in the League. 'Bob came home and said he was packing it in, that he'd had enough,' revealed Jessie Paisley. 'Clearly, he had a change of mind because I never heard any more about it!' Perhaps Liverpool's response to those successive defeats was one reason. They lost only once more in the League between then and the end of the season, a shock 1–0 home reverse to Brighton, who had Jimmy Case in their ranks and won in a mudbath through a Hansen own goal.

In harness with their First Division surge, Liverpool also reached the League Cup Final after defeating Exeter, Middlesbrough, Arsenal, Barnsley and Ipswich. Their Wembley opponents, Tottenham had Ray Clemence in goal and with three minutes left it seemed he was destined to collect a medal at his former club's expense. The north London side, still to concede a goal in the competition that season, were clinging to a lead provided by Steve Archibald's early strike and sensing victory. Then Liverpool's exciting new talent Ronnie Whelan, hailed by the hugely respected Joe Mercer as 'the new Peter Doherty', rifled an equaliser from a pass by substitute David Johnson, sent on by Paisley 11 minutes earlier with the objective of providing fresh impetus. In the short break prior to extra time, the Tottenham players lay sprawled on the turf. Their Liverpool counterparts, on Paisley's instruction, stood up waiting for the resumption. The psychology was again at work.

There was only one winner now and Whelan struck again in the 111th minute – a goal fashioned by the magic of Dalglish, who purveyed a glorious pass – with Rush adding a third eight minutes later to clinch Liverpool's second successive triumph in the competition. At the end, Souness collected his first trophy as captain by going up to receive the League Cup while deposed skipper Thompson was told by Paisley to collect the new Milk Cup trophy. 'It was as though the whole thing had been scripted,' said Souness, who had just had a script of his own to contend with by appearing with his moustachioed look-alike Yosser Hughes in the hit television series *Boys From the Black Stuff*.

Liverpool's Wembley celebrations swiftly gave way to preparation for their European Cup quarter-final return with CSKA in Sofia the following Wednesday. Although they had beaten CSKA at the same stage a year earlier, even then Paisley had noted their quality. His antennae had been raised. So when the draw pitted Liverpool against the Bulgarians yet again, he rated them a big threat.

'I'll never forget the days of Cup draws and Bob waiting to learn who we were going to play,' said Lawrenson. 'He had a little office at Melwood with a radiator which was always on in the winter and he would stand there warming his legs, watching us train while he waited for news of the draw. If we'd got a good draw he would come marching out across the pitch. We knew from 300 yards away it was a good draw. If he only took short strides we knew it was a tough one.' Paisley certainly rated CSKA a tough challenge, especially after they restricted Liverpool to a 1–0 first leg win obtained through a second-half goal from Whelan.

'The Anfield game was played in a strong wind and with our pitch being worn, it made it difficult for us to get our game together,' Paisley entered in his diary. 'We didn't get the score we required to make it easy in Bulgaria, but it wasn't for lack of effort. But we kept a clean sheet and it's a lead we must defend.'

Their St Patrick's Day return to the Levski Stadium brought only bad luck to Liverpool in general and Irish international Lawrenson in particular. He became the first Liverpool player to be sent off in the club's 18 consecutive seasons in Europe for alleged retaliation on Histvan Yonchev in extra time. 'He caught me off the ball and although I reacted, I never touched him But he went down like a sack of potatoes,' Lawrenson insisted.

Grobbelaar did not have an on-target shot to worry about until he made a fateful 78th-minute misjudgement. He came out too far and left himself stranded as substitute Nikola Velkov crossed from the left. Stoytcho Mladenov outjumped Alan Kennedy to bury the aggregate equaliser in Liverpool's net. Then in the 11th minute of extra time, the same combination that brought the Bulgarians their equaliser dislodged Liverpool's grip on the European Cup. After Yonchev's corner had been partially cleared, Velkov crossed and Mladenov's shot looped over Grobbelaar into the net. It was a bitterly disappointing and controversial exit for Liverpool. Austrian referee Franz Woehrer waved away three clear penalty claims for Paisley's side in a series of bizarre decisions. If there had been any doubt that the European lights were going out for Liverpool they were dispelled when a Whelan header and a Lawrenson shot hit the woodwork.

Paisley admitted that the Austrian official's display revived the haunting nightmare of Ortiz de Mendibil in the San Siro in Liverpool's 1965 semi-final return with Inter Milan. 'Memories of the Spanish referee in Milan came flooding back when I saw this fellow,' said Paisley. 'Ian Rush beat the goalkeeper with a header and as he turned away to acclaim the goal, the keeper clawed the ball out of the net and the referee waved play on! He also rejected several penalties and sent off Mark even though he was 25 yards away and didn't even consult his linesman. It was scandalous. Despite all that, we were on our way to a goalless draw that would have taken us through until Bruce's mistake. Because Ray Clemence left, Bruce was thrust into our team with no experience. His error was down to that: inexperience and a lack of understanding with his fellow defenders. It was all so disappointing.'

The team now had the task of picking themselves up to resume their League championship challenge against Sunderland at

Anfield three days later. The outcome was a hard-earned 1–0 win – through an early Rush goal – and a spat between Paisley and a section of supporters who jeered his decision to substitute Craig Johnston with David Johnson in the 71st minute. Pulling no punches, Paisley rounded on the boo-boys and declared: 'There were ten dead men out there, weary from midweek, while Craig, who played only half an hour as a substitute in Sofia, was fresh and more likely to cause us damage with his inexperience. It was impossible for the rest of the team to respond to a player bursting with energy and enthusiasm and keen to make an impression, as Craig is. I sent on David Johnson because he's more used to these situations, but that would be too intelligent for the few yobbos in the crowd to understand. Everyone's entitled to their opinion and I'm not labelling them all yobbos. I'm only speaking about three or four. But if any Liverpool fans think I've got it in for Craig, they're wrong. I did it because the rest of the lads were so tired they couldn't keep up with him.

'Because Sunderland were next to bottom, we were expected to trounce them. But the way they were fighting to stave off relegation – which they eventually did – I could see signs that they might snatch a draw. If we had dropped two points, it could have cost us title. When there's danger, you close ranks. But I got dog's abuse from a handful – and I stress a handful – of spectators. I was accused of being stupid for taking Craig off. I rate it as one of the key factors in our championship success.'

Earlier in the season, Paisley had the rare experience of missing two Liverpool games, a draw at West Brom and a home defeat by Southampton, because of an attack of pleurisy, the first he had missed in the League since joining forces with Shankly in 1959. His only other first-team absence had been for an FA Cup tie against Chelsea in 1966. Ultimately, though, it was Liverpool's challengers who were sickened by the pace of Anfield's title pursuit. It was too much for Ipswich, Manchester United, earlier leaders Swansea and all the rest. Paisley's fifth championship as manager, and Liverpool's 13th, was clinched in their penultimate fixture, a home clash with Tottenham which meant a reunion for Ray Clemence and the Kop.

Glenn Hoddle threatened to wreck the party with a spectacular long-range goal midway through the first half to give Tottenham hope of their first Anfield win since 1912. But Clemence, at the Kop end after the interval, was beaten by a Lawrenson header, a

Dalglish shot for his 22nd goal of the season after a superb link with 30-goal Rush, and a late third from Whelan which polished off Tottenham. It was a thrilling ascent to another championship, their campaign concluding three days later with a goalless draw at Middlesbrough, which gave Liverpool an automatic new points record of 87 under the new system. They had marched unbeaten through their last 16 games and plundered 63 points from a possible 75 since their Boxing Day demise against Manchester City.

During the campaign Phil Neal had a public clash with Paisley after the manager had blasted the team following a 2–0 defeat at eventual runners-up Ipswich. 'If players are going to play for us they must be professional. I don't want playboys or fly-by-nights,' he chided. When Neal, offended, took up the verbal cudgels with his manager, Paisley explained he was talking about their attitude and added: 'This idea of just saying "We're sorry" and thinking it's over and done with has got to change.'

As Neal, Anfield's 31-year-old senior professional, collected his fifth title medal after seeing off Tottenham, he reflected: 'At the end of my first season here we finished second and I was feeling great. Everyone else had long faces. That's when I realised what Liverpool are all about.'

The trophy was presented to Souness on the pitch by chairman John Smith as Paisley glowed with pride at a title win achieved against the odds. 'Considering where we had to come from and what we had to do, this is one of the most pleasing,' said Paisley. In what was a transitional season, he had used only 16 players – with one of them, Kevin Sheedy, making only two substitute appearances – and seen them confound the critics. For the first time Liverpool had lost more home games – four – than the three defeats they suffered on their travels. It had been a strange season but a wonderfully productive one, with another two trophies for the Anfield sideboard and the Paisley roll of honour.

He had proved again what a superb judge of football flesh he was, and amidst the congratulations he was asked about Hoddle, scorer of that magnificent Tottenham goal. 'Is he a luxury in a team?' asked a knowing journalist.

'You've got to be a good player to be a luxury,' was the withering reply, demonstrating that, for all Hoddle's undoubted skill, without commitment and consistency he was as much a Paisley player as Long John Silver was a tap dancer.

16

Farewell

Bob Paisley chose his native soil of Durham to announce that he would be spending just one more season in charge of Liverpool before passing the glittering baton to his successor. He told a football writers' dinner, staged in his honour: 'I'll give it another 12 months, which will see me complete 44 years at Liverpool, and then I'll hand it over. We've come through a transitional period and once I'm certain that things are running smoothly, it will be time to go.'

If retirement was in his mind, there was no drop in concentration or planning as he prepared for a final campaign in charge. He was also receptive to new ideas, such as the pre-season deployment of all three of his international centre-backs, with Hansen as a Continental-style sweeper alongside Lawrenson and 'spare man' Thompson, which had to be abandoned when Hansen missed the first eight games of the season through thigh damage. The Anfield pitch, heavily criticised in many quarters and blamed by Paisley for sabotaging his team on occasions, was ripped up and relaid in time for the 1982–83 season which also heralded a new shirt sponsorship deal, with Crown Paints injecting £500,000 over three years to succeed the club's pioneering link-up with Hitachi. John Smith took a swipe at the restrictions still placed on sponsor's names by TV and the FA. 'Why should football be handicapped unfairly in a way other sports are not? It's quite wrong,' he rapped.

Paisley said farewell to several players including David Johnson, who followed Kevin Sheedy by rejoining his first club Everton for £100,000, while late September saw Terry McDermott, who had figured in all three European Cup triumphs, return to Newcastle for £100,000. Reserve goalkeeper Steve Ogrizovic, who had only five senior outings in five years, joined Shrewsbury in a straight swap with Bob Wardle. Johnson's departure prompted Paisley to pay £450,000 for Middlesbrough's England Under-21 striker David Hodgson, although the new boy, true to Paisley's policy, had to be content with a seat on the bench at Wembley when a Rush goal gave Liverpool a 1–0 Charity Shield win over Tottenham.

If the previous title win had been almost a handicap chase for Liverpool, this one proved to be a procession, with Paisley's side establishing a pre-Christmas grip on the battle and at one stage opening up a 16-point lead over runners-up Watford. Elton John's top-flight newcomers, managed by Graham Taylor, took much of the First Division by storm but closed to within 11 points of Liverpool only because Paisley's team took their foot off the gas after becoming champions with five games to go.

British World Cup hopes in Spain during the summer had once again nose-dived, with Scotland not even making the second round and England and valiant Northern Ireland, surprise conquerors of the host nation, failing to reach the semi-finals. But those who called for more sophistication received a scornful response from Watford boss Taylor, who was destined one day to become England manager. 'Football's a game for the man on the terraces. I hate sophisticated football,' he proclaimed. His team, with their physical, long-ball game, were never in any danger of being called sophisticates. The clash of football philosophies when they visited Anfield in December went powerfully Liverpool's way, with two Phil Neal penalties, following an opening strike from Rush, giving Paisley's side a 3–1 win.

Following official confirmation that Paisley would step down at the end of the season, Liverpool ended feverish speculation over his successor by naming Joe Fagan as the man who, at 62, would follow the most successful manager in the history of the English game. Paisley would bow out, though, in style. Rush had become a master predator and his attacking alliance with Dalglish was honed to perhaps the finest ever witnessed in British club football. It was illustrated with a display that still sends a chill through Evertonians. Liverpool went to Goodison and won 5–0 with Rush scoring four, the biggest individual goal blitz in a Mersey derby since 1935. The Welshman then asked his compatriot, Everton defender Kevin Ratcliffe, to give him a lift home after the match!

If Rush was Everton's executioner, Dalglish supplied much of the ammunition. He had what appeared a splendid headed goal disallowed before his pace and trickery proved too much for Glenn Keeley, making his debut on a month's loan from Blackburn. Keeley pulled Dalglish's shirt so strongly he virtually disrobed the Scot and under the newly introduced disciplinary clampdown that meant one thing: dismissal. Referee Derek Civil gave Keeley his marching orders and he never kicked another ball for Everton, his Goodison career started and finished in just 32 minutes.

Rush's emergence as a goal plunderer had, Paisley believed, been influenced heavily by Dalglish. 'I think Kenny made all the difference to Ian in his early days because he had this rare quality of knowing where other players were without even looking and of finding them with a perfect pass,' Paisley said. 'He knew how to place the ball into the space where Ian was heading. It made them the most lethal pairing I've ever seen. The greatness in Kenny was that while he was a tremendous individual himself, he made others play too.'

Alan Hansen frankly admits that Rush's emergence mocked his early opinion of the lean and hungry Welshman. Said Hansen: 'When Rush first came, I watched him and thought: "No pace, can't head it, can't score...they'll get rid of him at the end of the season." It shows what a good judge I am!' Rush followed his foursome at Everton with a hat-trick against Coventry in his next League outing and Liverpool, who went top in October, were never dislodged from the summit, with Everton's April win over Manchester United clinching Anfield's 14th title and Paisley's sixth as manager. Dalglish, who contributed 20 of a 50-goal partnership with Rush in all competitions, was named Footballer of the Year by both the football writers and his fellow professionals, with his attacking accomplice taking the Young Player Award. Craig Johnston, transfer listed by Paisley at his own request earlier in the season because he wanted regular first-team action, earned his title medal by appearing in 33 of the 42 League games from which Liverpool amassed 82 points, Watford 71 and Manchester United a point further behind. Liverpool became champions with so much to spare they just strolled through their final fixtures, amazingly losing five and drawing two of their last seven League games.

Europe brought a second successive season of disappointment for Paisley, with another Champions' Cup quarter-final exit behind the Iron Curtain. Liverpool saw off Republic of Ireland side Dundalk and Finnish club Helsinki, both on 5–1 aggregates, although the latter only after an embarrassing 1–0 first-leg defeat in Finland which incurred Paisley's wrath. That was nothing, however, compared to his feelings the following March after another costly Continental bungle by Grobbelaar, this time in Poland, which gifted Widzew Lodz the initiative for a 4–3 aggregate knock-out of Paisley's side.

Paisley and the Liverpool party were involved in a terrifying drama as their aircraft was about to land at mist-shrouded, snow-covered Warsaw on their journey for the quarter-final first leg. Their Boeing 737 overshot and had to bank sharply, with its port wing only 30 feet from the ground. The pilot had to make an emergency climb and, finally, land safely. 'We've flown a few miles over the years but I've never experienced anything like that,' said captain Graeme Souness.

What happened in the match, however, was a sad case of deja vu. The contest was goalless when Grobbelaar rose early in the second half, attempting a right-handed catch from a left-wing cross, and dropped the ball. Polish international Miroslaw Thokinski snapped up the invitation by gleefully firing Lodz ahead. They doubled their lead through a diving header from Wieslaw Wraga ten minutes from the end for a 2–0 win. 'I have to blame myself for the first goal. I thought I had it covered,' admitted Grobbelaar, who also took the rap for his costly blunder in Sofia a year earlier.

Souness declared: 'It was a bad goal but Bruce has kept us in games many times in the past and I'm sure he will again.' Paisley, while publicly refusing to slate Grobbelaar and proclaiming the tie still winnable, privately sensed that the keeper's aberration would cost him the chance of a fourth European Cup triumph. 'I couldn't even look at Bruce afterwards,' he revealed. He realised that his side's second-leg task had become mountainous when the inspirational Dalglish was hit by a virus that was kept secret on Paisley's orders. The Scot's importance, though, persuaded Paisley to try to break his own rule of a lifetime by fielding an unfit player.

'Kenny meant so much to the team and put fear into the opposition, that I just wanted him out on the field,' said Paisley. 'I almost convinced him he was alright to play in the second leg. But he had no chance – he was so weak he could hardly stand up, let alone play football.'

Dalglish's absence ended his 35-game ever-present run in

Europe. Liverpool's adventure was also halted for another season and, in Paisley's case, for the last time as a manager. An early Neal penalty gave Liverpool hope of retrieving a two-goal first-leg deficit for the first time in their European history, but a Lodz spot kick, dispatched by first-leg scorer Tlokinski, and another from Smolarek early in the second half smashed those ambitions, even though goals from Rush and Dalglish's stand-in David Hodgson gave Liverpool a 3–2 win on the night.

Among the 44,000-plus crowd that evening was the coach of French club Lens who was watching Smolarek with a view to signing him. The man with a mission was Gerard Houllier. But what made an indelible impression on him was the sheer intensity of the occasion. 'One day I'd love to be coach of Liverpool,' he revealed to his Polish assistant, Joachim Marx.

Houllier had already had a spell teaching on Merseyside but that March night in 1983 sparked an ambition he realised more than 15 years later, when he was appointed joint-manager of Liverpool alongside Roy Evans in July 1998, taking sole charge the following November.

'At that European Cup game against Lodz I could see something was getting to Gerard,' recalled Marx. 'He seemed very excited and it was something more than just the football that was affecting him. It was the noise and the atmosphere, the stadium and its situation, surrounded by working-class houses.

'He was also deeply impressed at the way the supporters really cheered Liverpool even though their team were eliminated from the competition. After the match Gerard and I went to a pub, drank a few beers and talked to the fans. He was spellbound by the whole thing.'

Liverpool's exit ended England's six-year grip on the European Cup started by Liverpool in 1977, continued by Nottingham Forest then Liverpool again and extended the previous year by Aston Villa.

It was also the second time in less than a month that Liverpool had tasted Cup elimination following their 2–1 home FA Cup fifth-round defeat by Brighton in the first Sunday match at Anfield in the club's 91-year history. Gerry Ryan's 33rd-minute opener for the visitors, propping up the First Division and whose acting boss was former Liverpool forward Jimmy Melia, was cancelled out in the second half by substitute Craig Johnston's overhead kick. Yet within a minute, another Anfield old boy,

Jimmy Case, unleashed a 20-yard right-foot blast that flew past Grobbelaar to restore Brighton's shock advantage.

A subsequent Neal penalty miss, on his 32nd birthday, only confirmed that the football gods had decreed that the FA Cup would remain the one gap in Paisley's unprecedented array of silverware. It was Brighton's first away win over First Division opposition since their League triumph at Anfield 11 months earlier and with it went Liverpool's 63-game unbeaten home run in Cup competitions since November 1974 and their undefeated FA Cup record at Anfield, stretching back to Leicester's win in 1969.

Paisley took it philosophically, saying: 'This is what football is all about and what it can have in store for you. People say I don't smile. But even after this if I had a better set of teeth I'd have the biggest smile in the country. Those people who go on about winning four trophies are talking rubbish. I only wish the bookies had taken up my offer to give me £1,000 when they were offering 10–1 against us winning four trophies! I'd have been richer now.'

Said Melia: 'Bob was magnificent. He came straight into our dressing room at the end, wished us all the best and said he hoped we win the Cup.' But for an inexplicable late miss by Gordon Smith at Wembley, Melia's team would have done. But his failure meant that Brighton's collision with Manchester United ended in a 2–2 draw, with Ron Atkinson's side demolishing the rank outsiders 4–0 in the replay.

When United visited Wembley two months earlier, in the Milk Cup Final, their fate had been very different. The day belonged to Liverpool with Paisley the star of the show, his side again coming from behind to complete a unique hat-trick of triumphs. Referee George Courtney was widely criticised for failing to send off Grobbelaar for a professional foul on Gordon McQueen, although Atkinson did not complain and Paisley said: 'McQueen was waiting to be put down. If the RSPCA had come on then we'd all have got done for letting him play! He was so tired.'

Norman Whiteside struck early for United but Alan Kennedy equalised 15 minutes from the end. 'I preached patience to the players,' said Paisley. 'When we got that goal it was a question of taking the game into extra time before we killed them off. I felt like the bullfighter going for the last stab after the bull had 40 arrows in its back.' The fatal thrust was supplied by Wembley specialist Whelan, who struck a spectacular curler beyond Gary Bailey nine minutes into the extra period.

At the end Paisley, for once, acted on the orders of his players and backroom staff. As he walked across the Wembley stage, heading for the tunnel in his raincoat and flat cap, he was stopped by Joe Fagan, Ronnie Moran and Tom Saunders. They took his coat and cap and sent him for further instructions from Souness. The captain told him that as this was his last Wembley appearance in charge, the players wanted him to become the first manager to climb the 39 steps to be presented with a trophy.

'Bob at first said no,' Mark Lawrenson recalled, 'but Graeme insisted it was the players' wish that he did go up. I think that tells you something about what every player at Liverpool Football Club thought about Bob Paisley.'

Paisley did as he was told and as he climbed the steps in his grey suit, a fan threw a Liverpool scarf around his shoulders. For Paisley it was the seventh win in the 11 occasions he had led Liverpool to Wembley, with three draws and just a single defeat. 'I'm surprised they don't charge me rent and rates,' he quipped.

The following night, as guest of honour at the Professional Footballers Asociation annual awards dinner in London's West End, he received a standing ovation and urged the country's players to protect the interests of the game that had been his life. 'You've got the ball . . . don't drop it,' he told them.

Although Liverpool had already made certain of the title, they still felt the heat of Paisley's tongue after losing 2–0 at home to Norwich on St George's Day. 'The players were wearing roses in their button holes when they left the ground. They should have worn tulips the way they tried to tiptoe through the opposition,' Paisley barked.

The championship trophy was presented to Souness on the Anfield pitch by Football League president Jack Dunnett before the kick-off in Liverpool's final home game of the season, a 1–1 draw with Aston Villa, which was Paisley's managerial farewell to the Kop. The skipper immediately handed the prized pot to Paisley, who had also been presented with a Royal Doulton commemorative plate with the inscription: 'The greatest managerial record of all time.' Paisley, wearing his raincoat yet again, thrust the trophy in the air as the fans chanted his name. Then the 64-year-old, who had torn up all previous records of managerial achievement, was gone, walking down the tunnel for the last time as manager, one day short of his 44th anniversary of signing for Liverpool.

Liverpool poet Adrian Henri penned these moving lines:

There's a breathless hush in the Kop tonight
Bob Paisley's going away
At every turn they came to learn
To play the Paisley way

So fill the cup and raise it up
King Kenny leads the cheers
The Paisley name, the Paisley game
Will echo down the years

It was not quite Paisley's last public football appearance. The following August, by now a Liverpool director, he made his 17th Wembley visit in his various roles with the club. The occasion was the Charity Shield duel with Manchester United and, fittingly, Paisley did a motorised pre-match lap of honour on the back of a truck standing with Sir Matt Busby, the man who had been so helpful and welcoming to him as Liverpool captain when he had arrived in 1939.

When he received his sixth Manager of the Year award in eight seasons, plus a special award to take his total of Bell's presentations to a record 23 – he donated most of his whisky prizes either to charity or the Boot Room – Paisley, true to type, refused to dwell in the past. He was looking ahead even though he had relinquished the reins to Fagan. He told his audience at London's Cafe Royal: 'You may have found me mean and thirsty in my search for trophies, but the bad news is that the man who is taking my place is hungrier than me. Fagan's the name and I don't think he'll need any help from the Artful Dodger!'

His last signing was Jim Beglin, a £20,000 acquisition from Shamrock Rovers, and he officially handed over to Fagan on 1 July. 'I know that Joe feels, like me, that although I'm handing over a squad that's won things, we still need to look for players,' said Paisley. 'My policy has been to have five or six in the team around the 25 to 26 mark, a couple younger than that, two around 28 and one or two who have reached 30. But a team still needs a boost from youngsters competing for places in every area, and it's essential we have more of that.

'But I certainly won't be interfering with Joe's job. It will be a terrible wrench stepping down as manager. Bill Shankly did it far too soon and regretted it for the rest of his life. But I know this time is right for me. Bill and I were very close but completely different animals.'

Paisley was true to his pledge and Fagan true to his predecessor's forecast by landing an unprecedented treble of European Cup, League title and Milk Cup in his first season at the helm, 15 years before Manchester United became only the second English club to win three trophies in a season. With sad irony, Fagan died at the age of 80 in the summer of 2001 just a few weeks after Gerard Houllier had led Liverpool to the second treble in the club's history by lifting the UEFA Cup, FA Cup and Worthington Cup, the first time such a cup hat trick had been achieved in English football.

In November 1983, a unique football gathering paid tribute to Paisley at a gala dinner in Anfield's Trophy Room. A host of personalities, including his former team-mates, football administrators, sportswriters, and supporters, were present to salute the man who had devoted a lifetime to the club and made them kings of Europe on three occasions.

Paisley's long-time friend Sir Matt Busby, captain of Liverpool when he had arrived in 1939, was among the guests along with Everton manager Howard Kendall and his predecessor Gordon Lee and Bob's successor at Anfield, Joe Fagan. Also present were Bob's former playing colleagues Billy Liddell, Jack Balmer, Cyril Sidlow, Eddie Spicer, Bill Jones, Ray Lambert and Phil Taylor, who also managed Liverpool.

Graeme Souness, Liverpool captain at the time, was one of the speakers and I had the privilege of being master of ceremonies on an unforgettable occasion, crowned when my journalist colleague Colin Wood, then with the *Daily Mail*, presented Bob with a Royal Doulton figure of St George on horseback mounted on an inscribed plinth.

The personal honours piled up for Paisley. As well as a special award from the Professional Footballers' Association, he was made an honorary Master of Science by Liverpool University, an Honorary Fellow of John Moores University (then a Polytechnic), a Freeman of his adopted city of Liverpool and had an inscribed plaque erected in his honour above a supermarket in Hetton, standing on the site of Barrington School, which Paisley attended. He was also on the football wanted list of a number of countries. He coached for a month in Indonesia and had overtures to become national manager of Wales, Turkey and Israel, among others.

The most bizarre chapter, though, concerned the Republic of Ireland. 'Bob got a telephone call from one of the members of the Football Association of Ireland asking if he would be interested in becoming a candidate to be Ireland manager, which he said he would,' recalled Jessie Paisley. 'The selection process went to a committee ballot, which Bob won by a clear majority. Then, for some reason, they had another vote and Jack Charlton was installed! It was very strange but very fortuitous for all concerned, because Bob was soon quite ill and couldn't have done the job. And Jack didn't do badly for Ireland, did he!'

Prior to the onset of Alzheimer's Disease, Paisley, working closely with his friend, fellow director and later club vice-chairman Sydney Moss, continued his duties on the Liverpool board. But Fagan's decision to retire after two years in charge, a story which broke the day before the appalling 1985 European Cup Final tragedy at the Heysel Stadium in Brussels, meant yet another role for Paisley, as consultant to greenhorn manager Kenny Dalglish. The outcome was fairly satisfactory as the man Paisley rated the greatest Liverpool player he had ever seen swept the club to a League and FA Cup double in his first season as player-boss, a feat that had even eluded Paisley!

In 1989, the year Paisley celebrated a half century at Anfield, he was the victim of some cheap and nasty tabloid journalism when he was already suffering from the initial stages of Alzheimer's. He was asked by a photographer if he could assemble his vast array of cups and medals for a souvenir picture. An accompanying reporter chatted to him and the outcome was a sensationalised attack on the club he had served loyally and brilliantly for 50 years. The board accepted he never had any intention of being critical of Liverpool and the matter was closed. But it was a shameful, ignoble chapter which shocked other journalists as much as the Paisley family.

He accepted an invitation to be a manager again for just one day by returning to his native North East to take charge of a combined Liverpool and Juventus Under-21 team that met the Skol Northern League in their centenary match at Newcastle in September 1989. The Northern League was part of Paisley's football roots, having played in it for Bishop Auckland in the 1930s before joining Liverpool.

The cruel, progressive disease which had afflicted Paisley led to his resignation from the Liverpool board on 7 February 1992. In his letter, Paisley, who was made a life vice-president at Anfield, wrote: 'I have served the club for more than 50 years and to be elected to the board was the final accolade.'

Club chairman David Moores paid him this tribute: 'Bob's knowledge of players and the game in general is unsurpassed. Football has known no equal in management or prize-winning, but his modesty and dignity were overwhelming as he led this club from one triumph to another. His name will always be synonymous with Liverpool.'

Bob Paisley, whose last days were spent in Arncliffe Court nursing home, 'being wonderfully cared for,' in Jessie's words, died on Valentine's Day, 14 February 1996, at the age of 77.

'Football has lost a legend, a mountain of talent has left us,' was the tribute from Brian Clough, with sentiments echoed universally. 'Bob was a genius. His smile was as wide as Stockton High Street; he had the nicest face in football. How did he follow Bill Shankly? I once asked the late Eric Morecambe how he followed the likes of George Burns and Bob Hope. He replied: "With difficulty." Bob Paisley conquered the same problem.'

Paisley's last captain, Graeme Souness, said: 'I think I learned more about football from Bob Paisley than anyone else. He's the most successful manager in the history of the British game and someone who must have been very brave to take the Liverpool job when he did. He followed in the footsteps of a legend in Bill Shankly and not only matched what he did but bettered it. He is someone who should be remembered as long as Liverpool Football Club exists.'

Souness, then managing Turkish club Galatasaray after an unhappy spell in charge of Liverpool, flew in from Istanbul to attend Paisley's funeral service at St Peter's Church in Liverpool's Woolton district. Other luminaries of Paisley's great teams, including Dalglish, Rush and Hansen, and people from every era of his long association with Anfield, Roger Hunt and Ian Callaghan among them, were also present. So was Manchester United and England legend Sir Bobby Charlton, who said: 'Bob's deeds will never be surpassed, certainly not in my lifetime. He was a lovely, unforgettable man, who always made you feel welcome. It is a sad day.'

Hansen, one of Paisley's most inspired acquisitions for Liverpool, offered a fulsome salute to the legend whose leadership brought him astounding football success: 'He was a great manager. The record speaks for itself. I go by records and they show that he's the best. He was a very modest man who just wanted to get on with the game. He was also a ruthless manager. Everyone thought of him as a favourite uncle but the thing about Bob is that he never showed any sentiment. He just picked his best 11, which was one of the secrets of Liverpool success at that time. He kept everyone hungry, fresh and motivated. The biggest threat to a team is complacency, but there was never any danger of that while he was there.

'One year I was out for ten games, of which the team won nine and drew one. I didn't think I had a chance of getting back. But on the Thursday Bob came to me and told me I was playing. I realised then that he would always pick what he thought was his best 11. It's hard for a manager to be like that but it's imperative to have the strength of character to do that. Everyone knew where they stood with Bob. Possibly he learned from the Shankly era that you couldn't be loyal to players past their best. The minute they were past their best, they were on the way. He showed no sentiment even if a player had been there ten years and been a magnificent servant.

'Bob had a wealth of football knowledge second to none. He often said that football was about strengths and weaknesses. He could pinpoint them better than any manager I've ever played for or ever met. He wasn't great with words but when he did say something, you always took notice because 99 times out of a 100 he was spot-on. He had this great line about the first two yards at top level being in your head. When he first said it to me I thought it was utter rubbish. But the more I played the game, I realised it was so true.

'Another of his great lines was, "There hasn't been a player yet without a weakness."

'We'd say: "What about Pele? What was his weakness?"

'Bob would say: "He's got one somewhere. Everyone has."

'His approach was to play to your strengths and don't let anyone exploit your weaknesses. That's what his team meetings were all about. The meetings would be hilarious with Bob, because he would struggle to string two sentences together and he was always getting opposition names wrong. The laughter on a Friday morning was unbelievable. Terry Mac used to impersonate Bob before he came in and we all used to bite our lips trying not to laugh. But at the same time the respect we had for him was enormous and Bob did encourage us to have a laugh and enjoy ourselves.

'He wanted training to be enjoyable, which was a great tribute to Bob and Bill Shankly. They understood just how much team spirit meant and one of the secrets of Liverpool success was that they were in front before they went on the pitch because of the camaraderie that existed. You have to work to get that and unless you have a manager that wants to work at it then you're in trouble. This is where Kenny Dalglish learned a lot from Bob and Joe Fagan, that team spirit is vital, and wherever Kenny's gone he's tried to enhance the team spirit. Human nature dictates that if you have 16 players, two coaches and a manager, they won't all like each other. But that doesn't matter as long as you can rely on each other. The only way you can do that is by having a great team spirit, so that when you go on to the pitch you have a bond and unity that holds you together. If you've got that you're always in front.

'You heard so many stories about players in other teams fighting and disliking each other and of stars taking liberties. Bob Paisley brought in a lot of superstars but nobody in his teams ever took liberties. When you talk about great managers, Bob Paisley is number one.'

Another of Paisley's great signings, Mark Lawrenson, said of him: 'To the Europeans he had this mystique about him. They recognised that he was a great football man; he knew about players, he knew about winning matches and he knew how to set up teams. That was possibly the biggest compliment you could pay him. For me he's the greatest manager ever. I say that for what he did following Shankly and because of his great team-building ability. When you've got a really good team, the terrible temptation must be just to leave it. Bob seemed to have the timing right of when to leave players out. It's the hardest thing in football.

'Supporters would say: "Hey, you can't leave him out – he's won two European Cups and a couple of League championships!" But all of a sudden this other guy would come from nowhere – like Steve Nicol – and turn out to be a great player. In my time at Liverpool he had at least two exceptional sides.'

Paisley's towering contribution to British and European football was a reflection, too, of the happy, stable family background he had enjoyed as a foundation for his time-consuming commitment to football. In a BBC Radio Merseyside interview with Bob Azurdia in September 1980, he had the opportunity to say a public thank you to Jessie. 'I've been very fortunate to have such an understanding wife and family,' he told listeners. 'They've had to put up with a lot of trials and tribulations.

'One of Jessie's favourite songs, and one of mine, is Harry Secombe's' "If I Ruled The World". I'd like that played as a tribute to her for what she and the family have done for me.'

One of Bob Paisley's memorable phrases if his team were playing below peak efficiency and over-indulging in passing was: 'They're getting carried away with their own music.' Bob never got carried away with his own music although the chorus of praise will echo down the years for the genius who rests in the same Woolton graveyard as the unknown 'Eleanor Rigby'. It was originally thought that this provided the inspiration for the Beatles song written by John Lennon and Paul McCartney, who first met at that same church hall in July 1957. However, McCartney says that the name 'Eleanor' was taken from the actress, Eleanor Bron, who appeared in the film *Help!*, and that 'Rigby' came from a wine and spirit shipping company.

The rector of St Peter's, the Rev Canon John Roberts, supplied the perfect epitaph for Bob Paisley, and one which is etched on his gravestone, when he described him to the mourners in the packed church as 'an ordinary man amidst extraordinary achievement'.

The impact of Paisley and the fabled Boot Room rolls down the years. One of Sven Goran Eriksson's first public statements on being appointed as England's first ever foreign coach in November 2000 was to reveal the deep influence Anfield thinking has had on his approach to the game, which has brought him 16 major trophies in management including championships in Italy, Portugal and his native Sweden.

'I made my first visits to Anfield in the mid 1970s, when Liverpool were winning domestic and European trophies so regularly, and I met and talked with Bob Paisley and Joe Fagan, who succeeded Bob as manager,' Eriksson recalled. 'I was starting my own managerial career in Sweden at the time and I really admired the Liverpool coaches for their achievements. Their football philosophy was to keep the game very simple. That influenced me. I believe that is good advice to give to a coach.

'Liverpool FC is part of the story of football. Anfield is one of the most famous grounds in the world and to play there is always something special. But the only time I visited Anfield for a club match was in 1984 when I was coach of Benfica and we lost 1–0 in the first leg of the European Cup quarter final. As Liverpool were such a great team we thought that was a good result and gave us a chance of going through. But we lost 4–1 in Lisbon!'

Eriksson's compatriot and England assistant, Tord Grip, also points to Paisley's Liverpool side as torch bearers for his own football creed, which has carried him through spells as coach of the Norway and Sweden national sides. Said Grip: 'When I was with Sweden we finished third in the 1994 World Cup behind Brazil and Italy and we did that because we had a good team system. We did have some outstanding players – Tomas Brolin was very important to us – but the most vital thing is that we played as a team.

'We learned that from the Liverpool of the 1970s, from a team who did everything simple. One touch. Two touch. It worked so well. Liverpool had some good players but they didn't have great individuals then. Their strength was in their teamwork. We thought: We can use that. That can work for us.'

Fittingly, England's first competitive match under the new regime of Eriksson and Grip was at Anfield, the World Cup qualifier against Finland in March 2001, which the home nation won 2–1.

Captain of the Scandinavian visitors was another figure who salutes the inspirational effect Paisley's team had on him and helped persuade him to pursue a career in football rather than ice hockey. Jari Litmanen was signed by Liverpool from Barcelona shortly before the World Cup game and reflected:

'I grew up in my home town of Lahti watching Bob Paisley's team on television and I have supported Liverpool ever since. It was always my dream to play for Liverpool. Now it has come true and every day it's a special feeling to train or play for the club. I have also now met many of the old players I followed on television in the 1970s and 1980s. It's been a great thrill to meet them, something really special.'

Paisley's feats, and his unrivalled contribution to Liverpool, were hailed on an atmospheric, emotional Anfield evening in February 2001 at the UEFA Cup match against Roma which was dedicated to his memory as Paisley Flag Night. The stadium became a shrine as giant mosaics were created by fans holding cards to form images of Paisley's achievements. As a choir sang 'You'll Never Walk Alone' the Kop mosaic depicted the European Cup, League championship trophy, the UEFA Cup, League Cup and European Super Cup, all won during his fabulous reign.

The Centenary Stand mosaic created the legend 'Paisley' while the Anfield Road Stand was a sea of green and white, the colours of St Etienne, the French club who forged a lasting bond with Anfield after their tumultous European Cup quarter final visit in 1977, from which Liverpool progressed to win the trophy for the first time.

Two strikers, spanning the years from the Paisley era to the present, captured the essence of the evening. Current star Michael Owen, who was not even born for the first two of Paisley's three European Cup triumphs, declared: 'Bob Paisley is a legend at Liverpool and it's fitting that his achievements are still remembered by the club. As players we're hoping to pay the biggest possible tribute to him by enjoying some of the success he enjoyed as a manager.'

Wales legend Ian Rush, signed by Paisley to become a master goalscorer, said of his former boss: 'His knowledge of the game was unbelievable. He was a very quiet man but he knew how to handle people. His man-management was excellent. He is the greatest manager in the history of English football, his record at home and in Europe proves that. I don't think we'll ever see his like again.'

Jessie Paisley, who attended the Flag Night with her family, reflected: 'It's lovely to know that Bob still means so much to people and that something like this has been organised in his memory. Mind you, he'd have wondered what all the fuss was about. Bob didn't like fuss. He'd have said: "Let's get on with the game. That's our job."'

Jessie has been delighted, too, to see Bob's memory perpetuated by an annual football tournament for youngsters from England and Ireland. Merseyside-based club Halewood Juniors meet Ballinasloe Town juniors, from Bob's favourite Irish county of Galway, for the Bob Paisley Friendship Cup. His unprecedented feats at Liverpool are also being saluted by twenty-first century technology. A website dedicated to him – www. bob paisley. com – went on line in May 2001.

A month after Bob's death, Jessie accepted an invitation to be guest of honour at a Variety Club charity dinner in tribute to her late husband, whose brilliance at building football teams was reflected in the glittering assembly of playing talent who attended to salute the man whose OBE, according to Lawrie McMenemy, should stand for 'Our Bob's Extraordinary'.

'At first I was reluctant to come because I felt it was too close to Bob's death,' Jessie told the celebrity audience. 'But I'm glad I did. I've enjoyed every minute and I'd like to thank you all for coming and the work the Variety Club does for children's charities.' She also amused them by explaining something that had puzzled a host of famous players from Tommy Smith and Ian Callaghan to Graeme Souness and Alan Hansen, often prompting some dressing room mirth. 'To those people who have had a little laugh at Bob saying a player was "not quick but nippy", let me assure them that there is a big difference between the two. Quick means he runs like mad. Nippy means he goes in and out like Kenny!' Later that year, Liverpool's Anglican Cathedral staged a moving memorial service which included readings by Jessie and Ian Callaghan, who so admired the man he had known as a physiotherapist, trainer and manager for almost 40 years.

Jessie also performed the proud duty of officially opening Anfield's imposing Paisley Gateway in front of the Kop Stand in April 1999, which stands as a permanent memorial to Bob. The words 'The Paisley Gateway' are spelt out over the archway, above two massive gates, along with three European Cup symbols, as requested by Jessie. With a captivating address to an invited Anfield audience of football personalities, media representatives, club officials and guests, which included her sons Robert and Graham and daughter Christine, as well as Bob's brother Hughie and his wife Mary, who had travelled from Hetton. Jessie, who was presented with a ceremonial key to the Gateway, said: 'If this was an Oscar ceremony I would be expected to fling my arms around, burst into tears and say Bob didn't deserve it. But although the tears aren't far away, I'm not going to say that. If you ask me if Bob deserved it, I say, "Yes, 100 per cent."

'There are three features of the gates. The first is the crest of Hetton-le-Hole, where he was born and first learned to kick a football or, in those days, a pig's bladder! Then there is the crest of Liverpool, his adopted home. And then there are the three European Cups over the gateway, symbolising Bob's successes in 1977, 1978 and 1981. I may be putting my foot in it when I say this, but I believe the European Cup was much harder to win then than it is nowadays. You had to win the League to enter, not come second or third. And if you lost, that was it. There were no little leagues to give you a second chance like now. For Bob to win it three times was the jewel in his crown, but he didn't go round shouting about it.'

That, indeed, would have been alien to Bob Paisley's nature. As Kevin Keegan so significantly observed, Bob had no ego, although the massive scale of his deeds gave many others the chance to polish their own egos if they were so inclined. He had magic fingers as a physiotherapist and a magic wand as a manager. His genius opened up a Pandora's Box of trophies and medals. Yet, more mundanely, he would be as pleased as punch to know that the brass miner's safety lamp, presented to him in 1977 by the town council in his native Hetton in recognition of his achievements, is on permanent display in the Anfield Museum along with one of his flat caps. In another era, when football was more politically correct, the knighthood he so richly deserved would surely have been his. Posterity, though, has bestowed its own title on Bob Paisley: the Manager of the Millennium.

The Statistics

Bob Paisley's managerial record in figures

First Division	P	W	D	L	Goals for	Against	Points	Position
1974-75	42	20	11	11	60	39	51	2
1975-76	42	23	14	5	66	31	60	1
1976-77	42	23	11	8	62	33	57	1
1977-78	42	24	9	9	65	34	57	2
1978-79	42	30	8	4	85	16	68	1
1979-80	42	25	10	7	81	30	60	1
1980-81	42	17	17	8	62	42	51	5
1981-82	42	26	9	7	80	32	87	1
1982-83	42	24	10	8	87	37	82	1
Totals	**378**	**212**	**99**	**67**	**648**	**294**	**573**	

Other competitions totals

FA Cup	36	20	7	9	62	27
Europe	57	38	9	10	130	43
League/ Milk Cup	53	32	13	8	98	31
Charity Shield	5	4	1	0	6	1
World Club Championship	1	0	0	1	0	3
European Super Cup	4	2	1	1	10	5
Totals	**156**	**96**	**31**	**29**	**306**	**110**
Grand Total	**534**	**308**	**130**	**96**	**954**	**404**

Liverpool season by season under Paisley's management

Season	League position	FA Cup	League Cup	Europe	Charity Shield	European Super Cup	World Club Championship
1974-75	2	r4	r4	CWCr2	*		
1975-76	Champions	r4	r3	UEFA Winners			
1976-77	Champions	Finalists	r2	EC winners	Winners		
1977-78	2	r3	Finalists	EC winners	Jt winners	Winners	
1978-79	Champions	sf	r2	ECr1		Losers	
1979-80	Champions	sf	sf	ECr1	Winners		
1980-81	5	r4	Winners	EC winners	Winners		
1981-82	Champions	r5	Winners	ECqf			Losers
1982-83	Champions	r5	Winners	ECqf	Winners		

TROPHY TOTALS		KEY
League championship	6	EC = European Cup
European Cup	3	CWC = Cup-Winners' Cup
UEFA Cup	1	UEFA = UEFA Cup
League/Milk Cup	3	sf = semi-finals
Charity Shield	5	qf = quarter-finals
European Super Cup	1	rl = round one
Grand Total	**19**	

* Liverpool won the Charity Shield in August 1974 but Paisley, although appointed as the new manager, had not officially taken over as successor to Bill Shankly, who led out the team at Wembley. Paisley believed that a Charity Shield was a reflection of the previous season's achievements and did not claim the 1974 win on his record.

During Bob Paisley's managerial reign Liverpool set an all-time record of 85 home games unbeaten in all competitions. It included 63 in the League, also a record.

This remarkable undefeated sequence spanned three years from January 1978, when they lost 3-2 to Birmingham City, to January 1981 when Leicester City, then bottom of the old First Division, won 2-1, thereby completing the only home and away double defeat of Liverpool in six seasons.

The previous longest undefeated home League run in English football's top flight had been set by Nottingham Forest, who were undefeated in 49 matches at the City Ground between 1977 and

1980. The previous record for all divisions had been held by
Millwall, who played 59 home League games without losing in the
old Fourth, Third and Second Divisions between 1964 and 1967.

This is the game-by-game breakdown of Liverpool's three-year
unbeaten sequence, with figures on the extreme left denoting
League games:

League match number	Date	Opposition	Result	Goalscorers
	1978			
	7/2	Arsenal	W 2-1	R Kennedy, Dalglish
1	25/2	Manchester United	W 3-1	Souness, R Kennedy, Case
2	11/3	Leeds United	W 1-0	Dalglish
	15/3	Benfica (ECqf)	W 4-1	Callaghan, Dalglish, McDermott, Neal
3	8/4	Leicester City	W 3-2	Smith 2, Lee
	12/4	Bor Mnchngldbch (ECsf)	W 3-0	R Kennedy, Dalglish, Case
4	18/4	Ipswich Town	D 2-2	Dalglish, Souness
5	22/4	Norwich City	W 3-0	Ryan (og), Fairclough 2
6	25/4	Arsenal	W 1-0	Fairclough
7	1/5	Manchester City	W 4-0	Dalglish 3, Neal p
8	4/5	Nottingham Forest	D 0-0	
9	19/3	Queens Pk Rangers	W 2-1	Dalglish, Heighway
10	2/9	Tottenham Hotspur	W 7-0	Dalglish 2, R Kennedy, Johnson 2, Neal p, McDermott
11	16/9	Coventry City	W 1-0	Souness
	27/9	Nottingham Forest	D 0-0	
12	30/9	Bolton Wanderers	W 3-0	Case 3
13	14/10	Derby County	W 5-0	Johnson, R Kennedy 2, Dalglish 2 p
14	21/10	Chelsea	W 2-0	Johnson, Dalglish
15	4/11	Leeds Utd	D 1-1	McDermott p
16	18/11	Manchester City	W 1-0	Neal p
17	25/11	Middlesbrough	W 2-0	McDermott, Souness
18	9/12	Nottingham Forest	W 2-0	McDermott 2 1p
	19/12	Anderlecht (9ESC)	W 2-1	Hughes, Fairclough
	1979			
	17/1	Southend Utd (FAC3)	W 3-0	Case, Dalglish, R Kennedy
	30/1	Blackburn Rov (FAC4)	W 1-0	Dalglish
19	3/2	West Bromwich Alb	W 2-1	Dalglish, Fairclough
20	13/2	Birmingham City	W 1-0	Souness
21	21/2	Norwich City	W 6-0	Dalglish 2, Johnson 2, A Kennedy, R Kennedy

	28/2	Burnley (FAC5)	W 3-0	Johnson 2, Souness
22	13/3	Everton	D 1-1	Dalglish
23	20/3	Wolves	W 2-0	McDermott, Johnson
24	24/3	Ipswich Town	W 2-0	Dalglish, Johnson
25	7/4	Arsenal	W 3-0	Case, Dalglish, McDermott
26	14/4	Manchester Utd	W 2-0	Dalglish, Neal
27	21/4	Bristol City	W 1-0	Dalglish
28	5/5	Southampton	W 2-0	Neal 2
29	8/5	Aston Villa	W 3-0	A Kennedy, Dalglish, McDermott
30	21/8	Bolton Wand	D 0-0	
31	25/8	West Bromwich Alb	W 3-1	Johnson 2, McDermott
	4/9	Tranmere R (LC2)	W 4-0	Dalglish 2, Thompson, Fairclough
32	8/9	Coventry City	W 4-0	Johnson 2, Case, Dalglish
	19/9	DynamoTbilisi (EC1)	W 2-1	Johnson, Case
33	22/9	Norwich City	D 0-0	
	25/9	Chesterfield (LC3)	W 3-1	Fairclough, Dalglish, McDermott
34	6/10	Bristol City	W 4-0	Johnson, Dalglish, R Kennedy, McDermott
35	20/10	Everton	D 2-2	Lyons og, R Kennedy
	30/10	Exeter City (LC4)	W 2-0	Fairclough 2
36	3/11	Wolves	W 3-0	Dalglish 2, R Kennedy
37	17/11	Tottenham H.	W 2-1	McDermott 2
38	1/12	Middlesbrough	W 4-0	McDermott, Hansen, Johnson, R Kennedy
39	15/12	Crystal Palace	W 3-0	Case, Dalglish, McDermott
40	26/12	Manchester Utd	W 2-0	Hansen, Johnson

1980

	5/1	Grimsby Town (FAC3)	W 5-0	Souness, Johnson 3, Case
41	12/1	Southampton	D 1-1	McDermott p
	13/2	Nottingham F (LCsf)	D 1-1	Fairclough
	17/2	Bury (FAC5)	W 2-0	Fairclough 2
42	19/2	Notthingham Forest	W 2-0	McDermott, R Kennedy
43	23/2	Ipswich Town	D 1-1	Fairclough
44	11/3	Manchester City	W 2-0	Caton og, Souness
45	19/3	Leeds Utd	W 3-0	Johnson 2, A Kennedy
46	22/3	Brighton	W 1-0	Hansen
47	1/4	Stoke City	W 1-0	Dalglish
48	8/4	Derby County	W 3-0	Irwin, Johnson, Osgood og
49	19/4	Arsenal	D 1-1	Dalglish
50	3/5	Aston Villa	W 4-1	Johnson 2, Cohen, R Kennedy
51	16/8	Crystal Palace	W 3-0	Dalglish, R Kennedy, A Kennedy
52	30/8	Norwich City	W 4-1	Hansen, McDermott, A Kennedy, Johnson

	2/9	Bradford City (LC2)	W 4-0	Dalglish 2, R Kennedy, Johnson
53	13/9	West Bromwich Alb	W 4-0	McDermott p, Souness, Fairclough 2
	23/9	Swindon Town (LC3)	W 5-0	Lee 2, Dalglish, Cockerill og, Fairclough
54	27/9	Brighton	W 4-1	Souness 2, McDermott p, Fairclough
	1/10	Oulun Palloseura (EC1)	W 10-1	Souness 3 1p, McDermott 3, Fairclough 2, Lee, R Kennedy
55	7/10	Middlesbrough	W 4-2	McDermott 2 1p, R Kennedy, Dalglish
56	11/10	Ipswich Town	D 1-1	McDermott p
57	25/10	Arsenal	D 1-1	Souness
	28/10	Portsmouth (LC4)	W 4-1	Dalglish, Johnson 2, Souness
	5/11	Aberdeen (EC2)	W 4-0	Miller og, Neal, Dalglish, Hansen
58	8/11	Nottingham Forest	D 0-0	
59	11/11	Coventry City	W 2-1	Johnson 2
60	22/11	Aston Villa	W 2-1	Dalglish 2
	2/12	Birmingham (LCqf)	W 3-1	Dalglish, Johnson, McDermott
61	6/12	Tottenham	W 2-1	R Kennedy, Johnson
62	20/12	Wolves	W 1-0	R Kennedy
63	27/12	Leeds Utd	D 0-0	
1981	3/1	Altrincham (FAC3)	W 4-1	R Kennedy, Dalglish 2, McDermott

p denotes penalty, og denotes own goal

Analysis of the Record Run

	Played	Won	Drawn	Lost	For	Against
League Matches	63	49	14	0	142	26
FA Cup	6	6	0	0	18	1
League Cup	9	8	1	0	28	5
European Games	7	6	1	0	25	4
	85	**69**	**16**	**0**	**213**	**36**

Wembley Wizard

As manager, Paisley took Liverpool to Wembley 11 times, comprising one FA Cup Final, one European Cup Final, four League/Milk Cup Finals and five Charity Shield visits. He lost only one of those games, to Manchester United in the 1977 FA Cup Final. In all his various roles at Liverpool, Paisley went to Wembley on an incredible 27 occasions which comprise:

As player

1950 FA Cup Final v Arsenal (lost 2-0) (12th man)

As trainer and physiotherapist

1965 FA Cup Final v Leeds United (won 2-1 aet)

As assistant manager

1971 FA Cup Final v Arsenal (lost 2-1 aet)
1974 FA Cup Final v Newcastle (won 3-0)

As manager-elect

1974 Charity Shield v Leeds (1-1, Liverpool won on penalties)

As manager

1976 Charity Shield v Southampton (won 1-0)
1977 FA Cup Final v Manchester United (lost 2-1)
1977 Charity Shield v Manchester United (drawn 0-0)
1978 League Cup Final v Nottingham Forest (drawn 0-0 aet)
1978 European Cup Final v Bruges (won 1-0)
1979 Charity Shield v Arsenal (won 3-1)
1980 Charity Shield v West Ham United (won 1-0)
1981 League Cup Final v West Ham United (drawn 1-1 aet)
1982 Milk Cup Final v Tottenham (won 3-1 aet)
1982 Charity Shield v Tottenham (won 1-0)
1983 Milk Cup Final v Manchester United (won 2-1 aet)

As director

1983 Charity Shield v Manchester United (lost 2-0)
1984 Milk Cup Final v Everton (drawn 0-0 aet)
1984 Charity Shield v Everton (lost 1-0)
1988 FA Cup Final v Wimbledon (lost 1-0)
1988 Charity Shield v Wimbledon (won 2-1)
1989 FA Cup Final v Everton (won 3-2 aet)
1989 Charity Shield v Arsenal (won 1-0)
1990 Charity Shield v Manchester United (drawn 1-1)

As director and consultant to manager Kenny Dalglish

1986 FA Cup Final v Everton (won 3-1)
1986 Charity Shield v Everton (drawn 1-1)
1987 Littlewoods Cup Final v Arsenal (lost 2-1)

aet = after extra time

Paisley's semi-final record as manager

1975–76 UEFA Cup (won and lifted trophy)
1976–77 FA Cup (won but lost in final)
        European Cup (won and lifted trophy)
1977–78 European Cup (won and lifted trophy)
        League Cup (won but lost in final replay)
1978–79 FA Cup (lost)
1979–80 FA Cup (lost in third replay)
        League Cup (lost)
1980–81 League Cup (won and lifted trophy after final replay)
        European Cup (won and lifted trophy)
1981–82 League Cup (won and lifted trophy)
1982–83 League Cup (won and lifted trophy)

Total: Played 12, won 9, lost 3

Playing Days

Bob Paisley was a wing-half in the Bishop Auckland side that won the FA Amateur Cup in 1939, prior to signing for Liverpool on 8 May that year. He won a League championship medal in 1947 and retired as a player in 1954 after making a total of 278 first-team appearances for Liverpool, scoring 13 goals (League: 253, goals 10. FA Cup: 25, goals 3).

During his record-breaking period of management spanning nine seasons, Liverpool played a total of 259 home games in all competitions and lost only 16 of them. They comprise League 189 (lost 14), FA Cup 13 (lost 1), Europe 27 (lost O), League Cup 28 (lost 1), European Super Cup 2 (lost O).

In 1977 he was awarded an OBE for services to football.

Paisley's achievements earned him a total of 23 managerial awards from Bell's Whisky. They comprise:

1	December 1975	Manager of the Month	1	75/76
2	April 1976	Manager of the Month	2	75/76
3		**MANAGER OF THE YEAR 1976**		75/76
4	October 1976	Divisional Manager of the Month	1	76/77
5	March 1977	Manager of the Month	3	76/77
6	April 1977	Manager of the Month	4	76/77
7		**MANAGER OF THE YEAR 1977**		76/77
8	April 1978	Divisional Manager of the Month	2	77/78
9		**SPECIAL AWARD 1978**		77/78
10	February 1978	Manager of the Month	5	78/79
11		**MANAGER OF THE YEAR 1979**		78/79
12	December 1979	Manager of the Month	6	79/80
13		**MANAGER OF THE YEAR 1980**		79/80
14	April 1981	Manager of the Month	7	80/81
15		**SPECIAL AWARD 1981**		80/81
16	January 1982	Manager of the Month	8	81/82
17	March 1982	Manager of the Month	9	81/82
18		**MANAGER OF THE YEAR 1982**		81/82
19	November 1982	Manager of the Month	10	82/83
20	January 1983	Manager of the Month	11	82/83
21	March 1983	Divisional Manager of the Month	3	82/83
22		**MANAGER OF THE YEAR 1983**		82/83
23		**SPECIAL AWARD FOR OVERALL ACHIEVEMENT 1983**		